Living History
of Israel

Living History of Israel

A Paraphrase of
Joshua, Judges, I and II Samuel,
I and II Kings, I and II Chronicles,
Ezra, and Nehemiah

TYNDALE HOUSE PUBLISHERS
Wheaton, Illinois

Coverdale House Publishers Ltd.
London, England

Distributed in Canada by
Home Evangel Books Ltd.
Toronto, Ontario

Library of Congress Catalog Card No. 79-123032
SBN 8423-2460-7

Copyright © 1970 by Tyndale House Publishers,
Wheaton, Illinois 60187

Printed in the United States of America

Contents

From Wm. Tyndale's Prologue to the First Printed English New Testament:

Exhortynge instantly and besechynge those that are better sene in the tongues than I, and that have higher gifts of grace to interpret the sense of Scripture, and meaning of the Spirit, than I, to consider and ponder my labor, and that with the spirit of meekness. And if they perceive in any places that I have not attained the very sense of the tongue, or meaning of the Scripture, or have not given the right English word, that they put to their hands to amend it, remembering that so is their duty to do. For we have not received the gifts of God for ourselves only, or for to hide them; but for to bestow them unto the honoring of God and Christ and edifying of the congregation, which is the body of Christ.

At Last!

This is the final volume in the *Living* series of para-phrased Scriptures, and I thank God for allowing me to finish the project. This preface, being the last, will also be more personal than the others, so I hope those who feel uneasy (as I do) about people baring their souls in public, will be able to tolerate it this once. For now, at last, I lay down my commission and my pen — the task is finished to the best of my ability after these fourteen arduous years. In some strange way I look around again as one from prison, and see how the world has turned over many times since I bowed my head to begin *Living Letters,* the first volume in this series. Millions more of humanity now swarm the surface of the earth, with famine and chaos ever closer at hand. The church is moving forward in many areas as never before. History seems to be catapulting into its final phase.

I want to express appreciation to hundreds, most of them unknown to me, who have written to say they have been praying me through to the end. And equal thanks to those who have helped in this same way, though silently.

A friend recently remarked that he felt that these prefaces to the various volumes in the series have been in a way a spiritual biography of the paraphraser. Perhaps this is so. What then shall I say about the Scriptures in this volume, containing as they do so much of butchery of human life?

If I state my personal reaction to these blood-filled books, will I harm the faith of others? Will I be unfaithful to my God? Yet it is just because of silence here that some who are dear to me and to God have turned away in horror. If this is our God, they say, then let me burn in hell with those this God destroys.

So let me speak. I too am horrified at the God-ordained slaughter you will read about in the early pages of this book. As a pacifist, I am devastated that God is a God of war and judgment and vengeance. I wish He were only loving and kind — and how loving He always is to His people, and kind when they obey! From reading these books I came very close, I fear, to a spiritual collapse, especially on one bright autumn afternoon that I shall never forget as I sat in the grandstand with my children at a high school football game and watched not the players but the doomed and happy people all around me. Why did God create mankind with godliness, only to destroy them again in hell? Why allow the Canaanites to be born at all, victims of sinful hearts that worshiped other gods, thus meriting slaughter upon slaughter, even of their little children and their cattle?

I regret that I have not yet found the answers to these questions. I only know that I cannot live without God, and I worship Him alone, and I cannot testify enough of His personal kindness to me. I know that the world is sad and broken everywhere, and lonely, and I know that no one who comes to God is turned away. So I will spend my life helping them to find the universal solution for all troubled hearts — the Lord Jesus Christ. And I shall weep for those who cannot find Him.

O Christ of God, I worship and adore You. No one else but You can save and help me. No one else but You is truly good. I turn from the gloom of those things I do not understand, to the joy in sorrow of serving You and being used by You to snatch from the flames my fallen fellowmen. Oh, help me to help them to find in You what I have found — a Father, Brother, Savior, Guide, and Friend. Amen.

Kenneth N. Taylor

P.S. I challenge you to read this book without feeling some wild upsurges in your personal faith. The amazing miracles God did for His people in days long ago are an open invitation for us to ask Him to do the same again today. He is waiting for us to expect Him to do the incredible things we need to see done for God in the 1970s. Reading this book makes it easy to believe. For "faith comes by hearing . . . the Word of God."

Joshua

CHAPTER 1

A fter the death of Moses, the Lord's disciple, God spoke to Moses' assistant, whose name was Joshua (the son of Nun), and said to him,

2 "Now that My disciple is dead, [you are the new leader of Israel[1]]. Lead My people across the Jordan River into the Promised Land.

3 I say to you what I said to Moses: 'Wherever you go will be part of the land of Israel —

4 All the way from Negeb desert in the south to the Lebanon mountains in the north, and from the Mediterranean Sea in the west to the Euphrates River in the east, including all the land of the Hittites.'

5 No one will be able to oppose you as long as you live, for I will be with you just as I was with Moses; I will not abandon you or fail to help you.

6 Be strong and brave, for you will be a successful leader of My people; and they shall conquer all the land I promised to their ancestors.

7 You need only to be strong and courageous and to obey to the letter every law Moses gave you, for if you are careful to obey every one of them you will be successful in everything you do.

8 Constantly remind the people about these laws, and you yourself must think about them every day and every night so that you will be sure to obey all of

---

[1]Implied.

them. For only then will you succeed.

9 Yes, be bold and strong! Banish fear and doubt! For remember, the Lord your God is with you wherever you go."

10, 11 Then Joshua issued instructions to the leaders of Israel to tell the people to get ready to cross the Jordan River. "In three days we will go across and conquer and live in the land which God has given us!" he told them.

12, 13 Then he summoned the leaders of the tribes of Reuben, Gad, and the half-tribe of Manasseh and reminded them of their agreement with Moses: "The Lord your God has given you a homeland here on the east side of the Jordan River," Moses had told them,

14 "So your wives and children and cattle may remain here, but your troops, fully armed, must lead the other tribes across the Jordan River to help them conquer their territory on the other side;

15 Stay with them until they complete the conquest. Only then may you settle down here on the east side of the Jordan."

16 To this they fully agreed, and pledged themselves to obey Joshua as their commander-in-chief.

17, 18 "We will obey you just as we obeyed Moses," they assured him, "and may the Lord your God be with you as He was with Moses. If anyone, no matter who, rebels against your commands, he shall die. So lead on with courage and strength!"

CHAPTER 2

Then Joshua sent two spies from the Israeli camp at Acacia to cross the river and check out the situation on the other side, especially at Jericho. They arrived at an inn operated by a woman named Rahab, who was a prostitute. They were planning to spend the night there,

2   But someone informed the king of Jericho that two Israelis who were suspected of being spies had arrived in the city that evening.

3   He dispatched a police squadron to Rahab's home, demanding that she surrender them. "They are spies," he explained. "They have been sent by the Israeli leaders to discover the best way to attack us."

4   But she had hidden them, so she told the officer in charge, "The men were here earlier, but I didn't know they were spies.

5   They left the city at dusk as the city gates were about to close, and I don't know where they went. If you hurry you can probably catch up with them!"

6   But actually she had taken them up to the roof and hidden them beneath piles of flax that were drying there.

7   So the constable and his men went all the way to the Jordan River looking for them; meanwhile, the city gates were kept shut.

8   Rahab went up to talk to the men before they retired for the night.

9   "I know perfectly well that your God is going to give my country to you," she told them. "We are all afraid of you; everyone is terrified if the word *Israel* is even mentioned.

10   For we have heard how the Lord made a path through the Red Sea for you when you left Egypt! And we know what you did to Sihon and Og, the two Amorite kings east of the Jordan, and how you ruined their

land and completely destroyed their people.

11   No wonder we are afraid of you! No one has any fight left in him after hearing things like that, for your God is the supreme God of heaven, not just an ordinary god.

12, 13   Now I beg for this one thing: Swear to me by the sacred name of your God that when Jericho is conquered you will let me live, along with my father and mother, my brothers and sisters, and all their families. This is only fair after the way I have helped you."

14   The men agreed. "If you won't betray us, we'll see to it that you and your family aren't harmed," they promised.

15   "We'll defend you with our lives." Then, since her house was on top of the city wall, she let them down by a rope from a window.

16   "Escape to the mountains," she told them. "Hide there for three days until the men who are searching for you have returned; then go on your way."

17, 18   But before they left, the men had said to her, "We cannot be responsible for what happens to you unless this rope is hanging from this window and unless all your relatives — your father, mother, brothers, and anyone else — are here inside the house.

19   If they go out into the street we assume no responsibility whatsoever; but we swear that no one inside this house will be killed or injured.

20   However, if you betray us, then this oath will no longer bind us in any way."

21   "I accept your terms," she replied. And she left the scarlet rope hanging from the window.

22   The spies went up into the mountains and

stayed there three days, until the men who were chasing them had returned to the city after searching everywhere along the road without success.

23 Then the two spies came down from the mountain and crossed the river and reported to Joshua all that had happened to them.

24 "The Lord will certainly give us the entire land," they said, "for all the people over there are scared to death of us."

CHAPTER 3

Early the next morning Joshua and all the people of Israel left Acacia, and arrived that evening at the banks of the Jordan River, where they camped for a few days before crossing.

2, 3, 4 On the third day, officers went through the camp giving these instructions: "When you see the priests carrying the Ark of God,[1] follow them. You have never before been where we are going now, so they will guide you. However, stay about a half mile behind, with a clear space between you and the Ark; be sure that you don't get any closer."

5 Then Joshua told the people to perform the purification ceremony for themselves. "For tomorrow," he said, "the Lord will do a great miracle."

6 In the morning Joshua ordered the priests, "Take up the Ark and lead us across the river!" And so they started out.

7 "Today," the Lord told Joshua, "I will give you great honor, so that all Israel will know that I am with you just as I was with Moses.

---

[1]Literally, "the Ark of the covenant of the Lord."

8   Instruct the priests who are carrying the Ark to stop at the edge of the river."

9   Then Joshua summoned all the people and told them, "Come and listen to what the Lord your God has said.

10   Today you are going to know for sure that the living God is among you and that He will, without fail, drive out the Canaanites, Hittites, Hivites, Perizzites, Girgashites, Amorites, and Jebusites — all the people who now live in the land you will soon occupy.

11   Think of it! The Ark of God, who is Lord of the whole earth, will lead you across the river!

12   Now select twelve men, one from each tribe, for a special task.[2]

13, 14   When the priests who are carrying the Ark touch the water with their feet, the river will stop flowing as though held back by a dam, and will pile up as though against an invisible wall!" Now it was the harvest season and the Jordan was overflowing all its banks; but as the people set out to cross the river and as the feet of the priests who were carrying the Ark touched the water at the river's edge,

15, 16   Suddenly, far up the river at the city of Adam, near Zarethan, the water began piling up as though against a dam! And the water below that point flowed on to the Salt Sea until the riverbed was empty. Then all the people crossed at a spot where the river was close to the city of Jericho,

17   And the priests who were carrying the Ark stood on dry ground in the middle of the Jordan and waited as all the people passed by.

---

[2]Their duties are explained in chapter 4, verses 2-7.

CHAPTER 4

When all the people were safely across, the Lord said to Joshua,

2, 3 "Tell the twelve men chosen for a special task, one from each tribe, each to take a stone from where the priests are standing in the middle of the Jordan, and to carry them out and pile them up as a monument at the place where you camp tonight."

4 So Joshua summoned the twelve men,

5 And told them, "Go out into the middle of the Jordan where the Ark is. Each of you is to carry out a stone on your shoulder — twelve stones in all, one for each of the twelve tribes.

6 We will use them to build a monument so that in the future, when your children ask, 'What is this monument for?'

7 You can tell them, 'It is to remind us that the Jordan River stopped flowing when the Ark of God went across!' The monument will be a permanent reminder to the people of Israel of this amazing miracle."

8 So the men did as Joshua told them. They took twelve stones from the middle of the Jordan River — one for each tribe, just as the Lord had commanded Joshua. They carried them to the place where they were camped for the night and constructed a monument there.

9 Joshua also built another monument of twelve stones in the middle of the river, at the place where the priests were standing; and it is there to this day.

10 The priests who were carrying the Ark stood in the middle of the river until all these instructions of

the Lord, which had been given to Joshua by Moses, had been carried out. Meanwhile, the people had hurried across the riverbed,

11 And when everyone was over, the people watched the priests carry the Ark up out of the river.

12, 13 The troops of Reuben, Gad, and the half-tribe of Manasseh — fully armed as Moses had instructed, and forty thousand strong — led the other tribes of the Lord's army across to the plains of Jericho.

14 It was a tremendous day for Joshua! The Lord made him great in the eyes of all the people of Israel, and they revered him as much as they had Moses, and respected him deeply all the rest of his life.

15, 16 For it was Joshua who, at the Lord's command, issued the orders to the priests carrying the Ark.

"Come up from the riverbed," the Lord now told him to command them.

17 So Joshua issued the order.

18 And as soon as the priests came out, the water poured down again as usual and overflowed the banks of the river as before!

19 This miracle occurred on the 25th of March.[1] That day the entire nation crossed the Jordan River and camped in Gilgal at the eastern edge of the city of Jericho;

20 And there the twelve stones from the Jordan were piled up as a monument.

21 Then Joshua explained again the purpose of the stones: "In the future," he said, "when your chil-

---

[1]Literally, "The tenth day of the first month" (of the Jewish calendar).

dren ask you why these stones are here and what they mean,

22 You are to tell them that these stones are a reminder of this amazing miracle — that the nation of Israel crossed the Jordan River on dry ground!

23 Tell them how the Lord our God dried up the river right before our eyes, and then kept it dry until we were all across! It is the same thing the Lord did forty years ago[2] at the Red Sea!

24 He did this so that all the nations of the earth will realize that Jehovah is the mighty God, and so that all of you will worship Him forever."

CHAPTER 5

When the nations west of the Jordan River — the Amorites and Canaanites who lived along the Mediterranean coast — heard that the Lord had dried up the Jordan River so the people of Israel could cross, their courage melted away completely and they were paralyzed with fear.

2, 3 The Lord then told Joshua to set aside a day to circumcise the entire male population of Israel. (It was the second time in Israel's history that this was done.) The Lord instructed them to manufacture flint knives for this purpose. The place where the circumcision rite took place was named "The Hill of the Foreskins."

4, 5 The reason for this second circumcision ceremony was that although when Israel left Egypt all of the men who had been old enough to bear arms had been circumcised, that entire generation had died

---

[2]Implied.

during the years in the wilderness, and none of the
boys born since that time had been circumcised.

6 For the nation of Israel had traveled back and
forth across the wilderness for forty years until all
the men who had been old enough to bear arms when
they left Egypt were dead; they had not obeyed the
Lord, and He vowed that He wouldn't let them enter
the land He had promised to Israel — a land that
"flowed with milk and honey."

7 So now Joshua circumcised their children —
the men who had grown up to take their fathers' places.

8, 9 And the Lord said to Joshua, "Today I
have ended your shame of not being circumcised."[1]
So the place where this was done was called Gilgal
(meaning, "to end"[2]), and is still called that today.
After the ceremony the entire nation rested in camp
until the raw flesh of their wounds had been healed.

10 While they were camped at Gilgal on the
plains of Jericho, they celebrated the Passover during
the evening of the 14th day of the month.

11, 12 The next day they began to eat from the
gardens and grain fields which they invaded, and they
made unleavened bread. The following day no manna
fell, and it was never seen again! So from that time
on they lived on the crops of Canaan.

13 As Joshua was sizing up the city of Jericho, a
man appeared nearby with a drawn sword. Joshua
strode over to him and demanded, "Are you friend or
foe?"

14 "I am the Commander-in-Chief of the Lord's
army," He replied. Joshua fell to the ground before

---

[1] Literally, "the shame of Egypt."
[2] Literally, "to roll" (away).

Him and worshiped Him and said, "Give me Your commands."

15 "Take off your shoes," the Commander told him, "for this is holy ground." And Joshua did.

CHAPTER 6

The gates of Jericho were kept tightly shut because the people were afraid of the Israelis; no one was allowed to go in or out.

2 But the Lord said to Joshua, "Jericho and its king and all its mighty warriors are already defeated, for I have given them to you!

3, 4 Your entire army is to walk around the city once a day for six days, followed by seven priests walking ahead of the Ark, each carrying a trumpet made from a ram's horn. On the seventh day you are to walk around the city seven times, with the priests blowing their trumpets.

5 Then, when they give one long, loud blast, all the people are to give a mighty shout and the walls of the city will fall down; then move in upon the city from every direction."

6-9 So Joshua summoned the priests and gave them their instructions: the armed men would lead the procession followed by seven priests blowing continually on their trumpets. Behind them would come the priests carrying the Ark, followed by a rearguard.

10 "Let there be complete silence except for the trumpets," Joshua commanded. "Not a single word from any of you until I tell you to shout; then *shout!*"

11 The Ark was carried around the city once that day, after which everyone returned to the camp again and spent the night there.

12, 13, 14   At dawn the next morning they went around again, and returned again to the camp. They followed this pattern for six days.

15   At dawn of the seventh day they started out again, but this time they went around the city not once, but seven times.

16   The seventh time, as the priests blew a long, loud trumpet blast, Joshua yelled to the people, *"Shout! The Lord has given us the city!"*

17   (He had told them previously, "Kill everyone except Rahab the prostitute and anyone in her house, for she protected our spies.

18   Don't take any loot, for everything is to be destroyed. If it isn't, disaster will fall upon the entire nation of Israel.

19   But all the silver and gold and the utensils of bronze and iron will be dedicated to the Lord, and must be brought into His treasury.")

20   So when the people heard the trumpet blast, they shouted as loud as they could. And suddenly the walls of Jericho crumbled and fell before them, and the people of Israel poured into the city from every side and captured it!

21   They destroyed everything in it — men and women, young and old; oxen; sheep; donkeys — everything.

22   Then Joshua said to the two spies, "Keep your promise. Go and rescue the prostitute and everyone with her."

23   The young men found her and rescued her, along with her father, mother, brothers, and other relatives who were with her. Arrangements were made for them to live outside the camp of Israel.

24 Then the Israelis burned the city and everything in it except that the silver and gold and the bronze and iron utensils were kept for the Lord's treasury.

25 Thus Joshua saved Rahab the prostitute and her relatives who were with her in the house, and they still live among the Israelites because she hid the spies sent to Jericho by Joshua.

26 Then Joshua declared a terrible curse upon anyone who might rebuild Jericho, warning that when the foundation was laid, the builder's oldest son would die, and when the gates were set up, his youngest son would die.[1] *(cp. I Kings 16:34)*

27 So the Lord was with Joshua, and his name became famous everywhere.

CHAPTER 7

But there was sin among the Israelis. God's command to destroy everything except that which was reserved for the Lord's treasury was disobeyed. For Achan (the son of Carmi, grandson of Zabdi, and great-grandson of Zerah, of the tribe of Judah) took some loot for himself, and the Lord was very angry with the entire nation of Israel because of this.

2 Soon after Jericho's defeat, Joshua sent some of his men to spy on the city of Ai, east of Bethel.

3 Upon their return they told Joshua, "It's a small city and it won't take more than two or three thousand of us to destroy it; there's no point in all of us going there."

4 So approximately three thousand soldiers were sent — and they were soundly defeated.

5 About thirty-six of the Israelis were killed during

---

[1]See I Kings 16:34 for the fulfillment of this curse.

the attack, and many others died while being chased by the men of Ai as far as the quarries. The Israeli army was paralyzed with fear at this turn of events.

6 Joshua and the elders of Israel tore their clothing and lay prostrate before the Ark of the Lord until evening, with dust on their heads.

7 Joshua cried out to the Lord, "O Jehovah, why have You brought us over the Jordan River if You are going to let the Amorites kill us? Why weren't we content with what we had? Why didn't we stay on the other side?

8 O Lord, what am I to do now that Israel has fled from her enemies!

9 For when the Canaanites and the other nearby nations hear about it, they will surround us and attack us and wipe us out. And then what will happen to the honor of Your great name?"

10, 11 But the Lord said to Joshua, "Get up off your face! Israel has sinned and disobeyed My commandment and has taken loot when I said it was not to be taken; and they have not only taken it, they have lied about it and have hidden it among their belongings.

12 That is why the people of Israel are being defeated. That is why your men are running from their enemies — for they are cursed.[1] I will not stay with you any longer unless you completely rid yourselves of this sin.

13 Get up! Tell the people, 'Each of you must undergo purification rites in preparation for tomorrow, for the Lord your God of Israel says that someone has

---

[1]Literally, they have become "something which must be totally destroyed" or else become totally God's.

stolen from Him, and you cannot defeat your enemies until you deal with this sin.

14 In the morning you must come by tribes, and the Lord will point out the tribe to which the guilty man belongs. And that tribe must come by its clans and the Lord will point out the guilty clan; and the clan must come by its families, and then each member of the guilty family must come one by one.

15 And the one who has stolen that which belongs to the Lord shall be burned with fire, along with everything he has, for he has violated the covenant of the Lord and has brought calamity upon all of Israel.' "

16 So, early the next morning, Joshua brought the tribes of Israel before the Lord, and the tribe of Judah was indicated.

17 Then he brought the clans of Judah, and the clan of Zerah was singled out. Then the families of that clan were brought before the Lord and the family of Zabdi was indicated.

18 Zabdi's family was brought man by man, and his grandson Achan was found to be the guilty one.

19 Joshua said to Achan, "My son, give glory to the God of Israel and make your confession. Tell me what you have done."

20 Achan replied, "I have sinned against the Lord, the God of Israel.

21 For I saw a beautiful robe imported from Babylon, and some silver worth $200, and a bar of gold worth $500. I wanted them so much that I took them, and they are hidden in the ground beneath my tent, with the silver buried deeper than the rest."

22 So Joshua sent some men to search for the loot. They ran to the tent and found the stolen goods hidden

there just as Achan had said, with the silver buried beneath the rest.

23   They brought it all to Joshua and laid it on the ground in front of him.

24   Then Joshua and all the Israelites took Achan, the silver, the robe, the wedge of gold, his sons, his daughters, his oxen, donkeys, sheep, his tent, and everything he had, and brought them to the valley of Achor.

25   Then Joshua said to Achan, "Why have you brought calamity upon us? The Lord will now bring calamity upon you." And the men of Israel stoned them to death and burned their bodies,

26   And piled a great heap of stones upon them. The stones are still there to this day, and even today that place is called "The Valley of Calamity." And so the fierce anger of the Lord was ended.

CHAPTER 8

Then the Lord said to Joshua, "Don't be afraid or discouraged; take the entire army and go to Ai, for it is now yours to conquer. I have given the king of Ai and all of his people to you.

2   You shall do to them as you did to Jericho and her king; but this time you may keep the loot and the cattle for yourselves. Set an ambush behind the city."

3, 4   Before the main army left for Ai, Joshua sent thirty thousand of his bravest troops to hide in ambush close behind the city, alert for action.

5   "This is the plan," he explained to them. "When our main army attacks, the men of Ai will come out to fight as they did before, and we will run away.

6 We will let them chase us until they have all left the city; for they will say, 'The Israelis are running away again just as they did before!'

7 Then you will jump up from your ambush and enter the city, for the Lord will give it to you.

8 Set the city on fire, as the Lord has command-ed. You now have your instructions."

9 So they left that night and lay in ambush be-tween Bethel and the west side of Ai; but Joshua and the rest of the army remained in the camp at Jericho.

10 Early the next morning Joshua roused his men and started toward Ai, accompanied by the elders of Israel,

11, 12, 13 And stopped at the edge of a valley north of the city. That night Joshua sent another five thousand men to join the troops ambushed on the west side of the city.[1] He himself spent the night in the valley.

14 The King of Ai, seeing the Israeli across the valley, went out early the next morning and attacked at the Plain of Arabah. But of course he didn't realize that there was an ambush behind the city.

15 Joshua and the Israeli army fled across the wilderness as though badly beaten,

16 And all the soldiers in the city were called out to chase after them; so the city was left defenseless;

17 There was not a soldier left in Ai or Bethel and the city gates were left wide open.

18 Then the Lord said to Joshua, "Point your spear toward Ai, for I will give you the city." Joshua did.

---

[1]These were evidently additional to the thirty thousand men already hiding there. Perhaps the additional five thousand were to intercept the forces expected from Bethel (verse 17).

19 And when the men in ambush saw his signal, they jumped up and poured into the city and set it on fire.

20, 21 When the men of Ai looked behind them, smoke from the city was filling the sky, and they had nowhere to go. When Joshua and the troops who were with him saw the smoke, they knew that their men who had been in ambush were inside the city, so they turned upon their pursuers and began killing them.

22 Then the Israelis who were inside the city came out and began destroying the enemy from the rear. So the men of Ai were caught in a trap and all of them died; not one man survived or escaped,

23 Except for the king of Ai, who was captured and brought to Joshua.

24 When the army of Israel had finished slaughtering all the men outside the city, they went back and finished off everyone left inside.

25 So the entire population of Ai, twelve thousand in all, were wiped out that day.

26 For Joshua kept his spear pointed toward Ai until the last person was dead.

27 Only the cattle and the loot were not destroyed, for the armies of Israel kept these for themselves. (The Lord had told Joshua they could.)

28 So Ai became a desolate mound of refuse, as it still is today.

29 Joshua hanged the king of Ai on a tree until evening, but as the sun was going down, he took down the body and threw it in front of the city gate. There he piled a great heap of stones over it, which can still be seen.

30   Then Joshua built an altar to the Lord God of Israel at Mount Ebal,

31   As Moses had commanded[2] in the book of his laws: "Make Me an altar of boulders that have neither been broken nor carved," the Lord had said concerning Mount Ebal. Then the priests offered burnt sacrifices and peace offerings to the Lord on the altar.

32   And as the people of Israel watched, Joshua carved upon the stones of the altar each of the Ten Commandments.[3]

33   Then all the people of Israel — including the elders, officers, judges, and the foreigners living among them — divided into two groups, half of them standing at the foot of Mount Gerizim and half at the foot of Mount Ebal. Between them stood the priests with the Ark, ready to pronounce their blessing. (This was all done in accordance with the instructions given long before by Moses.)

34   Joshua then read to them all of the statements of blessing and curses that Moses had written in the book of God's laws.

35   Every commandment Moses had ever given was read before the entire assembly, including the women and children and the foreigners who lived among the Israelis.

CHAPTER 9

When the kings of the surrounding area heard what had happened to Jericho, they quickly combined their armies to fight for their lives against Joshua and the Israelis. These were the kings of the nations west

---

2See Deuteronomy 27:2-8.
3Literally, "the law of Moses."

of the Jordan River, along the shores of the Mediterranean as far north as the Lebanon mountains — the Hittites, Amorites, Canaanites, Perizzites, Hivites, and Jebusites.

3, 4, 5 But when the people of Gibeon heard what had happened to Jericho and Ai, they resorted to trickery to save themselves. They sent ambassadors to Joshua wearing worn-out clothing, as though from a long journey, with patched shoes, weatherworn saddlebags on their donkeys, old, patched wineskins and dry, moldy bread.

6 When they arrived at the camp of Israel at Gilgal, they told Joshua and the men of Israel, "We have come from a distant land to ask for a peace treaty with you."

7 The Israelis replied to these Hivites, "How do we know you don't live nearby? For if you do, we cannot make a treaty with you."

8 They replied, "We will be your slaves."

"But who are you?" Joshua demanded. "Where do you come from?"

9 And they told him, "We are from a very distant country; we have heard of the might of the Lord your God and of all that He did in Egypt,

10 And what you did to the two kings of the Amorites — Sihon, king of Heshbon, and Og, king of Bashan.

11 So our elders and our people instructed us, 'Prepare for a long journey; go to the people of Israel and declare our nation to be their servants, and ask for peace.'

12 This bread was hot from the ovens when we left, but now as you see, it is dry and moldy;

13   These wineskins were new, but now they are old and cracked; our clothing and shoes have become worn out from our long, hard trip."

14, 15   Joshua and the other leaders finally believed them. They did not bother to ask the Lord, but went ahead and signed a peace treaty. And the leaders of Israel ratified the agreement with a binding oath.

16   Three days later the facts came out — these men were close neighbors.

17   The Israeli army set out at once to investigate, and reached their cities in three days. (The names of the cities were Gibeon, Chephirah, Be-eroth, and Kiriath-jearim.)

18   But the cities were not harmed because of the vow which the leaders of Israel had made before the Lord God. The people of Israel were angry with their leaders because of the peace treaty,

19   But the leaders replied, "We have sworn before the Lord God of Israel that we will not touch them, and we won't.

20   We must let them live, for if we break our oath the wrath of Jehovah will be upon us."

21   So they became servants of the Israelis, chopping their wood and carrying their water.

22   Joshua summoned their leaders and demanded, "Why have you lied to us by saying that you lived in a distant land, when you were actually living right here among us?

23   Now a curse shall be upon you! From this moment you must always furnish us with servants to chop wood and carry water for the service of our God."

24   They replied, "We did it because we were told that Jehovah instructed His disciple Moses to conquer

this entire land and destroy all the people living in it. So we feared for our lives because of you; that is why we have done it.

25 But now we are in your hands; you may do with us as you wish."

26 So Joshua would not allow the people of Israel to kill them,

27 But they became wood-choppers and water-carriers for the people of Israel and for the altar of the Lord — wherever it would be built (for the Lord hadn't yet told them where to build it). This arrangement is still in force at the time of this writing.

CHAPTER 10

When Adoni-zedek, the king of Jerusalem, heard how Joshua had captured and destroyed Ai and had killed its king, the same as he had done at Jericho, and how the people of Gibeon had made peace with Israel and were now their allies,

2 He was very frightened. For Gibeon was a great city — as great as the royal cities and much larger than Ai — and its men were known as hard fighters.

3 So King Adoni-zedek of Jerusalem sent messengers to several other kings:

> King Hoham of Hebron,
> King Piram of Jarmuth,
> King Japhia of Lachish,
> King Debir of Eglon.

4 "Come and help me destroy Gibeon," he urged them, "for they have made peace with Joshua and the people of Israel."

5   So these five Amorite kings combined their armies for a united attack on Gibeon.

6   The men of Gibeon hurriedly sent messengers to Joshua at Gilgal. "Come and help your servants!" they demanded. "Come quickly and save us! For all the kings of the Amorites who live in the hills are here with their armies."

7   So Joshua and the Israeli army left Gilgal and went to rescue Gibeon.

8   "Don't be afraid of them," the Lord said to Joshua, "for they are already defeated! I have given them to you to destroy. Not a single one of them will be able to stand up to you."

9   Joshua traveled all night from Gilgal and took the enemy armies by surprise.

10   Then the Lord threw them into a panic so that the army of Israel slaughtered great numbers of them at Gibeon and chased the others all the way to Beth-horon and Azekah and Makkedah, killing them along the way.

11   And as the enemy was racing down the hill to Beth-horon, the Lord destroyed them with a great hailstorm that continued all the way to Azekah; in fact, more men died from the hail than by the swords of the Israelis.

12   As the men of Israel were pursuing and harassing the foe, Joshua prayed aloud, "Let the sun stand still over Gibeon, and let the moon stand in its place over the valley of Aijalon!"

13   And the sun and the moon didn't move until the Israeli army had finished the destruction of its enemies! This is described in greater detail in *The Book of Jashar*. So the sun stopped in the heavens and

stayed there for almost twenty-four hours!

14   There had never been such a day before, and there has never been another since, when the Lord stopped the sun and moon — all because of the prayer of one man. But the Lord was fighting for Israel.

15   (Afterwards Joshua and the Israeli army returned to Gilgal.)

16   During the battle the five kings escaped and hid in a cave at Makkedah.

17   When the news was brought to Joshua that they had been found,

18   He issued a command that a great stone be rolled against the mouth of the cave and that guards be placed there to keep the kings inside.

19   Then Joshua commanded the rest of the army, "Go on chasing the enemy and cut them down from the rear. Don't let them get back to their cities, for the Lord will help you to completely destroy them."

20   So Joshua and the Israeli army continued the slaughter and wiped out the five armies except for a tiny remnant that managed to reach their fortified cities.

21   Then the Israelis returned to their camp at Makkedah without having lost a single man! And after that no one dared to attack Israel.

22, 23   Joshua now instructed his men to remove the stone from the mouth of the cave and to bring out the five kings — of Jerusalem, Hebron, Jarmuth, Lachish, and Eglon.

24   Joshua told the captains of his army to put their feet on the kings' necks.

25   "Don't ever be afraid or discouraged," Joshua said to his men. "Be strong and courageous, for the

Lord is going to do this to all of your enemies."

26 With that, Joshua plunged his sword into each of the five kings, killing them. He then hanged them on five trees until evening.

27 As the sun was going down, Joshua instructed that their bodies be taken down and thrown into the cave where they had been hiding; and a great pile of stones was placed at the mouth of the cave. (The pile is still there today.)

28 On that same day Joshua destroyed the city of Makkedah and killed its king and everyone in it. Not one person in the entire city was left alive.

29 Then the Israelis went to Libnah.

30 There, too, the Lord gave them the city and its king. Every last person was slaughtered, just as at Jericho.

31 From Libnah they went to Lachish and attacked it.

32 And the Lord gave it to them on the second day; here, too, the entire population was slaughtered, just as at Libnah.

33 During the attack on Lachish, King Horam of Gezer arrived with his army to try to help defend the city, but Joshua's men killed him and destroyed his entire army.

34, 35 The Israeli army then captured Eglon on the first day and, as at Lachish, they killed everyone in the city.

36 After leaving Eglon they went to Hebron,

37 And captured it and all of its surrounding villages, slaughtering the entire population. Not one person was left alive.

38 Then they turned back to Debir,

39 Which they quickly captured with all of its outlying villages. And they killed everyone just as they had at Libnah.

40 So Joshua and his army conquered the whole country — the nations and kings of the hill country, the Negeb, the lowlands, and the mountain slopes. They destroyed everyone in the land, just as the Lord God of Israel had commanded,

41 Slaughtering them from Kadesh-barnea to Gaza, and from Goshen to Gibeon.

42 This was all accomplished in one campaign, for the Lord God of Israel was fighting for His people.

43 Then Joshua and his army returned to their camp at Gilgal.

CHAPTER 11

When King Jabin of Hazor heard what had happened, he sent urgent messages to the following kings:

> King Jobab of Madon;
> The king of Shimron;
> The king of Achshaph;
> All the kings of the northern hill country;
> The kings in the Arabah, south of Chinneroth;
> Those in the lowland;
> The kings in the mountain areas of Dor, on the west;

3   The kings of Canaan, both east and west;
> The kings of the Amorites;
> The kings of the Hittites;
> The kings of the Perizzites;
> The kings in the Jebusite hill country;

The Hivite kings in the cities on the slopes
of Mount Hermon, in the land of Mizpah.

4 All these kings responded by mobilizing their
armies, and uniting to crush Israel. Their combined
troops, along with a vast array of horses and chariots,
covered the landscape around the Springs of Merom
as far as one could see;

5 For they established their camp at the Springs
of Merom.

6 But the Lord said to Joshua, "Don't be afraid
of them, for by this time tomorrow they will all be
dead! Hamstring their horses and burn their chariots."

7 Joshua and his troops arrived suddenly at the
Springs of Merom and attacked.

8 And the Lord gave all that vast army to the
Israelis, who chased them as far as Great Sidon and a
place called the Salt Pits, and eastward into the valley
of Mizpah; so not one enemy troop survived the battle.

9 Then Joshua and his men did as the Lord had
instructed, for they hamstrung the horses and burned
all the chariots.

10 On the way back, Joshua captured Hazor and
killed its king. (Hazor had at one time been the
capital of the federation of all those kingdoms.)

11 Every person there was killed and the city was
burned.

12 Then he attacked and destroyed all the other
cities of those kings. All the people were slaughtered,
just as Moses had commanded long before.

13 (However, Joshua did not burn any of the cities
built on mounds except for Hazor.)

14 All the spoil and cattle of the ravaged cities

were taken by the Israelis for themselves, but they killed all the people.

15   For so the Lord had commanded His disciple Moses; and Moses had passed the commandment on to Joshua, who did as he had been told: he carefully obeyed all of the Lord's instructions to Moses.

16   So Joshua conquered the entire land — the hill country, the Negeb, the land of Goshen, the lowlands, the Arabah, and the hills and lowlands of Israel.

17   The Israeli territory now extended all the way from Mount Halak, near Seir, to Baal-gad in the valley of Lebanon, at the foot of Mount Hermon. And Joshua killed all the kings of those territories.

18   It took seven years[1] of war to accomplish all of this.

19   None of the cities was given a peace treaty except the Hivites of Gibeon; all of the others were destroyed.

20   For the Lord made the enemy kings want to fight the Israeli instead of asking for peace; so they were mercilessly killed, as the Lord had commanded Moses.

21   During this period Joshua routed all of the giants — the descendants of Anak who lived in the hill country in Hebron, Debir, Anab, Judah, and Israel; he killed them all and completely destroyed their cities.

22   None was left in all the land of Israel, though some still remained in Gaza, Gath, and Ashdod.

23   So Joshua took the entire land just as the Lord had instructed Moses; and he gave it to the people of

---

[1]Implied in other text. Literally, "a long time."

Israel as their inheritance, dividing the land among the tribes. So the land finally rested from its war.

CHAPTER 12

H ere is the list of the kings on the east side of the Jordan River whose cities were destroyed by the Israeli: (The area involved stretched all the way from the valley of the Arnon River to Mount Hermon, including the cities of the eastern desert.)

2 King Sihon of the Amorites, who lived in Heshbon. His kingdom extended from Aroer, on the edge of the Arnon Valley, and from the middle of the valley of the Arnon River to the Jabbok River, which is the boundary of the Ammonites. This includes half of the present area of Gilead, which lies north of the Jabbok River.

3 Sihon also controlled the Jordan River valley as far north as the western shores of the Lake of Galilee; and as far south as the Salt Sea and the slopes of Mount Pisgah.

4 King Og of Bashan, the last of the Rephaim, who lived at Ashtaroth and Edre-i:

5 He ruled a territory stretching from Mount Hermon in the north to Salecah on Mount Bashan in the east, and on the west, extending to the boundary of the kingdoms of Geshur and Ma-acah. His kingdom also stretched south to include the northern half of Gilead where the boundary touched the border of the kingdom of Sihon, king of Heshbon.

6 Moses and the people of Israel had destroyed these people, and Moses gave the land to the tribes of Reuben and the half-tribe of Manasseh.

7 Here is a list of the kings destroyed by Joshua

and the armies of Israel on the west side of the Jordan. (This land which lay between Baal-gad in the Valley of Lebanon and Mount Halak, west of Mount Seir, was allotted by Joshua to the other tribes of Israel.

8-24 The area included the hill country, the lowlands, the Arabah, the mountain slopes, the Judean Desert, and the Negeb. The people who lived there were the Hittites, the Amorites, the Canaanites, the Perizzites, the Hivites, and the Jebusites):

> The king of Jericho;
> The king of Ai, near Bethel;
> The king of Jerusalem;
> The king of Hebron;
> The king of Jarmuth;
> The king of Lachish;
> The king of Eglon;
> The king of Gezer;
> The king of Debir;
> The king of Geder;
> The king of Hormah;
> The king of Arad;
> The king of Libnah;
> The king of Adullam;
> The king of Makkedah;
> The king of Bethel;
> The king of Tappu-ah;
> The king of Hepher;
> The king of Aphek;
> The king of Lasharon;
> The king of Madon;
> The king of Hazor;
> The king of Shimron-meron;
> The king of Achshaph;

> The king of Taanach;
> The king of Megiddo;
> The king of Kedesh;
> The king of Jokne-am, in Carmel;
> The king of Dor in the city of Naphath-dor;
> The king of Goiim in Gilgal;
> The king of Tirzah.

So in all, thirty-one kings and their cities were destroyed.

CHAPTER 13

Joshua was now an old man. "You are growing old," the Lord said to him, "and there are still many nations to be conquered.

2-7 Here is a list of the areas still to be occupied:

> All the land of the Philistines;
> The land of the Geshurites;
> The territory now belonging to the Canaanites from the brook of Egypt to the southern boundary of Ekron;
> Five cities of the Philistines:
>> Gaza,
>> Ashdod,
>> Ashkelon,
>> Gath,
>> Ekron;
> The land of the Avvim in the south;
> In the north,[1] all the land of the Canaanites, including Me-arah (which belongs to the Sidonians), stretching northward[1] to Aphek at the boundary of the Amorites;

---

[1] Implied.

> The land of the Gebalites on the coast[2]
> and all of the Lebanon mountain
> area from Baal-gad beneath Mount
> Hermon in the south to the entrance
> of Hamath in the north;
>
> All the hill country from Lebanon to Mis-
> rephoth-maim, including all the land
> of the Sidonians.

I am ready to drive these people out from before the nation of Israel, so include all this territory when you divide the land to the nine tribes and the half-tribe of Manasseh as I have commanded you."

8   The other half of the tribe of Manasseh, and the tribes of Reuben and Gad, had already received their inheritance on the east side of the Jordan, for Moses had previously assigned this land to them.

9   Their territory ran from Aroer, on the edge of the valley of the Arnon River, included the city in the valley, and crossed the tableland of Medeba to Dibon;

10   It also included all the cities of King Sihon of the Amorites, who reigned in Heshbon, and extended as far as the borders of Ammon.

11   It included Gilead; the territory of the Geshur-ites and the Ma-acathites; all of Mount Hermon; Mount Bashan with its city of Salecah;

12   And all the territory of King Og of Bashan, who had reigned in Ashtaroth and Edre-i. (He was the last of the Rephaim, for Moses had attacked them and driven them out.

13   However, the people of Israel had not driven out the Geshurites or the Ma-acathites, who still live there among the Israelites to this day.)

---

[2]Implied.

14 The Territorial Assignments

The Land Given to the Tribe of Levi:

Moses hadn't assigned any land to the tribe of Levi; instead, they were given the offerings brought to the Lord.

15 *The Land Given to the Tribe of Reuben*:

Fitting the size of its territory to its size of population,[3] Moses had assigned the following area to the tribe of Reuben:

16 Their land extended from Aroer on the edge of the valley of the Arnon River, past the city of Arnon in the middle of the valley, to beyond the tableland near Medeba.

17 It included Heshbon and the other cities on the plain — Dibon, Bamoth-baal, Beth-baal-meon,

18 Jahaz, Kedemoth, Mepha-ath,

19 Kiriathaim, Sibmah, Zereth-shahar on the mountain above the valley,

20 Beth-peor, Beth-jeshimoth, and the slopes of Mount Pisgah.

21 The land of Reuben also included the cities of the tableland and the kingdom of Sihon. Sihon was the king who had lived in Heshbon and was killed by Moses along with the other chiefs of Midian — Evi, Rekem, Zur, Hur, and Reba.

22 The people of Israel also killed Balaam the magician, the son of Beor.

23 The Jordan River was the western boundary of the tribe of Reuben.

24 *The Land Given to the Tribe of Gad*:

Moses also assigned land to the tribe of Gad in proportion to its population.[3]

---

[3]Literally, "according to its families."

25 This territory included Jazer, all the cities of Gilead and half of the land of Ammon as far as Aroer near Rabbah.

26 It also extended from Heshbon to Ramath-mizpeh and Betonim, and from Mahanaim to Lo-de-bar.

27, 28 In the valley were Beth-haram, and Beth-nimrah, Succoth, Zaphon, and the rest of the kingdom of King Sihon of Heshbon. The Jordan River was the western border, extending as far as the Lake of Galilee; then the border turned east from the Jordan River.

29 *The Land Given to the Half-Tribe of Manasseh:* Moses has assigned the following territory to the half-tribe of Manasseh in proportion to its needs:[4]

30 Their territory extended north from Mahanaim, included all of Bashan, the former kingdom of King Og, and the sixty cities of Jair in Bashan.

31 Half of Gilead and King Og's royal cities of Ashteroth and Edre-i were given to half of the clan Machir, who was Manasseh's son.

32 That was how Moses divided the land east of the Jordan River where the people were camped at that time across from Jericho.

33 But Moses had given no land to the tribe of Levi for, as he had explained to them, the Lord God was their inheritance. He was all they needed. He would take care of them in other ways.

CHAPTER 14

The conquered lands of Canaan were allotted to the remaining nine and a half tribes of Israel. The decision as to which tribe would receive which area

---

[4]Literally, "according to its families."

> Hazar-shual, Beer-sheba, Biziothiah,
> Baalah, Iim, Ezem,
> Eltolad, Chesil, Hormah,
> Ziklag, Madmannah, Sansannah,
> Lebaoth, Shilhim, Ain, and Rimmon.

In all, there were twenty-nine of these cities with their surrounding villages.

33-36   The following cities situated in the lowlands were also given to Judah:

> Eshtaol, Zorah, Ashnah,
> Zanoah, En-gannim, Tappu-ah, Enam,
> Jarmuth, Adullam, Socoh, Azekah,
> Sha-araim, Adithaim, Gederah, and Gederothaim.

In all, there were fourteen of these cities with their surrounding villages.

37-44   The tribe of Judah also inherited twenty-five other cities with their villages:[2]

> Zenan, Hadashah, Migdal-gad,
> Dilean, Mizpeh, Jokthe-el,
> Lachish, Bozkath, Eglon,
> Cabbon, Lahmam, Chitlish,
> Gederoth, Beth-dagon, Naamah, Makkedah,
> Libnah, Ether, Ashan,
> Iphtah, Ashnah, Nezib,
> Keilah, Achzib, and Mareshah.

45   The territory of the tribe of Judah also included all the towns and villages of Ekron.

46   From Ekron the boundary extended to the Mediterranean, and included the cities along the borders of Ashdod with their nearby villages;

---

[2]Implied. See verses 41 and 44.

47   Also the city of Ashdod with its villages, and
Gaza with its villages as far as the Brook of Egypt;
also the entire Mediterranean coast from the mouth
of the Brook of Egypt on the south, to Tyre on the
north.

48-62   Judah also received these forty-four[3] cities
in the hill country with their surrounding villages:

>   Shamir, Jattir, Socoh,
>   Dannah, Kiriath-sannah (or, Debir),
>   Anab, Eshtemoh, Anim,
>   Goshen, Holon, Giloh,
>   Arab, Dumah, Eshan,
>   Janim, Beth-tappu-ah, Aphekah,
>   Humtah, Kiriath-arba (or, Hebron), Zior,
>   Maon, Carmel, Ziph, Juttah,
>   Jezreel, Jokde-am, Zanoah,
>   Kain, Gibe-ah, Timnah,
>   Halhul, Beth-zur, Gedor,
>   Maarath, Beth-anoth, Eltekon,
>   Kiriath-baal (also known as Kiriath-jear-
>   im), Rabbah,
>   Beth-arabah, Middin, Secacah,
>   Nibshan, The City of Salt, and En-gedi.

63   But the tribe of Judah could not drive out the
Jebusites who lived in the city of Jerusalem, so the
Jebusites live there among the people of Judah to this
day.

CHAPTER 16

The Southern Boundary of the Tribes of Joseph
(Ephraim and the Half-tribe of Manasseh):
This boundary extended from the Jordan River at

---

[3]Implied in verses 51, 54, 57, 59, 60, and 62, where the original text
indicates sub-totals of the number of cities assigned to Judah.

and the land north of the brook and east of the sea went to Manasseh. Manasseh's northern boundary was the territory of Asher and the eastern boundary was the territory of Issachar.

11   The half-tribe of Manasseh was also given the following cities which were situated in the areas assigned to Issachar and Asher: Beth-shean, Ible-am, Dor, En-dor, Taanach, Megiddo (where there are the three cliffs), with their respective villages.

12   But since the descendants of Manasseh could not drive out the people who lived in those cities, the Canaanites remained.

13   Later on, however, when the Israelis became strong enough, they forced the Canaanites to work as slaves.

14   Then the two tribes of Joseph came to Joshua and asked, "Why have you given us only one portion of land when the Lord has given us such large populations?"

15   "If the hill country of Ephraim is not large enough for you," Joshua replied, "and if you are able to do it, you may clear out the forest land where the Perizzites and Rephaim live."

16, 17, 18   "Fine," said the tribes of Joseph, "for the Canaanites in the lowlands around Beth-shean and the Valley of Jezreel have iron chariots and are too strong for us."

"Then you shall have the mountain forests," Joshua replied, "and since you are such a large, strong tribe you will surely be able to clear it all and live there. And I'm sure you can drive out the Canaanites from the valleys, too, even though they are strong and have iron chariots."

CHAPTER 18

After the conquest — although seven of the tribes of Israel had not yet entered and conquered the land God had given them — all Israel gathered at Shiloh to set up the Tabernacle.

3   Then Joshua asked them, "How long are you going to wait before clearing out the people living in the land which the Lord your God has given to you?

4   Select three men from each tribe and I will send them to scout the unconquered territory and bring back a report of its size and natural divisions so that I can divide it for you.

5, 6   The scouts will map it into seven sections, and then I will throw the sacred dice to decide which section will be assigned to each tribe.

7   However, remember that the Levites won't receive any land; they are priests of the Lord. That is their wonderful heritage. And of course the tribes of Gad and Reuben and the half-tribe of Manasseh won't receive any more, for they already have land on the east side of the Jordan where Moses promised them that they could settle."

8   So the scouts went out to map the country and to bring back their report to Joshua. Then the Lord could assign the sections of land to the tribes by the throw of the sacred dice.

9   The men did as they were told and divided the entire territory into seven sections, listing the cities in each section. Then they returned to Joshua and the camp at Shiloh.

10   There at the Tabernacle at Shiloh the Lord showed Joshua by the sacred lottery which tribe should have each section:

11   *The Land Given to the Tribe of Benjamin*:
The section of land assigned to the families of the
tribe of Benjamin lay between the territory previously
assigned to the tribes of Judah and Joseph.

12   The northern boundary began at the Jordan
River, went north of Jericho, then west through the hill
country and the Wilderness of Beth-aven.

13   From there the boundary went south to Luz
(also called Bethel) and proceeded down to Ataroth-
addar in the hill country south of Lower Beth-horon.

14   There the border turned south, passing the
mountain near Beth-horon and ending at the village of
Kiriath-baal (sometimes called Kiriath-jearim), one of
the cities of the tribe of Judah. This was the western
boundary.

15   The southern border ran from the edge of
Kiriath-baal, over Mount Ephron to the spring of
Naphtoah,

16   And down to the base of the mountain beside
the valley of Hinnom, north of the valley of Rephaim.
From there it continued across the valley of Hinnom,
crossed south of the old city of Jerusalem[1] where the
Jebusites lived, and continued down to En-rogel.

17   From En-rogel the boundary proceeded north-
east to En-shemesh and on to Geliloth (which is opposite the slope of Adummim). Then it went down to
the Stone of Bohan (who was a son of Reuben),

18   Where it passed along the north edge of the
Arabah. The border then went down into the Arabah,

19   Ran south past Beth-hoglah, and ended at the
north bay of the Salt Sea — which is the southern end
of the Jordan River.

---

[1]Implied.

20   The eastern border was the Jordan River. This was the land assigned to the tribe of Benjamin.

21-28   These twenty-six[2] cities were included in the land given to the tribe of Benjamin:

> Jericho, Beth-hoglah, Emek-keziz,
> Beth-arabah, Zimaraim, Bethel,
> Avvim, Parah, Ophrah,
> Chephar-ammoni, Ophni, Geba,
> Gibeon, Ramah, Be-eroth,
> Mizpeh, Chephirah, Mozah,
> Rekem, Irpeel, Taralah,
> Zela, Ha-eleph, Jebus (or, Jerusalem),
>   Gibe-ah, and Kiriath-jearim.

All of these cities and their surrounding villages were given to the tribe of Benjamin.

CHAPTER 19

The Land Given to the Tribe of Simeon:
   The tribe of Simeon received the next assignment of land — including part of the land previously assigned to Judah.

2-7   Their inheritance included these seventeen[1] cities with their respective villages:

> Beer-sheba, Sheba, Moladah,
> Hazar-shual, Balah, Ezem,
> Eltolad, Bethul, Hormah,
> Ziklag, Beth-marcaboth, Hazar-susah,
> Beth-lebaoth,
> Sharuhen, En-rimmon, Ether, and Ashan.

8   The cities as far south as Baalath-beer (also

---

[2]Implied in verses 24 and 28, where the original manuscript indicates sub-totals.

[1]Totaled from verses 6 and 7 of the original manuscripts, where sub-totals are indicated.

known as Ramah-in-the-Negeb) were also given to the tribe of Simeon.

9   So the Simeon tribe's inheritance came from what had earlier been given to Judah, for Judah's section had been too large for them.

10   *The Land Given to the Tribe of Zebulun*:
The third tribe to receive its assignment of land was Zebulun. Its boundary started on the south side of Sarid.

11   From there it circled to the west, going near Mareal and Dabbesheth until it reached the brook east of Jeokne-am.

12   In the other direction, the boundary line went east to the border of Chisloth-tabor, and from there to Daberath and Japhia;

13   Then it continued east of Gath-hepher, Eth-kazin, and Rimmon and turned toward Neah.

14   The northern boundary of Zebulun passed Hannathon and ended at the Valley of Iphtahel.

15, 16   The cities in these areas, besides those already mentioned,[2] included Kattath, Nahalal, Shimron, Idalah, Bethlehem, and each of their surrounding villages. Altogether there were twelve of these cities.

17-23   *The Land Given to the Tribe of Issachar*:
The fourth tribe to be assigned its land was Issachar. Its boundaries included the following cities:

Jezreel, Chesulloth, Shunem,
Hapharaim, Shion, Anaharath,
Rabbith, Kishion, Ebez,
Remeth, En-gannim, En-haddah, Beth-paz-zez,
Tabor, Shahazumah, and Beth-shemesh —

---

[2]Implied.

sixteen cities in all, each with its surrounding villages. The boundary of Issachar ended at the Jordan River.

24 *The Land Given to the Tribe of Asher*:
The fifth tribe to be assigned its land was Asher. The boundaries included these cities:

25 Helkath, Hali, Beten, Achshaph,

26 Allammelech, Amad, and Mishal.
The boundary on the west side went from Carmel to Shihor-libnath,

27 Turned east toward Beth-dagon, and ran as far as Zebulun in the Valley of Iphtahel, running north of Beth-emek and Neiel. It then passed to the east of Kabul,

28 Ebron, Rehob, Hammon, Kanah, and Greater Sidon.

29 Then the boundary turned toward Ramah and the fortified city of Tyre and came to the Mediterranean Sea at Hosah. The territory also included Mahalab, Achzib,

30, 31 Ummah, Aphek, and Rehob — an overall total of twenty-two cities and their surrounding villages.

32 *The Land Given to the Tribe of Naphtali*:
The sixth tribe to receive its assignment was the tribe of Naphtali.

33 Its boundary began at Judah, at the oak in Zaanannim, and extended across to Adami-nekeb, Jabneel, and Lakkum, ending at the Jordan River.

34 The western boundary began near Heleph and ran past Aznoth-tabor, then to Hukkok, and coincided with the Zebulun boundary in the south, and with the boundary of Asher on the west, and with the Jordan River at the east.

35-39   The fortified cities included in this territory were:

> Ziddim, Zer, Hammath, Rakkath, Chin-
> nereth,
> Adamah, Ramah, Hazor,
> Kedesh, Edre-i, Enhazor,
> Yiron, Migdal-el, Horem, Beth-anath, and
> Beth-shemesh.

So altogether the territory included nineteen cities with their surrounding villages.

40   *The Land Given to the Tribe of Dan*:
The last tribe to be assigned its land was Dan.

41-46   The cities within its area included:

> Zorah, Eshta-ol, Ir-shemesh,
> Sha-alabbin, Aijalon, Ithlah,
> Elon, Timnah, Ekron,
> Eltekeh, Gibbethon, Baalath,
> Jehud, Bene-berak, Gath-rimmon,
> Me-jarkon, and Rakkon, also the territory
> near Joppa.

47, 48   But some of this territory proved impossible to conquer, so the tribe of Dan captured the city of Leshem, slaughtered its people, and lived there; and they called the city "Dan," naming it after their ancestor.

49   So all the land was divided among the tribes, with the boundaries indicated; and the nation of Israel gave a special piece of land to Joshua,

50   For the Lord had said that he could have any city he wanted. He chose Timnath-serah in the hill country of Ephraim; he rebuilt it and lived there.

51   Eleazar the priest, Joshua, and the leaders of the tribes of Israel supervised the sacred lottery to

divide the land among the tribes. This was done in the Lord's presence at the entrance of the Tabernacle at Shiloh.

CHAPTER 20

The Lord said to Joshua,
2   "Tell the people of Israel to designate now the Cities of Refuge, as I instructed Moses.[1]

3   If a man is guilty of killing someone unintentionally, he can run to one of these cities and be protected from the relatives of the dead man, who may try to kill him in revenge.

4   When the innocent killer reaches any of these cities, he will meet with the city council and explain what happened, and they must let him come in and must give him a place to live among them.

5   If a relative of the dead man comes to kill him in revenge, the innocent slayer must not be released to them, for the death was accidental.

6   The man who caused the accidental death must stay in that city until he has been tried by the judges, and must live there until the death of the high priest who was in office at the time of the accident. But then he is free to return to his own city and home."

7   The cities chosen as Cities of Refuge were Kedesh of Galilee in the hill country of Naphtali; Shechem, in the hill country of Ephraim; and Kiriatharba (also known as Hebron) in the hill country of Judah.

8   The Lord also instructed that three cities be set aside for this purpose on the east side of the Jordan River, across from Jericho. They were Bezer, in the

---

[1]See Numbers 35 and I Chronicles 6.

wilderness of the land of the tribe of Reuben; Ramoth of Gilead, in the territory of the tribe of Gad; and Golan of Bashan, in the land of the tribe of Manasseh.

9   These Cities of Refuge were for foreigners living in Israel as well as for the Israelis themselves, so that anyone who accidentally killed another man could run to that place for a trial, and not be killed in revenge.

CHAPTER 21

Then the leaders of the tribe of Levi came to Shiloh to consult with Eleazar the priest and with Joshua and the leaders of the various tribes.

2   "The Lord instructed Moses to give cities to us Levites for our homes, and pastureland for our cattle," they said.

3   So they were given some of the recently conquered cities with their pasturelands.

4   Thirteen of these cities had been assigned originally to the tribes of Judah, Simeon, and Benjamin. These were given to some of the priests of the Kohath division (of the tribe of Levi, descendants of Aaron).

5   The other families of the Kohath division were given ten cities from the territories of Ephraim, Dan, and the half-tribe of Manasseh.

6   The Gershon division received thirteen cities, selected by sacred lot in the area of Bashan. These cities were given by the tribes of Issachar, Asher, Naphtali, and the half-tribe of Manasseh.

7   The Merari division received twelve cities from the tribes of Reuben, Gad, and Zebulun.

8   So the Lord's command to Moses was obeyed, and the cities and pasturelands were assigned by the toss of the sacred dice.

9-16   First to receive their assignment were the priests — the descendants of Aaron, who was a member of the Kohath division of the Levites. The tribes of Judah and Simeon gave them the nine[1] cities listed below, with their surrounding pasturelands:

Hebron, in the Judean hills, as a City of Refuge —it was also called Kiriath-arba (Arba was the father of Anak) — although the fields beyond the city and the surrounding villages were given to Caleb, the son of Jephunneh;

Libnah;

Jattir, Eshtemoa;

Holon, Debir;

Ain, Juttah, and Beth-shemesh.

17, 18   The tribe of Benjamin gave them these four cities and their pasturelands:

Gibeon, Gaba, Anathoth, and Almon.

19   So in all, thirteen cities were given to the priests — the descendants of Aaron.

20, 21, 22   The other families of the Kohath division received four[2] cities and pasturelands from the tribe of Ephraim:

Ephraim:

Shechem (a City of Refuge), Gezer, Kibza-im, and Beth-horon.

23, 24   The following four cities and pasturelands were given by the tribe of Dan:

Elteke, Gibbethon, Aijalon, and Gath-rimmon.

25   The half-tribe of Manasseh gave the cities of Taanach and Gath-rimmon with their surrounding pasturelands.

---

[1]Implied in verse 16, where a subtotal is indicated in the original text.
[2]Implied in verse 22, where the total appears in the text.

26　So the total number of cities and pasturelands given to the remainder of the Kohath division was ten.

27　The descendants of Gershon, another division of the Levites, received two cities and pasturelands from the half-tribe of Manasseh:

> Golan, in Bashan (a City of Refuge), and Be-eshterah.

28　The tribe of Issachar gave four cities:

> Kishion, Daberath,

29　　　Jarmuth, and Engannim.

30, 31　The tribe of Asher gave four cities and pasturelands:

> Mishal, Abdon, Helkath, and Rehob.

32　The tribe of Naphtali gave:

> Kedesh, in Galilee (a City of Refuge), Hammoth-dor, and Kartan.

33　So thirteen cities with their pasturelands were assigned to the division of Gershon.

34, 35　The remainder of the Levites — the Merari division — were given four cities by the tribe of Zebulun:

> Jokne-am, Kartah, Dimnah, and Nahalal.

36　Reuben gave them:

> Bezer, Jahaz,

37　　　Kedemoth, and Mepha-ath.

38, 39　Gad gave them four cities with pasturelands:

> Ramoth (a City of Refuge), Mahanaim, Heshbon, and Jazer,

40　So the Merari division of the Levites was given twelve cities in all.

41, 42　The total number of cities and pasturelands given to the Levites came to forty-eight.

43 So in this way the Lord gave to Israel all the land He had promised to their ancestors, and they went in and conquered it and lived there.

44 And the Lord gave them peace, just as He had promised, and no one could stand against them; the Lord helped them destroy all their enemies.

45 Every good thing the Lord had promised them came true.

CHAPTER 22

Joshua now called together the troops from the tribes of Reuben, Gad, and the half-tribe of Manasseh,

2, 3 And addressed them as follows: "You have done as the Lord's disciple Moses commanded you, and have obeyed every order I have given you — every order of the Lord your God. You have not deserted your brother tribes, even though the campaign has lasted for such a long time.

4 And now the Lord our God has given us success and rest as He promised He would. So go home now to the land given you by the Lord's servant Moses, on the other side of the Jordan River.

5 Be sure to continue to obey all of the commandments Moses gave you. Love the Lord and follow His plan for your lives. Cling to Him and serve Him enthusiastically."

6 So Joshua blessed them and sent them home.

7, 8 (Moses had assigned the land of Bashan to the half-tribe of Manasseh, although the other half of the tribe was given land on the west side of the Jordan.)

As Joshua sent away these troops, he blessed

them and told them to share their great wealth with their relatives back home — their booty of cattle, silver, gold, bronze, iron, and clothing.

9   So the troops of Reuben, Gad, and the half-tribe of Manasseh left the army of Israel at Shiloh in Canaan and crossed the Jordan River to their own homeland of Gilead.

10   Before they went across, while they were still in Canaan, they built a large monument for everyone to see, in the shape of an altar.

11   But when the rest of Israel heard about what they had done,

12   They mustered an army at Shiloh and prepared to go to war against their brother tribes.

13   First, however, they sent a delegation led by Phinehas, the son of Eleazar the priest. They crossed the river and talked to the tribes of Reuben, Gad, and Manasseh.

14   In this delegation were ten high officials of Israel, one from each of the ten tribes, and each a clan leader.

15   When they arrived in the land of Gilead they said to the tribes of Reuben, Gad, and the half-tribe of Manasseh,

16   "The whole congregation of the Lord demands to know why you are sinning against the God of Israel by turning away from Him and building an altar of rebellion against the Lord.

17, 18   Was our guilt at Peor — from which we have not even yet been cleansed despite the plague that tormented us — so little that you must rebel again? For you know that if you rebel today the Lord will be angry with all of us tomorrow.

19 If you need the altar because your land is defiled, then join us on our side of the river where the Lord lives among us in His Tabernacle, and we will share our land with you. But do not rebel against the Lord by building another altar in addition to the only true altar of our God.

20 Don't you remember that when Achan, the son of Zerah, sinned against the Lord, the entire nation was punished in addition to the one man who had sinned?"

21 This was the reply of the people of Reuben, Gad, and the half-tribe of Manasseh to these high officials:

22, 23 "We swear by Jehovah, the God of gods, that we have not built the altar in rebellion against the Lord. He knows (and let all Israel know it too) that we have not built the altar to sacrifice burnt offerings or grain offerings or peace offerings — may the curse of God be on us if we did.

24, 25 We have done it because we love the Lord and because we fear that in the future your children will say to ours, 'What right do you have to worship the Lord God of Israel? The Lord has placed the Jordan River as a barrier between our people and your people! You have no part in the Lord.' And your children may make our children stop worshiping Him.

26, 27 So we decided to build the altar as a symbol to show our children and your children that we, too, may worship the Lord with our burnt offerings and peace offerings and sacrifices, and your children will not be able to say to ours, 'You have no part in the Lord our God.'

28 If they say this, our children can reply, 'Look

at the altar of the Lord which our fathers made, patterned after the altar of Jehovah. It is not for burnt offerings or sacrifices, but is a symbol of the relationship with God that both of us have.'

29 Far be it from us to turn away from the Lord or to rebel against Him by building our own altar for burnt offerings, grain offerings, or sacrifices. Only the altar in front of the Tabernacle may be used for that."

30 When Phinehas the priest and the high officials heard this from the tribes of Reuben, Gad, and Manasseh, they were very happy.

31 Phinehas replied to them, "Today we know that the Lord is among us because you have not sinned against the Lord as we thought; instead, you have saved us from destruction!"

32 Then Phinehas and the ten ambassadors went back to the people of Israel and told them what had happened,

33 And all Israel rejoiced and praised God and spoke no more of war against Reuben and Gad.

34 The people of Reuben and Gad named the altar "The Altar of Witness," for they said, "It is a witness between us and them that Jehovah is our God, too."

CHAPTER 23

Long after this, when the Lord had given success to the people of Israel against their enemies and when Joshua was very old,

2 He called for the leaders of Israel — the elders, judges, and officers — and said to them, "I am an old man now,

3 And you have seen all that the Lord your God

has done for you during my lifetime. He has fought for you against your enemies and has given you their land.

4, 5 And I have divided to you the land of the nations yet unconquered as well as the land of those you have already destroyed. All the land from the Jordan River to the Mediterranean Sea shall be yours, for the Lord your God will drive out all the people living there now, and you will live there instead, just as He has promised you.

6 But be very sure to follow all the instructions written in the book of the laws of Moses; do not deviate from them the least little bit.

7 Be sure that you do not mix with the heathen people still remaining in the land; do not even mention the names of their gods, much less swear by them or worship them.

8 But follow the Lord your God just as you have until now.

9 He has driven out great, strong nations from before you, and no one has been able to defeat you.

10 Each one of you has put to flight a thousand of the enemy, for the Lord your God fights for you, just as He has promised.

11 So be very careful to keep on loving Him.

12 If you don't, and if you begin to intermarry with the nations around you,

13 Then know for a certainty that the Lord your God will no longer chase those nations from your land. Instead, they will be a snare and a trap to you, a pain in your side and a thorn in your eyes, and you will disappear from this good land which the Lord your God has given you.

14   Soon I will be going the way of all the earth —
I am going to die.

You know very well that God's promises to you
have all come true.

15, 16   But as certainly as the Lord has given you
the good things He promised, just as certainly He will
bring evil upon you if you disobey Him. For if you
worship other gods He will completely wipe you out
from this good land which the Lord has given you.
His anger will rise hot against you, and you will quickly
perish.

CHAPTER 24

Then Joshua summoned all the people of Israel to
him at Shechem, along with their leaders — the
elders, officers, and judges. So they came and presented themselves before God.

2   Then Joshua addressed them as follows: "The
Lord God of Israel says, 'Your ancestors, including
Terah the father of Abraham and Nahor, lived east of
the Euphrates River; and they worshiped other gods.

3   But I took your father Abraham from that
land across the river and led him into the land of
Canaan and gave him many descendants through
Isaac his son.

4   Isaac's children, whom I gave him, were Jacob
and Esau. To Esau I gave the area around Mount
Seir while Jacob and his children went into Egypt.

5   Then I sent Moses and Aaron to bring terrible
plagues upon Egypt; and afterwards I brought My people out as free men.

6   But when they arrived at the Red Sea, the
Egyptians chased after them with chariots and cavalry.

7 Then Israel cried out to Me and I put darkness between them and the Egyptians; and I brought the sea crashing in upon the Egyptians, drowning them. You saw what I did. Then Israel lived in the wilderness for many years.

8 Finally I brought you into the land of the Amorites on the other side of the Jordan; and they fought against you, but I destroyed them and gave you their land.

9 Then King Balak of Moab started a war against Israel, and he asked Balaam, the son of Beor, to curse you.

10 But I wouldn't listen to him. Instead I made him bless you; and so I delivered Israel from him.

11 Then you crossed the Jordan River and came to Jericho. The men of Jericho fought against you, and so did many others — the Perizzites, the Canaanites, the Hittites, the Girgashites, the Hivites, and the Jebusites. Each in turn fought against you but I destroyed them all.

12 And I sent hornets ahead of you to drive out the two kings of the Amorites and their people. It was not your swords or bows that brought you victory!

13 I gave you land you had not worked for and cities you did not build — these cities where you are now living. I gave you vineyards and olive groves for food, though you did not plant them.'

14 So revere Jehovah and serve Him in sincerity and truth. Put away forever the idols which your ancestors worshiped when they lived beyond the Euphrates River and in Egypt. Worship the Lord alone.

15 But if you are unwilling to obey the Lord, then decide today whom you will obey. Will it be the gods

of your ancestors beyond the Euphrates or the gods of the Amorites here in this land? But as for me and my family, we will serve the Lord."

16 And the people replied, "We would never forsake the Lord and worship other gods!

17 For the Lord our God is the one who rescued our fathers from their slavery in the land of Egypt. He is the God who did mighty miracles before the eyes of Israel, as we traveled through the wilderness, and preserved us from our enemies when we passed through their land.

18 It was the Lord who drove out the Amorites and the other nations living here in the land. Yes, we choose the Lord, for He alone is our God."

19 But Joshua replied to the people, "You can't worship the Lord God, for He is holy and jealous; He will not forgive your rebellion and sins.

20 If you forsake Him and worship other gods, He will turn upon you and destroy you, even though He has taken care of you for such a long time."

21 But the people answered, "We choose the Lord!"

22 "You have heard yourselves say it," Joshua said — "you have chosen to obey the Lord."

"Yes," they replied, "we are witnesses."

23 "All right," he said, "then you must destroy all the idols you now own, and you must obey the Lord God of Israel."

24 The people replied to Joshua, "Yes, we will worship and obey the Lord alone."

25 So Joshua made a covenant with them that day at Shechem, committing them to a permanent and binding contract between themselves and God.

26 Joshua recorded the people's reply in the book of the laws of God, and took a huge stone as a reminder and rolled it beneath the oak tree that was beside the Tabernacle.

27 Then Joshua said to all the people, "This stone has heard everything the Lord said, so it will be a witness to testify against you if you go back on your word."

28 Then Joshua sent the people away to their own sections of the country.

29 Soon after this he died at the age of 110.

30 He was buried on his own estate at Timnath-serah, in the hill country of Ephraim, on the north side of the mountains of Gaash.

31 Israel obeyed the Lord throughout the lifetimes of Joshua and the other old men who had personally witnessed the amazing deeds which the Lord had done for Israel.

32 The bones of Joseph, which the people of Israel had brought with them when they left Egypt, were buried in Shechem, in the parcel of ground which Jacob had bought for $200 from the sons of Hamor. (The land was located in the territory assigned to the tribes of Joseph.)

33 Eleazar, the son of Aaron, also died; he was buried in the hill country of Ephraim, at Gibe-ah, the city which had been given to his son Phinehas.

Judges

CHAPTER 1

After Joshua died, the nation of Israel went to the Lord to receive His instructions. "Which of our tribes should be the first to go to war against the Canaanites?" they inquired.

2 God's answer came, "Judah. And I will give them a great victory."

3 The leaders of the tribe of Judah, however, asked help from the tribe of Simeon. "Join us in clearing out the people living in the territory allotted to us," they said, "and then we will help you conquer yours." So the army of Simeon went with the army of Judah.

4, 5, 6 And the Lord helped them defeat the Canaanites and Perizzites, so that ten thousand of the enemy were slain at Bezek. King Adoni-bezek escaped, but the Israeli army soon captured him and cut off his thumbs and big toes.

7 "I have treated seventy kings in this same manner and have fed them the scraps under my table!" King Adoni-bezek said. "Now God has paid me back." He was taken to Jerusalem, and died there.

8 (Judah had conquered Jerusalem, and massacred its people, setting the city on fire.)

9 Afterwards the army of Judah fought the Canaanites in the hill country and in the Negeb, as well as on the coastal plains.

10 Then Judah marched against the Canaanites in Hebron (formerly called Kiriath-arba), destroying the cities of Sheshai, Ahiman, and Talmai.

11 Later they attacked the city of Debir (formerly called Kiriath-sepher).

12 "Who will lead the attack against Debir?" Caleb challenged them. "Whoever conquers it shall have my daughter Achsah as his wife!"

13 Caleb's nephew, Othni-el, son of his younger brother Kenaz, volunteered to lead the attack; and he conquered the city and won Achsah as his bride.

14 As they were leaving for their new home,[1] she urged him to ask her father for an additional[2] piece of land. She dismounted from her donkey to speak to Caleb about it. "What do you wish?" he asked.

15 And she replied, "You have been kind enough to give me land in the Negeb, but please give us springs of water too." So Caleb gave her the upper and lower springs.

16 When the tribe of Judah moved into its new land in the Negeb wilderness south of Arad, the descendants of Moses' father-in-law — members of the Kenite tribe — accompanied them. They left their homes in Jericho, "The City of Palm Trees," and the two tribes lived together after that.

17 Afterwards the army of Judah joined Simeon's and they fought the Canaanites at the city of Zephath and massacred all its people. So now the city is named Hormah (meaning, "massacred").

18 The army of Judah also conquered the cities of Gaza, Ashkelon, and Ekron, with their surrounding vil-

[1]Literally, "when she came to him."
[2]Implied.

lages.

19 The Lord helped the tribe of Judah exterminate the people of the hill country, though they failed in their attempt to conquer the people of the valley, who had iron chariots.

20 The city of Hebron was given to Caleb as the Lord had promised; so Caleb drove out the inhabitants of the city; they were descendants of the three sons of Anak.

21 The tribe of Benjamin failed to exterminate the Jebusites living in Jerusalem, so they still live there today, mingled with the Israelis.

22, 23 As for the tribe of Joseph, they attacked the city of Bethel, formerly known as Luz, and the Lord was with them. First they sent scouts,

24 Who captured a man coming out of the city. They offered to spare his life and that of his family if he would show them the entrance passage through the wall.[3]

25 So he showed them how to get in, and they massacred the entire population except for this man and his family.

26 Later the man moved to Syria and founded a city there, naming it Luz, too, as it is still known to-day.

27 The tribe of Manasseh failed to drive out the people living in Beth-shean, Taanach, Dor, Ibleam, Megiddo, with their surrounding towns; so the Canaanites stayed there.

28 In later years when the Israelis were stronger they put the Canaanites to work as slaves, but never

---

[3]Literally, "the way into the city." Obviously this does not mean via the city gates.

did force them to leave the country.

29 This was also true of the Canaanites living in Gezer; they still live among the tribe of Ephraim.

30 And the tribe of Zebulun did not massacre the people of Kitron or Nahalol, but made them their slaves;

31, 32 Nor did the tribe of Asher drive out the residents of Acco, Sidon, Ahlab, Achzib, Helbah, Aphik, or Rehob; so the Israelis still live among the Canaanites, who were the original people of that land.

33 And the tribe of Naphtali did not drive out the people of Beth-shemesh or of Beth-anath, so these people continue to live among them as servants.

34 As for the tribe of Dan, the Amorites forced them into the hill country and wouldn't let them come down into the valley;

35 But when the Amorites later spread into Mount Heres, Aijalon, and Sha-albim, the tribe of Joseph conquered them and made them their slaves.

36 The boundary of the Amorites begins at the ascent of Scorpion Pass, runs to a spot called The Rock, and continues upward from there.

CHAPTER 2

One day the Angel of the Lord arrived at Bochim, coming from Gilgal, and announced to the people of Israel, "I brought you out of Egypt into this land which I promised to your ancestors, and I said that I would never break My covenant with you,

2 If you, on your part, would make no peace treaties with the people living in this land; I told you to destroy their heathen altars. Why have you not

obeyed?

3 And now since you have broken the contract, it is no longer in effect, and I no longer promise to destroy the nations living in your land; rather, they shall be thorns in your sides, and their gods will be a constant temptation to you."

4 The people broke into tears as the Angel finished speaking;

5 So the name of that place was called "Bochim" (meaning, "the place where people wept"). Then they offered sacrifices to the Lord.

6 When Joshua finally disbanded the armies of Israel, the tribes moved into their new territories and took possession of the land.

7-9 Joshua, the man of God, died at the age of 110, and was buried at the edge of his property in Timnath-heres, in the hill country of Ephraim, north of Mount Gaash. The people had remained true to the Lord throughout Joshua's lifetime, and as long afterwards as the old men of his generation were still living — those who had seen the mighty miracles the Lord had done for Israel.

10 But finally all that generation died; and the next generation did not worship Jehovah as their God, and did not care about the mighty miracles He had done for Israel.

11 They did many things which the Lord had expressly forbidden, including the worshiping of heathen gods.

12-14 They abandoned Jehovah, the God loved and worshiped by their ancestors — the God who had brought them out of Egypt. Instead, they were worshiping and bowing low before the idols of the neighboring nations. So the anger of the Lord flamed out against all Israel. He left them to the mercy of their enemies, for they had departed from Jehovah and were worshiping Baal and the Ashtaroth idols.

15 So now when the nation of Israel went out to battle against its enemies, the Lord blocked their path. He had warned them about this, and in fact had vowed that He would do it. But when the people were in this terrible plight,

16 The Lord raised up judges to save them from their enemies.

17 Yet even then Israel would not listen to the judges, but broke faith with Jehovah by worshiping other gods instead. How quickly they turned away from the true faith of their ancestors, for they refused to obey God's commands.

18 Each judge rescued the people of Israel from their enemies throughout his lifetime, for the Lord was moved to pity by the groaning of His people under their crushing oppressions; so He helped them as long as that judge lived.

19 But when the judge died, the people turned from doing right and behaved even worse than their ancestors had. They prayed to heathen gods again, throwing themselves to the ground in humble worship. They stubbornly returned to the evil customs of the nations around them.

20 Then the anger of the Lord would flame out against Israel again. He declared, "Because these people have violated the treaty I made with their ancestors,

21 I will no longer drive out the nations left unconquered by Joshua when he died.

22 Instead, I will use these nations to test My

people, to see whether or not they will obey the Lord as their ancestors did."

23 So the Lord left those nations in the land and did not drive them out, nor let Israel destroy them.

CHAPTER 3

H ere is a list of the nations the Lord left in the land to test the new generation of Israel who had not experienced the wars of Canaan. For God wanted to give opportunity to the youth of Israel to exercise faith[1] and obedience[1] in conquering their enemies:[2]

3   The Philistines (five cities),
           The Canaanites,
           The Sidonians,
           The Hivites living in Mount Lebanon, from Baal-hermon to the entrance of Hamath.

4 These people were a test to the new generation of Israel, to see whether they would obey the commandments the Lord had given to them through Moses.

5 So Israel lived among the Canaanites, Hittites, Hivites, Perizzites, Amorites, and Jebusites.

6 But instead of destroying them, the people of Israel intermarried with them. The young men of Israel took their girls as wives, and the Israeli girls married their men. And soon Israel was worshiping their gods.

7 So the people of Israel were very evil in God's sight, for they turned against Jehovah their God and worshiped Baal and the goddess Asheroth.

---

[1]Implied in chapter 2, verse 22; and chapter 3, verse 4.
[2]Literally, "that . . . the people of Israel . . . might know war . . ."

8   Then the anger of the Lord flamed out against Israel, and He let King Cushan-rishathaim of eastern Syria conquer them. They were under his rule for eight years.

9   But when Israel cried out to the Lord, He gave them Caleb's nephew, Othni-el (son of Kenaz, Caleb's younger brother) to save them.

10   The Spirit of the Lord took control of him and he reformed and purged Israel so that when he led the forces of Israel against the army of King Cushan-rishathaim, the Lord helped Israel conquer him completely.

11   Then, for forty years under Othni-el, there was peace in the land. But when Othni-el died,

12   The people of Israel turned once again to their sinful ways, so God helped King Eglon of Moab to conquer part of Israel at that time.

13   Allied with him were the armies of the Ammonites and the Amalekites. These forces defeated the Israelis and took possession of Jericho, often called "The City of Palm Trees."

14   For the next eighteen years the people of Israel were required to pay crushing taxes to King Eglon.

15   But when they cried to the Lord, He sent them a savior, Ehud (son of Gera, a Benjaminite), who was left-handed. Ehud was the man chosen to carry Israel's annual tax money to the Moabite capital.

16   Before he went on this journey he made himself a double-edged dagger eighteen inches long and hid it in his clothing, strapped against his right thigh.

17, 18, 19   After delivering the money to King Eglon (who, by the way, was very fat!) he started home again. But outside the city, at the quarries of

Gilgal, he sent his companions on and returned alone to the king. "I have a secret message for you," he told him. The king immediately dismissed all those who were with him so that he could have a private interview.

20 Ehud walked over to him as he was sitting in a cool upstairs room and said to him, "It is a message from God!" King Eglon stood up at once to receive it,

21 Whereupon Ehud reached beneath his robe with his strong left hand, pulled out the double-bladed dagger strapped against his right thigh, and plunged it deep into the king's belly.

22, 23 The hilt of the dagger disappeared beneath the flesh, and the fat closed over it as the entrails oozed out. Leaving the dagger there, Ehud locked the doors behind him and escaped across an upstairs porch.

24 When the king's servants returned and saw that the doors were locked, they waited, thinking that perhaps he was using the bathroom.

25 But when, after a long time, he still didn't come out, they became concerned and got a key. And when they opened the door, they found their master dead on the floor.

26 Meanwhile Ehud had escaped past the quarries to Se-irah.

27 When he arrived in the hill country of Ephraim, he blew a trumpet as a call to arms and mustered an army under his own command.

28 "Follow me," he told them, "for the Lord has put your enemies, the Moabites, at your mercy!" The army then proceeded to seize the fords of the Jordan River near Moab, preventing anyone from crossing.

29 Then they attacked the Moabites and killed about ten thousand of the strongest and most skillful of their fighting men, letting not one escape.

30 So Moab was conquered by Israel that day, and the land was at peace for the next eighty years.

31 The next judge after Ehud was Shamgar (son of Anath). He once killed 600 Philistines with an ox goad, thereby saving Israel from disaster.

CHAPTER 4

After Ehud's death the people of Israel again sinned against the Lord,

2, 3 So the Lord let them be conquered by King Jabin of Hazor, in Canaan. The commander-in-chief of his army was Sisera, who lived in Harosheth-ha-goiim. He had 900 iron chariots, and made life unbearable for the Israelis for twenty years. But finally they begged the Lord for help.

4 Israel's leader at that time, the one who was responsible for bringing the people back to God, was Deborah, a prophetess, the wife of Lappidoth.

5 She held court at a place now called "Deborah's Palm Tree," between Ramah and Bethel, in the hill country of Ephraim; and the Israelites came to her to decide their disputes.[1]

6 One day she summoned Barak (son of Abinoam), who lived in Kedesh, in the land of Naphtali, and said to him, "The Lord God of Israel has commanded you to mobilize ten thousand men from the tribes of Naphtali and Zebulun. Lead them to Mount Tabor,

---

[1] Or, "to listen to her speak to them about God."

7   To fight King Jabin's mighty army with all his chariots, under General Sisera's command. The Lord says, 'I will draw them to the Kishon River, and you will defeat them there.'"

8   "I'll go, but only if you go with me!" Barak told her.

9   "All right," she replied, "I'll go with you; but I'm warning you now that the honor of conquering Sisera will go to a woman instead of to you!" So she went with him to Kedesh.

10   When Barak summoned the men of Zebulun and Naphtali to mobilize at Kedesh, ten thousand men volunteered. And Deborah marched with them.

11   (Heber, the Kenite — the Kenites were the descendants of Moses' father-in-law Hobab — had moved away from the rest of his clan, and had been living in various places as far away as the Oak of Za-anannim, near Kedesh.)

12   When General Sisera was told that Barak and his army were camped at Mount Tabor,

13   He mobilized his entire army, including the 900 iron chariots, and marched from Harosheth-ha-goiim to the Kishon River.

14   Then Deborah said to Barak, "Now is the time for action! The Lord leads on! He has already delivered Sisera into your hand!" So Barak led his ten thousand men down the slopes of Mount Tabor into battle.

15   Then the Lord threw the enemy into a panic, both the soldiers and the charioteers, and Sisera leaped from his chariot and escaped on foot.

16   Barak and his men chased the enemy and the chariots as far as Harosheth-ha-goiim, until all of Sis-

era's army was destroyed; not one man was left alive.

17   Meanwhile, Sisera had escaped to the tent of Jael, the wife of Heber the Kenite, for there was a mutual-assistance agreement between King Jabin of Hazor and the clan of Heber.

18   Jael went out to meet Sisera and said to him, "Come into my tent, sir. You will be safe here in our protection. Don't be afraid." So he went into her tent and she covered him with a blanket.

19   "Please give me some water," he said, "for I am very thirsty." So she gave him some milk and covered him again.

20   "Stand in the door of the tent," he told her, "and if anyone comes by looking for me, tell them that no one is here."

21   Then Jael took a sharp tent peg and a hammer and, quietly creeping up to him as he slept, she drove the peg through his temples and into the ground; and so he died, for he was fast asleep from weariness.

22   When Barak came by looking for Sisera, Jael went out to meet him and said, "Come, and I will show you the man you are looking for." So he followed her into the tent and found Sisera lying there dead, with the tent peg through his temples.

23   So that day the Lord used Israel to subdue King Jabin of Canaan.

24   And from that time on Israel became stronger and stronger against King Jabin, until he and all his people were destroyed.

CHAPTER 5

Then Deborah and Barak sang this song about the wonderful victory:

2 Praise the Lord!
Israel's leaders bravely led;
The people gladly followed!
Yes, bless the Lord!

3 Listen, O you kings and princes,
For I shall sing about the Lord,
The God of Israel.

4 When You led us out from Seir,
Out across the fields of Edom,
The earth trembled
And the sky poured down its rain.

5 Yes, even Mount Sinai quaked
At the presence of the God of Israel!

6 In the days of Shamgar and of Jael,
The main roads were deserted.
Travelers used the narrow, crooked side
    paths.

7 Israel's population dwindled,
Until Deborah became a mother to Israel.

8 When Israel chose new gods,
Everything collapsed.
Our masters would not let us have
A shield or spear.
Among forty thousand men of Israel,
Not a weapon could be found!

9 How I rejoice
In the leaders of Israel
Who offered themselves so willingly!
Praise the Lord!

10 Let all Israel, rich and poor,
Join in His praises —
Those who ride on white donkeys
And sit on rich carpets,

And those who are poor and must walk.

11 The village musicians
Gather at the village well
To sing of the triumphs of the Lord.
Again and again they sing the ballad
Of how the Lord saved Israel
With an army of peasants!
The people of the Lord
Marched through the gates!

12 Awake, O Deborah, and sing!
Arise, O Barak!
O son of Abino-am, lead away your captives!

13, 14 Down from Mount Tabor marched the noble remnant.
The people of the Lord
Marched down against great odds.
They came from Ephraim and Benjamin,
From Machir and from Zebulun.

15 Down into the valley
Went the princes of Issachar
With Deborah and Barak.
At God's command they rushed into the valley.
(But the tribe of Reuben
Didn't go.

16 Why did you sit at home among the sheepfolds,
Playing your shepherd pipes?
Yes, the tribe of Reuben has an uneasy conscience.

17 Why did Gilead remain across the Jordan,
And why did Dan remain with his ships?

And why did Asher sit unmoved
Upon the seashore,
At ease beside his harbors?)

18   But the tribes of Zebulun and Naphtali
Dared to die upon the fields of battle.

19   The kings of Canaan fought in Taanach
By Megiddo's springs,
But did not win the victory.

20   The very stars of heaven
Fought Sisera.

21   The rushing Kishon River
Swept them away.
March on, my soul, with strength!

22   Hear the stamping
Of the horsehoofs of the enemy!
See the prancing of his steeds!

23   But the Angel of Jehovah
Put a curse on Meroz.
"Curse them bitterly," He said,
"Because they did not come to help the
       Lord
Against His enemies."

24   Blessed be Jael,
The wife of Heber the Kenite —
Yes, may she be blessed
Above all women who live in tents.

25   He asked for water
And she gave him milk in a beautiful cup!

26   Then she took a tent pin and a workman's
       hammer
And pierced Sisera's temples,
Crushing his head.
She pounded the tent pin through his head,

27	And he lay at her feet, Dead.
28	The mother of Sisera watched through the window For his return. "Why is his chariot so long in coming? Why don't we hear the sound of the wheels?"
29	But her ladies-in-waiting — and she herself — replied,
30	"There is much loot to be divided, And it takes time. Each man receives a girl or two; And Sisera will get gorgeous robes, And he will bring home Many gifts for me."
31	O Lord, may all Your enemies Perish as Sisera did, But may those who love the Lord Shine as the sun!

After that there was peace in the land for forty years.

CHAPTER 6

Then the people of Israel began once again to worship other gods, and once again the Lord let their enemies harass them. This time it was by the people of Midian, for seven years.

2 The Midianites were so cruel that the Israelis took to the mountains, living in caves and dens.

3, 4 When they planted their seed, marauders from Midian, Amalek, and other neighboring nations came and destroyed their crops and plundered the countryside as far away as Gaza, leaving nothing to eat, and taking away all their sheep, oxen, and donkeys.

5 These enemy hordes arrived on droves of camels too numerous to count and stayed until the land was completely stripped and devastated.

6, 7 So Israel was reduced to abject poverty because of the Midianites. Then at last the people of Israel began to cry out to the Lord for help.

8 However, the Lord's reply through the prophet He sent to them was this: "The Lord God of Israel brought you out of slavery in Egypt,

9 And rescued you from the Egyptians and from all who were cruel to you, and drove out your enemies from before you, and gave you their land.

10 He told you that He is the Lord your God, and that you must not worship the gods of the Amorites who live around you on every side. But you have not listened to Him."

11 But one day the Angel of the Lord came and sat beneath the oak tree at Ophrah, on the farm of Joash the Abiezrite. Joash's son, Gideon, had been threshing wheat by hand in the bottom of a grape press — a pit where grapes were pressed to make wine — for he was hiding from the Midianites.

12 The Angel of the Lord appeared to him and said, "Mighty soldier, the Lord is with you!"

13 "Stranger," Gideon replied, "if the Lord is with us, why has all this happened to us? And where are all the miracles our ancestors have told us about — such as when God brought them out of Egypt? Now the Lord has thrown us away and has let the Midianites completely ruin us."

14 Then the Lord turned to him and said, "I will

make you strong! Go and save Israel from the Midianites! I am sending you!"

15 But Gideon replied, "Sir, how can *I* save Israel? My family is the poorest in the whole tribe of Manasseh, and I am the least thought of in the entire family!"

16 Whereupon the Lord said to him, "But I, Jehovah,[1] will be with you! And you shall quickly destroy the Midianite hordes!"

17 Gideon replied, "If it is really true that You are going to help me like that, then do some miracle to prove it! Prove that it is really Jehovah who is talking to me!

18 But stay here until I go and get a present for You."

"All right," the Angel agreed. "I'll stay here until you return."

19 Gideon hurried home and roasted a young goat, and baked some unleavened bread from a bushel of flour. Then, carrying the meat in a basket and broth in a pot, he took it out to the Angel, who was beneath the oak tree, and presented it to Him.

20 The Angel said to him, "Place the meat and the bread upon that rock over there, and pour the broth over it." When Gideon had followed these instructions,

21 The Angel touched the meat and bread with His staff, and fire flamed up from the rock and consumed them! And suddenly the Angel was gone!

22 When Gideon realized that it had indeed been

---

[1]Literally, "I Am will be with you." The same name is used here as in Exodus 3:14. God is telling Gideon that the same one who appeared to Moses and rescued Israel from Egypt (much on Gideon's mind: see verse 13) will now do it again, rescuing Israel from Midian.

the Angel of the Lord, he cried out, "Alas, O Lord God, for I have seen the Angel of the Lord face to face!"

23   "It's all right," the Lord replied, "don't be afraid! You shall not die."

24   And Gideon built an altar there and named it "The Altar of Peace with Jehovah." (The altar is still there in Ophrah in the land of the Abiezrites.)

25   That night the Lord told Gideon to hitch his father's best ox to the family altar of Baal, and pull it down, and to cut down the wooden idol of the goddess Asherah that stood nearby.

26   "Replace it with an altar for the Lord your God, built here on this hill, laying the stones carefully. Then sacrifice the ox as a burnt offering to the Lord, using the wooden idol as wood for the fire on the altar."

27   So Gideon took ten of his servants and did as the Lord had commanded. But he did it at night for fear of the other members of his father's household, and for fear of the men of the city; for he knew what would happen if they found out who did it!

28   Early the next morning, as the city began to stir, someone discovered that the altar of Baal was knocked apart, the idol beside it was gone, and a new altar had been built instead, with the remains of a sacrifice on it.

29   "Who did this?" everyone demanded. Finally they learned that it was Gideon, the son of Joash.

30   "Bring out your son," they shouted to Joash. "He must die for insulting the altar of Baal, and for cutting down the Asherah idol."

31   But Joash retorted to the whole mob, "Does Baal need *your* help? What an insult to a god! You

are the ones who should die for insulting Baal! If
Baal is really a god, let him take care of himself and
destroy the one who broke apart his altar!"

32   From then on Gideon was called "Jerubbaal,"
a nickname meaning "let Baal take care of himself!"[2]

33   Soon afterward the armies of Midian, Amalek,
and other neighboring nations united in one vast alliance against Israel. They crossed the Jordan and
camped in the valley of Jezreel.

34   Then the Spirit of the Lord came upon Gideon,
and he blew a trumpet as a call to arms, and the men
of Abiezer came to him.

35   He also sent messengers throughout Manasseh,
Asher, Zebulun, and Naphtali, summoning their fighting forces, and all of them responded.

36   Then Gideon said to God, "If You are really
going to use me to save Israel as You promised,

37   Prove it to me in this way: I'll put some wool
on the threshing floor tonight, and if, in the morning,
the fleece is wet and the ground is dry, I will know
You are going to help me!"

38   And it happened just that way! When he got
up the next morning he pressed the fleece together and
wrung out a whole bowlful of water!

39   Then Gideon said to the Lord, "Please don't
be angry with me, but let me make one more test:
this time let the fleece remain dry while the ground
around it is wet!"

40   So the Lord did as he asked; that night the
fleece stayed dry, but the ground was covered with
dew!

---

[2]Literally, "let Baal bring charges," or, used mockingly, "let Baal be
honored!"

CHAPTER 7

Jerubbaal (that is, Gideon — his other name) and his army got an early start and went as far as the spring of Harod. The armies of Midian were camped north of them, down in the valley beside the hill of Moreh.

2 The Lord then said to Gideon, "There are too many of you! I can't let all of you fight the Midianites, for then the people of Israel will boast to Me that they saved themselves by their own strength!

3 Send home any of your men who are timid and frightened." So twenty-two thousand of them left, and only ten thousand remained who were willing to fight.

4 But the Lord told Gideon, "There are still too many! Bring them down to the spring and I'll show you which ones shall go with you and which ones shall not."

5, 6 So Gideon assembled them at the water. There the Lord told him, "Divide them into two groups decided by the way they drink. In Group I will be all the men who cup the water in their hands to get it to their mouths and lap it like dogs. In Group II will be those who kneel, with their mouths in the stream."

Only 300 of the men drank from their hands; all the others drank with their mouths to the stream.

7 "I'll conquer the Midianites with these 300!" the Lord told Gideon. "Send all the others home!"

8, 9 So after Gideon had collected all the clay jars and trumpets they had among them, he sent them home, leaving only 300 men with him.

During the night, with the Midianites camped in the valley just below, the Lord said to Gideon,

"Get up! Take your troops and attack the Midianites, for I will cause you to defeat them!

10   But if you are afraid, first go down to the camp alone — take along your servant Purah if you like —

11   And listen to what they are saying down there! You will be greatly encouraged and be eager to attack!" So he took Purah and crept down through the darkness to the outposts of the enemy camp.

12, 13   The vast armies of Midian, Amalek, and the other nations of the East were crowded across the valley like locusts — yes, like the sand upon the seashore — and there were too many camels even to count!

Gideon crept up to one of the tents just as a man inside had wakened from a nightmare and was telling his tent-mate about it. "I had this strange dream," he was saying, "and there was this huge loaf of barley bread that came tumbling down into our camp. It hit our tent and knocked it flat!"

14   The other soldier replied, "Your dream can mean only one thing! Gideon, the son of Joash, the Israeli, is going to come and massacre all the allied forces of Midian!"

15   When Gideon heard the dream and the interpretation, all he could do was just stand there worshiping God! Then he returned to his men and shouted, "Get up! For the Lord is going to use you to conquer all the vast armies of Midian!"

16   He divided the 300 men into three groups and gave each man a trumpet and a clay jar with a torch in it.

17   Then he explained his plan. "When we arrive

at the outer guardposts of the camp," he told them, "do just as I do.

18   As soon as I and the men in my group blow our trumpets, you blow yours on all sides of the camp and shout, 'We fight for God and for Gideon!' "

19, 20   It was just after midnight and the change of guards when Gideon and the hundred men with him crept to the outer edge of the camp of Midian. Suddenly they blew their trumpets and broke their clay jars so that their torches blazed into the night. Then the other 200 of his men did the same, blowing the trumpets in their right hands, and holding the flaming torches in their left hands, all yelling, "For the Lord and for Gideon!"

21   Then they just stood and watched as the whole vast enemy army began rushing around in a panic, shouting and running away.

22   For in the confusion the Lord caused the enemy troops to begin fighting and killing each other from one end of the camp to the other, and they fled into the night to places as far away as Beth-shittah near Zererah, and to the border of Abel-meholah near Tabbath.

23   Then Gideon sent for the troops of Naphtali, Asher, and Manasseh and told them to come and chase and destroy the fleeing army of Midian.

24   Gideon also sent messengers throughout the hill country of Ephraim summoning troops who seized the fords of the Jordan River at Beth-barah, thus preventing the Midianites from escaping by going across.

25   Oreb and Zeeb, the two generals of Midian, were captured. Oreb was killed at the rock now known by his name, and Zeeb at the winepress of Zeeb, as it

is now called; and the Israelis took the heads of Oreb and Zeeb across the Jordan to Gideon.

CHAPTER 8

But the tribal leaders of Ephraim were violently angry with Gideon. "Why didn't you send for us when you first went out to fight the Midianites?" they demanded.

2, 3 But Gideon replied, "God let you capture Oreb and Zeeb, the generals of the army of Midian! What have I done in comparison with that? Your actions at the end of the battle were more important than ours at the beginning!"[1] So they calmed down.

4 Gideon now crossed the Jordan River with his 300 men. They were very tired, but still chasing the enemy.

5 He asked the men of Succoth for food. "We are weary from chasing after Zebah and Zalmunna, the kings of Midian," he said.

6 But the leaders of Succoth replied, "You haven't caught them yet! If we feed you and you fail, they'll return and destroy us."[2]

7 Then Gideon warned them, "When the Lord has delivered them to us, I will return and tear your flesh with the thorns and briers of the wilderness."

8 Then he went up to Penuel and asked for food there, but got the same answer.

9 And he said to them also, "When this is all over, I will return and break down this tower."

10 By this time King Zebah and King Zalmunna

---

[1]More literally, "Are not the last grapes of Ephraim better than the entire crop of Abiezer?"
[2]Literally, "are Zebah and Zalmunna already in your hand . . . ?"

with a remnant of fifteen thousand troops were in Karkor. That was all that was left of the allied armies of the east; for one hundred twenty thousand had already been killed.

11   Then Gideon circled around by the caravan route east of Nobah and Jogbehah, striking at the Midianite army in surprise raids.

12   The two kings fled, but Gideon chased and captured them, routing their entire force.

13   Later, Gideon returned by way of Heres Pass.

14   There he captured a young fellow from Succoth and demanded that he write down the names of all the seventy-seven political and religious leaders of the city.

15   He then returned to Succoth. "You taunted me that I would never catch King Zebah and King Zalmunna, and you refused to give us food when we were tired and hungry," he said. "Well, here they are!"

16   Then he took the leaders of the city and scraped them to death[3] with wild thorns and briers.

17   He also went to Penuel and knocked down the city tower and killed the entire male population.

18   Then Gideon asked King Zebah and King Zalmunna, "The men you killed at Tabor — what were they like?"

They replied, "They were dressed just like you — like sons of kings!"

19   "They must have been my brothers!" Gideon exclaimed. "I swear that if you hadn't killed them I wouldn't kill you."

20   Then, turning to Jether, his oldest son, he in-

---

[3]Literally, "he taught the men of Succoth."

structed him to kill them. But the boy was only a lad
and was afraid to.

21 Then Zebah and Zalmunna said to Gideon,
"You do it; we'd rather be killed by a man!"[4] So
Gideon killed them and took the ornaments from their
camels' necks.

22 Now the men of Israel said to Gideon, "Be our
king! You and your sons and all your descendants
shall be our rulers, for you have saved us from Midian."

23, 24 But Gideon replied, "I will not be your
king, nor shall my son; the Lord is your king! However, I have one request. Give me all the earrings
collected from your fallen foes," — for the troops of
Midian, being Ishmaelites, all wore golden earrings.

25 "Gladly!" they replied, and spread out a sheet
for everyone to throw in the gold earrings he had
gathered.

26 Their value was estimated at $25,000, not in-
cluding the crescents and pendants or the royal clothing of the kings, or the chains around the camels'
necks.

27 Gideon made an ephod[5] from the gold and put
it in Ophrah, his home town. But all Israel soon began worshiping it, so it became an evil deed that
Gideon and his family did.

28 That is the true account of how Midian was
subdued by Israel. Midian never recovered, and the
land was at peace for forty years — all during Gideon's

---

[4]Literally, "For as the man is, so is his strength." Perhaps the meaning is, "A quick death is less painful."
[5]An ephod was usually a linen pouch worn by priests on their chests.
In this case the ephod evidently was highly decorated with gold, and
probably, because of its weight, hung upon a wall.

lifetime.

29 He returned home,

30 And eventually had seventy sons, for he married many wives.

31 He also had a concubine in Shechem, who presented him with a son named Abimelech.

32 Gideon finally died, an old, old man, and was buried in the sepulchre of his father Joash in Ophrah, in the land of the Abiezrites.

33 But as soon as Gideon was dead, the Israeli began to worship the idols Baal and Baal-berith.

34 They no longer considered the Lord as their God, though He had rescued them from all their enemies on every side.

35 Nor did they show any kindness to the family of Gideon despite all he had done for them.

CHAPTER 9

One day Gideon's son Abimelech visited his uncles — his mother's brothers — in Shechem.

2 "Go and talk to the leaders of Shechem," he requested, "and ask them whether they want to be ruled by seventy kings — Gideon's seventy sons — or by one man — meaning me, your own flesh and blood!"[1]

3 So his uncles went to the leaders of the city and proposed Abimelech's scheme; and they decided that since his mother was a native of their town they would go along with it.

4 They gave him money from the temple offer-

---

[1] Of all of Gideon's wives, only Abimelech's mother was from Shechem (Judges 8:30-31), so Abimelech felt close kinship there.

ings of the idol Baal-berith, which he used to hire some worthless loafers who agreed to do whatever he told them to.

5 He took them to his father's home at Ophrah and there, upon one stone, they slaughtered all seventy of his half-brothers, except for the youngest, Jotham, who escaped and hid.

6 Then the citizens of Shechem and Beth-millo called a meeting under the oak beside the garrison at Shechem, and Abimelech was acclaimed king of Israel.

7 When Jotham heard about this, he stood at the top of Mount Gerizim and shouted across to the men of Shechem, "If you want God's blessing, listen to me!

8 Once upon a time the trees decided to elect a king. First they asked the olive tree,

9 But it refused. 'Should I quit producing the olive oil that blesses God and man, just to wave to and fro over the other trees?' it asked.

10 Then they said to the fig tree, 'You be our king!'

11 But the fig tree also refused. 'Should I quit producing sweetness and fruit just to lift my head above all the other trees?' it asked.

12 Then they said to the grapevine, 'You reign over us!'

13 But the grapevine replied, 'Shall I quit producing the wine that cheers both God and man, just to be mightier than all the other trees?'

14 Then all the trees finally turned to the thorn bush. 'You be our king!' they exclaimed.

15 And the thorn bush replied, 'If you really want me, come and humble yourselves beneath my shade! If you refuse, let fire flame forth from me and burn

down the great cedars of Lebanon!'

16   Now make sure that you have done the right
thing in making Abimelech your king, that you have
done right by Gideon and all of his descendants.

17   For my father fought for you and risked his
life and delivered you from the Midianites,

18   Yet you have revolted against him and killed
his seventy sons upon one stone. And now you have
chosen his slave girl's son, Abimelech, to be your king
just because he is your relative.

19   If you are sure that you have done right by
Gideon and his descendants, then may you and Abimelech have a long and happy life together.

20   But if you have not been fair to Gideon, then
may Abimelech destroy the citizens of Shechem and
Beth-millo; and may they destroy Abimelech!"

21   Then Jotham escaped and lived in Beer for
fear of his brother Abimelech.

22, 23   Three years later God stirred up trouble
between King Abimelech and the citizens of Shechem,
and they revolted.

24   In the events that followed, both Abimelech
and the citizens of Shechem who aided him in butchering Gideon's seventy sons were given their just punishment for these murders.

25   For the men of Shechem set an ambush for
Abimelech along the trail at the top of the mountain.
(While they were waiting for him to come along, they
robbed everyone else who passed that way.) But
someone warned Abimelech about their plot.

26   At that time Gaal (the son of Ebed) moved
to Shechem with his brothers, and he became one of
the leading citizens.

27   During the harvest feast at Shechem that year,
held in the temple of the local god, the wine flowed
freely and everyone began cursing Abimelech.

28   "Who is Abimelech," Gaal shouted, "and why
should he be our king? Why should we be his servants? He and his friend Zebul should be *our* servants.
Down with Abimelech!

29   Make me your king and you'll soon see what
happens to Abimelech! I'll tell Abimelech, 'Get up an
army and come on out and fight!' "

30   But when Zebul, the mayor of the city, heard
what Gaal was saying, he was furious.

31   He sent messengers to Abimelech in Arumah
telling him, "Gaal, son of Ebed, and his relatives have
come to live in Shechem, and now they are arousing
the city to rebellion against you.

32   Come by night with an army and hide out in
the fields;

33   And in the morning, as soon as it is daylight,
storm the city. When he and those who are with him
come out against you, you can do with them as you
wish!"

34   So Abimelech and his men marched through
the night and split into four groups, stationing themselves around the city.

35   The next morning as Gaal sat at the city gates,
discussing various issues with the local leaders, Abimelech and his men began their march upon the city.

36   When Gaal saw them, he exclaimed to Zebul,
"Look over at that mountain! Doesn't it look like people coming down?"

      "No!" Zebul said. "You're just seeing shadows
that look like men!"

37   "No, look over there," Gaal said. "I'm sure I see people coming towards us. And look! There are others coming along the road past the oak of Meonenim!"

38   Then Zebul turned on him triumphantly. "Now where is that big mouth of yours?" he demanded. "Who was it who said, 'Who is Abimelech, and why should he be our king?' The men you taunted and cursed are right outside the city! Go on out and fight!"

39   So Gaal led the men of Shechem into the battle and fought with Abimelech,

40   But was defeated, and many of the men of Shechem were left wounded all the way to the city gate.

41   Abimelech was living at Arumah at this time, and Zebul drove Gaal and his relatives out of Shechem, and wouldn't let them live there any longer.

42   The next day the men of Shechem went out to battle again. However, someone had told Abimelech about their plans,

43   So he had divided his men into three groups hiding in the fields. And when the men of the city went out to attack, he and his men jumped up from their hiding places and began killing them.

44   Abimelech stormed the city gate to keep the men of Shechem from getting back in, while his other two groups cut them down in the fields.

45   The battle went on all day before Abimelech finally captured the city, killed its people, and leveled it to the ground.

46   The people at the nearby town of Migdal saw what was happening and took refuge in the fort next to the temple of Baal-berith.

47, 48   When Abimelech learned of this, he led his forces to Mount Zalmon where he began chopping a bundle of firewood, and placed it upon his shoulder. "Do as I have done," he told his men.

49   So each of them quickly cut a bundle and carried it back to the town where, following Abimelech's example, the bundles were piled against the walls of the fort and set on fire. So all the people inside died, about a thousand men and women.

50   Abimelech next attacked the city of Thebez, and captured it.

51   However there was a fort inside the city and the entire population fled into it, barricaded the gates, and climbed to the top of the roof to watch.

52   But as Abimelech was preparing to burn it,

53   A woman on the roof threw down a millstone. It landed on Abimelech's head, crushing his skull.

54   "Kill me!" he groaned to his youthful armor-bearer. "Never let it be said that a woman killed Abimelech!" So the young man pierced him with his sword, and he died.

55   When his men saw that he was dead, they disbanded and returned to their homes.

56, 57   Thus God punished both Abimelech and the men of Shechem for their sin of murdering Gideon's seventy sons. So the curse of Jotham, Gideon's son, came true.

CHAPTER 10

After Abimelech's death, the next judge of Israel was Tola (son of Puah and grandson of Dodo). He was from the tribe of Issachar, but lived in the city of Shamir in the hill country of Ephraim.

2 He was Israel's judge for twenty-three years. When he died, he was buried in Shamir,

3 And was succeeded by Jair, a man from Gilead, who judged Israel for twenty-two years.

4 His thirty sons rode around together on thirty donkeys, and they owned thirty cities in the land of Gilead which are still called "The Cities of Jair."

5 When Jair died he was buried in Kamon.

6 Then the people of Israel turned away from the Lord again, and worshiped the heathen gods Baal and Ashtaroth, and the gods of Syria, Sidon, Moab, Ammon and Philistia. Not only this, but they no longer worshiped Jehovah at all.

7, 8 This made Jehovah very angry with His people, so He immediately permitted the Philistines and the Ammonites to begin tormenting them. These attacks took place east of the Jordan River in the land of the Amorites (that is, in Gilead),

9 And also in Judah, Benjamin, and Ephraim. For the Ammonites crossed the Jordan to attack the Israelis. This went on for eighteen years.

10 Finally the Israelis turned to Jehovah again and begged Him to save them. "We have sinned against You and have forsaken You as our God and have worshiped idols," they confessed.

11 But the Lord replied, "Didn't I save you from the Egyptians, the Amorites, the Ammonites, the Philistines,

12 The Sidonians, the Amalekites, and the Maonites? Has there ever been a time when you cried out to Me that I haven't rescued you?

13 Yet you continue to abandon Me and to wor-

ship other gods. So go away; I won't save you any more.

14 Go and cry to the new gods you have chosen! Let them save you in your hour of distress!"

15 But they pleaded with Him again and said, "We have sinned. Punish us in any way You think best, only save us once more from our enemies."

16 Then they destroyed their foreign gods and worshiped only the Lord; and He was grieved by their misery.

17 The armies of Ammon were mobilized in Gilead at that time, preparing to attack Israel's army at Mizpah.

18 "Who will lead our forces against the Ammonites?" the leaders of Gilead asked each other. "Whoever volunteers shall be our king!"

CHAPTER 11

Now Jephthah was a great warrior from the land of Gilead, but his mother was a prostitute. His father (whose name was Gilead) had several other sons by his legitimate wife, and when these half-brothers grew up, they chased Jephthah out of the country. "You son of a whore!" they said, "You'll not get any of our father's estate."

3 So Jephthah fled from his father's home and lived in the land of Tob. Soon he had quite a band of malcontents as his followers, living off the land as bandits.

4 It was about this time that the Ammonites began their war against Israel.

5 The leaders of Gilead sent for Jephthah,

6 Begging him to come and lead their army against the Ammonites.

7 But Jephthah said to them, "Why do you come to me when you hate me and have driven me out of my father's house? Why come now when you're in trouble?"

8 "Because we need you," they replied. "If you will be our commander-in-chief against the Ammonites, we will make you the king of Gilead."

9 "Sure!" Jephthah exclaimed. "Do you expect me to believe that?"

10 "We swear it," they replied. "We promise with a solemn oath."

11 So Jephthah accepted the commission and was made commander-in-chief and king. The contract was ratified before the Lord in Mizpah at a general assembly of all the people.

12 Then Jephthah sent messengers to the king of Ammon, demanding to know why Israel was being attacked.

13 The king of Ammon replied that the land belonged to the people of Ammon; it had been stolen from them, he said, when the Israelis came from Egypt; the whole territory from the Arnon River to the Jabbok and the Jordan was his, he claimed. "Give us back our land peaceably," he demanded.

14, 15 Jephthah replied, "Israel did not steal the land.

16 What happened was this: When the people of Israel arrived at Kadesh, on their way from Egypt to the Red Sea,

17 They sent a message to the king of Edom asking permission to pass through his land. But their

petition was denied. Then they asked the king of Moab for similar permission. It was the same story there, so the people of Israel stayed in Kadesh.

18 Finally they went around Edom and Moab through the wilderness, and traveled along the eastern border until at last they arrived beyond the boundary of Moab at the Arnon River; but they never once crossed into Moab.

19 Then Israel sent messengers to King Sihon of the Amorites, who lived in Heshbon, and asked permission to cross through his land to get to their destination.

20 But King Sihon didn't trust Israel, so he mobilized an army at Jahaz and attacked them.

21, 22 But the Lord our God helped Israel defeat King Sihon and all your people, so Israel took over all of your land from the Arnon River to the Jabbok, and from the wilderness to the Jordan River.

23 So you see, it was the Lord God of Israel who took away the land from you Amorites and gave it to Israel. Why, then, should we return it to you?

24 You keep whatever your god Chemosh gives you, and we will keep whatever Jehovah our God gives us!

25 And besides, just who do you think you are? Are you better than King Balak, the king of Moab? Did he try to recover his land after Israel defeated him? No, of course not.

26 But now after three hundred years you make an issue of this! Israel has been living here for all that time, spread across the land from Heshbon to Aroer, and all along the Arnon River. Why have you made no effort to recover it before now?

27 No, I have not sinned against you; rather, you have wronged me by coming to war against me; but Jehovah the Judge will soon show which of us is right — Israel or Ammon."

28 But the king of Ammon paid no attention to Jephthah's message.

29 At that time the Spirit of the Lord came upon Jephthah and he led his army across the land of Gilead and Manasseh, past Mizpah in Gilead, and attacked the army of Ammon.

30, 31 Meanwhile Jephthah had vowed to the Lord that if God would help Israel conquer the Ammonites, then when he returned home in peace, the first person coming out of his house to meet him would be sacrificed as a burnt offering to the Lord!

32 So Jephthah led his army against the Ammonites, and the Lord gave him the victory.

33 He destroyed the Ammonites with a terrible slaughter all the way from Aroer to Minnith, including twenty cities, and as far away as Vineyard Meadow. Thus the Ammonites were subdued by the people of Israel.

34 When Jephthah returned home his daughter — his only child — ran out to meet him, playing on a tambourine and dancing for joy.

35 When he saw her he tore his clothes in anguish. "Alas, my daughter!" he cried out. "You have brought me to the dust. For I have made a vow to the Lord and I cannot take it back."

36 And she said, "Father, you must do whatever you promised the Lord, for He has given you a great victory over your enemies, the Ammonites.

37 But first let me go up into the hills and roam

with my girl friends for two months, weeping because
I'll never marry."

38 "Yes," he said. "Go." And so she did, bewailing her fate with her friends for two months.

39 Then she returned to her father, who did as he had vowed. So she was never married.[1] And after that it became a custom in Israel,

40 That the young girls went away for four days each year to lament the fate of Jephthah's daughter.

CHAPTER 12

Then the tribe of Ephraim mobilized its army at Zaphon and sent this message to Jephthah: "Why didn't you call for us to help you fight against Ammon? We are going to burn down your house, with you in it!"

2 "I summoned you, but you refused to come!" Jephthah retorted. "You failed to help us in our time of need,

3 So I risked my life and went to battle without you, and the Lord helped me to conquer the enemy. Is that anything for you to fight us about?"

4 Then Jephthah, furious at the taunt of Ephraim that the men of Gilead were mere outcasts[1] and the scum of the earth, mobilized his army and attacked the army of Ephraim.

5 He captured the fords of the Jordan behind the army of Ephraim, and whenever a fugitive from Ephraim tried to cross the river, the Gilead guards

---

[1]It is not clear whether he killed her or satisfied his vow by consecrating her to perpetual virginity.
[1]Literally, "fugitives of Ephraim . . ."

challenged him. "Are you a member of the tribe of Ephraim?" they asked. If the man replied that he was not,

6 Then they demanded, "Say, 'Shibboleth.'" But if he couldn't pronounce the H and said, "Sibboleth" instead of "Shibboleth," he was dragged away and killed. So forty-two thousand people of Ephraim died there at that time.

7 Jephthah was Israel's judge for six years. At his death he was buried in one of the cities of Gilead.

8 The next judge was Ibzan, who lived in Bethlehem.

9, 10 He had thirty sons and thirty daughters. He married his daughters to men outside his clan, and brought in thirty girls to marry his sons. He judged Israel for seven years before he died, and was buried at Bethlehem.

11, 12 The next judge was Elon from Zebulun. He judged Israel for ten years and was buried at Aijalon in Zebulun.

13 Next was Abdon (son of Hillel) from Pirathon.

14 He had forty sons and thirty grandsons, who rode on seventy donkeys. He was Israel's judge for eight years.

15 Then he died and was buried in Pirathon, in Ephraim, in the hill country of the Amalekites.

CHAPTER 13

Once again Israel sinned by worshiping other gods, so the Lord let them be conquered by the Philistines, who kept them in subjection for forty years.

2, 3 Then one day the Angel of the Lord appeared to the wife of Manoah, of the tribe of Dan, who lived in the city of Zorah. She had no children, but the Angel said to her, "Even though you have been barren so long, you will soon conceive and have a son!

4　Don't drink any wine or beer, and don't eat any food that isn't kosher.

5　Your son's hair must never be cut, for he shall be a Nazirite, a special servant of God from the time of his birth; and he will begin to rescue Israel from the Philistines."

6　The woman ran and told her husband, "A man from God appeared to me and I think He must be the Angel of the Lord, for He was almost too glorious to look at. I didn't ask where He was from, and He didn't tell me His name,

7　But He told me, 'You are going to have a baby boy!' And He told me not to drink any wine or beer, and not to eat food that isn't kosher, for the baby is going to be a Nazirite — he will be dedicated to God from the moment of his birth until the day of his death!"

8　Then Manoah prayed, "O Lord, please let the man from God come back to us again and give us more instructions about the child You are going to give us."

9　The Lord answered his prayer, and the Angel of God appeared once again to his wife as she was sitting in the field. But again she was alone — Manoah was not with her —

10　So she quickly ran and found her husband and told him, "The same man is here again!"

11　Manoah ran back with his wife and asked, "Are You the man who talked to my wife the other day?"

"Yes," He replied, "I am."

12 So Manoah asked Him, "Can You give us any special instructions about how we should raise the baby after he is born?"

13, 14 And the Angel replied, "Be sure that your wife follows the instructions I gave her. She must not eat grapes or raisins, or drink any wine or beer, or eat anything that isn't kosher."

15 Then Manoah said to the Angel, "Please stay here until we can get You something to eat."

16 "I'll stay," the Angel replied, "but I'll not eat anything. However, if you wish to bring something, bring an offering to sacrifice to the Lord." (Manoah didn't yet realize that He was the Angel of the Lord.)

17 Then Manoah asked Him for His name. "When all this comes true and the baby is born," he said to the Angel, "we will certainly want to tell everyone that You predicted it!"

18 "Don't even ask my name," the Angel replied, "for it is a secret."

19 Then Manoah took a young goat and a grain offering and offered it as a sacrifice to the Lord; and the Angel did a strange and wonderful thing,

20 For as the flames from the altar were leaping up toward the sky, and as Manoah and his wife watched, the Angel ascended in the fire! Manoah and his wife fell face downward to the ground,

21 And that was the last they ever saw of Him. It was then that Manoah finally realized that it had been the Angel of the Lord.

22 "We will die," Manoah cried out to his wife, "for we have seen God!"

23 But his wife said, "If the Lord were going to

kill us He wouldn't have accepted our burnt offerings
and wouldn't have appeared to us and told us this
wonderful thing and done these miracles."

24   When her son was born they named him Samson, and the Lord blessed him as he grew up.

25   And the Spirit of the Lord began to excite him
whenever he visited the parade grounds of the army of
the tribe of Dan, located between the cities of Zorah
and Eshta-ol.

CHAPTER 14

One day when Samson was in Timnah, he noticed
a certain Philistine girl,

2   And when he got home he told his father and
mother that he wanted to marry her.

3   They objected strenuously. "Why don't you
marry a Jewish girl?" they asked. "Why must you go
and get a wife from these heathen Philistines? Isn't
there one girl among all the people of Israel you
could marry?"

But Samson told his father, "She is the one I
want. Get her for me."

4   His father and mother didn't realize that the
Lord was behind the request, for God was setting a trap
for the Philistines, who at that time were the rulers of
Israel.

5   As Samson and his parents were going to Timnah, a young lion attacked Samson in the vineyards on
the outskirts of the town.

6   At that moment the Spirit of the Lord came
mightily upon him and since he had no weapon, he
ripped the lion's jaws apart, and did it as easily as

though it were a young goat!

But he didn't tell his father or mother about it.

7 Upon arriving at Timnah he talked with the girl and found her to be just what he wanted, so the arrangements were made.[1]

8 When he returned for the wedding, he turned off the path to look at the carcass of the lion. And he found a swarm of bees in it, and some honey!

9 He took some of the honey with him, eating as he went, and gave some of it to his father and mother. But he didn't tell them where he had gotten it.

10, 11 As his father was making final arrangements for the marriage, Samson threw a party for thirty young men of the village, as was the custom of the day.

12 When Samson asked if they would like to hear a riddle, they replied that they would. "If you solve my riddle during these seven days of the celebration," he said, "I'll give you thirty plain robes and thirty fancy robes.

13 But if you can't solve it, then you must give the robes to me!"

"All right," they agreed, "let's hear it."

14 This was his riddle: "Food came out of the eater, and sweetness from the strong!" Three days later they were still trying to figure it out.

15 On the fourth day they said to his new wife, "Get the answer from your husband, or we'll burn down your father's house with you in it. Were we invited to this party just to make us poor?"

16 So Samson's wife broke down in tears before

---

[1]Implied.

him and said, "You don't love me at all; you hate me, for you have told a riddle to my people and haven't told me the answer!"

"I haven't even told it to my father or mother; why should I tell you?" he replied.

17 So she cried whenever she was with him and kept it up for the remainder of the celebration. At last, on the seventh day, he told her the answer and she, of course, gave the answer to the young men.

18 So before sunset of the seventh day they gave him their reply. "What is sweeter than honey?" they asked, "and what is stronger than a lion?"

"If you hadn't plowed with my heifer, you wouldn't have found the answer to my riddle!" he retorted.

19 Then the Spirit of the Lord came upon him and he went to the city of Ashkelon, killed thirty men, took their clothing, and gave it to the young men who had told him the answer to his riddle. But he was furious about it and abandoned his wife and went back home to live with his father and mother.

20 So his wife was married instead to the fellow who had been best man at Samson's wedding.

CHAPTER 15

L ater on, during the wheat harvest, Samson took a young goat as a present to his wife, intending to sleep with her; but her father wouldn't let him in.

2 "I really thought you hated her," he explained, "so I married her to your best man. But look, her sister is prettier than she is. Marry her instead."

3 Samson was furious. "You can't blame me for whatever happens now," he shouted.

4 So he went out and caught three hundred foxes and tied their tails together in pairs, with a torch between each pair.

5 Then he lit the torches and let the foxes run through the fields of the Philistines, burning the grain to the ground along with all the sheaves and shocks of grain, and destroying the olive trees.

6 "Who did this?" the Philistines demanded. "Samson," was the reply, "because his wife's father gave her to another man." So the Philistines came and got the girl and her father and burned them alive.

7 "Now my vengeance will strike again!" Samson vowed.

8 So he attacked them with great fury and killed many of them. Then he went to live in a cave in the rock of Etam.

9 The Philistines in turn sent a huge posse into Judah and raided Lehi.

10 "Why have you come here?" the men of Judah asked. And the Philistines replied, "To capture Samson and do to him as he has done to us."

11 So three thousand men of Judah went down to get Samson at the cave in the rock of Etam. "What are you doing to us?" they demanded of him. "Don't you realize that the Philistines are our rulers?"

But Samson replied, "I only paid them back for what they did to me."

12, 13 "We have come to capture you and take you to the Philistines," the men of Judah told him. "All right," Samson said, "but promise me that you won't kill me yourselves."

"No," they replied, "we won't do that." So they tied him with two new ropes and led him away.

14 As Samson and his captors arrived at Lehi, the Philistines shouted with glee; but then the strength of the Lord came upon Samson, and the ropes with which he was tied snapped like thread and fell from his wrists!

15 Then he picked up a donkey's jawbone that was lying on the ground and killed a thousand Philistines with it.

16, 17 Tossing away the jawbone, he remarked,

"Heaps upon heaps,
All with a donkey's jaw!
I've killed a thousand men,
All with a donkey's jaw!"

(The place has been called "Jawbone Hill" ever since.)

18 But now he was very thirsty and he prayed to the Lord and said, "You have given Israel such a wonderful deliverance through me today! Must I now die of thirst, and fall to the mercy of these heathen?"

19 So the Lord caused water to gush out from a hollow in the ground and Samson's spirit was revived as he drank. Then he named the place "The Spring of the Man Who Prayed," and the spring is still there today.

20 Samson was Israel's judge for the next twenty years, but the Philistines still controlled the land.

CHAPTER 16

One day Samson went to the Philistine city of Gaza and spent the night with a prostitute.

2 Word soon spread that he had been seen in the city, so the police were alerted and many men of the city lay in wait all night at the city gate to capture

him if he tried to leave. "In the morning," they thought, "when there is enough light, we'll find him and kill him."

3   Samson stayed in bed with the girl until midnight, then went out to the city gates and lifted them, with the two gateposts, right out of the ground. He put them on his shoulders and carried them to the top of the mountain across from Hebron!

4   Later on he fell in love with a girl named Delilah over in the valley of Sorek.

5   The five heads of the Philistine nation went personally to her and demanded that she find out from Samson what made him so strong, so that they would know how to overpower and subdue him and put him in chains. "Each of us will give you a thousand dollars for this job," they promised.

6   So Delilah begged Samson to tell her his secret. *"Please* tell me, Samson, why you are so strong," she pleaded. "I don't think anyone could ever capture you!"

7   "Well," Samson replied, "if I were tied with seven raw-leather bowstrings, I would become as weak as anyone else."

8   So they brought her the seven bowstrings, and while he slept[1] she tied him with them.

9   Some men were hiding in the next room, so as soon as she had tied him up she exclaimed, "Samson! the Philistines are here!" Then he snapped the bowstrings like cotton thread,[2] and so his secret was not discovered.

10   Afterwards Delilah said to him, "You are

---

[1]Implied in verse 14.
[2]Literally, "like a string of tow snaps when it touches the fire."

making fun of me! You told me a lie! *Please* tell me how you can be captured!"

11　"Well," he said, "if I am tied with brand new ropes which have never been used, I will be as weak as other men."

12　So that time, as he slept,[3] Delilah took new ropes and tied him with them. The men were hiding in the next room, as before. Again Delilah exclaimed, "Samson! The Philistines have come to capture you!" But he broke the ropes from his arms like spiderwebs!

13　"You have mocked me again, and told me more lies!" Delilah complained. "Now tell me how you can *really* be captured."

"Well," he said, "if you weave my hair into your loom . . . !"

14　So while he slept, she did just that and then screamed, "The Philistines have come, Samson!" And he woke up and yanked his hair away, breaking the loom.

15　"How can you say you love me when you don't confide in me?" she whined. "You've made fun of me three times now, and you still haven't told me what makes you so strong!"

16, 17　She nagged at him every day until he couldn't stand it any longer and finally told her his secret. "My hair has never been cut," he confessed, "for I've been a Nazirite to God since before my birth. If my hair were cut, my strength would leave me, and I would become as weak as anyone else."

18　Delilah realized that he had finally told her the truth, so she sent for the five Philistine leaders.

---

[3]Implied.

"Come just this once more," she said, "for this time he has told me everything." So they brought the money with them.

19 She lulled him to sleep with his head in her lap, and they brought in a barber and cut off his hair. Delilah began to hit him, but she could see that his strength was leaving him.

20 Then she screamed, "The Philistines are here to capture you, Samson!" And he woke up and thought, "I will do as before; I'll just shake myself free." But he didn't realize that the Lord had left him.

21 So the Philistines captured him and gouged out his eyes and took him to Gaza, where he was bound with bronze chains and made to grind grain in the prison.

22 But before long his hair began to grow again.

23, 24 The Philistine leaders declared a great festival to celebrate the capture of Samson. The people made sacrifices to their god Dagon and excitedly praised him. "Our god has delivered our enemy Samson to us!" they thrilled as they saw him there in chains. "The scourge of our nation who killed so many of us is now in our power!"

25, 26 Half-drunk by now, the people demanded, "Bring out Samson so we can have some fun with him!" So he was brought from the prison and made to stand at the center of the temple, between the two pillars supporting the roof. Samson said to the boy who was leading him by the hand, "Place my hands against the two pillars. I want to rest against them."

27 By then the temple was completely filled with people. The five Philistine leaders were there as well

as three thousand people in the balconies[4] who were watching Samson and making fun of him.

28   Then Samson prayed to the Lord and said, "O Lord Jehovah, remember me again — please strengthen me one more time, so that I may pay back the Philistines for the loss of at least one of my eyes."

29   Then Samson pushed against the pillars with all his might.

30   "Let me die with the Philistines," he prayed. And the temple crashed down upon the Philistine leaders and all the people. So those he killed at the moment of his death were more than those he had killed during his entire lifetime.

31   Later, his brothers and other relatives came down to get his body, and they brought him back home and buried him between Zorah and Eshta-ol, where his father, Manoah, was buried. He had judged Israel for twenty years.

CHAPTER 17

In the hill country of Ephraim lived a man named Micah.

2   One day he said to his mother, "That thousand dollars you thought was stolen from you, and you were cursing about — well, I stole it!"

"God bless you for confessing it," his mother replied.

3   So he returned the money to her. "I am going to give it to the Lord as a credit for your account," she declared. "I'll have an idol carved for you and plate it with the silver."

---

[4]Literally, "on the roof."

4, 5   So his mother took a fifth of it to a silver-smith, and the idol he made from it was placed in Micah's shrine. Micah had many idols in his collection, also an ephod and some teraphim, and he installed one of his sons as the priest.

6   (For in those days Israel had no king, so everyone did whatever he wanted to — whatever seemed right in his own eyes.)

7, 8   One day a young priest[1] from the town of Bethlehem, in Judah, arrived in that area of Ephraim, looking for a good place to live. He happened to stop at Micah's house as he was traveling through.

9   "Where are you from?" Micah asked him.

And he replied, "I am a priest[1] from Bethlehem, in Judah, and I am looking for a place to live."

10, 11   "Well, stay here with me," Micah said, "and you can be my priest. I will give you ten dollars a year plus a new suit and your board and room." The young man agreed to this, and became as one of Micah's sons.

12   So Micah consecrated him as his personal priest.

13   "I know the Lord will really bless me now," Micah exclaimed, "because now I have a genuine priest working for me!"[2]

CHAPTER 18

A s has already been stated, there was no king in Israel at that time. The tribe of Dan was trying to find a place to settle, for they had not yet driven out the people living in the land assigned to them.

---

[1]Literally, "a Levite."
[2]Literally, "a Levite as a priest."

2 So the men of Dan chose five army heroes from the cities of Zorah and Eshta-ol as scouts to go and spy out the land they were supposed to settle in. Arriving in the hill country of Ephraim, they stayed at Micah's home.

3 Noticing the young Levite's accent, they took him aside and asked him, "What are you doing here? Why did you come?"

4 He told them about his contract with Micah, and that he was his personal priest.

5 "Well, then," they said, "ask God whether or not our trip will be successful."

6 "Yes," the priest replied, "all is well. The Lord is taking care of you."

7 So the five men went on to the town of Laish, and noticed how secure everyone felt. Their manner of life was Phoenician, and they were wealthy. They lived quietly, and were unprepared for an attack, for there were no tribes in the area strong enough to try it. They lived a great distance from their relatives in Sidon, and had little or no contact with the nearby villages.

8 So the spies returned to their people in Zorah and Eshta-ol. "What about it?" they were asked. "What did you find?"

9, 10 And the men replied, "Let's attack! We have seen the land and it is ours for the taking — a broad, fertile, wonderful place — a real paradise. The people aren't even prepared to defend themselves! Come on, let's go! For God has given it to us!"

11 So six hundred armed troops of the tribe of Dan set out from Zorah and Eshta-ol.

12 They camped first at a place west of Kiriath-

jearim in Judah (which is still called "The Camp of Dan"),

13 Then they went on up into the hill country of Ephraim. As they passed the home of Micah,

14 The five spies told the others, "There is a shrine in there with an ephod, some teraphim, and many plated idols. It's obvious what we ought to do!"

15, 16 So the five men went over to the house and with all of the armed men standing just outside the gate, they talked to the young priest, and asked him how he was getting along.

17 Then the five spies entered the shrine and took the idols, the ephod, and the teraphim.

18 "What are you doing?" the young priest demanded when he saw them carrying them out.

19 "Be quiet and come with us," they said. "Be a priest to all of us. Isn't it better for you to be a priest to a whole tribe in Israel instead of just to one man in his private home?"

20 The young priest was then quite happy to go with them, and he took along the ephod, the teraphim, and the idols.

21 They started on their way again, placing their children, cattle, and household goods at the front of the column.

22 When they were quite a distance from Micah's home, Micah and some of his neighbors came chasing after them,

23 Yelling at them to stop. "What do you want, chasing after us like this?" the men of Dan demanded.

24 "What do you mean, 'What do I want'!" Micah retorted. "You've taken away all my gods and my priest, and I have nothing left!"

25 "Be careful how you talk, mister," the men of Dan replied. "Somebody's apt to get angry and kill every one of you."

26 So the men of Dan kept going. When Micah saw that there were too many of them for him to handle, he turned back home.

27 Then, with Micah's idols and the priest, the men of Dan arrived at the city of Laish. There weren't even any guards, so they went in and slaughtered all the people and burned the city to the ground.

28 There was no one to help the inhabitants, for they were too far away from Sidon, and they had no local allies, for they had no dealings with anyone. This happened in the valley next to Beth-rehob. Then the people of the tribe of Dan rebuilt the city and lived there.

29 The city was named "Dan" after their ancestor, Israel's son, but it had originally been called Laish.

30 Then they set up the idols and appointed a man named Jonathan (son of Gershom and grandson of Moses!) and his sons as their priests. This family continued as priests until the city was finally conquered by its enemies.

31 So Micah's idols were worshiped by the tribe of Dan as long as the Tabernacle remained at Shiloh.

CHAPTER 19

At this time before Israel had a king, there was a man of the tribe of Levi living on the far side of the hill country of Ephraim, who brought home a girl from Bethlehem in Judah to be his concubine.

2 But she became angry with him and ran away,

and returned to her father's home in Bethlehem, and was there about four months.

3   Then her husband, taking along a servant and an extra donkey, went to see her to try to win her back again. When he arrived at her home, she let him in and introduced him to her father, who was delighted to meet him.

4   Her father urged him to stay awhile, so he stayed three days, and they all had a very pleasant time.

5   On the fourth day they were up early, ready to leave, but the girl's father insisted on their having breakfast first.

6   Then he pleaded with him to stay one more day, as they were having such a good time.

7   At first the man refused, but his father-in-law kept urging him until finally he gave in.

8   The next morning they were up early again, and again the girl's father pleaded, "Stay just today and leave sometime this evening." So they had another day of feasting.

9   That afternoon as he and his wife and servant were preparing to leave, his father-in-law said, "Look, it's getting late. Stay just tonight, and we will have a pleasant evening together and tomorrow you can get up early and be on your way."

10   But this time the man was adamant, so they left, getting as far as Jerusalem (also called Jebus) before dark.

11   His servant said to him, "It's getting too late to travel; let's stay here tonight."

12, 13   "No," his master said, "we can't stay in this heathen city where there are no Israelites — we will go on to Gibe-ah, or possibly Ramah."

14 So they went on. The sun was setting just as they came to Gibe-ah, a village of the tribe of Benjamin,

15 So they went there for the night. But as no one invited them in, they camped in the village square.

16 Just then an old man came by on his way home from his work in the fields. (He was originally from the hill country of Ephraim, but was living now in Gibe-ah, even though it was in the territory of Benjamin.)

17 When he saw the travelers camped in the square, he asked them where they were from, and where they were going.

18 "We're on the way home from Bethlehem, in Judah," the man replied. "I live on the far edge of the Ephraim hill country, near Shiloh. But no one has taken us in for the night,

19 Even though we have fodder for our donkeys, and plenty of food and wine for ourselves."

20 "Don't worry," the old man said, "be my guests; for you mustn't stay here in the square. It's too dangerous."

21 So he took them home with him. He fed their donkeys while they rested, and afterwards they had supper together.

22 Just as they were beginning to warm to the occasion, a gang of sex perverts gathered around the house and began beating at the door and yelling at the old man to bring out the man who was staying with him, so they could rape him.

23 The old man stepped outside to talk to them. "No, my brothers, don't do such a dastardly act," he

begged, "for he is my guest.

24   Here, take my virgin daughter and this man's
wife. I'll bring them out and you can do whatever
you like to them — but don't do such a thing to this
man."

25   But they wouldn't listen to him. Then the
girl's husband pushed her out to them, and they abused
her all night, taking turns raping her until morning.
Finally, just at dawn, they let her go.

26   She fell down at the door of the house and lay
there until it was light.

27   When her husband opened the door to be on
his way, he found her there, fallen down in front of
the door with her hands digging into the threshhold.

28   "Well, come on," he said. "Let's get going."
But there was no answer, for she was dead; so he
threw her across the donkey's back and took her home.

29   When he got there he took a knife and cut her
body into twelve parts and sent one piece to each
tribe of Israel.

30   Then the entire nation was roused to action
against the men of Benjamin because of this awful
deed. "There hasn't been such a horrible crime since
Israel left Egypt," everyone said. "We've got to do
something about it."

CHAPTER 20

Then the entire nation of Israel sent their leaders
and 450,000 troops to assemble with one mind
before the Lord at Mizpah. They came from as far
away as Dan and Beersheba, and everywhere between,
and from across the Jordan in the land of Gilead.

3 (Word of the mobilization of the Israeli forces at Mizpah soon reached the land of Benjamin.) The chiefs of Israel now called for the murdered woman's husband and asked him just what had happened.

4 "We arrived one evening at Gibe-ah, a village in Benjamin," he began.

5 "That night the men of Gibe-ah surrounded the house, planning to kill me, and they raped my wife until she was dead.

6 So I cut her body into twelve pieces and sent the pieces throughout the land of Israel, for these men have committed a terrible crime.

7 Now then, sons of Israel, express your mind and give me your counsel!"

8, 9, 10 And as one man they replied, "Not one of us will return home until we have punished the village of Gibe-ah. A tenth of the army will be selected by lot as a supply line to bring us food, and the rest of us will destroy Gibe-ah for this horrible deed."

11 So the whole nation united in this task.

12 Then messengers were sent to the tribe of Benjamin, asking, "Did you know about the terrible thing that was done among you?

13 Give up these evil men from the city of Gibe-ah so that we can execute them and purge Israel of her evil." But the people of Benjamin wouldn't listen.

14, 15 Instead, twenty-six thousand of them arrived in Gibe-ah to join the seven hundred local men in their defense against the rest of Israel.

16 (Among all these there were seven hundred men who were left-handed sharpshooters. They could hit a target within a hair's breadth, never missing!)

17 The army of Israel, not counting the men of Benjamin, numbered 400,000 men.

18 Before the battle the Israeli army went to Bethel first to ask counsel from God. "Which tribe shall lead us against the people of Benjamin?" they asked.

And the Lord replied, "Judah shall go first."

19, 20 So the entire army left early the next morning to go to Gibe-ah, to attack the men of Benjamin.

21 But the men defending the village stormed out and killed twenty-two thousand Israelis that day.

22, 23, 24 Then the Israeli army wept before the Lord until evening and asked Him, "Shall we fight further against our brother Benjamin?"

And the Lord said, "Yes." So the men of Israel took courage and went out again the next day to fight at the same place.

25 And that day they lost another eighteen thousand men, all experienced swordsmen.

26 Then the entire army went up to Bethel and wept before the Lord and fasted until evening, offering burnt sacrifices and peace offerings.

27, 28 (The Ark of God was in Bethel in those days. Phinehas, the son of Eleazar and grandson of Aaron, was the priest.) The men of Israel asked the Lord, "Shall we go out again and fight against our brother Benjamin, or shall we stop?"

And the Lord said, "Go, for tomorrow I will see to it that you defeat the men of Benjamin."

29 So the Israeli army set an ambush all around the village,

30 And went out again on the third day and set themselves in their usual battle formation.

31 When the army of Benjamin came out of the

town to attack, the Israeli forces retreated and Benjamin was drawn away from the town as they chased after Israel. And as they had done previously, Benjamin began to kill the men of Israel along the roadway running between Bethel and Gibe-ah, so that about thirty of them died.

32   Then the army of Benjamin shouted, "We're defeating them again!" But the armies of Israel had agreed in advance to run away so that the army of Benjamin would chase them and be drawn away from the town.

33   But when the main army of Israel reached Baal-tamar, it turned and attacked, and the ten thousand men in ambush west of Geba jumped up from where they were,

34   And advanced against the rear of the army of Benjamin, who still didn't realize the impending disaster.

35-39   So the Lord helped Israel defeat Benjamin, and the Israeli army killed 25,100 men of Benjamin that day, leaving but a tiny remnant of their forces.

Summary of the Battle:

The army of Israel retreated from the men of Benjamin in order to give the ambush more room for maneuvering. When the men of Benjamin had killed about thirty of the Israelis, they were confident of a massive slaughter just as on the previous days. But then the men in ambush rushed into the village and slaughtered everyone in it, and set it on fire. The great cloud of smoke pouring into the sky was the signal for the Israeli army to turn around and attack the army of Benjamin,

40, 41   Who now looked behind them and were

terrified to discover that their city was on fire, and that they were in serious trouble.

42   So they ran toward the wilderness, but the Israelis chased after them, and the men who had set the ambush came out and joined the slaughter from the rear.

43   They encircled the army of Benjamin east of Gibe-ah, and killed most of them there.

44   Eighteen thousand of the Benjamin troops died in that day's battle.

45   The rest of the army fled into the wilderness toward the rock of Rimmon, but five thousand were killed along the way, and two thousand more near Gidom.

46, 47   So the tribe of Benjamin lost twenty-five thousand brave warriors that day, leaving only six hundred men who escaped to the rock of Rimmon, where they lived for four months.

48   Then the Israeli army returned and slaughtered the entire population of the tribe of Benjamin — men, women, children, and cattle — and burned down every city and village in the entire land.

CHAPTER 21

The leaders of Israel had vowed at Mizpah never to let their daughters marry a man from the tribe of Benjamin.

2   And now the Israeli leaders met at Bethel and sat before God until evening, weeping bitterly.

3   "O Lord God of Israel," they cried out, "why has this happened, that now one of our tribes is missing?"

4   The next morning they were up early and built an altar, and offered sacrifices and peace offerings on it.

5   And they said among themselves, "Was any tribe of Israel not represented when we held our council before the Lord at Mizpah?" For at that time it was agreed by solemn oath that anyone who refused to come must die.

6   There was deep sadness throughout all Israel for the loss of their brother tribe, Benjamin. "Gone," they kept saying to themselves, "gone — an entire tribe of Israel has been cut off, and is gone.

7   And how shall we get wives for the few who remain, since we have sworn by the Lord that we will not give them our daughters?"

8, 9   Then they thought again of their oath to kill anyone who refused to come to Mizpah, and discovered that no one had attended from Jabesh-gilead.

10, 11, 12   So they sent twelve thousand of their best soldiers to destroy the people of Jabesh-gilead. All the men, married women, and children were slain, but the young virgins of marriageable age were saved. There were four hundred of these, and they were brought to the camp at Shiloh.

13   Then Israel sent a peace delegation to the little remnant of the men of Benjamin at Rimmon Rock.

14   The four hundred girls were given to them as wives, and they returned to their homes; but there were not enough of these girls for all of them.

15   (What a sad time it was in Israel in those days, because the Lord had made a breach in the tribes of Israel.)

16   "What shall we do for wives for the others,

since all the women of the tribe of Benjamin are dead?" the leaders of Israel asked.

17 "There must be some way to get wives for them, so that an entire tribe of Israel will not be lost forever.

18 But we can't give them our own daughters. We have sworn with a solemn oath that anyone who does this shall be cursed of God."

19 Suddenly someone thought of the annual religious festival held in the fields of Shiloh, between Lebonah and Bethel, along the east side of the road that goes from Bethel to Shechem.

20 They told the men of Benjamin who still needed wives, "Go and hide in the vineyards,

21 And when the girls of Shiloh come out for their dances, rush out and catch them and take them home with you to be your wives!

22 And when their fathers and brothers come to us in protest, we will tell them, 'Please be understanding and let them have your daughters, for we didn't find enough wives for them when we destroyed Jabesh-gilead, and you couldn't have given your daughters to them without being guilty.' "

23 So the men of Benjamin did as they were told and kidnapped the girls who took part in the celebration, and carried them off to their own land. Then they rebuilt their cities and lived in them.

24 So the people of Israel returned to their homes.

25 (There was no king in Israel in those days, and every man did whatever he thought was right.)

I Samuel

CHAPTER 1

This is the story of Elkanah, a man of the tribe of Ephraim who lived in Ramathaim-zophim, in the hills of Ephraim.

> His father's name was Jeroham,
> His grandfather was Elihu,
> His great-grandfather was Tohu,
> His great-great-grandfather was Zuph.

2 He had two wives, Hannah and Peninnah. Peninnah had some children, but Hannah didn't.

3 Each year Elkanah and his families journeyed to the Tabernacle at Shiloh to worship the Lord of the heavens and to sacrifice to Him. (The priests on duty at that time were the two sons of Eli — Hophni and Phinehas.)

4 On the day he presented his sacrifice, Elkanah would celebrate the happy occasion by giving presents to Peninnah and her children;

5 But although he loved Hannah very much, he could give her only one present, for the Lord had sealed her womb; so she had no children to give presents to.

6 Peninnah made matters worse by taunting Hannah because of her barrenness.

7 Every year it was the same — Peninnah scof-

fing and laughing at her as they went to Shiloh, making her cry so much she couldn't eat.

8 "What's the matter, Hannah?" Elkanah would exclaim. "Why aren't you eating? Why make such a fuss over having no children? Isn't having me better than having ten sons?"

9 One evening after supper, when they were at Shiloh, Hannah went over to the Tabernacle. Eli the priest was sitting at his customary place beside the entrance.

10 She was in deep anguish and was crying bitterly as she prayed to the Lord.

11 And she made this vow: "O Lord of heaven, if You will look down upon my sorrow and answer my prayer and give me a son, then I will give him back to You, and he'll be Yours for his entire lifetime, and his hair shall never be cut."[1]

12, 13 Eli noticed her mouth moving as she was praying silently and, hearing no sound, thought she had been drinking.

14 "Must you come here drunk?" he demanded. "Throw away your bottle."

15, 16 "Oh, no, sir!" she replied, "I'm not drunk! But I am very sad and I was pouring out my heart to the Lord. Please don't think that I am just some drunken bum!"

17 "In that case," Eli said, "cheer up! May the Lord of Israel grant you your petition, whatever it is!"

18 "Oh, thank you, sir!" she exclaimed, and went happily back, and began to take her meals again.

---

[1]This was an approved custom for those who were wholly dedicated to God.

19, 20   The entire family was up early the next morning and went to the Tabernacle to worship the Lord once more. Then they returned home to Ramah, and when Elkanah slept with Hannah, the Lord remembered her petition; in the process of time, a baby boy was born to her. She named him Samuel (meaning[2] "asked of God") because, as she said, "I asked the Lord for him."

21, 22   The next year Elkanah and Peninnah and her children went on the annual trip to the Tabernacle without Hannah, for she told her husband, "Wait until the baby is weaned, and then I will take him to the Tabernacle and leave him there."

23   "Well, whatever you think best," Elkanah agreed. "May the Lord's will be done." So she stayed home until the baby was weaned.

24   Then, though he was still so small, they took him to the Tabernacle in Shiloh, along with a three-year-old bull for the sacrifice, and a bushel of flour and some wine.

25   After the sacrifice they took the child to Eli.

26   "Sir, do you remember me?" Hannah asked him. "I am the woman who stood here that time praying to the Lord!

27   I asked Him to give me this child, and He has given me my request;

28   And now I am giving him to the Lord for as long as he lives." So she left him there at the Tabernacle for the Lord to use.

---

[2]This was a play on words. The word Samuel in Hebrew sounds like the word "to ask".

CHAPTER 2

This was Hannah's prayer:
> "How I rejoice in the Lord!
> How He has blessed me!
> Now I have an answer for my enemies,
> For the Lord has solved my problem.
> How I rejoice!

2   No one is as holy as the Lord!
There is no other God,
Nor any Rock like our God.

3   Quit acting so proud and arrogant!
The Lord knows what you have done,
And He will judge your deeds.

4   Those who were mighty are mighty no
more!
Those who were weak are now strong.

5   Those who were well are now starving;
Those who were starving are fed.
The barren woman now has seven children;
She with many children has no more!

6   The Lord kills,
The Lord gives life.

7   Some He causes to be poor
And others to be rich.
He cuts one down
And lifts another up.

8   He lifts the poor from the dust —
Yes, from a pile of ashes —
And treats them as princes
Sitting in the seats of honor.
For all the earth is the Lord's

And He has set the world in order.

9   He will protect His godly ones,
But the wicked shall be silenced in darkness.

No one shall succeed by strength alone.

10   Those who fight against the Lord shall be broken;
He thunders against them from heaven.
He judges throughout the earth.
He gives mighty strength to His King,
And gives great glory to His anointed One."

11   So they returned home to Ramah without Samuel; and the child became the Lord's helper, for he assisted Eli the priest.

12   Now the sons of Eli were evil men who didn't love the Lord.

13, 14   It was their regular practice to send out a servant whenever anyone was offering a sacrifice, and while the flesh of the sacrificed animal was boiling, the servant would put a three-pronged fleshhook into the pot and demand that whatever it brought up be given to Eli's sons. They treated all of the Israelites in this way when they came to Shiloh to worship.

15   Sometimes the servant would come even before the rite of burning the fat on the altar had been performed, and he would demand raw meat before it was boiled, so that it could be used for roasting.

16   If the man offering the sacrifice replied, "Take as much as you want, but the fat must first be burned," [as the law requires[1]], then the servant would say,

---

[1]Implied.

"No, give it to me now or I'll take it by force."

17 So the sin of these young men was very great in the eyes of the Lord; for they treated the people's offerings to the Lord with contempt.

18 Samuel, though only a child, was the Lord's helper and wore a little linen robe just like the priest's.[2]

19 Each year his mother made a little coat for him and brought it to him when she came with her husband for the sacrifice.

20 Before they returned home Eli would bless Elkanah and Hannah and ask God to give them other children to take the place of this one they had given to the Lord.

21 And the Lord gave Hannah three sons and two daughters. Meanwhile Samuel grew up in the service of the Lord.

22 Eli was now very old, but he was aware of what was going on around him. He knew, for instance, that his sons were seducing the young women who assisted at the entrance to the Tabernacle.

23, 24, 25 "I have been hearing terrible reports from the Lord's people about what you are doing," Eli told his sons. "It is an awful thing to make the Lord's people sin. Ordinary sin receives heavy punishment, but how much more this sin of yours which has been committed against the Lord?" But they wouldn't listen to their father, for the Lord was already planning to kill them.

26 Little Samuel was growing in two ways — he was getting taller, and he was becoming everyone's favorite (and he was a favorite of the Lord's, too!)

---

[2]Literally, "wore a linen ephod."

27   One day a prophet[3] came to Eli and gave him this message from the Lord: "Didn't I demonstrate My power when the people of Israel were slaves in Egypt?

28   Didn't I choose your ancestor Levi from among all his brothers to be My priest, and to sacrifice upon My altar, and to burn incense, and to wear a priestly robe[4] as he served Me? And didn't I assign the sacrificial offerings to you priests?

29   Then why are you so greedy for all the other offerings which are brought to Me? Why have you honored your sons more than Me — for you and they have become fat from the best of the offerings of My people!

30   Therefore, I, the Lord God of Israel, declare that although I promised that your branch of the tribe of Levi could always be My priests, it is ridiculous to think that what you are doing can continue. I will honor only those who honor Me, and I will despise those who despise Me.

31   I will put an end to your family, so that it will no longer serve as priests. Every member will die before his time. None shall live to be old.

32   You will envy the prosperity I will give My people, but you and your family will be in distress and need. Not one of them will live out his days.

33   Those who are left alive will live in sadness and grief; and their children shall die by the sword.

34   And to prove that what I have said will come true, I will cause your two sons, Hophni and Phinehas, to die on the same day!

---

[3]Literally, "man of God."
[4]Literally, "wear an ephod."

35 Then I will raise up a faithful priest who will serve Me and do whatever I tell him to do. I will bless his descendants, and his family shall be priests to My kings forever.

36 Then all of your descendants shall bow before him, begging for money and food. 'Please,' they will say, 'give me a job among the priests so that I will have enough to eat.' "

CHAPTER 3

Meanwhile little Samuel was helping the Lord by assisting Eli. Messages from the Lord were very rare in those days,

2, 3 But one night after Eli had gone to bed (he was almost blind with age by now), and Samuel was sleeping in the Temple near the Ark,

4, 5 The Lord called out, "Samuel! Samuel!"

"Yes?" Samuel replied. "What is it?" He jumped up and ran to Eli. "Here I am. What do you want?" he asked.

"I didn't call you," Eli said. "Go on back to bed." So he did.

6 Then the Lord called again, "Samuel!" And again Samuel jumped up and ran to Eli.

"Yes?" he asked. "What do you need?"

"No, I didn't call you, my son," Eli said. "Go on back to bed."

7 (Samuel had never had a message from Jehovah before.[1])

8 So now the Lord called the third time, and

---

[1]Literally, "did not yet know Jehovah."

once more Samuel jumped up and ran to Eli. "Yes?" he asked, "what do you need?" Then Eli realized it was the Lord who had spoken to the child.

9　So he said to Samuel, "Go and lie down again, and if He calls again, say, 'Yes, Lord, I'm listening.' " So Samuel went back to bed.

10　And the Lord came and called as before, "Samuel! Samuel!"

And Samuel replied, "Yes, I'm listening."

11　Then the Lord said to Samuel, "I am going to do a shocking thing in Israel.

12　I am going to do all of the dreadful things I warned Eli about.

13　I have continually threatened him and his entire family with punishment because his sons are blaspheming God, and he doesn't stop them.

14　So I have vowed that the sins of Eli and of his sons shall never be forgiven by sacrifices and offerings."

15　Samuel stayed in bed until morning, then opened the doors of the Temple as usual, for he was afraid to tell Eli what the Lord had said to him.

16, 17　But Eli called him. "My son," he said, "what did the Lord say to you? Tell me everything. And may God punish you if you hide anything from me!"

18　So Samuel told him what the Lord had said.

"It is the Lord's will," Eli replied; "let Him do what He thinks best."

19　As Samuel grew, the Lord was with him and people listened carefully to his advice.

20　And all Israel from Dan to Beer-sheba knew that Samuel was going to be a prophet of the Lord.

21, 4:1 Then the Lord began to give messages to him there at the Tabernacle in Shiloh, and he passed them on to the people of Israel.

CHAPTER 4

At that time Israel was at war with the Philistines. The Israeli army was camped near Ebenezer, the Philistines at Aphek.

2 And the Philistines defeated Israel, killing four thousand of them.

3 After the battle was over, the army of Israel returned to their camp and their leaders discussed why the Lord had let them be defeated.

"Let's bring the Ark here from Shiloh," they said. "If we carry it into battle with us, the Lord will be among us and He will surely save us from our enemies."

4 So they sent for the Ark of the Lord of heaven who is enthroned above the angels. Hophni and Phinehas, the sons of Eli, accompanied it into the battle.

5 When the Israelis saw the Ark coming, their shout of joy was so loud that it almost made the ground shake!

6 "What's going on?" the Philistines asked. "What's all the shouting about over in the camp of the Hebrews?" When they were told it was because the Ark of the Lord had arrived,

7 They panicked. "God has come into their camp!" they cried out. "Woe upon us, for we have never had to face anything like this before!

8 Who can save us from these mighty gods of Israel? They are the same gods who destroyed the

Egyptians with plagues when Israel was in the wilderness.

9   Fight as you never have before, O Philistines, or we will become their slaves just as they have been ours."

10   So the Philistines fought desperately and Israel was defeated again. Thirty thousand men of Israel died that day and the remainder fled to their tents.

11   And the Ark of God was captured and Hophni and Phinehas were killed.

12   A man from the tribe of Benjamin ran from the battle and arrived at Shiloh the same day with his clothes torn and dirt on his head.[1]

13   Eli was waiting beside the road to hear the news of the battle, for his heart trembled for the safety of the Ark of God. As the messenger from the battlefront arrived and told what had happened, a great cry arose throughout the city.

14   "What is all the noise about?" Eli asked. And the messenger rushed over to Eli and told him what had happened.

15   (Eli was ninety-eight years old and was blind.)

16   "I have just come from the battle — I was there today," he told Eli,

17   "And Israel has been defeated and thousands of the Israeli troops are dead on the battlefield. Hophni and Phinehas were killed too, and the Ark has been captured."

18   When the messenger mentioned what had happened to the Ark, Eli fell backward from his seat be-

---

[1]This was a common expression of grief in that day.

side the gate and his neck was broken by the fall and he died (for he was old and fat). He had judged Israel for forty years.

19 When Eli's daughter-in-law, Phinehas's wife, who was pregnant, heard that the Ark had been captured and that her husband and father-in-law were dead, her labor pains suddenly began.

20 Just before she died, the women who were attending her told her that everything was all right and that the baby was a boy. But she did not reply or respond in any way.

21, 22 Then she murmured, "Name the child 'Ichabod,' for Israel's glory is gone." (Ichabod means "there is no glory." She named him this because the Ark of God had been captured and because her husband and her father-in-law were dead.)

CHAPTER 5

The Philistines took the captured Ark of God from the battleground at Ebenezer to the temple of their idol Dagon in the city of Ashdod.

3 But when the local citizens went to see it the next morning, Dagon had fallen with his face to the ground before the Ark of Jehovah! They set him up again,

4 But the next morning the same thing had happened — the idol had fallen face down before the Ark of the Lord again. This time his head and hands had been cut off and were lying in the doorway; only the trunk of his body was left intact.

5 (That is why to this day neither the priests of Dagon nor his worshipers will walk on the threshhold

of the temple of Dagon in Ashdod.)

6   Then the Lord began to destroy the people of Ashdod and the nearby villages with a plague of boils.

7   When the people realized what was happening, they exclaimed, "We can't keep the Ark of the God of Israel here any longer. We will all perish along with our god Dagon."

8   So they called a conference of the mayors of the five cities of the Philistines to decide how to dispose of the Ark. The decision was to take it to Gath.

9   But when the Ark arrived at Gath, the Lord began destroying its people, young and old, with the plague, and there was a great panic.

10   So they sent the Ark to Ekron, but when the people of Ekron saw it coming they cried out, "They are bringing the Ark of the God of Israel here to kill us too!"

11   So they summoned the mayors again and begged them to send the Ark back to its own country, lest the entire city die. For the plague had already begun and great fear was sweeping across the city.

12   Those who didn't die were deathly ill; and there was weeping everywhere.

CHAPTER 6

The Ark remained in the Philistine country for seven months in all.

2   Then the Philistines called for their priests and diviners and asked them, "What shall we do about the Ark of God? What sort of gift shall we send with it when we return it to its own land?"

3   "Yes, send it back with a gift," they were told.

"Send a guilt offering so that the plague will stop. Then, if it doesn't, you will know God didn't send the plague upon you after all."

4, 5 "What guilt offering shall we send?" they asked. And they were told, "Send five gold models of the tumor caused by the plague, and five gold models of the rats that have ravaged the whole land — the capital cities and villages alike. If you send these gifts and then praise the God of Israel, perhaps He will stop persecuting you and your god.

6 Don't be stubborn and rebellious as Pharaoh and the Egyptians were. They wouldn't let Israel go until God had destroyed them with dreadful plagues.

7 Now build a new cart and hitch to it two cows that have just had calves — cows that never before have been yoked — and shut their calves away from them in the barn.

8 Place the Ark of God on the cart beside a chest containing the gold models of the rats and tumors, and let the cows go wherever they want to.

9 If they cross the border of our land and go into Beth-shemesh, then you will know that it was God who brought this great evil upon us; if they don't, [but return to their calves,[1]] then we will know that the plague was simply a coincidence and was not sent by God at all."

10 So these instructions were carried out. Two fresh cows were hitched to the cart and their calves were shut up in the barn.

11 Then the Ark of the Lord and the chest containing the gold rats and tumors were placed upon the cart.

---

[1] Implied.

12 And sure enough, the cows went straight along the road toward Beth-shemesh, lowing as they went; and the Philistine mayors followed them as far as the border of Beth-shemesh.

13 The people of Beth-shemesh were reaping wheat in the valley, and when they saw the Ark they went wild with joy!

14 The cart came into the field of a man named Joshua and stopped beside a large rock. So the people broke up the wood of the cart for a fire and killed the cows and sacrificed them to the Lord as a burnt offering.

15 Several men of the tribe of Levi lifted the Ark and the chest containing the golden rats and tumors from the cart and laid them on the rock. And many burnt offerings and sacrifices were offered to the Lord that day by the men of Beth-shemesh.

16 After the five Philistine mayors had watched for awhile, they returned to Ekron that same day.

17 The five gold models of tumors which had been sent by the Philistines as a guilt offering to the Lord were gifts from the mayors of the capital cities, Ashdod, Gaza, Ashkelon, Gath, and Ekron.

18 The gold rats were to placate God for the other Philistine cities, both the fortified cities and the country villages controlled by the five capitals. (By the way, that large rock at Beth-shemesh can still be seen in the field of Joshua.)

19 But the Lord killed seventy of the men of Beth-shemesh because they looked into the Ark. And the people mourned because of the many people whom the Lord had killed.

20 "Who is able to stand before Jehovah, this holy

God?" they cried out. "Where can we send the Ark from here?"

21 So they sent messengers to the people at Kiriath-jearim and told them that the Philistines had brought back the Ark of the Lord. "Come and get it!" they begged.

CHAPTER 7

So the men of Kiriath-jearim came and took the Ark to the hillside home of Abinadab; and installed his son Eleazar to be in charge of it.

2 The Ark remained there for twenty years, and during that time all Israel was in sorrow because the Lord had seemingly abandoned them.

3 At that time Samuel said to them, "If you are really serious about wanting to return to the Lord, get rid of your foreign gods and your Ashtaroth idols. Determine to obey only the Lord; then He will rescue you from the Philistines."

4 So they destroyed their idols of Baal and Ashtaroth and worshiped only the Lord.

5 Then Samuel told them, "Come to Mizpah, all of you, and I will pray to the Lord for you."

6 So they gathered there and, in a great ceremony, drew water from the well and poured it out before the Lord. They also went without food all day as a sign of sorrow for their sins. So it was at Mizpah that Samuel became Israel's judge.

7 When the Philistine leaders heard about the great crowds at Mizpah, they mobilized their army and advanced. The Israelis were badly frightened when they learned that the Philistines were approaching.

8   "Plead with God to save us!" they begged Samuel.

9   So Samuel took a suckling lamb and offered it to the Lord as a whole burnt offering and pleaded with Him to help Israel. And the Lord responded.

10   Just as Samuel was sacrificing the burnt offering, the Philistines arrived for battle, but the Lord spoke with a mighty voice of thunder from heaven, and they were thrown into confusion, and the Israelis routed them,

11   And chased them from Mizpah to Beth-car, killing them all along the way.

12   Samuel then took a stone and placed it between Mizpah and Jeshanah and named it Ebenezer (meaning, "the Stone of Help"), for he said, "The Lord has certainly helped us!"

13   So the Philistines were subdued and didn't invade Israel again at that time, because the Lord was against them throughout the remainder of Samuel's lifetime.

14   The Israeli cities between Ekron and Gath, which had been conquered by the Philistines, were now returned to Israel, for the Israeli army rescued them from their Philistine captors. And there was peace between Israel and the Amorites in those days.

15   Samuel continued as Israel's judge for the remainder of his life.

16   He rode circuit annually, setting up his court first at Bethel, then Gilgal, and then Mizpah, and cases of dispute were brought to him in each of those three cities from all the surrounding territory.

17   Then he would come back to Ramah, for his

home was there, and he would hear cases there, too. And he built an altar to the Lord at Ramah.

CHAPTER 8

In his old age, Samuel retired and appointed his sons as judges in his place.

2   Joel and Abijah, his oldest sons, held court in Beer-sheba;

3   But they were not like their father, for they were greedy for money. They accepted bribes and were very corrupt in the administration of justice.

4   Finally the leaders of Israel met in Ramah to discuss the matter with Samuel.

5   They told him that since his retirement things hadn't been the same, for his sons were not good men. "Give us a king like all the other nations have," they pleaded.

6   Samuel was terribly upset and went to the Lord for advice.

7   "Do as they say," the Lord replied, "for I am the one they are rejecting, not you — they don't want Me to be their king any longer.

8   Ever since I brought them from Egypt they have continually forsaken Me and followed other gods. And now they are giving you the same treatment.

9   Do as they ask, but warn them about what it will be like to have a king!"

10   So Samuel told the people what the Lord had said:

11   "If you insist on having a king, he will conscript your sons and make them run before his chariots;

12   Some will be made to lead his troops into battle, while others will be slave laborers; they will be forced to plow in the royal fields, and harvest his crops without pay; and make his weapons and chariot equipment.

13   He will take your daughters from you and force them to cook and bake and make perfumes for him.

14   He will take away the best of your fields and vineyards and olive groves and give them to his friends.

15   He will take a tenth of your harvest and distribute it to his favorites.

16   He will demand your slaves and the finest of your youth and will use your animals for his personal gain.

17   He will demand a tenth of your flocks, and you shall be his slaves.

18   You will shed bitter tears because of this king you are demanding, but the Lord will not help you."

19   But the people refused to listen to Samuel's warning. "Even so, we still want a king," they said,

20   "For we want to be like the nations around us. He will govern us and lead us to battle."

21   So Samuel told the Lord what the people had said,

22   And the Lord replied again, "Then do as they say and give them a king." So Samuel agreed and sent the men home again.

CHAPTER 9

K ish was a rich, influential man from the tribe of Benjamin. He was the son of Abiel, grandson of

Zeror, great-grandson of Becorath, and great-great-grandson of Aphiah.

2 His son Saul was the most handsome man in Israel. And he was head and shoulders taller than anyone else in the land!

3 One day Kish's donkeys strayed away, so he sent Saul and a servant to look for them.

4 They traveled all through the hill country of Ephraim, the land of Shalisha, the Shaalim area, and the entire land of Benjamin, but couldn't find them anywhere.

5 Finally, after searching in the land of Zuph, Saul said to the servant, "Let's go home; by now my father will be more worried about us than about the donkeys!"

6 But the servant said, "I've just thought of something! There is a prophet who lives here in this city; he is held in high honor by all the people because everything he says comes true; let's go and find him and perhaps he can tell us where the donkeys are."

7 "But we don't have anything to pay him with," Saul replied. "Even our food is gone and we don't have a thing to give him."

8 "Well," the servant said, "I have a dollar! We can at least offer it to him and see what happens!"

9, 10, 11 "All right," Saul agreed, "let's try it!" So they started into the city where the prophet lived. As they were climbing a hill toward the city, they saw some young girls going out to draw water and asked them if they knew whether the seer was in town. (In those days prophets were called seers. "Let's go and ask the seer," people would say, rather than, "Let's go and ask the prophet," as we would say now.)

12, 13   "Yes," they replied, "stay right on this road. He lives just inside the city gates. He has just arrived back from a trip to take part in a public sacrifice up on the hill. So hurry, because he'll probably be leaving about the time you get there; the guests can't eat until he arrives and blesses the food."

14   So they went into the city, and as they were entering the gates they saw Samuel coming out towards them to go up the hill.

15   The Lord had told Samuel the previous day,

16   "About this time tomorrow I will send you a man from the land of Benjamin. You are to anoint him as the leader of My people. He will save them from the Philistines, for I have looked down on them in mercy and have heard their cry."

17   When Samuel saw Saul the Lord said, "That's the man I told you about! He will rule My people."

18   Just then Saul approached Samuel and asked, "Can you please tell me where the seer's house is?"

19   "I am the seer!" Samuel replied. "Go on up the hill ahead of me and we'll eat together; in the morning I will tell you what you want to know and send you on your way.

20   And don't worry about those donkeys that were lost three days ago, for they have been found. And anyway, you own all the wealth of Israel now!"

21   "Pardon me, sir," Saul replied. "I'm from the tribe of Benjamin, the smallest in Israel, and my family is the least important of all the families of the tribe! You must have the wrong man!"

22   Then Samuel took Saul and his servant into the great hall and placed them at the head of the table, honoring them above the thirty special guests.

23   Samuel then instructed the chef to bring Saul the choicest cut of meat, the piece that had been set aside for the guest of honor.

24   So the chef brought it in and placed it before Saul. "Go ahead and eat it," Samuel said, "for I was saving it for you, even before I invited these others!" So Saul ate with Samuel.

25   After the feast, when they had returned to the city, Samuel took Saul up to the porch on the roof and talked with him there.

26, 27   At daybreak the next morning, Samuel called up to him, "Get up; it's time you were on your way!" So Saul got up and Samuel accompanied him to the edge of the city. When they reached the city walls Samuel told Saul to send the servant on ahead. Then he told him, "I have received a special message for you from the Lord."

CHAPTER 10

Then Samuel took a flask of olive oil and poured it over Saul's head and kissed him on the cheek and said, "I am doing this because the Lord has appointed you to be the king of His people, Israel!

2   When you leave me, you will see two men beside Rachel's tomb at Zelzah, in the land of Benjamin; they will tell you that the donkeys have been found and that your father is worried about you and is asking, 'How am I to find my son?'

3   And when you get to the oak of Tabor you will see three men coming toward you who are on their way to worship God at the altar at Bethel; one will be carrying three young goats, another will have three loaves of bread, and the third will have a bottle

of wine.

4   They will greet you and offer you two of the loaves, which you are to accept.

5   After that you will come to Gibeath-elohim, also known as "God's Hill," where the garrison of the Philistines is. As you arrive there you will meet a band of prophets coming down the hill playing a psaltery, a timbrel, a flute, and a harp, and prophesying as they come.

6   At that time the Spirit of the Lord will come mightily upon you, and you will prophesy with them and you will feel and act like a different person.

7   From that time on your decisions should be based on whatever seems best under the circumstances, for the Lord will guide you.

8   Go to Gilgal and wait there seven days for me, for I will be coming to sacrifice burnt offerings and peace offerings. I will give you further instructions when I arrive."

9   As Saul said good-bye and started to go, God gave him a new attitude, and all of Samuel's prophecies came true that day.

10   When Saul and the servant arrived at the Hill of God they saw the prophets coming toward them, and the Spirit of God came upon him, and he too began to prophesy.

11   When his friends heard about it, they exclaimed, "What? Saul a prophet?"

12   And one of the neighbors added, "With a father like his?" So that is the origin of the proverb, "Is Saul a prophet, too?"[1]

----

[1]This was an expression of surprise concerning worldly Saul becoming religious, equivalent to our "He got religion."

13　When Saul had finished prophesying he climbed the hill to the altar.

*　　*　　*　　*　　*

14　"Where in the world did you go?" Saul's uncle asked him.

And Saul replied, "We went to look for the donkeys, but we couldn't find them; so we went to the prophet Samuel to ask him where they were."

15　"Oh? And what did he say?" his uncle asked.

16　"He said the donkeys had been found!" Saul replied. (But he didn't tell him that he had been anointed as king!)

17　Samuel now called a convocation of all Israel at Mizpah,

18, 19　And gave them this message from the Lord God: "I brought you from Egypt and rescued you from the Egyptians and from all of the nations that were torturing you. But although I have done so much for you, you have rejected Me and have said, 'We want a king instead!' All right, then, present yourselves before the Lord by tribes and clans."

20　So Samuel called the tribal leaders together before the Lord, and the tribe of Benjamin was chosen by sacred lot.

21　Then he brought each family of the tribe of Benjamin before the Lord, and the family of the Matrites was chosen. And finally, the sacred lot selected Saul, the son of Kish. But when they looked for him, he had disappeared!

22　So they asked the Lord, "Where is he? Is he here among us?"

And the Lord replied, "He is hiding in the baggage."

23 So they found him and brought him out, and he stood head and shoulders above anyone else.

24 Then Samuel said to all the people, "This is the man the Lord has chosen as your king. There isn't his equal in all of Israel!"

And all the people shouted, "Long live the king!"

25 Then Samuel told the people again what the rights and duties of a king were; he wrote them in a book and put it in a special place before the Lord. Then Samuel sent the people home again.

26 When Saul returned to his home at Gibe-ah, a band of men whose hearts the Lord had touched became his constant companions.

27 There were, however, some bums and loafers who exclaimed, "How can this man save us?" And they despised him and refused to bring him presents, but he took no notice.

CHAPTER 11

At this time Nahash led the army of the Ammonites against the Israeli city of Jabesh-gilead. But the citizens of Jabesh asked for peace. "Leave us alone and we will be your servants," they pleaded.

2 "All right," Nahash said, "but only on one condition: I will gouge out the right eye of every one of you as a disgrace upon all Israel!"

3 "Give us seven days to see if we can get some help!" replied the elders of Jabesh. "If none of our brothers will come and save us, we will agree to your terms."

4 When a messenger came to Gibe-ah, Saul's

home town, and told the people about their plight, everyone broke into tears.

5 Saul was plowing in the field, and when he returned to town he asked, "What's the matter? Why is everyone crying?" So they told him about the message from Jabesh.

6 Then the Spirit of God came strongly upon Saul and he became very angry.

7 He took two oxen and cut them into pieces and sent messengers to carry them throughout all Israel. "This is what will happen to the oxen of anyone who refuses to follow Saul and Samuel to battle!" he announced. And God caused the people to be afraid of Saul's anger, and they came to him as one man.

8 He counted them in Bezek and found that there were three hundred thousand of them in addition to thirty thousand from Judah.

9 So he sent the messengers back to Jabesh-gilead to say, "We will rescue you before tomorrow noon!" What joy there was throughout the city when that message arrived!

10 The men of Jabesh then told their enemies, "We surrender. Tomorrow we will come out to you and you can do to us as you wish."

11 But early the next morning Saul arrived, having divided his army into three detachments, and launched a surprise attack against the Ammonites and slaughtered them all morning. The remnant of their army was so badly scattered that no two of them were left together.

12 Then the people exclaimed to Samuel, "Where are those men who said that Saul shouldn't be our king? Bring them here and we will kill them!"

13   But Saul replied, "No one will be executed to-day; for today the Lord has rescued Israel!"

14   Then Samuel said to the people, "Come, let us all go to Gilgal and reconfirm Saul as our king."

15   So they went to Gilgal and in a solemn ceremony before the Lord they crowned him king. Then they offered peace offerings to the Lord, and Saul and all Israel were very happy.

CHAPTER 12

Then Samuel addressed the people again: "Look," he said, "I have done as you asked. I have given you a king.

2   I have selected him ahead of my own sons and now I stand here, an old, grey-haired man who has been in public service from the time he was a lad.

3   Now tell me as I stand before the Lord and before His anointed king — whose ox or donkey have I stolen? Have I ever defrauded you? Have I ever oppressed you? Have I ever taken a bribe? Tell me and I will make right whatever I have done wrong."

4   "No," they replied, "you have never defrauded or oppressed us in any way and you have never taken even one single bribe."

5   "The Lord and His anointed king are my witnesses," Samuel declared, "that you can never accuse me of robbing you."

"Yes, it is true," they replied.

6   "It was the Lord who appointed Moses and Aaron," Samuel continued. "He brought your ancestors out of the land of Egypt.

7   Now stand here quietly before the Lord as I

remind you of all the good things He has done for you and for your ancestors:

8 When the Israelites were in Egypt and cried out to the Lord, He sent Moses and Aaron to bring them into this land.

9 But they soon forgot about the Lord their God, so He let them be conquered by Sisera, the general of King Hazor's army, and by the Philistines and the king of Moab.

10 Then they cried to the Lord again and confessed that they had sinned by turning away from Him and worshiping the Baal and Ashtaroth idols. And they pleaded, 'We will worship You and You alone if You will only rescue us from our enemies.'

11 Then the Lord sent Gideon, Barak, Jephthah, and Samuel to save you, and you lived in safety.

12 But when you were afraid of Nahash, the king of Ammon, you came to me and said that you wanted a king to reign over you. But the Lord your God was already your King, for He has always been your King.

13 All right, here is the king you have chosen. Look him over. You have asked for him, and the Lord has answered your request.

14 Now if you will fear and worship the Lord and listen to His commandments and not rebel against the Lord, and if both you and your king follow the Lord your God, then all will be well.

15 But if you rebel against the Lord's commandments and refuse to listen to Him, then His hand will be as heavy upon you as it was upon your ancestors.

16 Now watch as the Lord does great miracles.

17 You know that it does not rain at this time of the year, during the wheat harvest; I will pray for

the Lord to send thunder and rain today, so that you will realize the extent of your wickedness in asking for a king!"

18 So Samuel called to the Lord, and the Lord sent thunder and rain; and all the people were very much afraid of the Lord and of Samuel.

19 "Pray for us lest we die!" they cried out to Samuel. "For now we have added to all our other sins by asking for a king."

20 "Don't be frightened," Samuel reassured them. "You have certainly done wrong, but make sure now that you worship the Lord with true enthusiasm, and that you don't turn your back on Him in any way.

21 Other gods can't help you.

22 The Lord will not abandon His chosen people, for that would dishonor His great name. He made you a special nation for Himself — just because He wanted to!

23 As for me, far be it from me that I should sin against the Lord by ending my prayers for you; and I will continue to teach you those things which are good and right.

24 Trust the Lord and sincerely worship Him; think of all the tremendous things He has done for you.

25 But if you continue to sin, you and your king will be destroyed."

CHAPTER 13

By this time Saul had reigned for one year.[1] In the second year of his reign,

---

[1] The Hebrew, from which the numbers have evidently dropped out in copying, reads: "Saul was . . . years old when he began to reign, and he reigned . . . and two years over Israel."

2   He selected three thousand special troops and took two thousand of them with him to Michmash and Mount Bethel while the other thousand remained with Jonathan, Saul's son, in Gibe-ah in the land of Benjamin. The rest of the army was sent home.

3, 4   Then Jonathan attacked and destroyed the garrison of the Philistines at Geba. The news spread quickly throughout the land of the Philistines, and Saul sounded the call to arms throughout Israel. He announced that he had destroyed the Philistine garrison and warned his troops that they stank to high heaven as far as the Philistines were concerned. So the entire Israeli army mobilized again and joined at Gilgal.

5   The Philistines recruited a mighty army of three thousand chariots, six thousand horsemen, and so many soldiers that they were as thick as sand along the seashore; and they camped at Michmash east of Beth-aven.

6   When the men of Israel saw the vast mass of enemy troops, they lost their nerve entirely and tried to hide in caves, thickets, coverts, among the rocks, and even in tombs and cisterns.

7   Some of them crossed the Jordan River and escaped to the land of Gad and Gilead. Meanwhile, Saul stayed at Gilgal, and those who were with him trembled with fear at what awaited them.

8   Samuel had told Saul earlier to wait seven days for his arrival, but when he still didn't come, and Saul's troops were rapidly slipping away,

9   He decided to sacrifice the burnt offering and the peace offerings himself.

10   But just as he was finishing, Samuel arrived.

Saul went out to meet him and to receive his blessing,

11　But Samuel said, "What is this you have done?"

"Well," Saul replied, "when I saw that my men were scattering from me, and that you hadn't arrived by the time you said you would, and that the Philistines were at Michmash, ready for battle,

12　I said, 'The Philistines are ready to march against us and I haven't even asked for the Lord's help!' So I reluctantly offered the burnt offering without waiting for you to arrive."

13　"You fool!" Samuel exclaimed. "You have disobeyed the commandment of the Lord your God. He was planning to make you and your descendants kings of Israel forever,

14　But now your dynasty must end; for the Lord wants a man who will obey Him. And He has discovered the man He wants and has already appointed him as king over His people; for you have not obeyed the Lord's commandment."

15　Samuel then left Gilgal and went to Gibe-ah in the land of Benjamin.

When Saul counted the soldiers who were still with him, he found that there were only about six hundred left!

16　Saul and Jonathan and these six hundred men set up their camp in Geba in the land of Benjamin; but the Philistines stayed at Michmash.

17　Three companies of raiders soon left the camp of the Philistines; one went toward Ophrah in the land of Shual,

18　Another went to Beth-horon, and the third moved toward the border above the valley of Zeboim near the desert.

19 There were no blacksmiths at all in the land of Israel in those days, for the Philistines wouldn't allow them for fear of their making swords and spears for the Hebrews.

20 So whenever the Israelites needed to sharpen their plowshares, discs, axes, or sickles, they had to take them to a Philistine blacksmith.

21 (The schedule of charges was as follows:

For sharpening a plow point	60¢
For sharpening a disc	60¢
For sharpening an axe	30¢
For sharpening a sickle	30¢
For sharpening an ox goad	30¢)

22 So there was not a single sword or spear in the entire "army" of Israel that day, except for Saul's and Jonathan's.

23 The mountain pass at Michmash had meanwhile been secured by a contingent of the Philistine army.

CHAPTER 14

A day or so later, Prince Jonathan said to his young bodyguard, "Come on, let's cross the valley to the garrison of the Philistines." But he didn't tell his father that he was leaving.

2 Saul and his six hundred men were camped at the edge of Gibe-ah, around the pomegranate tree at Migron.

3 Among his men was Ahijah the priest (the son of Ahitub, Ichabod's brother; Ahitub was the grandson of Phinehas and the great-grandson of Eli, the priest of the Lord in Shiloh.)

No one realized that Jonathan had gone.

4   To reach the Philistine garrison, Jonathan had to go over a narrow pass between two rocky crags which had been named Bozez and Seneh.

5   The crag on the north was in front of Michmash and the southern one was in front of Geba.

6   "Yes, let's go across to those heathen," Jonathan had said to his bodyguard. "Perhaps the Lord will do a miracle for us. For it makes no difference to Him how many enemy troops there are!"

7   "Fine!" the youth replied. "Do as you think best; I'm with you heart and soul, whatever you decide."

8   "All right, then this is what we'll do," Jonathan told him.

9   "When they see us, if they say, 'Stay where you are or we'll kill you!' then we will stop and wait for them.

10   But if they say, 'Come on up and fight!' then we will do just that; for it will be God's signal that He will help us defeat them!"

11   When the Philistines saw them coming they shouted, "Look! The Israelis are crawling out of their holes!"

12   Then they shouted to Jonathan, "Come on up here and we'll show you how to fight!"

"Come on, climb right behind me," Jonathan exclaimed to his bodyguard, "for the Lord will help us defeat them!"

13   So they clambered up on their hands and knees, and the Philistines fell back as Jonathan and the lad killed them right and left,

14   About twenty men in all, and their bodies

were scattered over about half an acre of land.

15 Suddenly panic broke out throughout the entire Philistine army, and even among the raiders. And just then there was a great earthquake, increasing the terror.

16 Saul's lookouts in Gibe-ah saw a strange sight — the vast army of the Philistines began to melt away in all directions.

17 "Find out who isn't here," Saul ordered. And when they had checked, they found that Jonathan and his bodyguard were gone.

18 "Bring the Ark of God," Saul shouted to Ahijah. (For the Ark was among the people of Israel at that time.)

19 But while Saul was talking to the priest, the shouting and the tumult in the camp of the Philistines grew louder and louder. "Quick! What does God say?" Saul demanded.

20 Then Saul and his six hundred men rushed out to the battle and found the Philistines killing each other, and there was terrible confusion everywhere.

21 And now the Hebrews who had been drafted into the Philistine army revolted and joined with the Israelis.

22 Finally even the men hiding in the hills joined the chase when they saw that the Philistines were running away.

23 So the Lord saved Israel that day, and the battle continued out beyond Beth-aven.

24, 25 Saul had declared, "A curse upon anyone who eats anything before evening — before I have full revenge on my enemies." So no one ate anything all day, even though they found honeycomb on the ground in the forest,

26   For they all feared Saul's curse.

27   Jonathan, however, had not heard his father's command; so he dipped a stick into a honeycomb, and when he had eaten the honey he felt much better.

28   Then someone told him that his father had laid a curse upon anyone who ate food that day, and everyone was weary and faint as a result.

29   "That's ridiculous!" Jonathan exclaimed, "A command like that only hurts us. See how much better I feel now that I have eaten this little bit of honey.

30   If the people had been allowed to eat freely from the food they found among our enemies, think how many more we could have slaughtered!"

31   But hungry as they were, they chased and killed the Philistines all day from Michmash to Aijalon, growing more and more faint.

32   That evening[1] they flew upon the spoils of battle and butchered the sheep, oxen, and calves, and ate the raw, bloody meat.

33   Someone reported to Saul what was happening, that the people were sinning against the Lord by eating blood. "That is very wrong," Saul said. "Roll a great stone over here,

34   And go out among the troops and tell them to bring the oxen and sheep here to kill and drain them, and not to sin against the Lord by eating the blood." So that is what they did.

35   And Saul built an altar to the Lord — his first.

36   Afterwards Saul said, "Let's chase the Philistines all night and destroy every last one of them."

---

[1] Implied.

"Fine!" his men replied, "Do as you think best."

But the priest said, "Let's ask God first."

37   So Saul asked God, "Shall we go after the Philistines? Will You help us defeat them?" But the Lord made no reply all night.

38   Then Saul said to the leaders, "Something's wrong![2] We must find out what sin was committed today.

39   I vow by the name of the God who saved Israel that though the sinner be my own son Jonathan, he shall surely die!" But no one would tell him what the trouble was.

40   Then Saul proposed, "Jonathan and I will stand over here, and all of you stand over there." And the people agreed.

41   Then Saul said, "O Lord God of Israel, why haven't You answered my question? What is wrong? Are Jonathan and I guilty, or is the sin among the others? O Lord God, show us who is guilty." And Jonathan and Saul were chosen by sacred lot as the guilty ones, and the people were declared innocent.

42   Then Saul said, "Now draw lots between me and Jonathan." And Jonathan was chosen as the guilty one.

43   "Tell me what you've done," Saul demanded of Jonathan.

"I tasted a little honey," Jonathan admitted. "It was only a little bit on the end of a stick; but now I must die."

44   "Yes, Jonathan," Saul said, "You must die; may

2Implied.

God strike me dead if you are not executed for this."

45   But the troops retorted, "Jonathan, who saved Israel today, shall die? Far from it! We vow by the life of God that not one hair on his head will be touched, for he has been used of God to do a mighty miracle today." So the people rescued Jonathan.

46   Then Saul called back the army, and the Philistines returned home.

47   And now, since he was securely in the saddle as king of Israel, Saul sent the Israeli army out in every direction against Moab, Ammon, Edom, the kings of Zobah, and the Philistines. And wherever he turned, he was successful.

48   He did great deeds and conquered the Amalekites and saved Israel from all those who had been their conquerors.

49   Saul had three sons, Jonathan, Ishvi, and Malchishua; and two daughters, Merab and Michal.

50, 51   Saul's wife was Ahino-am, the daughter of Ahima-az. And the general-in-chief of his army was his cousin Abner, his uncle Ner's son. (Abner's father, Ner, and Saul's father, Kish, were brothers; both were the sons of Abiel.)

52   The Israelis fought constantly with the Philistines throughout Saul's lifetime. And whenever Saul saw any brave, strong young man, he conscripted him into his army.

CHAPTER 15

One day Samuel said to Saul, "I crowned you king of Israel because God told me to. Now be sure that you obey Him.

2   Here is His commandment to you: 'I have decided to settle accounts with the nation of Amalek for refusing to allow My people to cross their territory when Israel came from Egypt.

3   Now go and completely destroy the entire Amalek nation — men, women, babies, little children, oxen, sheep, camels, and donkeys.' "

4   So Saul mobilized his army at Telaim. There were two hundred thousand troops in addition to ten thousand men from Judah.

5   The Amalekites were camped in the valley below them.

6   Saul sent a message to the Kenites, telling them to get out from among the Amalekites or else die with them. "For you were kind to the people of Israel when they came out of the land of Egypt," he explained. So the Kenites packed up and left.

7   Then Saul butchered the Amalekites from Havilah all the way to Shur, east of Egypt.

8   He captured Agag, the king of the Amalekites, but killed everyone else.

9   However, Saul and his men kept the best of the sheep and oxen and the fattest of the lambs — everything, in fact, that appealed to them. They destroyed only what was worthless or of poor quality.

10   Then the Lord said to Samuel,

11   "I am sorry that I ever made Saul king, for he has again refused to obey Me." Samuel was so deeply moved when he heard what God was saying, that he cried to the Lord all night.

12   Early the next morning he went out to find Saul. Someone said that he had gone to Mount Carmel to erect a monument to himself, and had then gone

on to Gilgal.

13   When Samuel finally found him, Saul greeted him cheerfully. "Hello there," he said. "Well, I have carried out the Lord's command!"

14   "Then what was all the bleating of sheep and lowing of oxen I heard?" Samuel demanded.

15   "It's true that the army spared the best of the sheep and oxen," Saul admitted, "but they are going to sacrifice them to the Lord your God; and we have destroyed everything else."

16   Then Samuel said to Saul, "Stop! Listen to what the Lord told me last night!"

"What was it?" Saul asked.

17   And Samuel told him, "When you didn't think much of yourself, God made you king of Israel.

18   And He sent you on an errand and told you, 'Go and completely destroy the sinners, the Amalekites, until they are all dead.'

19   Then why didn't you obey the Lord? Why did you rush for the loot and do exactly what God said not to?"

20   "But I *have* obeyed the Lord," Saul insisted. "I did what He told me to; and I brought King Agag but killed everyone else.

21   And it was only when my troops demanded it that I let them keep the best of the sheep and oxen and loot to sacrifice to the Lord."

22   Samuel replied, "Has the Lord as much pleasure in your burnt offerings and sacrifices as in your obedience? Obedience is far better than sacrifice. He is much more interested in your listening to Him than in your offering the fat of rams to Him.

23   For rebellion is as bad as the sin of witchcraft,

and stubbornness is as bad as worshiping idols. And now because you have rejected the word of Jehovah, He has rejected you from being king."

24 "I have sinned," Saul finally admitted. "Yes, I have disobeyed your instructions and the command of the Lord, for I was afraid of the people and did what they demanded.

25 Oh, please pardon my sin now and go with me to worship the Lord."

26 But Samuel replied, "It's no use! Since you have rejected the commandment of the Lord, He has rejected you from being the king of Israel."

27 As Samuel turned to go, Saul grabbed at him to try to hold him back, and tore his robe.

28 And Samuel said to him, "See? The Lord has torn the kingdom of Israel from you today and has given it to a countryman of yours who is better than you are.

29 And He who is the glory of Israel is not lying, nor will He change His mind, for He is not a man!"

30 Then Saul pleaded again, "I have sinned; but oh, at least honor me before the leaders and before my people by going with me to worship the Lord your God."

31 So Samuel finally agreed and went with him.

32 Then Samuel said, "Bring King Agag to me." Agag arrived all full of smiles, for he thought, "Surely the worst is over and I have been spared!"

33 But Samuel said, "As your sword has killed the sons of many mothers, now your mother shall be child-less." And Samuel chopped him in pieces before the Lord at Gilgal.

34 Then Samuel went home to Ramah, and Saul

returned to Gibe-ah.

35 Samuel never saw Saul again, but he mourned constantly for him; and the Lord was sorry that He had ever made Saul king of Israel.

CHAPTER 16

Finally the Lord said to Samuel, "You have mourned long enough for Saul, for I have rejected him as king of Israel. Now take a vial of olive oil and go to Bethlehem and find a man named Jesse, for I have selected one of his sons to be the new king."

2 But Samuel asked, "How can I do that? If Saul hears about it, he will kill me."

"Take a heifer with you," the Lord replied, "and say that you have come to make a sacrifice to the Lord.

3 Then call Jesse to the sacrifice and I will show you which of his sons to anoint."

4 So Samuel did as the Lord had told him to. When he arrived at Bethlehem, the elders of the city came trembling to meet him. "What is wrong?" they asked. "Why have you come?"

5 But he replied, "All is well. I have come to sacrifice to the Lord. Purify yourselves and come with me to the sacrifice." And he performed the purification rite on Jesse and his sons, and invited them too.

6 When they arrived, Samuel took one look at Eliab and thought, "Surely this is the man the Lord has chosen!"

7 But the Lord said to Samuel, "Don't judge by a man's face or height, for this is not the one. I don't make decisions the way you do! Men judge by outward

appearance, but I look at a man's thoughts and intentions."

8   Then Jesse told his son Abinadab to step forward and walk in front of Samuel. But the Lord said, "This is not the right man either."

9   Next Jesse summoned Shammah, but the Lord said, "No, this is not the one." In the same way all seven of his sons presented themselves to Samuel and were rejected.

10, 11   "The Lord has not chosen any of them," Samuel told Jesse; "are these all there are?"

"Well, there is the youngest," Jesse replied. "But he's out in the fields watching the sheep."

"Send for him at once," Samuel said, "for we will not sit down to eat until he arrives."

12   So Jesse sent for him. He was a fine looking boy, ruddy-faced, and with pleasant eyes. And the Lord said, "This is the one; anoint him."

13   So as David stood there among his brothers, Samuel took the olive oil he had brought and poured it upon David's head; and the Spirit of Jehovah came upon him and gave him great power from that day onward. Then Samuel returned to Ramah.

14   But the Spirit of the Lord had left Saul, and instead, the Lord had sent a tormenting spirit that filled him with depression and fear.

15, 16   Some of Saul's aides suggested a cure. "We'll find a good harpist to play for you whenever the tormenting spirit is bothering you," they said. "The harp music will quiet you and you'll soon be well again."

17   "All right," Saul said. "Find me a harpist."

18   One of them said he knew a young fellow in

Bethlehem, the son of a man named Jesse, who was not only a talented harp player, but was handsome, brave, and strong, and had good, solid judgment. "What's more," he added, "the Lord is with him."

19 So Saul sent messengers to Jesse, asking that he send his son David the shepherd.

20 Jesse responded by sending not only David but a young goat and a donkey carrying a load of food and wine.

21 From the instant he saw David, Saul admired and loved him; and David became his bodyguard.

22 Then Saul wrote to Jesse, "Please let David join my staff, for I am very fond of him."

23 And whenever the tormenting spirit from God troubled Saul, David would play the harp and Saul would feel better, and the evil spirit would go away.

CHAPTER 17

The Philistines now mustered their army for battle and camped between Socoh in Judah and Azekah in Ephes-dammim.

2 Saul countered with a buildup of forces at Elah Valley.

3 So the Philistines and Israelis faced each other on opposite hills, with the valley between them.

4-7 Then Goliath, a Philistine champion from Gath, came out of the Philistine ranks to face the forces of Israel. He was a giant of a man, measuring over nine feet tall! He wore a bronze helmet, a two-hundred-pound coat of mail, bronze leggings, and carried a bronze javelin several inches thick, tipped with a twenty-five-pound iron spearhead, and his armor bearer walked ahead of him with a huge shield.

8 He stood and shouted across to the Israelis, "Do you need a whole army to settle this? I will represent the Philistines, and you choose someone to represent you, and we will settle this in single combat!

9 If your man is able to kill me, then we will be your slaves. But if I kill him, then you must be our slaves!

10 I defy the armies of Israel! Send me a man who will fight with me!"

11 When Saul[1] and the Israeli army heard this, they were dismayed and frightened.

12 David (the son of aging Jesse, a member of the tribe of Ephraim who lived in Bethlehem-Judah) had seven older brothers.

13 The three oldest — Eliab, Abinadab, and Shammah — had already volunteered for Saul's army to fight the Philistines.

14, 15 David was the youngest son, and was on Saul's staff on a part-time basis. He went back and forth to Bethlehem to help his father with the sheep.

16 For forty days, twice a day, morning and evening the Philistine giant strutted before the armies of Israel.

17 One day Jesse said to David, "Take this bushel of roasted grain and these ten loaves of bread to your brothers.

18 Give this cheese to their captain and see how the boys are getting along; and bring us back a letter[2] from them!"

---

[1] Probably King Saul was especially worried, for he was the tallest of the Israelites, and was obviously the best match!
[2] Literally, "take their pledge."

19 (Saul and the Israeli army were camped at the valley of Elah.)

20 So David left the sheep with another shepherd and took off early the next morning with the gifts. He arrived at the outskirts of the camp just as the Israeli army was leaving for the battlefield with shouts and battle cries.

21 Soon the Israeli and Philistine forces stood facing each other, army against army.

22 David left his luggage with a baggage officer and hurried out to the ranks to find his brothers.

23 As he was talking with them, he saw Goliath the giant step out from the Philistine troops and shout his challenge to the army of Israel.

24 As soon as they saw him the Israeli army began to run away in fright.

25 "Have you seen the giant?" the soldiers were asking. "He has insulted the entire army of Israel. And have you heard about the huge reward the king has offered to anyone who kills him? And the king will give him one of his daughters for a wife, and his whole family will be exempted from paying taxes!"

26 David talked to some others standing there to verify the report. "What will a man get for killing this Philistine and ending his insults to Israel?" he asked them. "Who is this heathen Philistine, anyway, that he is allowed to defy the armies of the living God?"

27 And he received the same reply as before.

28 But when David's oldest brother, Eliab, heard David talking like that, he was angry. "What are you doing around here, anyway?" he demanded. "What about the sheep you're supposed to be taking care

of? I know what a cocky brat you are; you just want to see the battle!"

29 "What have I done now?" David replied. "I was only asking a question!"

30 And he walked over to some others and asked them the same thing and received the same answer.

31 When it was finally realized what David meant, someone told King Saul, and the king sent for him.

32 "Don't worry about a thing," David told him, "I'll take care of this Philistine!"

33 "Don't be ridiculous!" Saul replied. "How can a kid like you fight with a man like him? You are only a boy and he has been in the army *since* he was a boy!"

34 But David persisted. "When I am taking care of my father's sheep," he said, "and a lion or a bear comes and grabs a lamb from the flock,

35 I go after it with a club and take the lamb from its mouth. If it turns on me I catch it by the jaw and club it to death.

36 I have done this to both lions and bears, and I'll do it to this heathen Philistine too, for he has defied the armies of the living God!

37 The Lord who saved me from the claws and teeth of the lion and the bear will save me from this Philistine!"

Saul finally consented, "All right, go ahead"; he said, "and may the Lord be with you!"

38, 39 Then Saul gave David his own armor — a bronze helmet and a coat of mail. David put it on, strapped the sword over it, and took a step or two to see what it was like, for he had never worn such things before. "I can hardly move!" he exclaimed, and took them off again.

40 Then he picked up five smooth stones from a stream and put them in his shepherd's bag and, armed only with his shepherd's staff and sling, started across to Goliath.

41, 42 Goliath walked out towards David with his shield bearer ahead of him, sneering in contempt at this nice little red-cheeked boy!

43 "Am I a dog," he roared at David, "that you come at me with a stick?" And he cursed David by the names of his gods.

44 "Come over here and I'll give your flesh to the birds and wild animals," Goliath yelled.

45 David shouted in reply, "You come to me with a sword and a spear, but I come to you in the name of the Lord of the armies of heaven and of Israel — the very God whom you have defied.

46 Today the Lord will conquer you and I will kill you and cut off your head; and then I will give the dead bodies of *your* men to the birds and wild animals, and the whole world will know that there is a God in Israel!

47 And Israel will learn that the Lord does not depend on weapons to fulfill His plans — He works without regard to human means! He will give you to us!"

48, 49 As Goliath approached, David ran out to meet him and, reaching into his shepherd's bag, took out a stone, hurled it from his sling, and hit the Philistine in the forehead. The stone sank in, and the man fell on his face to the ground.

50, 51 So David conquered the Philistine giant with a sling and a stone. Since he had no sword, he ran over and pulled Goliath's from its sheath and killed him with it, and then cut off his head. When the Philistines saw that their champion was dead, they turned and ran.

52   Then the Israelis gave a great shout of triumph and rushed after the Philistines, chasing them as far as Gath and the gates of Ekron. The bodies of the dead and wounded Philistines were strewn all along the road to Shaaraim.

53   Then the Israeli army returned and plundered the deserted Philistine camp.

54   (Later David took Goliath's head to Jerusalem, but stored his armor in his tent.)

55   As Saul was watching David go out to fight Goliath, he asked Abner, the general of his army, "Abner, what sort of family does this young fellow come from?"[3]

"I really don't know," Abner said.

56   "Well, find out!" the king told him.

57   After David had killed Goliath, Abner brought him to Saul with the Philistine's head still in his hand.

58   "Tell me about your father, my boy," Saul said.

And David replied, "His name is Jesse and we live in Bethlehem."

CHAPTER 18

After King Saul had finished his conversation with David, David met Jonathan, the king's son, and there was an immediate bond of love between them.

---

[3]Literally, "Whose son is this?" Since David was, if successful, scheduled to marry Saul's daughter, Saul wanted to know more about his family! The other explanation of this confusing passage is that Saul's unstable mental condition caused forgetfulness, so that he didn't recognize David.

Jonathan swore to be his blood brother,

4 And sealed the pact by giving him his robe, sword, bow, and belt. King Saul now kept David at Jerusalem and wouldn't let him return home any more.

5 He was Saul's special assistant, and he always carried out his assignments successfully. So Saul made him commander of his troops, an appointment which was applauded by the army and general public alike.

6 But something had happened when the victorious Israeli army was returning home after David had killed Goliath. Women came out from all the towns along the way to celebrate and to cheer for King Saul, and were singing and dancing for joy with tambourines and cymbals.

7 However, this was their song: "Saul has slain his thousands, and David his ten thousands!"

8 Of course Saul was very angry. "What's this?" he said to himself. "They credit David with ten thousands and me with only thousands. Next they'll be making him their king!"

9 So from that time on King Saul kept a jealous watch on David.

10 The very next day, in fact, a tormenting spirit from God overwhelmed Saul, and he began to rave like a madman. David began to soothe him by playing the harp, as he did whenever this happened. But Saul, who was fiddling with his spear,

11, 12 Suddenly hurled it at David, intending to pin him to the wall. But David jumped aside and escaped. This happened another time, too, for Saul was afraid of him and jealous because the Lord had left him and was now with David.

13 Finally Saul banned him from his presence and

demoted him to the rank of captain. But the controversy put David more than ever in the public eye.

14 David continued to succeed in everything he undertook, for the Lord was with him.

15, 16 When King Saul saw this, he became even more afraid of him; but all Israel and Judah loved him, for he was as one of them.

17 One day Saul said to David, "I am ready to give you my oldest daughter Merab as your wife. But first you must prove yourself to be a real soldier by fighting the Lord's battles." For Saul thought to himself, "I'll send him out against the Philistines and let them kill him rather than doing it myself."

18 "Who am I that I should be the king's son-in-law?" David exclaimed. "My father's family is nothing!"

19 But when the time arrived for the wedding, Saul married her to Adriel, a man from Meholath, instead.

20 In the meantime Saul's daughter Michal had fallen in love with David, and Saul was delighted when he heard about it.

21 "Here's another opportunity to see him killed by the Philistines!" Saul said to himself. But to David he said, "You can be my son-in-law after all, for I will give you my youngest daughter."

22 Then Saul instructed his men to say confidentially to David that the king really liked him a lot, and that they all loved him and thought he should accept the king's proposition and become his son-in-law.

23 But David replied, "How can a poor man like me from an unknown family find enough dowry to marry the daughter of a king?"

24   When Saul's men reported this back to him,

25   He told them, "Tell David that the only dowry I need is one hundred dead Philistines![1] Vengeance on my enemies is all I want." But what Saul had in mind was that David would be killed in the fight.

26   David was delighted to accept the offer. So, before the time limit expired,

27   He and his men went out and killed two hundred Philistines and presented their foreskins to King Saul. So Saul gave Michal to him.

28   When the king realized how much the Lord was with David and how immensely popular he was with all the people,

29   He became even more afraid of him, and grew to hate him more with every passing day.

30   Whenever the Philistine army attacked, David was more successful against them than all the rest of Saul's officers. So David's name became very famous throughout the land.

CHAPTER 19

S aul now urged his aides and his son Jonathan to assassinate David. But Jonathan, because of his close friendship with David,

2   Told him what his father was planning. "Tomorrow morning," he warned him, "you must find a hiding place out in the fields.

3   I'll ask my father to go out there with me, and I'll talk to him about you; then I'll tell you everything I can find out."

4   The next morning[1] as Jonathan and his father

---

[1]Literally, "one hundred foreskins of the Philistines."
[1]Implied.

were talking together, he spoke well of David and begged him not to be against David. "He's never done anything to harm you," Jonathan pleaded. "He has always helped you in any way he could.

5 Have you forgotten about the time he risked his life to kill Goliath, and how the Lord brought a great victory to Israel as a result? You were certainly happy about it then. Why should you now murder an innocent man by killing him? There is no reason for it at all!"

6 Finally Saul agreed, and vowed, "As the Lord lives, he shall not be killed."

7 Afterwards Jonathan called David and told him what had happened. Then he took David to Saul and everything was as it had been before.

8 War broke out shortly after that and David led his troops against the Philistines and slaughtered many of them, and put to flight their entire army.

9, 10 But one day as Saul was sitting at home, listening to David playing the harp, suddenly the tormenting spirit from the Lord attacked him. He had his spear in his hand, and hurled it at David in an attempt to kill him. But David dodged out of the way and fled into the night, leaving the spear imbedded in the timber of the wall.

11 Saul sent troops to watch David's house and kill him when he came out in the morning. "If you don't get away tonight," Michal warned him, "you'll be dead by morning."

12 So she helped him get down to the ground through a window.

13 Then she took an idol[2] and put it in his bed,

---

[2]Literally, "teraphim."

and covered it with blankets, with its head on a pillow of goat's hair.

14 When the soldiers came to arrest David and take him to Saul,[3] she told them he was sick and couldn't get out of bed.

15 Saul said to bring him in his bed, then, so that he could kill him.

16 But when they came to carry him out, they discovered that it was only an idol!

17 "Why have you deceived me and let my enemy escape?" Saul demanded of Michal.

"I had to," Michal replied. "He threatened to kill me if I didn't help him."

18 In that way David got away and went to Ramah to see Samuel, and told him all that Saul had done to him. So Samuel took David with him to live at Naioth.

19 When the report reached Saul that David was at Naioth in Ramah,

20 He sent soldiers to capture him; but when they arrived and saw Samuel and the other prophets prophesying, the Spirit of God came upon them and they also began to prophesy.

21 When Saul heard what had happened, he sent other soldiers, but they too prophesied! The same thing happened a third time!

22 Then Saul himself went to Ramah and arrived at the great well in Secu. "Where are Samuel and David?" he demanded. Someone told him they were at Naioth.

23 But on the way to Naioth the Spirit of God came upon Saul, and he too began to prophesy!

3Implied.

24 He tore off his clothes and lay naked all day and all night, prophesying with Samuel's prophets. Saul's men were incredulous! "What!" they exclaimed, "is Saul a prophet, too?"[4]

CHAPTER 20

D avid now fled from Naioth in Ramah, and found Jonathan.

"What have I done?" he exclaimed. "Why is your father so determined to kill me?"

2 "That's not true!" Jonathan protested. "I'm sure he's not planning any such thing, for he always tells me everything he's going to do, even little things, and I know he wouldn't hide something like this from me. It just isn't so."

3 "Of course you don't know about it!" David fumed. "Your father knows perfectly well about our friendship, so he has said to himself, 'I'll not tell Jonathan — why should I hurt him?' But the truth is that I am only a step away from death! I swear it by the Lord and by your own soul!"

4 "Tell me what I can do," Jonathan begged.

5 And David replied, "Tomorrow is the beginning of the celebration of the new moon. Always before, I've been with your father for this occasion, but tomorrow I'll hide in the field and stay there until the evening of the third day.

6 If your father asks where I am, tell him that I asked permission to go home to Bethlehem for an annual family reunion.

4Implied. Literally, "hence it is said, 'Is Saul also among the prophets?'" (See I Samuel 10:10-12.)

7 If he says, 'Fine!' then I'll know that all is well. But if he is angry, then I'll know that he is planning to kill me.

8 Do this for me as my sworn brother. Or else kill me yourself if I have sinned against your father, but don't betray me to him!"

9 "Of course not!" Jonathan exclaimed. "Look, wouldn't I say so if I knew that my father was planning to kill you?"

10 Then David asked, "How will I know whether or not your father is angry?"

11 "Come out to the field with me," Jonathan replied. And they went out there together.

12 Then Jonathan told David, "I promise by the Lord God of Israel that about this time tomorrow, or the next day at the latest, I will talk to my father about you and let you know at once how he feels about you.

13 If he is angry and wants you killed, then may the Lord kill me if I don't tell you, so you can escape and live. May the Lord be with you as He used to be with my father.

14 And remember, you must demonstrate the love and kindness of the Lord not only to me during my own lifetime,

15 But also to my children after the Lord has destroyed all of your enemies."

16 So Jonathan made a covenant with the family of David, and David swore to it with a terrible curse against himself and his descendants, should he be unfaithful to his promise.

17 But Jonathan made David swear to it again, this time by his love for him, for he loved him as much

as he loved himself.

18 Then Jonathan said, "Yes, they will miss you tomorrow when your place at the table is empty.

19 By the day after tomorrow, everyone will be asking about you, so be at the hideout where you were before, over by the stone pile.

20 I will come out and shoot three arrows in front of the pile as though I were shooting at a target.

21 Then I'll send a lad to bring the arrows back. If you hear me tell him, 'They're on this side,' then you will know that all is well and that there is no trouble.

22 But if I tell him, 'Go farther — the arrows are still ahead of you,' then it will mean that you must leave immediately.

23 And may the Lord make us keep our promises to each other, for He has witnessed them.[1]

24, 25 So David hid himself in the field.

When the new moon celebration began, the king sat down to eat at his usual place against the wall. Jonathan sat opposite him and Abner was sitting beside Saul, but David's place was empty.

26 Saul didn't say anything about it that day, for he supposed that something had happened so that David was ceremonially impure. Yes, surely that must be it!

27 But when his place was still empty the next day, Saul asked Jonathan, "Why hasn't David been here for dinner either yesterday or today?"

28, 29 "He asked me if he could go to Bethlehem to take part in a family celebration," Jonathan re-

---

[1]Literally, "The Lord is our mediator forever."

plied. "His brother demanded that he be there, so I told him to go ahead."

30 Saul boiled with rage. "You son of a bitch!"[2] he yelled at him. "Do you think I don't know that you want this son of a nobody[3] to be king in your place, shaming yourself and your mother?

31 As long as that fellow is alive, you'll never be king. Now go and get him so I can kill him!"

32 "But what has he done?" Jonathan demanded. "Why should he be put to death?"

33 Then Saul hurled his spear at Jonathan, intending to kill him; so at last Jonathan realized that his father really meant it when he said that David must die.

34 Jonathan left the table in fierce anger and refused to eat all that day, for he was hurt by his father's shameful behavior toward David.

35 The next morning, as agreed, Jonathan went out into the field and took a young boy with him to gather his arrows.

36 "Start running," he told the boy, "so that you can find the arrows as I shoot them." So the boy ran and Jonathan shot an arrow beyond him.

37 When the boy had almost reached the arrow, Jonathan shouted, "The arrow is still ahead of you.

38 Hurry, hurry, don't wait." So the boy quickly gathered up the arrows and ran back to his master.

39 He, of course, didn't understand what Jonathan meant; only Jonathan and David knew.

40 Then Jonathan gave his bow and arrows to

---

[2]Literally, "son of a perverse, rebellious woman." This paraphrase is the modern equivalent.
[3]Literally, "son of Jesse."

the boy and told him to take them back to the city.

41   As soon as he was gone, David came out from where he had been hiding near the south edge of the field and they sadly shook hands, tears running down their cheeks until David could weep no more.[4]

42   At last Jonathan said to David, "Cheer up, for we have entrusted each other and each other's children into God's hands for ever." So they parted, David going away and Jonathan returning to the city.

CHAPTER 21

David went to the city of Nob to see Ahimelech, the priest. Ahimelech trembled when he saw him. "Why are you alone?" he asked. "Why is no one with you?"

2   "The king has sent me on a private matter," David lied. "He told me not to tell anybody why I am here. I have told my men where to meet me later.

3   Now, what is there to eat? Give me five loaves of bread, or anything else you can."

4   "We don't have any regular bread," the priest replied, "but there is the holy bread, which I guess you can have if only your young men have not slept with any women for awhile."

5   "Rest assured," David replied. "I never let my men run wild when they are on an expedition, and since they stay clean even on ordinary trips, how much more so on this one!"

6   So, since there was no other food available,

---

[4]Literally, "David . . . bowed himself three times and they kissed each other and wept until David exceeded."

the priest gave him the holy bread — the Bread of the Presence that was placed before the Lord in the Tabernacle. It had just been replaced that day with fresh bread.

7 (Incidentally, Doeg the Edomite, Saul's chief herdsman, was there at that time for ceremonial purification.[1])

8 David asked Ahimelech if he had a spear or sword he could use. "The king's business required such haste, and I left in such a rush that I came away without a weapon!" David explained.

9 "Well," the priest replied, "I have the sword of Goliath, the Philistine — the fellow you killed in the valley of Elah. It is wrapped in a cloth in the clothes closet.[2] Take that if you want it, for there is nothing else here."

"Just the thing!" David replied. "Give it to me!"

10 Then David hurried on, for he was fearful of Saul, and went to King Achish of Gath.

11 But Achish's officers weren't happy about his being there. "Isn't he the top leader of Israel?" they asked. "Isn't he the one the people honor at their dances, singing, 'Saul has slain his thousands and David his ten thousands'?"

12 David heard these comments and was afraid of what King Achish might do to him,

13 So he pretended to be insane! He scratched on doors and let his spittle flow down his beard,

14, 15 Until finally King Achish said to his men, "Must you bring me a madman? We already have

---

[1] Literally, "detained before the Lord."
[2] Literally, "behind the ephod."

enough of them around here! Should such a fellow as this be my guest?"

CHAPTER 22

S o David left Gath and escaped to the cave of Adullam, where his brothers and other relatives soon joined him.

2　Then others began coming — those who were in any kind of trouble, such as being in debt, or merely discontented — until David was the leader of about four hundred men.

3　(Later David went to Mizpah in Moab to ask permission of the king for his father and mother to live there under royal protection until David knew what God was going to do for him.

4　They stayed in Moab during the entire period when David was living in the cave.)

5　One day the prophet Gad told David to leave the cave and return to the land of Judah. So David went to the forest of Hereth.

6　The news of his arrival in Judah soon reached Saul. He was in Gibe-ah at the time, sitting beneath an oak tree playing with his spear, surrounded by his officers.

7　"Listen here, you men of Benjamin!" Saul exclaimed when he heard the news. "Has David promised you fields and vineyards and commissions in his army?

8　Is that why you are against me? For not one of you has ever told me that my own son is on David's side. You're not even sorry for me. Think of it! My own son — encouraging David to come and kill me!"

9, 10   Then Doeg the Edomite, who was standing there with Saul's men, spoke up. "When I was at Nob," he said, "I saw David talking to Ahimelech the priest. Ahimelech consulted the Lord to find out what David should do, and then gave him food and the sword of Goliath the Philistine."

11, 12   King Saul immediately summoned Ahimelech and all his family and all the other priests at Nob. When they arrived Saul shouted at him, "Listen to me, you son of Ahitub!"

"What is it?" quavered Ahimelech.

13   "Why have you and David conspired against me?" Saul demanded. "Why did you give him food and a sword and talk to God for him? Why did you encourage him to revolt against me and to come here and attack me?"

14   "But sir," Ahimelech replied, "is there anyone among all your servants who is as faithful as David your son-in-law? Why, he is the captain of your bodyguard and a highly honored member of your own household!

15   This was certainly not the first time I had consulted God for him! It's unfair for you to accuse me and my family in this matter, for we knew nothing of any plot against you."

16   "You shall die, Ahimelech, along with your entire family!" the king shouted.

17   He ordered his bodyguards, "Kill these priests, for they are allies and conspirators with David; they knew he was running away from me, but they didn't tell me!" But the soldiers refused to harm the clergy.

18   Then the king said to Doeg, "You do it." So Doeg turned on them and killed them, eighty-five

priests in all, all wearing their priestly robes.

19 Then he went to Nob, the city of the priests, and killed the priests' families — men, women, children, and babies, and also all the oxen, donkeys, and sheep.

20 Only Abiathar, one of the sons of Ahimelech, escaped and fled to David.

21 When he told him what Saul had done,

22 David exclaimed, "I knew it! When I saw Doeg there, I knew he would tell Saul. Now I have caused the death of all of your father's family.

23 Stay here with me, and I'll protect you with my own life. Any harm to you will be over my dead body."

CHAPTER 23

One day news came to David that the Philistines were at Keilah robbing the threshing floors.

2 David asked the Lord, "Shall I go and attack them?"

"Yes, go and save Keilah," the Lord told him.

3 But David's men said, "We're afraid even here in Judah; we certainly don't want to go to Keilah to fight the whole Philistine army!"

4 David asked the Lord again, and the Lord again replied, "Go down to Keilah, for I will help you conquer the Philistines."

5 They went to Keilah and slaughtered the Philistines and confiscated their cattle, and so the people of Keilah were saved.

6 (Abiathar the priest went to Keilah with David, taking his ephod with him to get answers for David from the Lord.)

7   Saul soon learned that David was at Keilah. "Good!" he exclaimed. "We've got him now! God has delivered him to me, for he has trapped himself in a walled city!"

8   So Saul mobilized his entire army to march to Keilah and besiege David and his men.

9   But David learned of Saul's plan and told Abiathar the priest to bring the ephod and to ask the Lord what he should do.

10   "O Lord God of Israel," David said, "I have heard that Saul is planning to come and destroy Keilah because I am here.

11   Will the men of Keilah surrender me to him? And will Saul actually come, as I have heard? O Lord God of Israel, please tell me."

And the Lord said, "He will come."

12   "And will these men of Keilah betray me to Saul?" David persisted.

And the Lord replied, "Yes, they will betray you."

13   So David and his men — about six hundred of them now — left Keilah and began roaming the countryside. Word soon reached Saul that David had escaped, so he didn't go there after all.

14, 15   David now lived in the wilderness caves in the hill country of Ziph. One day near Horesh he received the news that Saul was on the way to Ziph to search for him and kill him. Saul hunted him day after day, but the Lord didn't let him find him.

16   (Prince Jonathan now went to find David; he met him at Horesh and encouraged him in his faith in God.

17   "Don't be afraid," Jonathan reassured him.

"My father will never find you! You are going to be the king of Israel and I will be next to you, as my father is well aware."

18 So the two of them renewed their pact of friendship; and David stayed at Horesh while Jonathan returned home.)

19 But now the men of Ziph went to Saul in Gibeah and betrayed David to him. "We know where he is hiding," they said. "He is in the caves of Horesh on Hachilah Hill, down in the southern part of the wilderness.

20 Come on down, sir, and we will catch him for you and your fondest wish will be fulfilled!"

21 "Well, praise the Lord!" Saul said. "At last someone has had pity on me!

22 Go and check again to be sure of where he is staying and who has seen him there, for I know that he is very crafty.

23 Discover his hiding places and then come back and give me a more definite report. Then I'll go with you. And if he is in the area at all, I'll find him if I have to search every inch of the entire land!"

24, 25 So the men of Ziph returned home. But when David heard that Saul was on his way to Ziph, he and his men went even further into the wilderness of Maon in the south of the desert. But Saul followed them there.

26 He and David were now on opposite sides of a mountain. As Saul and his men began to close in, David tried his best to escape, but it was no use.

27 But just then a message reached Saul that the Philistines were raiding Israel again,

28 So Saul quit the chase and returned to fight the

Philistines. Ever since that time the place where David was camped has been called, "The Rock of Escape!"

29   David then went to live in the caves of Engedi.

CHAPTER 24

After Saul's return from his battle with the Philistines, he was told that David had gone into the wilderness of Engedi;

2   So he took three thousand special troops and went to search for him among the rocks and wild goats of the desert.

3   At the place where the road passes some sheepfolds, Saul went into a cave to go to the bathroom, but as it happened, David and his men were hiding in the cave!

4   "Now's your time!" David's men whispered to him. "Today is the day the Lord was talking about when He said, 'I will certainly put Saul into your power, to do with as you wish'!" Then David crept forward and quietly slit off the bottom of Saul's robe!

5   But then his conscience began bothering him.

6   "I shouldn't have done it," he said to his men. "It is a serious sin to attack God's chosen king in any way."

7, 8   These words of David persuaded his men not to kill Saul.

After Saul had left the cave and gone on his way, David came out and shouted after him, "My lord the king!" And when Saul looked around, David bowed low before him.

9, 10   Then he shouted to Saul, "Why do you listen to the people who say that I am trying to harm you? This very day you have seen that it isn't true. The Lord placed you at my mercy back there in the cave and some of my men told me to kill you, but I spared you. For I said, 'I will never harm him — he is the Lord's chosen king.'

11 See what I have in my hand? It is the hem of your robe! I cut it off, but I didn't kill you! Doesn't this convince you that I am not trying to harm you and that I have not sinned against you, even though you have been hunting for my life?

12 The Lord will decide between us. Perhaps He will kill you for what you are trying to do to me, but I will never harm you.

13 As that old proverb says, 'Wicked is as wicked does,' but despite your wickedness, I'll not touch you.

14 And who is the king of Israel trying to catch, anyway? Should he spend his time chasing one who is as worthless as a dead dog or a flea?

15 May the Lord judge as to which of us is right and punish whichever one of us is guilty. He is my lawyer and defender, and He will rescue me from your power!"

16 Saul called back, "Is it really you, my son David?" Then he began to cry.

17 And he said to David, "You are a better man than I am, for you have repaid me good for evil.

18 Yes, you have been wonderfully kind to me today, for when the Lord delivered me into your hand, you didn't kill me.

19 Who else in all the world would let his enemy get away when he had him in his power? May the Lord reward you well for the kindness you have shown

me today.

20   And now I realize that you are surely going to be king, and Israel shall be yours to rule.

21   Oh, swear to me by the Lord that when that happens you will not kill my family and destroy my line of descendants!"

22   So David promised, and Saul went home, but David and his men went back to their cave.

CHAPTER 25

Shortly afterwards, Samuel died and all Israel gathered for his funeral and buried him in his family plot at Ramah. Meanwhile David went down to the wilderness of Paran.

2   A wealthy man from Maon owned a sheep ranch there, near the village of Carmel. He had three thousand sheep and a thousand goats, and was at his ranch at this time for the sheep shearing.

3   His name was Nabal and his wife, a beautiful and very intelligent woman, was named Abigail. But the man, who was a descendant of Caleb, was uncouth, churlish, stubborn, and ill-mannered.

4   When David heard that Nabal was shearing his sheep,

5   He sent ten of his young men to Carmel to give him this message:

6   "May God prosper you and your family and multiply everything you own.

7   I am told that you are shearing your sheep and goats. While your shepherds have lived among us, we have never harmed them, nor stolen anything from them the whole time they have been in Carmel.

8 Ask your young men and they will tell you whether or not this is true. Now I have sent my men to ask for a little contribution from you, for we have come at a happy time of holiday. Please give us a present of whatever is at hand."

9 The young men gave David's message to Nabal and waited for his reply.

10 "Who is this fellow David?" he asked. "Who does this son of Jesse think he is? There are lots of servants these days who run away from their masters.

11 Should I take my bread and my water and my meat that I've slaughtered for my shearers and give it to a gang who suddenly appear from nowhere?"[1]

12 So David's messengers returned and told him what Nabal had said.

13 "Get your swords!" was David's reply as he strapped on his own. Four hundred of them started off with David and two hundred remained behind to guard their gear.

14 Meanwhile one of Nabal's men went and told Abigail, "David sent men from the wilderness to talk to our master, but he insulted them and railed at them.

15, 16 But David's men were very good to us and we never suffered any harm from them; in fact, day and night they were like a wall of protection to us and the sheep, and nothing was stolen from us the whole time they were with us.

17 You'd better think fast, for there is going to be trouble for our master and his whole family — he's such a stubborn lout that no one can even talk to him!"

---

[1] Literally, "to men who come from God knows where."

18 Then Abigail hurriedly took two hundred loaves of bread, two barrels of wine, five dressed sheep, two bushels of roasted grain, one hundred raisin cakes, and two hundred fig cakes, and packed them onto donkeys.

19 "Go on ahead," she said to her young men, "and I will follow." But she didn't tell her husband what she was doing.

20 As she was riding down the trail on her donkey, she met David coming towards her.

21 David had been saying to himself, "A lot of good it did us to help this fellow. We protected his flocks in the wilderness so that not one thing was lost or stolen, but he has repaid me bad for good. All that I get for my trouble is insults.

22 May God curse me if even one of his men remains alive by tomorrow morning!"

23 When Abigail saw David, she quickly dismounted and bowed low before him.

24 "I accept all blame in this matter, my lord," she said. "Please listen to what I want to say.

25 Nabal is a bad-tempered boor, but please don't pay any attention to what he said. He is a fool — just like his name means. But I didn't see the messengers you sent.

26 Sir, since the Lord has kept you from murdering and taking vengeance into your own hands, I pray by the life of God, and by your own life too, that all your enemies shall be as cursed as Nabal is.

27 And now, here is a present I have brought to you and your young men.

28 Forgive me for my boldness in coming out here. The Lord will surely reward you with eternal

royalty for your descendants, for you are fighting His battles; and you will never do wrong throughout your entire life.

29 Even when you are chased by those who seek your life, you are safe in the care of the Lord your God, just as though you were safe inside his purse! But the lives of your enemies shall disappear like stones from a sling!

30, 31 When the Lord has done all the good things He promised you and has made you king of Israel, you won't want the conscience of a murderer who took the law into his own hands! And when the Lord has done these great things for you, please remember me!"

32 David replied to Abigail, "Bless the Lord God of Israel who has sent you to meet me today!

33 Thank God for your good sense! Bless you for keeping me from murdering the man and carrying out vengeance with my own hands.

34 For I swear by the Lord, the God of Israel who has kept me from hurting you, that if you had not come out to meet me, not one of Nabal's men would be alive tomorrow morning."

35 Then David accepted her gifts and told her to return home without fear, for he would not kill her husband.

36 When she arrived home she found that Nabal had thrown a big party. He was roaring drunk, so she didn't tell him anything about her meeting with David until the next morning.

37, 38 By that time he was sober, and when his wife told him what had happened, he had a stroke and lay paralyzed[2] for about ten days, then died, for

---

[2]Literally, "his heart died within him and he became as stone."

the Lord killed him.

39   When David heard that Nabal was dead, he said, "Praise the Lord! God has paid back Nabal and kept me from doing it myself; he has received his punishment for his sin." Then David wasted no time in sending messengers to Abigail to ask her to become his wife.

40   When the messengers arrived at Carmel and told her why they had come,

41   She readily agreed to his request.

42   Quickly getting ready, she took along five of her serving girls as attendants, mounted her donkey, and followed the men back to David. So she became his wife.

43   David also married Ahino-am from Jezreel.

44   King Saul, meanwhile, had forced David's wife Michal, Saul's daughter, to marry a man from Gallim named Palti (the son of Laish).

CHAPTER 26

Now the men from Ziph came back to Saul at Gibeah to tell him that David had returned to the wilderness and was hiding on Hachilah Hill.

2   So Saul took his elite corps of three thousand troops and went to hunt him down.

3, 4   Saul camped along the road at the edge of the wilderness where David was hiding, but David knew of Saul's arrival and sent out spies to watch his movements.

5, 6, 7   David slipped over to Saul's camp one night to look around. King Saul and General Abner were sleeping inside a ring formed by the slumbering sol-

diers. "Any volunteers to go down there with me?"
David asked Ahimelech (the Hittite) and Abishai
(Joab's brother and the son of Zeruiah). "I'll go with
you," Abishai replied. So David and Abishai went to
Saul's camp and found him asleep, with his spear in
the ground beside his head.

8   "God has put your enemy within your power
this time for sure," Abishai whispered to David. "Let
me go and put that spear through him. I'll pin him
to the earth with it — I'll not need to strike a second
time!"

9   "No," David said. "Don't kill him, for who
can remain innocent after attacking the Lord's chosen
king?

10   Surely God will strike him down some day, or
he will die in battle or of old age.

11   But God forbid that I should kill the man He
has chosen to be king! But I'll tell you what — we'll
take his spear and his jug of water and then get out of
here!"

12   So David took the spear and jug of water, and
they got away without anyone seeing them or even
waking up, because the Lord had put them sound
asleep.

13   They climbed the mountain slope opposite
the camp until they were at a safe distance.

14   Then David shouted down to Abner and Saul,
"Wake up, Abner!"

"Who is it?" Abner demanded.

15   "Well, Abner, you're a great fellow, aren't you?"
David taunted. "Where in all Israel is there anyone as
wonderful? So why haven't you guarded your master
the king when someone came to kill him?

16 This isn't good at all! I swear by the Lord that you ought to die for your carelessness. Where is the king's spear and the jug of water that was beside his head? Look and see!"

17, 18 Saul recognized David's voice and said, "Is that you, my son David?"

And David replied, "Yes sir, it is. Why are you chasing me? What have I done? What is my crime?

19 If the Lord has stirred you up against me, then let Him accept my peace offering. But if this is simply the scheme of a man, then may he be cursed by God. For you have driven me out of my home so that I can't be with the Lord's people, and you have sent me away to worship heathen gods.

20 Must I die on foreign soil, far from the presence of Jehovah? Why should the king of Israel come out to hunt my life like a partridge on the mountains?"

21 Then Saul confessed, "I have done wrong. Come back home, my son, and I'll no longer try to harm you; for you saved my life today. I have been a fool, and very, very wrong."

22 "Here is your spear, sir," David replied. "Let one of your young men come over and get it.

23 The Lord gives His own reward for doing good and for being loyal, and I refused to kill you even when the Lord placed you in my power.

24 Now may the Lord save my life, even as I have saved yours today. May He rescue me from all my troubles."

25 And Saul said to David, "Blessings on you, my son David. You shall do heroic deeds and be a great conqueror." Then David went away and Saul returned home.

CHAPTER 27

But David kept thinking to himself, "Some day Saul is going to get me. I'll try my luck among the Philistines until Saul gives up and quits hunting for me; then I will finally be safe again."

2, 3 So David took his six hundred men and their families to live at Gath under the protection of King Achish. He had his two wives with him — Ahino-am of Jezreel and Abigail of Carmel, Nabal's widow.

4 Word soon reached Saul that David had fled to Gath, so he quit hunting for him.

5 One day David said to Achish, "My lord, if it is all right with you, we would rather live in one of the country towns instead of here in the royal city."

6 So Achish gave him Ziklah (which still belongs to the kings of Judah to this day),

7 And they lived there among the Philistines for a year and four months.

8 He and his men spent their time raiding the Geshurites, the Girzites, and the Amalekites — people who had lived near Shur along the road to Egypt ever since ancient times.

9 They didn't leave one person alive in the villages they hit, and took for themselves the sheep, oxen, donkeys, camels, and clothing before returning to their homes.

10 "Where did you make your raid today?" Achish would ask. And David would reply, "Against the south of Judah and the people of Jerahmeel and the Kenites."

11 No one was left alive to come to Gath and tell where he had really been. This happened again and

again while he was living among the Philistines.

12 Achish believed David and thought that the people of Israel must hate him bitterly by now. "Now he will have to stay here and serve me forever!" the king thought.

CHAPTER 28

About that time the Philistines mustered their armies for another war with Israel. "Come and help us fight," King Achish said to David and his men.

2 "Good," David agreed. "You will soon see what a help we can be to you."

"If you are, you shall be my personal body-guard for life," Achish told him.

3 (Meanwhile, Samuel had died and all Israel had mourned for him. He was buried in Ramah, his home town. King Saul had banned all mediums and wizards from the land of Israel.)

4 The Philistines set up their camp at Shunem, and Saul and the armies of Israel were at Gilboa.

5, 6 When Saul saw the vast army of the Philistines, he was frantic with fear and asked the Lord what he should do. But the Lord refused to answer him, either by dreams, or by Urim,[1] or by the prophets.

7, 8 Saul then instructed his aides to try to find a medium so that he could ask her what to do, and they found one at Endor. Saul disguised himself by wearing ordinary clothing instead of his royal robes. He went to the woman's home at night, accompanied by two of his men. "I've got to talk to a dead man," he pleaded. "Will you bring his spirit up?"

[1]The Urim and Thummim were holy instruments which were used as lots in determining the will of God. See Exodus 28:30.

9 "Are you trying to get me killed?" the woman demanded. "You know that Saul has had all of the mediums and fortune-tellers executed. You are spying on me."

10 But Saul took a solemn oath that he wouldn't betray her.

11 Finally the woman said, "Well, whom do you want me to bring up?"

"Bring me Samuel," Saul replied.

12 When the woman saw Samuel, she screamed, "You've deceived me! You are Saul!"

13 "Don't be frightened!" the king told her. "What do you see?"

"I see a specter coming up out of the earth," she said.

14 "What does he look like?"

"He is an old man wrapped in a robe."

Saul realized that it was Samuel and bowed low before him.

15 "Why have you disturbed me by bringing me back?" Samuel asked Saul.

"Because I am in deep trouble," he replied. "The Philistines are at war with us, and God has left me and won't reply by prophets or dreams; so I have called for you to ask you what to do."

16 But Samuel replied, "Why ask me if the Lord has left you and has become your enemy?

17 He has done just as He said He would and has taken the kingdom from you and given it to your rival, David.

18 All this has come upon you because you did not obey the Lord's instructions when He was so angry with Amalek.

19 What's more, the entire Israeli army will be routed and destroyed by the Philistines tomorrow, and you and your sons will be here with me."

20 Saul now fell full length upon the ground, paralyzed with fright because of Samuel's words. He was also faint with hunger, for he had eaten nothing all day.

21 When the woman saw how distraught he was, she said, "Sir, I obeyed your command at the risk of my life.

22 Now do what I say, and let me give you something to eat so you'll regain your strength for the trip back."

23 But he refused. The men who were with him added their pleas to that of the woman until he finally yielded and got up and sat on the bed.

24 The woman had been fattening a calf, so she hurried out and killed it and kneaded dough and baked unleavened bread.

25 She brought the meal to the king and his men, and they ate it. Then they went out into the night.

CHAPTER 29

The Philistine army now mobilized at Aphek, and the Israelis camped at the springs in Jezreel.

2 As the Philistine captains were leading out their troops by battalions and companies, David and his men marched at the rear with King Achish.

3 But the Philistine commanders demanded, "What are these Israelis doing here?"

And King Achish told them, "This is David, the runaway servant of King Saul of Israel. He's been with me for years, and I've never found one fault in him since he arrived."

4 But the Philistine leaders were angry. "Send them back!" they demanded. "They aren't going into the battle with us — they'll turn against us. Is there any better way for him to reconcile himself with his master than by turning against us in the battle?

5 This is the same man the women of Israel sang about in their dances: 'Saul has slain his thousands and David his ten thousands!' "

6 So Achish finally summoned David and his men.

"I swear by the Lord," he told them, "you are some of the finest men I've ever met, and I think you should go with us, but my commanders say no.

7 Please don't upset them, but go back quietly."

8 "What have I done to deserve this treatment?" David demanded. "Why can't I fight your enemies?"

9 But Achish insisted, "As far as I'm concerned, you're as perfect as an angel of God. But my commanders are afraid to have you with them in the battle.

10 Now get up early in the morning and leave as soon as it is light."

11 So David headed back into the land of the Philistines while the Philistine army went on to Jezreel.

CHAPTER 30

Three days later, when David and his men arrived home at their city of Ziklag, they found that the Amalekites had raided the city and burned it to the ground,

2 Carrying off all the women and children.

3   As David and his men looked at the ruins and realized what had happened to their families,

4   They wept until they could weep no more.

5   (David's two wives, Ahino-am and Abigail, were among those who had been captured.)

6   David was seriously worried, for in their bitter grief for their children, his men began talking of killing him. But David took strength from the Lord.

7   Then he said to Abiathar the priest, "Bring me the ephod!" So Abiathar brought it.

8   David asked the Lord, "Shall I chase them? Will I catch them?"

And the Lord told him, "Yes, go after them; you will recover everything that was taken from you!"

9, 10   So David and his six hundred men set out after the Amalekites. When they reached Besor Brook, two hundred of the men were too exhausted to cross, but the other four hundred kept going.

11, 12   Along the way they found an Egyptian youth in a field and brought him to David. He had not had anything to eat or drink for three days and nights, so they gave him part of a fig cake, two clusters of raisins, and some water, and his strength soon returned.

13   "Who are you and where do you come from?" David asked him.

"I am an Egyptian — the servant of an Amalekite," he replied. "My master left me behind three days ago because I was sick.

14   We were on our way back from raiding the Cherethites in the Nebeg, and had raided the south of Judah and the land of Caleb, and had burned Ziklag."

15   "Can you tell me where they went?" David

asked. The young man replied, "If you swear by God's name that you will not kill me or give me back to my master, then I will guide you to them."

16 So he led them to the Amalekite encampment. They were spread out across the fields, eating and drinking and dancing with joy because of the vast amount of loot they had taken from the Philistines and from the men of Judah.

17 David and his men rushed in among them and slaughtered them all that night and the entire next day until evening. No one escaped except four hundred young men who fled on camels.

18, 19 David got back everything they had taken. The men recovered their families and all of their belongings, and David rescued his two wives.

20 His troops rounded up all the flocks and herds and drove them on ahead of them. "These are all yours personally, as your reward!" they told David.

21 When they reached Bezor Brook and the two hundred men who had been too exhausted to go on, David greeted them joyfully.

22 But some of the ruffians among David's men declared, "They didn't go with us, so they can't have any of the loot. Give them their wives and their children and tell them to be gone."

23 But David said, "No, my brothers! The Lord has kept us safe and helped us defeat the enemy.

24 Do you think that anyone will listen to you when you talk like this? We share and share alike — those who go to battle and those who guard the equipment."

25 From then on David made this a law for all of Israel, and it is still followed.

26   When he arrived at Ziklag, he sent part of the loot to the elders of Judah. "Here is a present for you, taken from the Lord's enemies," he wrote them.

27-31   The gifts were sent to the elders in the following cities where David and his men had been:

> Bethel,
> South Ramoth,
> Jattir,
> Aroer,
> Siphmoth,
> Eshtemoa,
> Racal,
> The cities of the Jerahmeelites,
> The cities of the Kenites,
> Hormah,
> Borashan,
> Athach,
> Hebron.

CHAPTER 31

Meanwhile the Philistines had begun the battle against Israel, and the Israelis fled from them and were slaughtered wholesale on Mount Gilboa.

2   The Philistines closed in on Saul, and killed his sons Jonathan, Abinidab, and Malchishua.

3, 4   Then the archers overtook Saul and wounded him badly. He groaned to his armor bearer, "Kill me with your sword before these heathen Philistines capture me and torture me." But his armor bearer was afraid to, so Saul took his own sword and fell upon the point of the blade, and it pierced him through.

5   When his armor bearer saw that he was dead,

he also fell upon his sword and died with him.

6　So Saul, his armor bearer, his three sons, and his troops died together that same day.

7　When the Israelis on the other side of the valley and beyond the Jordan heard that their comrades had fled and that Saul and his sons were dead, they abandoned their cities; and the Philistines lived in them.

8　The next day when the Philistines went out to strip the dead, they found the bodies of Saul and his three sons on Mount Gilboa.

9　They cut off Saul's head and stripped off his armor and sent the wonderful news of Saul's death to their idols and to the people throughout their land.

10　His armor was placed in the temple of Ashtaroth, and his body was fastened to the wall of Bethshan.

11　But when the people of Jabesh-gilead heard what the Philistines had done,

12　Warriors from that town traveled all night to Bethshan and took down the bodies of Saul and his sons from the wall and brought them to Jabesh, where they cremated them.

13　Then they buried their remains beneath the oak tree at Jabesh and fasted for seven days.

II Samuel

CHAPTER 1

Saul was dead and David had returned to Ziklag after slaughtering the Amalekites. Three days later a man arrived from the Israeli army with his clothes torn and with dirt on his head as a sign of mourning. He fell to the ground before David in deep respect.

3 "Where do you come from?" David asked.

"From the Israeli army," he replied.

4 "What happened?" David demanded. "Tell me how the battle went."

And the man replied, "Our entire army fled. Thousands of men are dead and wounded on the field, and Saul and his son Jonathan have been killed."

5 "How do you know they are dead?"

6 "Because I was on Mount Gilboa and saw Saul leaning against his spear with the enemy chariots closing in upon him.

7 When he saw me he cried out for me to come to him.

8 'Who are you?' he asked.

'An Amalekite,' I replied.

9 'Come and put me out of my misery,' he begged, 'for I am in terrible pain but life lingers on.'

10 So I killed him, for I knew he couldn't live.[1] Then I took his crown and one of his bracelets to

[1]He was evidently lying. See I Samuel 31:3, 4 for the true account. Probably he had found Saul dead upon the field and thought David would reward him for killing his rival.

bring to you, my lord."

11 David and his men tore their clothes in sorrow when they heard the news.

12 They mourned and wept and fasted all day for Saul and his son Jonathan, and for the Lord's people, and for the men of Israel who had died that day.

13 Then David said to the young man who had brought the news, "Where are you from?"

And he replied, "I am an Amalekite."

14 "Why did you kill God's chosen king?" David demanded.

15 Then he said to one of his young men, "Kill him!" So he ran him through with his sword and he died.

16 "You die self-condemned," David said, "for you yourself confessed that you killed God's appointed king."

17, 18 Then David composed a dirge for Saul and Jonathan and afterward commanded that it be sung throughout Israel. It is quoted here from the book, *Heroic Ballads*.

19 O Israel, your pride and joy lies dead upon
    the hills;

   Mighty heroes have fallen.

20 Don't tell the Philistines, lest they re-
    joice.

   Hide it from the cities of Gath and Ash-
    kelon,

   Lest the heathen nations laugh in triumph.

21 O Mount Gilboa,

   Let there be no dew nor rain upon you,

   Let no crops of grain grow on your slopes.[2]

---

[2]The text is uncertain in the original manuscripts.

For there the mighty Saul has died;
He is God's appointed king no more.

22 Both Saul and Jonathan slew their strongest foes,
And did not return from battle empty-
handed.

23 How much they were loved, how wonder-
ful they were —
Both Saul and Jonathan!
They were together in life and in death.
They were swifter than eagles, stronger
than lions.

24 But now, O women of Israel, weep for
Saul;
He enriched you
With fine clothing and golden ornaments.

25 These mighty heroes have fallen in the
midst of the battle.
Jonathan is slain upon the hills.

26 How I weep for you, my brother Jona-
than;
How much I loved you!
And your love for me was deeper
Than the love of women!

27 The mighty ones have fallen,
Stripped of their weapons, and dead.

CHAPTER 2

David then asked the Lord, "Shall I move back to
Judah?"
And the Lord replied, "Yes."
"Which city shall I go to?"

And the Lord replied, "Hebron."

2 So David and his wives — Ahino-am from Jezreel and Abigail the widow of Nabal from Carmel —

3 And his men and their families all moved to Hebron.

4 Then the leaders of Judah came to David and crowned him king of the Judean confederacy.

When David heard that the men of Jabesh-gilead had buried Saul,

5 He sent them this message: "May the Lord bless you for being so loyal to your king and giving him a decent burial.

6 May the Lord be loyal to you in return, and reward you with many demonstrations of His love! And I too will be kind to you because of what you have done.

7 And now I ask you to be my strong and loyal subjects, now that Saul is dead. Be like the tribe of Judah who have appointed me as their new king."

8 But Abner, Saul's commander-in-chief, had gone to Mahanaim to crown Saul's son Ish-bosheth as king.

9 His territory included Gilead, Ashuri, Jezreel, Ephraim, the tribe of Benjamin, and all the rest of Israel.

10, 11 Ish-bosheth was forty years old at the time. He reigned in Mahanaim for two years; meanwhile, David was reigning in Hebron as king of the Judean confederacy for seven and one-half years.

12 One day General Abner led some of Ish-bosheth's troops to Gibeon from Mahanaim,

13 And General Joab (the son of Zeruiah) led David's troops out to meet them. They met at the pool

of Gibeon, where they sat facing each other on opposite sides of the pool.

14 Then Abner suggested to Joab, "Let's watch some sword play between our young men!" Joab agreed,

15 So twelve men were chosen from each side to fight in mortal combat.

16 Each one grabbed his opponent by the hair and thrust his sword into the other's side, so that all of them died. The place has been known ever since as Sword Field.

17 The two armies then began to fight each other, and by the end of the day Abner and the men of Israel had been defeated by Joab[1] and the forces of David.

18 Joab's brothers, Abishai and Asahel, were also in the battle. Asahel could run like a deer,

19 And he began chasing Abner. He wouldn't stop for anything, but kept on, singleminded, after Abner alone.

20 When Abner looked behind and saw him coming, he called out to him, "Is that you, Asahel?"

"Yes," he called back, "it is."

21 "Go after someone else!" Abner warned. But Asahel refused and kept on coming.

22 Again Abner shouted to him, "Get away from here. I could never face your brother Joab if I have to kill you!"

23 But he refused to turn away, so Abner pierced him through the belly with the butt end of his spear. It went right through his body and came out his back. He stumbled to the ground and died there, and every-

---

[1]Implied.

one stopped when they came to the place where he lay.

24   Now Joab and Abishai set out after Abner. The sun was just going down as they arrived at Ammah Hill near Giah, along the road into the Gibeon desert.

25   Abner's troops from the tribe of Benjamin regrouped there at the top of the hill,

26   And Abner shouted down to Joab, "Must our swords continue to kill each other forever? How long will it be before you call off your people from chasing their brothers?"

27   Joab shouted back, "I swear by God that even if you hadn't spoken, we would all have gone home tomorrow morning."

28   Then he blew his trumpet and his men stopped chasing the troops of Israel.

29   That night Abner and his men retreated across the Jordan Valley, crossed the river, and traveled all the next morning until they arrived at Mahanaim.

30   Joab and the men who were with him returned home too, and when he counted his casualties, he learned that only nineteen men were missing, in addition to Asahel.

31   But three hundred and sixty of Abner's men (all from the tribe of Benjamin) were dead.

32   Joab and his men took Asahel's body to Bethlehem and buried him beside his father; then they traveled all night and reached Hebron at daybreak.

CHAPTER 3

That was the beginning of a long war between the followers of Saul and of David. David's position now became stronger and stronger, while Saul's dynasty became weaker and weaker.

2 Several sons were born to David while he was at Hebron. The oldest was Amnon, born to his wife Ahino-am.

3 His second son, Chileab, was born to Abigail, the widow of Nabal of Carmel. The third was Absalom, born to Maacah, the daughter of King Talmai of Geshur.

4 The fourth was Adonijah, who was born to Haggith. Then Shephatiah was born to Abital, and

5 Ithream was born to Eglah.

6 As the war went on, Abner became a very powerful political leader among the followers of Saul.

7 He took advantage of his position by sleeping with one of Saul's concubines, a girl named Rizpah. But when Ish-bosheth accused Abner of this,

8 Abner was furious. "Am I a Judean dog to be kicked around like this?" he shouted. "After all I have done for you and for your father by not betraying you to David, is this my reward — to find fault with me about some woman?

9, 10 May God curse me if I don't do everything I can to take away the entire kingdom from you, all the way from Dan to Beer-sheba, and give it to David, just as the Lord predicted."

11 Ish-bosheth made no reply, for he was afraid of Abner.

12 Then Abner sent messengers to David to dis-

cuss a deal — to surrender the kingdom of Israel to him in exchange for becoming commander-in-chief of the combined armies of Israel and Judah.

13 "All right," David replied, "but I will not negotiate with you unless you bring me my wife Michal, Saul's daughter."

14 David then sent this message to Ish-bosheth: "Give me back my wife Michal, for I bought her with the lives of one hundred Philistines."

15 So Ish-bosheth took her away from her husband Palti.[1]

16 He followed along behind her as far as Behurim, weeping as he went. Then Abner told him, "Go on home now." So he returned.

17 Meanwhile Abner consulted with the leaders of Israel and reminded them that for a long time they had wanted David as their king.

18 "Now is the time!" he told them. "For the Lord has said, 'It is David by whom I will save My people from the Philistines and from all their other enemies.' "

19 Abner also talked to the leaders of the tribe of Benjamin; then he went to Hebron and reported to David his progress with the people of Israel and Benjamin.

20 Twenty men accompanied him, and David entertained them with a feast.

21 As Abner left, he promised David, "When I get back I will call a convention of all the people of Israel, and they will elect you as their king, as you've so long desired." So David let Abner return in safety.

22 But just after Abner left, Joab and some of

[1]See I Samuel 25:44.

David's troops returned from a raid, bringing much loot with them.

23 When Joab was told that Abner had just been there visiting the king and had been sent away in peace,

24, 25 He rushed to the king, demanding, "What have you done? What do you mean by letting him get away? You know perfectly well that he came to spy on us and that he plans to return and attack us!"

26 Then Joab sent messengers to catch up with Abner and tell him to come back. They found him at the well of Sirah and he returned with them; but David knew nothing about it.

27 When Abner arrived at Hebron, Joab took him aside at the city gate as if to speak with him privately; but then he pulled out a dagger and killed him in revenge for the death of his brother Asahel.

28 When David heard about it he declared, "I vow by the Lord that I and my people are innocent of this crime against Abner.

29 Joab and his family are the guilty ones. May each of his children be victims of cancer, or be lepers, or be sterile, or die of starvation, or be killed by the sword!"

30 So Joab and his brother Abishai killed Abner because of the death of their brother Asahel at the battle of Gibeon.

31 Then David said to Joab and to all those who were with him, "Go into deep mourning for Abner." And King David accompanied the bier to the cemetery.

32 They buried Abner in Hebron. And the king and all the people wept at the graveside.

33   "Should Abner have died like a fool?" the king lamented.

34   "Your hands were not bound,
         Your feet were not tied —
         You were murdered —
         The victim of a wicked plot."
And all the people wept again for him.

35, 36   David had refused to eat anything the day of the funeral, and now everyone begged him to take a bite of supper. But David vowed that he would eat nothing until sundown. This pleased his people, just as everything else he did pleased them!

37   Thus the whole nation, both Judah and Israel, understood from David's actions that he was in no way responsible for Abner's death.

38   And David said to his people, "A great leader and a great man has fallen today in Israel;

39   And even though I am God's chosen king, I can do nothing with these two sons of Zeruiah. May the Lord repay wicked men for their wicked deeds."

CHAPTER 4

When King Ish-bosheth heard about Abner's death at Hebron, he was paralyzed with fear, and his people too were badly frightened.

2, 3   The command of the Israeli troops then fell to two brothers, Baanah and Rechab, who were captains of King Ish-bosheth's raiding bands. They were the sons of Rimmon, who was from Be-eroth in Benjamin. (People from Be-eroth are counted as Benjaminites even though they fled to Gittaim,[1] where they now live.)

---

[1]Gittaim is not in Benjamin.

4 (There was a little lame grandson of King Saul's named Mephibosheth, who was the son of Prince Jonathan. He was five years old at the time Saul and Jonathan were killed at the battle of Jezreel. When the news of the outcome of the battle reached the capital, the child's nurse grabbed him and fled, but she fell and dropped him as she was running, and he became lame.)

5 Rechab and Baanah arrived at King Ish-bosheth's home one noon as he was taking a nap.

6, 7 They walked into the kitchen as though to get a sack of wheat, but then sneaked into his bedroom and murdered him and cut off his head. Taking his head with them, they fled across the desert that night and escaped.

8 They presented the head to David at Hebron. "Look!" they exclaimed, "here is the head of Ish-bosheth, the son of your enemy Saul who tried to kill you. Today the Lord has given you revenge upon Saul and upon his entire family!"

9 But David replied, "I swear by the Lord who saved me from my enemies,

10 That when someone told me, 'Saul is dead,' thinking he was bringing me good news, I killed him; that is how I rewarded him for his 'glad tidings.'

11 And how much more shall I do to wicked men who kill a good man in his own house and on his bed! Shall I not demand your lives?"

12 So David ordered his young men to kill them, and they did. They cut off their hands and feet and hanged their bodies beside the pool in Hebron. And they took Ish-bosheth's head and buried it in Abner's tomb in Hebron.

CHAPTER 5

Then representatives of all the tribes of Israel came to David at Hebron and gave him their pledge of loyalty. "We are your blood brothers," they said.

2 "And even when Saul was our king you were our real leader. The Lord has said that you should be the shepherd and leader of His people."

3 So David made a contract before the Lord with the leaders of Israel there at Hebron, and they crowned him king of Israel.

4, 5 (He had already been the king of Judah for seven years, since the age of thirty. He then ruled thirty-three years in Jerusalem as king of both Israel and Judah; so he reigned for forty years altogether.)

6 David now led his troops to Jerusalem to fight against the Jebusites who lived there. "You'll never come in here," they told him. "Even the blind and lame could keep you out!" For they thought they were safe.

7 But David and his troops defeated them and captured the stronghold of Zion, now called the City of David.

8 When the insulting message from the defenders of the city reached David, he told his troops, "Go up through the water tunnel into the city and destroy those 'lame' and 'blind' Jebusites. How I hate them." (That is the origin of the saying, "Even the blind and the lame could conquer you!")

9 So David made the stronghold of Zion (also called the City of David) his headquarters. Then, beginning at the old Millo section of the city, he built northward toward the present city center.

10   So David became greater and greater, for the Lord God of heaven was with him.

11   Then King Hiram of Tyre sent cedar lumber, carpenters, and masons to build a palace for David.

12   David now realized why the Lord had made him the king and blessed his kingdom so greatly — it was because God wanted to pour out His kindness on Israel, His chosen people.

13   After moving from Hebron to Jerusalem, David married additional wives and concubines, and had many sons and daughters.

14   These are his children who were born at Jerusalem:

>   Shammu-a,
>   Shobab,
>   Nathan,
>   Solomon,
> 15   Ibhar,
>   Elishu-a,
>   Nepheg,
>   Japhia,
> 16   Elishama,
>   Eliada,
>   Eliphelet.

17   When the Philistines heard that David had been crowned king of Israel, they tried to capture him; but David was told that they were coming and went into the stronghold.

18   The Philistines arrived and spread out across the valley of Rephaim.

19   Then David asked the Lord, "Shall I go out and fight against them? Will you defeat them for me?"

And the Lord replied, "Yes, go ahead, for I will give them to you."

20 So David went out and fought with them at Baal-perazim, and defeated them. "The Lord did it!" he exclaimed. "He burst through my enemies like a raging flood." So he named the place "Bursting."

21 At that time David and his troops confiscated many idols which had been abandoned by the Philistines.

22 But the Philistines returned and again spread out across the valley of Rephaim.

23 When David asked the Lord what to do, He replied, "Don't make a frontal attack. Go behind them and come out by the balsam trees.

24 When you hear a sound like marching feet in the tops of the balsam trees, attack! for it will signify that the Lord has prepared the way for you and will destroy them."

25 So David did as the Lord had instructed him and destroyed the Philistines all the way from Geba to Gezer.

CHAPTER 6

Then David mobilized thirty thousand special troops and led them to Baal-judah to bring home the Ark of the Lord of heaven enthroned above the cherubim.

3 The Ark was placed upon a new cart and taken from the hillside home of Abinadab. It was driven by Abinadab's sons, Uzzah and Ahio.

4 Ahio was walking in front,

5 And was followed by David and the other leaders of Israel, who were joyously waving branches of juniper trees and playing every sort of musical instru-

ment before the Lord — lyres, harps, tambourines, castanets, and cymbals.

6 But when they arrived at the threshing floor of Nacon, the oxen stumbled and Uzzah put out his hand to steady the Ark.

7 Then the anger of the Lord flared out against Uzzah and He killed him for doing this, so he died there beside the Ark.

8 David was angry at what the Lord had done, and named the spot "The Place of Wrath upon Uzzah" (which it is still called to this day).

9 David was now afraid of the Lord and asked, "How can I ever bring the Ark home?"

10 So he decided against taking it into the City of David, but carried it instead to the home of Obed-edom, who had come from Gath.

11 It remained there for three months, and the Lord blessed Obed-edom and all his household.

12 When David heard this, he brought the Ark to the City of David with a great celebration.

13 After the men who were carrying it had gone six paces, they stopped and waited so that he could sacrifice an ox and a fat lamb.

14 And David danced before the Lord with all his might, and was wearing priests' clothing.[1]

15 So Israel brought home the Ark of the Lord with much shouting and blowing of trumpets.

16 (But as the procession came into the city, Michal, Saul's daughter, watched from a window and saw King David leaping and dancing before the Lord; and she was filled with contempt for him.)

17 The Ark was placed inside the tent which Da-

---

[1]Literally, "David was girded with a linen ephod."

vid had prepared for it; and he sacrificed burnt offerings and peace offerings to the Lord.

18 Then he blessed the people in the name of the Lord of heaven,

19 And gave a present to everyone — men and women alike — of a loaf of bread, some wine, and a cake of raisins. When it was all over, and everyone had gone home,

20 David returned to bless his family. But Michal came out to meet him and exclaimed in disgust, "How glorious the king of Israel looked today! He exposed himself to the girls along the street like a common pervert!"

21 David retorted, "I was dancing before the Lord who chose me above your father and his family and who appointed me as leader of Israel, the people of the Lord! So I am willing to act like a fool in order to show my joy in the Lord.

22 Yes, and I am willing to look even more foolish than this, but I will be respected by the girls of whom you spoke!"

23 So Michal was childless throughout her life.

CHAPTER 7

When the Lord finally sent peace upon the land, and Israel was no longer at war with the surrounding nations,

2 David said to Nathan the prophet, "Look! Here I am living in this beautiful cedar palace while the Ark of God is out in a tent!"

3 "Go ahead with what you have in mind," Nathan replied, "for the Lord is with you."

4   But that night the Lord said to Nathan,

5   "Tell My servant David not to do it![1]

6   For I have never lived in a Temple. My home has been a tent ever since the time I brought Israel out of Egypt.

7   And I have never once complained to Israel's leaders, the shepherds of My people. Have I ever asked them, 'Why haven't you built Me a beautiful cedar Temple?'

8   Now go and give this message to David from the Lord of heaven: 'I chose you to be the leader of My people Israel when you were a mere shepherd, tending your sheep in the pastureland.

9   I have been with you wherever you have gone and have destroyed your enemies. And I will make your name greater yet, so that you will be one of the most famous men in the world!

10, 11   I have selected a homeland for My people from which they will never have to move. It will be their own land where the heathen nations won't bother them as they did when the judges ruled My people. There will be no more wars against you; and your descendants shall rule this land for generations to come!

12   For when you die, I will put one of your sons upon your throne and I will make his kingdom strong.

13   He is the one who shall build Me a Temple. And I will continue his kingdom into eternity.

14   I will be his father and he shall be My son. If he sins, I will use other nations to punish him,

15   But My love and kindness shall not leave him as I took it from Saul, your predecessor.

---

[1]Literally, "Shall you build Me a house to dwell in?"

16   Your family shall rule My kingdom forever.' "

17   So Nathan went back to David and told him everything the Lord had said.

18   Then David went into the Tabernacle and sat before the Lord and prayed, "O Lord God, why have You showered Your blessings on such an insignificant person as I am?

19   And now, in addition to everything else, You speak of giving me an eternal dynasty! Such generosity is far beyond any human standard! Oh, Lord God!

20   What can I say? For You know what I am like!

21   You are doing all these things just because You promised to and because You want to!

22   How great You are, Lord God! We have never heard of any other god like You. And there is no other god.

23   What other nation in all the earth has received such blessings as Israel, Your people? For You have rescued Your chosen nation in order to bring glory to Your name. You have done great miracles to destroy Egypt and its gods.

24   You chose Israel to be Your people forever, and You became our God.

25   And now, Lord God, do as You have promised concerning me and my family.

26   And may You be eternally honored when You have established Israel as Your people and have established my dynasty before You.

27   For You have revealed to me, O Lord of heaven, God of Israel, that I am the first of a dynasty which will rule Your people forever; that is why I

have been bold enough to pray this prayer of acceptance.

28 For You are indeed God, and Your words are truth; and You have promised me these good things —

29 So do as You have promised! Bless me and my family forever! May our dynasty continue on and on before You; for You, Lord God, have promised it.

CHAPTER 8

After this David subdued and humbled the Philistines by conquering Gath, their largest city.

2 He also devastated the land of Moab. He divided his victims by making them lie down side by side in rows. Two-thirds of each row, as measured with a tape, were butchered, and one-third were spared to become David's servants — they paid him tribute each year.

3 He also destroyed the forces of King Hadadezer (son of Rehob) of Zobah in a battle at the Euphrates River, for Hadadezer had attempted to regain his power.

4 David captured seventeen hundred cavalry and twenty thousand infantry; then he lamed all of the chariot horses except for one hundred teams.

5 He also slaughtered twenty-two thousand Syrians from Damascus when they came to help Hadadezer.

6 David placed several army garrisons in Damascus, and the Syrians became David's subjects and brought him annual tribute money. So the Lord gave him victories wherever he turned.

7 David brought the gold shields to Jerusalem which King Hadadezer's officers had used.

8   He also carried back to Jerusalem a very large amount of bronze from Hadadezer's cities of Betah and Berothai.

9   When King Toi of Hamath heard about David's victory over the army of Hadadezer,

10   He sent his son Joram to congratulate him, for Hadadezer and Toi were enemies. He gave David presents made from silver, gold, and bronze.

11, 12   David dedicated all of these to the Lord, along with the silver and gold he had taken from Syria, Moab, Ammon, the Philistines, Amalek, and King Hadadezer.

13   So David became very famous. After his return he destroyed eighteen thousand Edomites[1] at the Valley of Salt,

14   And then placed garrisons throughout Edom, so that the entire nation was forced to pay tribute to Israel — another example of the way the Lord made him victorious wherever he went.

15   David reigned with justice over Israel and was fair to everyone.

16   The general of his army was Joab (son of Zeruiah), and his secretary of state was Jehoshaphat (son of Ahilud).

17   Zadok (son of Ahitub) and Ahimelech (son of Abiathar) were the High Priests, and Seraiah was the king's private secretary.

18   Benaiah (son of Jehoiada) was captain of his bodyguard,[2] and David's sons were his assistants.[3]

---

[1]Literally, "Syrians."
[2]Literally, "the Cherethites and Pelethites."
[3]Literally, "were priests." See I Chronicles 18:17.

CHAPTER 9

O ne day David began wondering if any of Saul's family was still living, for he wanted to be kind to them, as he had promised Prince Jonathan.

2 He heard about a man named Ziba who had been one of Saul's servants, and summoned him.

"Are you Ziba?" the king asked.

"Yes, sir, I am," he replied.

3 The king then asked him, "Is anyone left from Saul's family? If so, I want to fulfill a sacred vow by being kind to him."

"Yes," Ziba replied, "Jonathan's lame son is still alive."

4 "Where is he?" the king asked.

"In Lo-debar," Ziba told him. "At the home of Machir."

5, 6 So King David sent for Mephibosheth — Jonathan's son and Saul's grandson. Mephibosheth arrived in great fear and greeted the king in deep humility, bowing low before him.

7 But David said, "Don't be afraid! I've asked you to come so that I can be kind to you because of my vow to your father Jonathan. I will restore to you all the land of your grandfather Saul, and you shall live here at the palace!"

8 Mephibosheth fell to the ground before the king. "Should the king show kindness to a dead dog like me?" he exclaimed.

9 Then the king summoned Saul's servant Ziba. "I have given your master's grandson everything that belonged to Saul and his family," he said.

10, 11 "You and your sons and servants are to

farm the land for him, to produce food for his family; but he will live here with me."

Ziba, who had fifteen sons and twenty servants, replied, "Sir, I will do all that you have commanded." And from that time on, Mephibosheth ate regularly with King David, as though he were one of his own sons.

12 Mephibosheth had a young son, Mica. All the household of Ziba became Mephibosheth's servants,

13 But Mephibosheth (who was lame in both feet) moved to Jerusalem to live at the palace.

CHAPTER 10

Sometime after this the Ammonite king died and his son Hanun replaced him.

2 "I am going to show special respect for him," David said, "because his father Nahash was always so loyal and kind to me." So David sent ambassadors to express regrets to Hanun about his father's death.

3 But Hanun's officers told him, "These men aren't here to honor your father! David has sent them to spy out the city before attacking it!"

4 So Hanun took David's men and shaved off half their beards and cut their robes off at the buttocks and sent them home half naked.

5 When David heard what had happened he told them to stay at Jericho until their beards grew out; for the men were very embarrassed over their appearance.

6 Now the people of Ammon realized how seriously they had angered David, so they hired twenty thousand Syrian mercenaries from the lands of Rehob

and Zobah, one thousand from the king of Maacah, and ten thousand from the land of Tob.

7, 8   When David heard about this, he sent Joab and the entire Israeli army to attack them. The Ammonites defended the gates of their city while the Syrians from Zobah, Rehob, Tob, and Maacah fought in the fields.

9   When Joab realized that he would have to fight on two fronts, he selected the best fighters in his army, placed them under his personal command, and took them out to fight the Syrians in the fields.

10   He left the rest of the army to his brother Abishai, who was to attack the city.

11   "If I need assistance against the Syrians, come out and help me," Joab instructed him. "And if the Ammonites are too strong for you, I will come and help you.

12   Courage! We must really act like men today if we are going to save our people and the cities of our God. May the Lord's will be done."

13   And when Joab and his troops attacked, the Syrians began to run away.

14   Then, when the Ammonites saw the Syrians running, they ran too, and retreated into the city. Afterwards Joab returned to Jerusalem.

15, 16   The Syrians now realized that they were no match for Israel. So when they regrouped, they were joined by additional Syrian troops summoned by Hadadezer from the other side of the Euphrates River. These troops arrived at Helam under the command of Shobach, the commander-in-chief of all of Hadadezer's forces.

17   When David heard what was happening, he per-

sonally led the Israeli army to Helam, where the Syrians attacked him.

18 But again the Syrians fled from the Israelis, this time leaving seven hundred charioteers dead on the field, also forty thousand cavalrymen, including General Shobach.

19 When Hadadezer's allies saw that the Syrians had been defeated, they surrendered to David and became his servants. And the Syrians were afraid to help the Ammonites anymore after that.

CHAPTER 11

In the spring of the following year, at the time when wars begin, David sent Joab and the Israeli army to destroy the Ammonites. They began by laying siege to the city of Rabbah. But David stayed in Jerusalem.

2 One night he couldn't get to sleep[1] and went for a stroll on the roof of the palace. As he looked out over the city, he noticed a woman of unusual beauty taking her evening bath.

3 He sent to find out who she was and was told that she was Bath-sheba, the daughter of Eliam and the wife of Uriah.

4 Then David sent for her and when she came he slept with her. (She had just completed the purification rites after menstruation.) Then she returned home.

5 When she found that he had gotten her pregnant she sent a message to inform him.

6 So David dispatched a memo to Joab: "Send me Uriah the Hittite."

---

[1]Literally, "arose from his bed."

7 When he arrived, David asked him how Joab and the army were getting along and how the war was prospering.

8 Then he told him to go home and relax, and he sent a present to him at his home.

9 But Uriah didn't go there. He stayed that night at the gateway of the palace with the other servants of the king.

10 When David heard what Uriah had done, he summoned him and asked him, "What's the matter with you? Why didn't you go home to your wife last night after being away for so long?"

11 Uriah replied, "The Ark and the armies and the general and his officers are camping out in open fields, and should I go home to wine and dine and sleep with my wife? I swear that I will never be guilty of acting like that."

12 "Well, stay here tonight," David told him, "and tomorrow you may return to the army." So Uriah stayed around the palace.

13 David invited him to dinner and got him drunk; but even so he didn't go home that night, but again he slept at the entry to the palace.

14 Finally the next morning David wrote a letter to Joab and gave it to Uriah to deliver.

15 The letter instructed Joab to put Uriah at the front of the hottest part of the battle — and then pull back and leave him there to die!

16 So Joab assigned Uriah to a spot close to the besieged city where he knew that the enemies' best men were fighting;

17 And Uriah was killed along with several other Israeli soldiers.

18   When Joab sent a report to David of how the battle was going,

19, 20, 21   He told his messenger, "If the king is angry and asks, 'Why did the troops go so close to the city? Didn't they know there would be shooting from the walls? Wasn't Abimelech killed at Thebez by a woman who threw down a millstone on him?' — then tell him, 'Uriah was killed, too.'"

22   So the messenger arrived at Jerusalem, and gave the report to David.

23   "The enemy came out against us," he said, "and as we chased them back to the city gates,

24   The men on the wall attacked us; and some of our men were killed, and Uriah the Hittite is dead too."

25   "Well, tell Joab not to be discouraged," David said. "The sword kills one as well as another![2] Fight harder next time, and conquer the city; tell him he is doing well."

26   When Bath-sheba heard that her husband was dead, she mourned for him;

27   Then, when the period of mourning was over, David sent for her and brought her to the palace and she became one of his wives; and she gave birth to his son. But the Lord was very displeased with what David had done.

CHAPTER 12

So the Lord sent the prophet Nathan to tell David this story: "There were two men in a certain city, one very rich, owning many flocks of sheep and herds of goats;

---

[2]Literally, "the sword devours now one and now another."

3   And the other very poor, owning nothing but a little lamb he had managed to buy. It was his children's pet and he fed it from his own plate and let it drink from his own cup; he cuddled it in his arms like a baby daughter.

4   Recently a guest arrived at the home of the rich man. But instead of killing a lamb from his own flocks for food for the traveler, he took the poor man's lamb and roasted it and served it."

5   David was furious. "I swear by the living God," he vowed, "any man who would do a thing like that should be put to death;

6   He shall repay four lambs to the poor man for the one he stole, and for having no pity."

7   Then Nathan said to David, *"You* are that rich man! The Lord God of Israel says, 'I made you king of Israel and saved you from the power of Saul.

8   I gave you his palace and his wives and the kingdoms of Israel and Judah; and if that had not been enough, I would have given you much, much more.

9   Why, then, have you despised the laws of God and done this horrible deed? For you have murdered Uriah and stolen his wife.

10   Therefore murder shall be a constant threat in your family from this time on, because you have insulted Me by taking Uriah's wife.

11   I vow that because of what you have done I will cause your own household to rebel against you. I will give your wives to another man, and he will go to bed with them in public view.[1]

12   You did it secretly, but I will do this to you

[1] Literally, "under this sun."

openly, in the sight of all Israel.' "

13 "I have sinned against the Lord," David confessed to Nathan.

Then Nathan replied, "Yes, but the Lord has forgiven you, and you won't die for this sin.

14 But you have given great opportunity to the enemies of the Lord to despise and blaspheme Him, so your child shall die."

15 Then Nathan returned to his home. And the Lord made Bath-sheba's baby deathly sick.

16 David begged Him to spare the child, and went without food and lay all night before the Lord on the bare earth.

17 The leaders of the nation pleaded with him to get up and eat with them, but he refused.

18 Then, on the seventh day, the baby died. David's aides were afraid to tell him. "He was so broken up about the baby being sick," they said, "what will he do to himself when we tell him the child is dead?"

19 But when David saw them whispering, he realized what had happened. "Is the baby dead?" he asked.

"Yes," they replied, "he is."

20 Then David got up off the ground, washed himself, brushed his hair, changed his clothes, and went into the Tabernacle and worshiped the Lord. Then he returned to the palace and ate.

21 His aides were amazed. "We don't understand you," they told him. "While the baby was still living, you wept and refused to eat; but now that the baby is dead, you have stopped your mourning and are eating again."

22 David replied, "I fasted and wept while the

child was alive, for I said, 'Perhaps the Lord will be gracious to me and let the child live.'

23 But why should I fast when he is dead? Can I bring him back again? I shall go to him, but he shall not return to me."

24 Then David comforted Bath-sheba; and when he slept with her, she conceived and gave birth to a son and named him Solomon. And the Lord loved the baby,

25 And sent congratulations[1] and blessings through Nathan the prophet. David nicknamed the baby Jedidiah, (meaning, "Beloved of Jehovah") because of the Lord's interest.[2]

26, 27 Meanwhile Joab and the Israeli army were successfully ending their siege of Rabbah the capital of Ammon. Joab sent messengers to tell David, "Rabbah and its beautiful harbor are ours![3]

28 Now bring the rest of the army and finish the job, so that you will get the credit for the victory instead of me."

29, 30 So David led his army to Rabbah and captured it. Tremendous amounts of loot were carried back to Jerusalem, and David took the king of Rabbah's crown — a $50,000 treasure made from solid gold set with gems — and placed it on his own head.

31 He made slaves of the people of the city and made them labor with saws, picks, and axes and work in the brick kilns;[4] that is the way he treated all of

---

[1]Literally, "Jehovah sent word by Nathan the prophet."

[2]Literally, "because of the Lord."

[3]"I have taken the City of Waters."

[4]Or, "killed them with saws and iron harrows, and in brick kilns."

the cities of the Ammonites. Then David and the army returned to Jerusalem.

CHAPTER 13

Prince Absalom, David's son, had a beautiful sister named Tamar. And Prince Amnon (her half-brother) fell desperately in love with her.

2   Amnon became so tormented by his love for her that he became ill. He had no way of talking to her, for the girls and young men were kept strictly apart.[1]

3   But Amnon had a very crafty friend — his cousin Jonadab (the son of David's brother Shime-ah).

4   One day Jonadab said to Amnon, "What's the trouble? Why should the son of a king look so haggard morning after morning?" So Amnon told him, "I am in love with Tamar, my half-sister."

5   "Well," Jonadab said, "I'll tell you what to do. Go back to bed and pretend you are sick; when your father comes to see you, ask him to let Tamar come and prepare some food for you. Tell him you'll feel better if she feeds you."

6   So Amnon did. And when the king came to see him, Amnon asked him for this favor — that his sister Tamar be permitted to come and cook a little something for him to eat.

7   David agreed, and sent word to Tamar to go to Amnon's quarters and prepare some food for him.

8   So she did, and went into his bedroom so that he could watch her mix some dough; then she baked some special bread for him.

---

[1]Literally, "for she was a virgin, and it seemed impossible to Amnon to do anything to her."

9 But when she set the serving tray before him, he refused to eat! "Everyone get out of here," he told his servants; so they all left the apartment.

10 Then he said to Tamar, "Now bring me the food again here in my bedroom and feed it to me." So Tamar took it to him.

11 But as she was standing there before him, he grabbed her and demanded, "Come to bed with me, my darling."

12 "Oh, Amnon," she cried. "Don't be foolish! Don't do this to me! You know what a serious crime it is in Israel.[2]

13 Where could I go in my shame? And you would be called one of the greatest fools in Israel. Please, just speak to the king about it, for he will let you marry me."

14 But he wouldn't listen to her; and since he was stronger than she, he forced her.

15 Then suddenly his love turned to hate, and now he hated her more than he had loved her. "Get out of here!" he snarled at her.

16 "No, no!" she cried. "To reject me now is a greater crime than the other you did to me." But he wouldn't listen to her.

17, 18 He shouted for his valet and demanded, "Throw this woman out and lock the door behind her." So he put her out. She was wearing a long robe with sleeves, as was the custom in those days for virgin daughters of the king.

19 Now she tore the robe and put ashes on her

---

[2]Literally, "No such thing ought to be done in Israel; do not this folly."

head and with her head in her hands went away crying.

20　　Her brother Absalom asked her, "Is it true that
Amnon raped you? Don't be so upset, since it's all
in the family anyway. It's not anything to worry
about!" So Tamar lived as a desolate woman in her
brother Absalom's quarters.

21-24　　When King David heard what had happened, he was very angry, but Absalom said nothing
one way or the other about this to Amnon. However,
he hated him with a deep hatred because of what he
had done to his sister. Then, two years later, when
Absalom's sheep were being sheared at Baal-hazor in
Ephraim, Absalom invited his father and all his brothers to come to a feast to celebrate the occasion.

25　　The king replied, "No, my boy; if we all came,
we would be too much of a burden on you." Absalom
pressed him, but he wouldn't come, though he sent
his thanks.

26　　"Well, then," Absalom said, "if you can't come,
how about sending my brother Amnon instead?"

"Why Amnon?" the king asked.

27　　Absalom kept on urging the matter until finally the king agreed, and let all of his sons attend,
including Amnon.

28　　Absalom told his men, "Wait until Amnon gets
drunk, then, at my signal, kill him! Don't be afraid.
I'm the one who gives the orders around here, and
this is a command. Take courage and do it!"

29, 30　　So they murdered Amnon. Then the other
sons of the king jumped on their mules and fled. As
they were on the way back to Jerusalem, the report
reached David: "Absalom has killed all of your sons,

and not one is left alive!"

31   The king jumped up, ripped off his robe, and fell prostrate to the ground. His aides also tore their clothes in horror and sorrow.

32, 33   But just then Jonadab (the son of David's brother Shime-ah) arrived and said, "No, not all have been killed! It was only Amnon! Absalom has been plotting this ever since Amnon raped Tamar. No, no! Your sons aren't all dead! It was only Amnon."

34   (Absalom got away.) Now the watchman on the Jerusalem wall saw a great crowd coming toward the city along the road at the side of the hill.

35   "See!" Jonadab told the king, "There they are now! Your sons are coming, just as I said."

36   They soon arrived, weeping and sobbing, and the king and his officials wept with them.

37, 38, 39   Absalom fled to King Talmai of Geshur[3] (the son of Ammihud) and stayed there three years. Meanwhile David, now reconciled to Amnon's death, longed day after day for fellowship with his son Absalom.

CHAPTER 14

When General Joab realized how much the king was longing to see Absalom,

2, 3   He sent for a woman of Tekoa who had a reputation for great wisdom and told her to ask for an appointment with the king. He told her what to say to him. "Pretend you are in mourning," Joab instructed her. "Wear mourning clothes, and dishevel your hair as though you have been in deep sorrow for a long time."

---

[3]King Talmai was his grandfather — his mother's father.

4　When the woman approached the king, she fell face downward on the floor in front of him, and cried out, "O king! Help me!"

5, 6　"What's the trouble?" he asked.

"I am a widow," she replied, "and my two sons had a fight out in the field, and since no one was there to part them, one of them was killed.

7　Now the rest of the family is demanding that I surrender my other son to them to be executed for murdering his brother. But if I do that, I will have no one left, and my husband's name will be destroyed from the face of the earth."

8　"Leave it with me," the king told her, "I'll see to it that no one touches him."

9　"Oh, thank you, my lord," she replied. "And I'll take the responsibility if you are criticized for helping me like this."

10　"Don't worry about that!" the king replied. "If anyone objects, bring him to me; I can assure you he will never complain again!"

11　Then she said, "Please swear to me by God that you won't let anyone harm my son. I want no more bloodshed."

"I vow by God," he replied, "that not a hair of your son's head shall be disturbed!"

12　"Please let me ask one more thing of you!" she said.

"Go ahead," he replied. "Speak!"

13　"Why don't you do as much for all the people of God as you have promised to do for me?" she asked. "You have convicted yourself in making this decision, because you have refused to bring home your own banished son.

14   All of us must die eventually; our lives are like water that is poured out on the ground — it can't be gathered up again. But God will bless you with a longer life if you will find a way to bring your son back from his exile.[1]

15, 16   But I have come to plead with you for my son because my life and my son's life have been threatened, and I said to myself, 'Perhaps the king will listen to me and rescue us from those who would end our existence in Israel.

17   Yes, the king will give us peace again.' I know that you are like the angel of God and can discern good from evil. May God be with you."

18   "I want to know one thing," the king replied. "Yes, my lord?" she asked.

19   "Did Joab send you here?"

And the woman replied, "How can I deny it? Yes, Joab sent me and told me what to say.

20   He did it in order to place the matter before you in a different light. But you are as wise as an angel of God, and you know everything that happens!"

21   So the king sent for Joab and told him, "All right, go and bring back Absalom."

22   Joab fell to the ground before the king and blessed him and said, "At last I know that you like me! For you have granted me this request!"

23   Then Joab went to Geshur and brought Absalom back to Jerusalem.

24   "He may go to his own quarters," the king ordered, "but he must never come here. I refuse to see him."

1Or, "God does not sweep life away, but has made provision to bring back those he banishes, so that they will not be forever exiles."

25 Now no one in Israel was such a handsome specimen of manhood as Absalom, and no one else received such praise.

26 He cut his hair only once a year — and then only because it weighed three pounds and was too much of a load to carry around!

27 He had three sons and one daughter, Tamar, who was a very beautiful girl.

28 After Absalom had been in Jerusalem for two years and had not yet seen the king,

29 He sent for Joab to ask him to intercede for him; but Joab wouldn't come. Absalom sent for him again, but again he refused to come.

30 So Absalom said to his servants, "Go and set fire to that barley field of Joab's next to mine," and they did.

31 Then Joab came to Absalom and demanded, "Why did your servants set my field on fire?"

32 And Absalom replied, "Because I wanted you to ask the king why he brought me back from Geshur if he didn't intend to see me. I might as well have stayed there. Let me have an interview with the king; then if he finds that I am guilty of murder, let him execute me."

33 So Joab told the king what Absalom had said. Then at last David summoned Absalom, and he came and bowed low before the king, and David kissed him.

CHAPTER 15

A bsalom then bought a magnificent chariot and chariot horses, and hired fifty footmen to run ahead of him.

2   He got up early every morning and went out to the gate of the city; and when anyone came to bring a case to the king for trial, Absalom called him over and expressed interest in his problem.

3   He would say, "I can see that you are right in this matter; it's unfortunate that the king doesn't have anyone to assist him in hearing these cases.

4   I surely wish I were the judge; then anyone with a lawsuit could come to me, and I would give him justice!"

5   And when anyone came to bow to him, Absalom wouldn't let him, but shook his hand instead![1]

6   So in this way Absalom stole the hearts of all the people of Israel.

7, 8   After four years, Absalom said to the king, "Let me go to Hebron to sacrifice to the Lord in fulfillment of a vow I made to Him while I was at Geshur — that if He would bring me back to Jerusalem, I would sacrifice to Him."

9   "All right," the king told him, "Go and fulfill your vow." So Absalom went to Hebron.[2]

10   But while he was there, he sent spies to every part of Israel to incite rebellion against the king. "As soon as you hear the trumpets," his message read, "you will know that Absalom has been crowned in Hebron."

11   He took two hundred men from Jerusalem with him as guests, but they knew nothing of his intentions.

12   While he was offering the sacrifice, he sent for Ahithophel, one of David's counselors who lived in Giloh. Ahithophel declared for Absalom, as did more

---

[1]Literally, "took hold of him and kissed him."

[2]Hebron was King David's first capital, and it was also Absalom's home town, its people doubtless very proud of him.

and more others. So the conspiracy became very strong.

13 A messenger soon arrived in Jerusalem to tell King David, "All Israel has joined Absalom in a conspiracy against you!"

14 "Then we must flee at once or it will be too late!" was David's instant response to his men. "If we get out of the city before he arrives, both we and the city of Jerusalem will be saved."

15 "We are with you," his aides replied. "Do as you think best."

16 So the king and his household set out at once. He left no one behind except ten of his young wives to keep the palace in order.

17, 18 David paused at the edge of the city to let his troops move past him to lead the way — six hundred Gittites who had come with him from Gath, and the Cherethites and Pelethites.

19, 20 But suddenly the king turned to Ittai, the captain of the six hundred Gittites, and said to him, "What are you doing here? Go on back with your men to Jerusalem, to your king, for you are a guest in Israel, a foreigner in exile. It seems but yesterday that you arrived, and now today should I force you to wander with us, who knows where? Go on back and take your troops with you, and may the Lord be merciful to you."

21 But Ittai replied, "I vow by God and by your own life that wherever you go, I will go, no matter what happens — whether it means life or death."

22 So David replied, "All right, come with us." Then Ittai and his six hundred men and their families went along.

23 There was deep sadness throughout the city as the king and his retinue passed by, crossed **Kidron** Brook, and went out into the country.

24 Abiathar and Zadok and the Levites took the Ark of the Covenant of God and set it down beside the road until everyone had passed.

25, 26 Then, following David's instructions, Zadok took the Ark back into the city. "If the Lord sees fit," David said, "He will bring me back to see the Ark and the Tabernacle again. But if He is through with me, well, let Him do what seems best to Him."

27 Then the king told Zadok, "Look, here is my plan. Return quietly to the city with your son Ahimaaz and Abiathar's son Jonathan.

28 I will stop at the ford of the Jordan River and wait there for a message from you. Let me know what happens in Jerusalem before I disappear into the wilderness."

29 So Zadok and Abiathar carried the Ark of God back into the city and stayed there.

30 David walked up the road that led to the Mount of Olives, weeping as he went. His head was covered and his feet were bare as a sign of mourning. And the people who were with him covered their heads and wept as they climbed the mountain.

31 When someone told David that Ahithophel, his advisor, was backing Absalom, David prayed, "O Lord, please make Ahithophel give Absalom foolish advice!"

32 As they reached the spot at the top of the Mount of Olives where people worshiped God, David found Hushai the Archite waiting for him with torn clothing and earth upon his head.

33, 34   But David told him, "If you go with me, you will only be a burden; return to Jerusalem and tell Absalom, 'I will counsel you as I did your father.' Then you can frustrate and counter Ahithophel's advice.

35, 36   Zadok and Abiathar, the priests, are there. Tell them the plans that are being made to capture me, and they will send their sons Ahima-az and Jonathan to find me and tell me what is going on."

37   So David's friend Hushai returned to the city, getting there just as Absalom arrived.

CHAPTER 16

D avid was just past the top of the hill when Ziba, the manager of Mephibosheth's household, caught up with him. He was leading two donkeys loaded with two hundred loaves of bread, one hundred clusters of raisins, one hundred bunches of grapes, and a small barrel of wine.

2   "What are these for?" the king asked Ziba.

And Ziba replied, "The donkeys are for your people to ride on, and the bread and summer fruit are for the young men to eat; the wine is to be taken with you into the wilderness for any who become faint."

3   "And where is Mephibosheth?" the king asked him.

"He stayed at Jerusalem," Ziba replied. "He said, 'Now I'll get to be king! Today I will get back the kingdom of my father, Saul.'[1]

4   "In that case," the king told Ziba, "I give you everything he owns."

"Thank you, thank you, sir," Ziba replied.

---

[1] Saul was Mephibosheth's grandfather.

5   As David and his party passed Bahurim, a man came out of the village cursing them. It was Shime-i, the son of Gera, a member of Saul's family.

6   He threw stones at the king and the king's officers and all the mighty warriors who surrounded them!

7, 8   "Get out of here, you murderer, you scoundrel!" he shouted at David. "The Lord is paying you back for murdering King Saul and his family; you stole his throne and now the Lord has given it to your son Absalom! At last you will taste some of your own medicine, you murderer!"

9   "Why should this dead dog curse my lord the king?" Abishai demanded. "Let me go over and strike off his head!"

10   "No!" the king said. "If the Lord has told him to curse me, who am I to say no?

11   My own son is trying to kill me, and this Benjaminite is merely cursing me. Let him alone, for no doubt the Lord has told him to do it.

12   And perhaps the Lord will see that I am being wronged and will bless me because of these curses."

13   So David and his men continued on, and Shime-i kept pace with them on a nearby hillside, cursing as he went and throwing stones at David and tossing dust into the air.

14   The king and all those who were with him were weary by the time they reached Bahurim, so they stayed there awhile and rested.

15   Meanwhile, Absalom and his men arrived at Jerusalem, accompanied by Ahithophel.

16   When David's friend, Hushai the Archite, arrived, he went immediately to see Absalom. "Long

live the king!" he exclaimed, "long live the king!"

17 "Is this the way to treat your friend David?" Absalom asked him. "Why aren't you with him?"

18 "Because I work for the man who is chosen by the Lord and by Israel," Hushai replied.

19 "And anyway, why shouldn't I? I helped your father, and now I will help you!"

20 Then Absalom turned to Ahithophel and asked him, "What shall I do next?"

21 Ahithophel told him, "Go and sleep with your father's wives, for he has left them here to keep the house. Then all Israel will know that you have insulted him beyond the possibility of reconciliation, and they will all close ranks behind you."[1]

22 So a tent was erected on the roof of the palace where everybody could see it, and Absalom went into the tent to lie with his father's wives.

23 (Absalom did whatever Ahithophel told him to, just as David had; for every word Ahithophel spoke was as wise as though it had come directly from the mouth of God.)

CHAPTER 17

"Now," Ahithophel said, "give me twelve thousand men to start out after David tonight.

2, 3 I will come upon him while he is weary and discouraged, and he and his troops will be thrown into a panic and everyone will run away; and I will kill only the king, and let all those who are with him live, and restore them to you.

4 Absalom and all the elders of Israel approved of the plan,

---

[1]Literally, "the hands of all who are with you will be strengthened."

5   But Absalom said, "Ask Hushai the Archite what he thinks about this."

6   When Hushai arrived, Absalom told him what Ahithophel had said. "What is your opinion?" Absalom asked him. "Should we follow Ahithophel's advice? If not, speak up."

7   "Well," Hushai replied, "this time I think Ahithophel has made a mistake.

8   You know your father and his men; they are mighty warriors and are probably as upset as a mother bear who has been robbed of her cubs. And your father is an old soldier and isn't going to be spending the night among the troops;

9   He has probably already hidden in some pit or cave. And when he comes out and attacks and a few of your men fall, there will be panic among your troops and everyone will start shouting that your men are being slaughtered.

10   Then even the bravest of them, though they have hearts of lions, will be paralyzed with fear; for all Israel knows what a mighty man your father is and how courageous his soldiers are.

11   What I suggest is that you mobilize the entire army of Israel, bringing them from as far away as Dan and Beer-sheba, so that you will have a huge force. And I think that you should personally lead the troops.

12   Then when we find him we can destroy his entire army so that not one of them is left alive.

13   And if David has escaped into some city, you will have the entire army of Israel there at your command, and we can take ropes and drag the walls of the city into the nearest valley until every stone is torn down."

14 Then Absalom and all the men of Israel said, "Hushai's advice is better than Ahithophel's." For the Lord had arranged to defeat the counsel of Ahithophel, which really was the better plan, so that He could bring disaster upon Absalom!

15 Then Hushai reported to Zadok and Abiathar, the priests, what Ahithophel had said and what he himself had suggested instead.

16 "Quick!" he told them. "Find David and urge him not to stay at the ford of the Jordan River tonight. He must go across at once into the wilderness beyond; otherwise he will die, and his entire army with him."

17 Jonathan and Ahima-az had been staying at En-rogel so as not to be seen entering and leaving the city. Arrangements had been made for a servant girl to carry to them the messages they were to take to King David.

18 But a boy saw them leaving En-rogel to go to David, and he told Absalom about it. Meanwhile, they escaped to Bahurim where a man hid them inside a well in his backyard.

19 The man's wife put a cloth over the top of the well with grain on it to dry in the sun; so no one suspected they were there.

20 When Absalom's men arrived and asked her if she had seen Ahima-az and Jonathan, she said they had crossed the brook and were gone. They looked for them without success and returned to Jerusalem.

21 Then the two men crawled out of the well and hurried on to King David. "Quick!" they told him, "cross the Jordan tonight!" And they told him how Ahithophel had advised that he be captured and killed.

22 So David and all the people with him went

across during the night and were all on the other bank before dawn.

23 Meanwhile, Ahithophel — publicly disgraced when Absalom refused his advice — saddled his donkey, went to his home town, set his affairs in order, and hanged himself; so he died and was buried beside his father.

24 David soon arrived at Mahanaim. Meanwhile, Absalom had mobilized the entire army of Israel and was leading the men across the Jordan River.

25 Absalom had appointed Amasa as general of the army, replacing Joab. (Amasa was Joab's second cousin; his father was Ithra, an Ishmaelite, and his mother was Abigal, the daughter of Nahash, who was the sister of Joab's mother Zeruiah.)

26 Absalom and the Israeli army now camped in the land of Gilead.

27 When David arrived at Mahanaim, he was warmly greeted by Shobi (son of Nahash of Rabbah, an Ammonite) and Machir, (son of Ammiel of Lodebar) and Barzillai (a Gileadite of Rogelim).

28, 29 They brought him and those who were with him mats to sleep on, cooking pots, serving bowls, wheat and barley flour, parched grain, beans, lentils, honey, butter, and cheese. For they said, "You must be very tired and hungry and thirsty after your long march through the wilderness."

CHAPTER 18

David now appointed regimental colonels and company commanders over his troops.

2 A third were placed under Joab's brother, Abishai (the son of Zeruiah); and a third under Ittai, the

Gittite. The king planned to lead the army himself, but his men objected strongly.

3　"You mustn't do it," they said, "for if we have to turn and run, and half of us die, it will make no difference to them — they will be looking only for you. You are worth ten thousand of us, and it is better that you stay here in the city and send us help if we need it."

4　"Well, whatever you think best," the king finally replied. So he stood at the gate of the city as all the troops passed by.

5　And the king commanded Joab, Abishai, and Ittai, "For my sake, deal gently with young Absalom." And all the troops heard the king give them this charge.

6　So the battle began in the forest of Ephraim,

7　And the Israeli troops were beaten back by David's men. There was a great slaughter and twenty thousand men laid down their lives that day.

8　The battle raged all across the countryside, and more men disappeared in the forest than were killed.

9　During the battle Absalom came upon some of David's men and as he fled[1] on his mule, it went beneath the thick boughs of a great oak tree, and his hair caught in the branches. He mule went on, leaving him dangling in the air.

10　One of David's men saw him and told Joab.

11　"What? You saw him there and didn't kill him?" Joab demanded. "I would have rewarded you handsomely and made you a commissioned officer."[2]

---

[1]Implied.

[2]Literally, "Given you ten pieces of silver and a belt." There is no way of knowing the value of the silver. The belt was probably that worn by a commissioned officer.

12 "For a million dollars I wouldn't do it," the man replied. "We all heard the king say to you and Abishai and Ittai, 'For my sake, please don't harm young Absalom.'

13 And if I had betrayed the king by killing his son (and the king would certainly find out who did it), you yourself would be the first to accuse me."

14 "Enough of this nonsense," Joab said. Then he took three daggers and plunged them into the heart of Absalom as he dangled alive from the oak.

15 Ten of Joab's young armor bearers then surrounded Absalom and finished him off.

16 Then Joab blew the trumpet, and his men returned from chasing the army of Israel.

17 They threw Absalom's body into a deep pit in the forest and piled a great heap of stones over it. And the army of Israel fled to their homes.

18 (Absalom had built a monument to himself in the King's Valley, for he said, "I have no sons to carry on my name." He called it "Absalom's Monument," as it is still known today.)

19 Then Zadok's son Ahima-az said, "Let me run to King David with the good news that the Lord has saved him from his enemy Absalom."

20 "No," Joab told him, "it wouldn't be good news to the king that his son is dead. You can be my messenger some other time."

21 Then Joab said to a man from Cush, "Go tell the king what you have seen." The man bowed and ran off.

22 But Ahima-az pleaded with Joab, "Please let me go, too."

"No, we don't need you now, my boy." Joab

replied. "There is no further news to send."

23   "Yes, but let me go anyway," he begged.

And Joab finally said, "All right, go ahead." Then Ahima-az took a short cut across the plain and got there ahead of the man from Cush.

24   David was sitting at the gate of the city. When the watchman climbed the stairs to his post at the top of the wall, he saw a lone man running towards them.

25   He shouted the news down to David, and the king replied, "If he is alone, he has news." As the messenger came closer,

26   The watchman saw another man running towards them. He shouted down, "Here comes another one."

And the king replied, "He will have more news."

27   "The first man looks like Ahima-az, the son of Zadok," the watchman said.

"He is a good man and comes with good news," the king replied.

28   Then Ahima-az cried out to the king, "All is well!" He bowed low with his face to the ground and said, "Blessed be the Lord your God who has destroyed the rebels who dared to stand against you."

29   "What of young Absalom?" the king demanded. "Is he all right?"

"When Joab told me to come, there was a lot of shouting; but I didn't know what was happening,"[3] Ahima-az answered.

30   "Wait here," the king told him. So Ahima-az stepped aside.

---

[3]Ahima-az apparently was afraid to tell the king what actually had happened.

31   Then the man from Cush arrived and said, "I have good news for my lord the king. Today Jehovah has rescued you from all those who rebelled against you."

32   "What about young Absalom? Is he all right?" the king demanded.

And the man replied, "May all of your enemies be as that young man is!"

33   Then the king broke into tears, and went up to his room over the gate, crying as he went. "O my son Absalom, my son, my son Absalom. If only I could have died for you! O Absalom, my son, my son."

CHAPTER 19

Word soon reached Joab that the king was weeping and mourning for Absalom.

2   As the people heard of the king's deep grief for his son, the joy of that day's wonderful victory was turned into deep sadness.

3   The entire army crept back into the city as though they were ashamed and had been beaten in battle.

4   The king covered his face with his hands and kept on weeping, "O my son Absalom! O Absalom my son, my son!"

5   Then Joab went to the king's room and said to him, "We saved your life today and the lives of your sons, your daughters, your wives and concubines; and yet you act like this, making us feel ashamed, as though we had done something wrong.

6   You seem to love those who hate you, and hate those who love you. Apparently we don't mean any-

thing to you; if Absalom had lived and all of us had died, you would be happy.

7 Now go out there and congratulate the troops, for I swear by Jehovah that if you don't, not a single one of them will remain here during the night; then you will be worse off than you have ever been in your entire life."

8, 9, 10 So the king went out and sat at the city gates, and as the news spread throughout the city that he was there, everyone went to him.

Meanwhile, there was much discussion and argument going on all across the nation: "Why aren't we talking about bringing the king back?" was the great topic everywhere. "For he saved us from our enemies, the Philistines; and Absalom whom we made our king instead, chased him out of the country, but now Absalom is dead. Let's ask David to return and be our king again."

11, 12 Then David sent Zadok and Abiathar the priests to say to the elders of Judah, "Why are you the last ones to reinstate the king? For all Israel is ready, and only you are holding out. Yet you are my own brothers, my own tribe, my own flesh and blood!"

13 And he told them to tell Amasa, "Since you are my nephew, may God strike me dead if I do not appoint you as commander-in-chief of my army in place of Joab."

14 Then Amasa convinced all the leaders of Judah, and they responded as one man. They sent word to the king, "Return to us and bring back all those who are with you."

15 So the king started back to Jerusalem. And when he arrived at the Jordan River, it seemed as if

everyone in Judah had come to Gilgal to meet him and escort him across the river!

16   Then Shime-i (the son of Gera the Benjamin-ite), the man from Bahurim, hurried across with the men of Judah to welcome King David.

17   A thousand men from the tribe of Benjamin were with him, including Ziba, the servant of Saul, and Ziba's fifteen sons and twenty servants; they rushed down to the Jordan to arrive ahead of the king.

18   They all worked hard ferrying the king's household and troops across, and helped them in every way they could. As the king was crossing, Shime-i fell down before him,

19   And pleaded, "My lord the king, please forgive me and forget the terrible thing I did when you left Jerusalem;

20   For I know very well how much I sinned. That is why I have come here today, the very first person in all the tribe of Joseph to greet you."

21   Abishai asked, "Shall not Shime-i die, for he cursed the Lord's chosen king!"

22   "Don't talk to me like that!" David exclaimed. "This is not a day for execution but for celebration! I am once more king of Israel!"

23   Then, turning to Shime-i, he vowed, "Your life is spared."

24, 25   Now Mephibosheth, Saul's grandson, arrived from Jerusalem to meet the king. He had not washed his feet or clothes nor trimmed his beard since the day the king left Jerusalem. "Why didn't you come with me, Mephibosheth?" the king asked him.

26   And he replied, "My lord, O king, my servant Ziba deceived me. I told him, 'Saddle my donkey

so that I can go with the king.' For as you know I am lame.

27 But Ziba has slandered me by saying that I refused to come.[1] But I know that you are as an angel of God, so do what you think best.

28 I and all my relatives could expect only death from you, but instead you have honored me among all those who eat at your own table! So how can I complain?"

29 "All right," David replied. "My decision is that you and Ziba will divide the land equally between you."

30 "Give him all of it," Mephibosheth said. "I am content just to have you back again!"

31, 32 Barzillai, who had fed the king and his army during their exile in Mahanaim, arrived from Rogelim to conduct the king across the river. He was very old now, about eighty, and very wealthy.

33 "Come across with me and live in Jerusalem," the king said to Barzillai. "I will take care of you there."

34 "No," he replied, "I am far too old for that.

35 I am eighty years old today, and life has lost its excitement.[2] Food and wine are no longer tasty, and entertainment is not much fun; I would only be a burden to my lord the king.

36 Just to go across the river with you is all the honor I need!

37 Then let me return again to die in my own city, where my father and mother are buried. But here is Chimham.[3] Let him go with you and receive

---

[1]Implied.
[2]Literally, "can I discern between good and bad?"
[3]According to Josephus, Chimham was Barzillai's son.

whatever good things you want to give him."

38   "Good," the king agreed. "Chimham shall go with me, and I will do for him whatever I would have done for you."

39   So all the people crossed the Jordan with the king; and after David had kissed and blessed Barzillai, he returned home.

40   The king then went on to Gilgal, taking Chimham with him. And most of Judah and half of Israel were there to greet him.

41   But the men of Israel complained to the king because only men from Judah had ferried him and his household across the Jordan.

42   "Why not?" the men of Judah replied. "The king is one of our own tribe. Why should this make you angry? We have charged him nothing — he hasn't fed us or given us gifts!"

43   "But there are ten tribes in Israel," the others replied, "so we have ten times as much right in the king as you do; why didn't you invite the rest of us? And, remember, we were the first to speak of bringing him back to be our king again." The argument continued back and forth, and the men of Judah were very rough in their replies.

CHAPTER 20

Then a hot-head whose name was Sheba (son of Bichri, a Benjaminite) blew a trumpet and yelled, "We want nothing to do with David. Come on, you men of Israel, let's get out of here. He's not our king!"

2   So all except Judah and Benjamin turned around and deserted David and followed Sheba! But the men of Judah stayed with their king, accompany-

ing him from the Jordan to Jerusalem.

3　When he arrived at his palace in Jerusalem, the king instructed that his ten wives he had left to keep house should be placed in seclusion. Their needs were to be cared for, he said, but he would no longer sleep with them as his wives. So they remained in virtual widowhood until their deaths.

4　Then the king instructed Amasa to mobilize the army of Judah within three days and to report back at that time.

5　So Amasa went out to notify the troops, but it took him longer than the three days he had been given.

6　Then David said to Abishai, "That fellow Sheba is going to hurt us more than Absalom did. Quick, take my bodyguard and chase after him before he gets into a fortified city where we can't reach him."

7　So Abishai and Joab set out after Sheba with an elite guard from Joab's army and the king's own bodyguard.

8, 9, 10　As they arrived at the great stone in Gibeon, they came face to face with Amasa. Joab was wearing his uniform with a dagger strapped to his side. As he stepped forward to greet Amasa, he stealthily slipped the dagger from its sheath. "I'm glad to see you, my brother," Joab said, and took him by the beard with his right hand as though to kiss him. Amasa didn't notice the dagger in his left hand, and Joab stabbed him in the stomach with it, so that his bowels gushed out onto the ground. He did not need to strike again, and he died there. Joab and his brother Abishai left him lying there and continued after Sheba.

11   One of Joab's young officers shouted to Amasa's troops, "If you are for David, come and follow Joab."

12   But Amasa lay in his blood in the middle of the road, and when Joab's young officers saw that a crowd was gathering around to stare at him, they dragged him off the road into a field and threw a garment over him.

13   With the body out of the way, everyone went on with Joab to capture Sheba.

14   Meanwhile Sheba had traveled across Israel to mobilize his own clan of Bichri at the city of Abel in Beth-maacah.

15   When Joab's forces arrived, they besieged Abel and built a mound to the top of the city wall and began battering it down.

16   But a wise woman in the city called out to Joab, "Listen to me, Joab. Come over here so I can talk to you."

17   As he approached, the woman asked, "Are you Joab?"

And he replied, "I am."

18   So she told him, "There used to be a saying, 'If you want to settle an argument, ask advice at Abel.' For we always give wise counsel.

19   You are destroying an ancient, peace-loving city, loyal to Israel. Should you destroy what is the Lord's?"

20   And Joab replied, "That isn't it at all.

21   All I want is a man named Sheba from the hill country of Ephraim, who has revolted against King David. If you will deliver him to me, we will leave the city in peace."

"All right," the woman replied, "we will throw his head over the wall to you."

22 Then the woman went to the people with her wise advice, and they cut off Sheba's head and threw it out to Joab. And he blew the trumpet and called his troops back from the attack, and they returned to the king at Jerusalem.

23 Joab was commander-in-chief of the army, and Benaiah was in charge of the king's bodyguard.[1]

24 Adoram was in charge of the forced labor battalions, and Jehoshaphat was the historian who kept the records.

25 Sheva was the secretary, and Zadok and Abiathar were the chief priests.

26 Ira the Jairite was David's personal chaplain.

CHAPTER 21

There was a famine during David's reign that lasted year after year for three years, and David spent much time in prayer about it. Then the Lord said, "The famine is because of the guilt of Saul and his family, for they murdered the Gibeonites."

2 So King David summoned the Gibeonites. They were not part of Israel, but were what was left of the nation of the Amorites. Israel had sworn not to kill them; but Saul, in his nationalistic zeal, had tried to wipe them out.

3 David asked them, "What can I do for you, to rid ourselves of this guilt and to induce you to ask God to bless us?"

4 "Well, money won't do it," the Gibeonites re-

---

[1]Literally, "the Cherethites and Pelethites."

plied, "and we don't want to see Israelites executed in revenge."

"What can I do, then?" David asked. "Just tell me and I will do it for you."

5, 6 "Well, then," they replied, "give us seven of Saul's sons — the sons of the man who did his best to destroy us. We will hang them before the Lord in Gibeon, the city of King Saul.

"All right," the king said, "I will do it."

7 He spared Jonathan's son Mephibosheth, who was Saul's grandson, because of the oath between himself and Jonathan.

8 But he gave them the two sons of Rizpah — Armoni and Mephibosheth — who were grandsons of Saul by his wife Aiah. He also gave them the five adopted sons of Michal that she brought up for Saul's daughter Merab, the wife of Adri-el.

9 The men of Gibeon impaled them in the mountain before the Lord. So all seven of them died together at the beginning of the barley harvest.

10 Then Rizpah, the mother of two of the men,[1] spread sackcloth upon a rock and stayed there through the entire harvest season[2] to prevent the vultures from tearing at their bodies during the day and the wild animals from eating them at night.

11 When David learned what she had done,

12, 13, 14 He arranged for the men's bones to be buried in the grave of Saul's father, Kish. At the same time he sent a request to the men of Jabesh-gilead, asking them to bring him the bones of Saul and Jonathan. They had stolen their bodies from the public

---

[1] Implied.

[2] The harvest lasted six months, from April until October.

square at Beth-shan where the Philistines had impaled them after they had died in battle on Mount Gilboa. So their bones were brought to him.

Then at last God answered prayer and ended the famine.

*   *   *   *   *

15 Once when the Philistines were at war with Israel and David and his men were in the thick of the battle, David became weak and exhausted.

16 Ishbi-benob, a giant whose speartip weighed more than twelve pounds and who was sporting a new suit of armor, closed in on David and was about to kill him.

17 But Abishai the son of Zeruiah came to his rescue and killed the Philistine. After that David's men declared, "You are not going out to battle again! Why should we risk snuffing out the light of Israel?"

18 Later, during a war with the Philistines at Gob, Sibbecai the Hushathite killed Saph, another giant.

19 At still another time and at the same place, Elhanan killed the brother of Goliath the Gittite,[3] whose spearhandle was as huge as a weaver's beam!

20, 21 And once when the Philistines and the Israelis were fighting at Gath, a giant with six fingers on each hand and six toes on each foot defied Israel, and David's nephew Jonathan — the son of David's brother Shime-i — killed him.

22 These four were from the tribe of giants in Gath, and were killed by David's troops.

---

[3]Literally, "slew Goliath of Gath." (See I Chronicles 20:5.)

CHAPTER 22

David sang this song to the Lord after He had rescued him from Saul and from all his other enemies:

2   Jehovah is my rock,
       My fortress and my Savior.

3   I will hide in God,
       Who is my rock and my refuge.
       He is my shield
       And my salvation,
       My refuge and high tower.
       Thank you, O my Savior,
       For saving me from all my enemies.

4   I will call upon the Lord,
       Who is worthy to be praised;
       He will save me from all my enemies.

5   The waves of death surrounded me;
       Floods of evil burst upon me;

6   I was trapped, and bound
       By hell and death;

7   But I called upon the Lord in my distress,
       And He heard me from His Temple.
       My cry reached His ears.

8   Then the earth shook and trembled;
       The foundations of the heavens quaked
       Because of His wrath.

9   Smoke poured from His nostrils;
       Fire leaped from His mouth
       And burned up all before Him,
       Setting fire to the world.[1]

10   He bent the heavens down and came to
           earth;

---

[1] Literally, "coals were kindled by it."

He walked upon dark clouds.

11   He rode upon the glorious —
On the wings of the wind.

12   Darkness surrounded Him,
And clouds were thick around Him;

13   The earth was radiant with His brightness.

14   The Lord thundered from heaven;
The God above all gods gave out a mighty
     shout.

15   He shot forth His arrows of lightning
And routed His enemies.

16   By the blast of His breath
Was the sea split in two.
The bottom of the sea appeared.

17   From above, He rescued me.
He drew me out from the waters;

18   He saved me from powerful enemies,
From those who hated me
And from those who were too strong for
     me.

19   They came upon me
In the day of my calamity,
But the Lord was my salvation.

20   He set me free and rescued me,
For I was His delight.

21   The Lord rewarded me for my goodness,
For my hands were clean;

22   And I have not departed from my God.

23   I knew His laws,
And I obeyed them.

24   I was perfect in obedience
And kept myself from sin.

25   That is why the Lord has done so much
          for me,
       For He sees that I am clean.

26   You are merciful to the merciful;
       You show your perfections
       To the blameless.

27   To those who are pure,
       You show Yourself pure;
       But You destroy those who are evil.

28   You will save those in trouble,
       But You bring down the haughty;
       For You watch their every move.

29   O Lord, You are my light!
       You make my darkness bright.

30   By Your power I can crush an army;
       By Your strength I leap over a wall.

31   As for God, His way is perfect;
       The word of the Lord is true.
       He shields all who hide behind Him.

32   Our Lord alone is God;
       We have no other Savior.[2]

33   God is my strong fortress;
       He has made me safe.

34   He causes the good to walk a steady tread
       Like mountain goats upon the rocks.

35   He gives me skill in war
       And strength to bend a bow of bronze.

36   You have given me the shield of Your
          salvation;
       Your gentleness has made me great.

37   You have made wide steps for my feet,
       To keep them from slipping.

[2]Literally, "who is a rock save our God?"

38　I have chased my enemies
　　And destroyed them.
　　I did not stop 'til all were gone.

39　I have destroyed them
　　So that none can rise again.
　　They have fallen beneath my feet.

40　For You have given me strength for the
　　　　battle
　　And have caused me to subdue
　　All those who rose against me.

41　You have made my enemies
　　Turn and run away;
　　I have destroyed them all.

42　They looked in vain for help;
　　They cried to God,
　　But He refused to answer.

43　I beat them into dust;
　　I crushed and scattered them
　　Like dust along the streets.

44　You have preserved me
　　From the rebels of my people;
　　You have preserved me
　　As the head of the nations.
　　Foreigners shall serve me

45　And shall quickly submit to me
　　When they hear of my power.

46　They shall lose heart
　　And come, trembling,
　　From their hiding places.

47　The Lord lives.
　　Blessed be my Rock.
　　Praise to Him —
　　The Rock of my salvation.

48   Blessed be God
      Who destroys those who oppose me
49   And rescues me from my enemies.
      Yes, You hold me safe above their heads.
      You deliver me from violence.
50   No wonder I give thanks to You, O Lord,
            among the nations,
      And sing praises to Your name.
51   He gives wonderful deliverance to his king,
      And shows mercy to His anointed —
      To David and his family,
      Forever.

CHAPTER 23

These are the last words of David:
      David, the son of Jesse, speaks.
      David, the man to whom God gave
      Such wonderful success;
      David, the anointed of the God of Jacob;
      David, sweet psalmist of Israel:
2   The Spirit of the Lord spoke by me,
      And His word was on my tongue.
3   The Rock of Israel said to me:
      "One shall come who rules righteously,
      Who rules in the fear of God.
4   He shall be as the light of the morning;
      A cloudless sunrise
      When the tender grass
      Springs forth upon the earth;
      As sunshine after rain."
5   And it is my family
      He has chosen!

Yes, God has made
An everlasting covenant with me;
His agreement is eternal, final, sealed.
He will constantly look after
My safety and success.[1]

6　　But the godless are as thorns to be thrown
　　　　away,
For they tear the hand that touches them.

7　　One must be armed to chop them down;
They shall be burned.

*　　*　　*　　*　　*

8　These are the names of the Top Three — the most heroic men in David's army: the first was Josheb-basshebeth from Tah-chemon, known also as Adino, the Eznite. He once killed eight hundred men in one battle.

9　Next in rank was Eleazar, the son of Dodo and grandson of Ahohi. He was one of the three men who, with David, held back the Philistines that time when the rest of the Israeli army fled.

10　He killed the Philistines until his hand was too tired to hold his sword; and the Lord gave him a great victory. (The rest of the army did not return until it was time to collect the loot!)

11, 12　After him was Shammah, the son of Agee from Harar. Once during a Philistine attack, when all his men deserted him and fled, he stood alone at the center of a field of lentils and beat back the Philistines; and God gave him a great victory.

13　One time when David was living in the cave of Adullam and the invading Philistines were at the valley

---

[1]Literally, "He will cause my help and my desire to sprout."

of Rephaim, three of The Thirty — the top-ranking officers of the Israeli army — went down at harvest time to visit him.

14 David was in the stronghold at the time, for Philistine marauders had occupied the nearby city of Bethlehem.

15 David remarked, "How thirsty I am for some of that good water in the city well!" (The well was near the city gate.)

16 So the three men broke through the Philistine ranks and drew water from the well and brought it to David. But he refused to drink it! Instead, he poured it out before the Lord.

17 "No, my God," he exclaimed, "I cannot do it! This is the blood of these men who have risked their lives."

18, 19 Of those three men, Abishai, the brother of Joab (son of Zeruiah), was the greatest. Once he took on three hundred of the enemy singlehanded and killed them all. It was by such feats that he earned a reputation equal to The Three, though he was not actually one of them. But he was the greatest of The Thirty — the top-ranking officers of the army — and was their leader.

20 There was also Benaiah (son of Jehoiada), a heroic soldier from Kabzeel. Benaiah killed two giants,[2] sons of Ariel of Moab. Another time he went down into a pit and, despite the slippery snow on the ground, took on a lion that was caught there and killed it.

21 Another time, armed only with a staff, he killed an Egyptian warrior who was armed with a spear;

2The meaning of the Hebrew wording is uncertain.

he wrenched the spear from the Egyptian's hand and killed him with it.

22　These were some of the deeds that gave Benaiah almost as much renown as the Top Three.

23　He was one of the greatest of The Thirty, but was not actually one of the Top Three. And David made him chief of his bodyguard.

24　Asahel, the brother of Joab, was also one of The Thirty. Others were:

Elhanan (son of Dodo) from Bethlehem;
25　Shammah from Harod;
　　Elika from Harod;
26　Helez from Palti;
　　Ira (son of Ikkesh) from Tekoa;
27　Abi-ezer from Anathoth;
　　Mebunnai from Hushath;
28　Zalmon from Ahoh;
　　Maharai from Netophah;
29　Heleb (son of Baanah) from Netophah;
　　Ittai (son of Ribai) from Gibe-ah, of the tribe of Benjamin;
30　Benaiah of Pirathon;
　　Hiddai from the brooks of Gaash;
31　Abi-albon from Arbath;
　　Azmaveth from Bahurim;
32　Eliahba from Sha-albon;
　　The sons of Jashen;
　　Jonathan;
33　Shammah from Harar;
　　Ahiam (the son of Sharar) from Harar;
34　Eliphelet (son of Ahasbai) from Maacah;
　　Eliam (the son of Ahithophel) from Gilo;
35　Hezro from Carmel;

Paarai from Arba;

36 Igal (son of Nathan) from Zobah;

Bani from Gad;

37 Zelek from Ammon;

Naharai from Be-eroth, the armor bearer of Joab (son of Zeruiah);

38 Ira from Ithra;

Gareb from Ithra;

39 Uriah the Hittite — thirty-seven[3] in all.

CHAPTER 24

Once again the anger of the Lord flared against Israel, and David was moved to harm them by taking a national census.

2 The king said to Joab, commander-in-chief of his army, "Take a census of all the people from one end of the nation to the other, so that I will know how many of them there are."

3 But Joab replied, "God grant that you will live to see the day when there will be a hundred times as many people in your kingdom as there are now! But you have no right to rejoice in their strength."[1]

4 But the king's command overcame Joab's remonstrance; so Joab and the other army officers went out to count the people of Israel.

5 First they crossed the Jordan and camped at Aroer, south of the city that lies in the middle of the valley of Gad, near Jazer;

6 Then they went to Gilead in the land of Tahtim-hodshi and to Dan-jaan and around to Sidon;

---

[3]The Thirty, plus the Top Three, plus Generals Joab, Abishai, Asahel, and Benaiah. Apparently new names were elected to this hall of fame to replace those who died.

[1]Literally, "but why does my lord the king delight in this thing?"

7 And then to the stronghold of Tyre, and all the cities of the Hivites and Canaanites, and south to Judah as far as Beer-sheba.

8 Having gone through the entire land, they completed their task in nine months and twenty days.

9 And Joab reported the number of the people to the king — 800,000 men of conscription age in Israel, and 500,000 in Judah.

10 But after he had taken the census, David's conscience began to bother him, and he said to the Lord, "What I did was very wrong. Please forgive this foolish wickedness of mine."

11 The next morning the word of the Lord came to the prophet Gad, who was David's contact with God. The Lord said to Gad,

12 "Tell David that I will give him three choices."

13 So Gad came to David and asked him, "Will you choose seven years of famine across the land, or to flee for three months before your enemies, or to submit to three days of plague? Think this over and let me know what answer to give to God."

14 "This is a hard decision," David replied, "but it is better to fall into the hand of the Lord (for His mercy is great) than into the hands of men."

15 So the Lord sent a plague upon Israel that morning, and it lasted for three days; and seventy thousand men died throughout the nation.

16 But as the death angel was preparing to destroy Jerusalem, the Lord was sorry for what was happening and told him to stop. He was by the threshing floor of Araunah the Jebusite at the time.

17 When David saw the angel, he said to the Lord, "Look, I am the one who has sinned! What

have these sheep done? Let Your anger be only against me and my family."

18   That day Gad came to David and said to him, "Go and build an altar to the Lord on the threshing floor of Araunah the Jebusite."

19   So David went to do what the Lord had commanded him.

20   When Araunah saw the king and his men coming towards him, he came forward and fell flat on the ground with his face in the dust.

21   "Why have you come?" Araunah asked.

And David replied, "To buy your threshing floor, so that I can build an altar to the Lord, and He will stop the plague."

22   "Use anything you like," Araunah told the king. "Here are oxen for the burnt offering, and you can use the threshing instruments and ox yokes for wood to build a fire on the altar.

23   I will give it all to you, and may the Lord God accept your sacrifice."

24   But the king said to Araunah, "No, I will not have it as a gift. I will buy it, for I don't want to offer to the Lord my God burnt offerings that have cost me nothing." So David paid him[1] for the threshing floor and the oxen.

25   And David built an altar there to the Lord and offered burnt offerings and peace offerings. And the Lord answered his prayer, and the plague was stopped.

---

[1]Literally, "paid him fifty shekels of silver."

I Kings

CHAPTER 1

In his old age King David was confined to his bed; but no matter how many blankets were heaped upon him, he was always cold.

2 "The cure for this," his aides told him, "is to find a young virgin to be your concubine and nurse. She will lie in your arms and keep you warm."

3, 4 So they searched the country from one end to the other to find the most beautiful girl in all the land. Abishag, from Shunam, was finally selected. They brought her to the king and she lay in his arms to warm him (but he had no sexual relations with her).

5 At about that time, David's son[1] Adonijah (his mother was Haggith) decided to crown himself king in place of his aged father. So he hired chariots and drivers and recruited fifty men to run down the streets before him as royal footmen.

6 Now his father, King David, had never disciplined him at any time — not so much as by a single scolding! He was a very handsome man, and was Absalom's younger brother.

7 He took General Joab and Abiathar the priest into his confidence, and they agreed to help him become king.

---

1 Implied.

8 But among those who remained loyal to King David and refused to endorse Adonijah were the priests Zadok and Benaiah, the prophet Nathan, Shime-i, Rei, and David's army chiefs.

9 Adonijah went to En-rogel where he sacrificed sheep, oxen, and fat young goats at the Serpent's Stone. Then he summoned all of his brothers — the other sons of King David — and all the royal officials of Judah, requesting that they come to his coronation.

10 But he didn't invite Nathan the prophet, Benaiah, the loyal army officers, or his brother Solomon.

11 Then Nathan the prophet went to Bath-sheba, Solomon's mother, and asked her, "Do you realize that Haggith's son, Adonijah, is now the king and that our lord David doesn't even know about it?

12 If you want to save your own life and the life of your son Solomon — do exactly as I say!

13 Go at once to King David and ask him, 'My lord, didn't you promise me that my son Solomon would be the next king and would sit upon your throne? Then why is Adonijah reigning?'

14 And while you are still talking with him, I'll come and confirm everything you've said."

15 So Bath-sheba went into the king's bedroom. He was an old, old man now, and Abishag was caring for him.

16 Bath-sheba bowed low before him. "What do you want?" he asked her.

17 She replied, "My lord, you vowed to me by the Lord your God that my son Solomon would be the next king and would sit upon your throne.

18 But instead, Adonijah is the new king, and you don't even know about it.

19   He has celebrated his coronation by sacrificing oxen, fat goats, and many sheep and has invited all your sons and Abiathar the priest and General Joab. But he didn't invite Solomon.

20   And now, my lord the king, all Israel is waiting for your decision as to whether Adonijah is the one you have chosen to succeed you.

21   If you don't act, my son Solomon and I will be arrested and executed as criminals as soon as you are dead."

22, 23   While she was speaking, the king's aides told him, "Nathan the prophet is here to see you."

Nathan came in and bowed low before the king,

24   And asked, "My lord, have you appointed Adonijah to be the next king? Is he the one you have selected to sit upon your throne?

25   Today he celebrated his coronation by sacrificing oxen and fat goats and many sheep, and has invited your sons to attend the festivities. He also invited General Joab and Abiathar the priest; and they are feasting and drinking with him and shouting, 'Long live King Adonijah!'

26   But Zadok the priest and Benaiah and Solomon and I weren't invited.

27   Has this been done with your knowledge? For you haven't said a word as to which of your sons you have chosen to be the next king."

28   "Call Bath-sheba," David said. So she came back in and stood before the king.

29   And the king vowed, "As the Lord lives who has rescued me from every danger,

30   I decree that your son Solomon shall be the next king and shall sit upon my throne, just as I swore

to you before by the Lord God of Israel."

31 Then Bath-sheba bowed low before him again[2] and exclaimed, "Oh, thank you, sir. May my lord the king live forever!"

32 "Call Zadok the priest," the king ordered, "and Nathan the prophet, and Benaiah." When they arrived,

33 He said to them, "Take Solomon and my officers to Gihon. Solomon is to ride on my personal mule,

34 And Zadok the priest and Nathan the prophet are to anoint him there as king of Israel. Then blow the trumpets and shout, 'Long live King Solomon!'

35 When you bring him back here, place him upon my throne as the new king; for I have appointed him king of Israel and Judah."

36 "Amen! Praise God!" replied Benaiah, and added,

37 "May the Lord be with Solomon as He has been with you, and may God make Solomon's reign ever greater than yours!"

38 So Zadok the priest, Nathan the prophet, Benaiah, and David's bodyguard took Solomon to Gihon, riding on King David's own mule.

39 At Gihon, Zadok took a flask of sacred oil from the Tabernacle and poured it over Solomon; and the trumpets were blown and all the people shouted, "Long live King Solomon!"

40 Then they all returned with him to Jerusalem, making a joyous and noisy celebration all along the way.

41 Adonijah and his guests heard the commotion

---

[2]Literally, "did reverence to the king."

and shouting just as they were finishing their banquet.

"What's going on?" Joab demanded; "why is the city in such an uproar?"

42 And while he was still speaking, Jonathan, the son of Abiathar the priest, rushed in.

"Come in," Adonijah said to him, "for you are a good man; you must have good news."

43 "Our lord King David has declared Solomon as king!" Jonathan shouted.

44, 45 "The king sent him to Gihon with Zadok the priest and Nathan the prophet and Benaiah, protected by the king's own bodyguard; and he rode on the king's own mule. And Zadok and Nathan have anointed him as the new king! They have just returned, and the whole city is celebrating and rejoicing. That's what all the noise is.

46, 47 Solomon is sitting on the throne, and all the people are congratulating King David, saying, 'May God bless you even more through Solomon than He has blessed you personally! May God make Solomon's reign even greater than yours!' And the king is lying in bed, acknowledging their blessings.

48 He is saying, 'Blessed be the Lord God of Israel who has selected one of my sons to sit upon my throne while I am still alive to see it.' "

49, 50 Then Adonijah and his guests jumped up from the banquet table and fled in panic; for they were fearful for their lives. Adonijah rushed into the Tabernacle and caught hold of the horns of the sacred altar.

51 When word reached Solomon that Adonijah was claiming sanctuary in the Tabernacle, and pleading for clemency,

52 Solomon replied, "If he behaves himself, he

will not be harmed; but if he does not, he shall die."

53 So King Solomon summoned him, and they brought him down from the altar. He came to bow low before the king; and then Solomon curtly dismissed him. "Go on home" he said.

CHAPTER 2

As the time of King David's death approached, he gave this charge to his son Solomon:

2 "I am going where every man on earth must some day go. I am counting on you to be a strong and worthy successor.

3 Obey the laws of God and follow all His ways; keep each of His commands written in the law of Moses so that you will prosper in everything you do, wherever you turn.

4 If you do this, then the Lord will fulfill the promise He gave me, that if my children and their descendants watch their step and are faithful to God, one of them shall always be the king of Israel — my dynasty will never end.

5 Now listen to my instructions. You know that Joab murdered my two generals, Abner and Amasa. He pretended that it was an act of war, but it was done in a time of peace.

6 You are a wise man and will know what to do — don't let him die in peace.

7 But be kind to the sons of Barzillai the Gileadite. Make them permanent guests of the king, for they took care of me when I fled from your brother Absalom.

8 And do you remember Shime-i, the son of

Gera the Benjaminite from Bahurim? He cursed me with a terrible curse as I was going to Mahanaim; but when he came down to meet me at the Jordan River I promised I wouldn't kill him.

9 But that promise doesn't bind you! You are a wise man, and you will know how to arrange a bloody death for him."

10 Then David died and was buried in Jerusalem.

11 He had reigned over Israel for forty years, seven of them in Hebron and thirty-three in Jerusalem.

12 And Solomon became the new king, replacing his father David; and his kingdom prospered.

13 One day Adonijah the son of Haggith came to see Solomon's mother, Bath-sheba.

"Have you come to make trouble?" she asked him.

"No," he replied, "I come in peace.

14 As a matter of fact, I have a favor to ask of you."

"What is it?" she asked.

15 "Everything was going well for me," he said, "and the kingdom was mine: everyone expected me to be the next king. But the tables were turned, and everything went to my brother instead; for that is the way the Lord wanted it.

16 But now I have just a small favor to ask of you; please don't turn me down."

"What is it?" she asked.

17 He replied, "Speak to King Solomon on my behalf (for I know he will do anything you request) and ask him to give me Abishag, the Shunammite, as my wife."

18 "All right," Bath-sheba replied, "I'll ask him."

19 So she went to ask the favor of King Solomon. The king stood up from his throne as she entered and bowed low to her. He ordered that a throne for his mother be placed beside his; so she sat at his right hand.

20 "I have one small request to make of you," she said. "I hope you won't turn me down."

"What is it, my mother?" he asked. "You know I won't refuse you."

21 "Then let your brother Adonijah marry Abishag," she replied.

22 "Are you crazy?" he asked her. "If I were to give him Abishag, I would be giving him the kingdom too! For he is my older brother! He and Abiathar the priest and General Joab would take over!"

23, 24 Then King Solomon swore with a great oath, "May God strike me dead if Adonijah does not die this very day for this plot against me! I swear it by the living God who has given me the throne of my father David and this kingdom he promised me."

25 So King Solomon sent Benaiah to execute him, and he killed him with a sword.

26 Then the king said to Abiathar the priest, "Go back to your home in Anathoth. You should be killed, too, but I won't do it now. For you carried the Ark of the Lord during my father's reign, and you suffered right along with him in all of his troubles."

27 So Solomon forced Abiathar to give up his position as the priest of the Lord, thereby fulfilling the decree of Jehovah at Shiloh concerning the descendants of Eli.[1]

---

[1]See I Samuel 2:31-35.

28 When Joab heard about Adonijah's death (Joab had joined Adonijah's revolt, though not Absalom's) he ran to the Tabernacle for sanctuary and caught hold of the horns of the altar.

29 When news of this reached King Solomon, he sent Benaiah to execute him.

30 Benaiah went into the Tabernacle and said to Joab, "The king says to come out!"

"No," he said, "I'll die here."

So Benaiah returned to the king for further instructions.

31 "Do as he says," the king replied. "Kill him there beside the altar and bury him. This will remove the guilt of his senseless murders from me and from my father's family.

32 Then Jehovah will hold him personally responsible for the murders of two men who were better than he. For my father was no party to the deaths of General Abner, commander-in-chief of the army of Israel, and General Amasa, commander-in-chief of the army of Judah.

33 May Joab and his descendants be forever guilty of these murders, and may the Lord declare David and his descendants guiltless concerning their deaths."

34 So Benaiah returned to the Tabernacle and killed Joab; and he was buried beside his house in the desert.

35 Then the king appointed Benaiah as commander-in-chief, and Zadok as priest instead of Abiathar.

36, 37 The king now sent for Shime-i and told him, "Build a house here in Jerusalem, and don't step outside the city on pain of death.

The moment you go beyond Kidron Brook, you die; and it will be your own fault."

38　"All right," Shime-i replied, "whatever you say." So he lived in Jerusalem for a long time.

39　But three years later two of Shime-i's slaves escaped to King Achish of Gath. When Shime-i learned where they were,

40　He saddled a donkey and went to Gath to visit the king. And when he had found his slaves, he took them back to Jerusalem.

41　When Solomon heard that Shime-i had left Jerusalem and had gone to Gath and returned,

42　He sent for him and demanded, "Didn't I command you in the name of God to stay in Jerusalem or die? You replied, 'Very well, I will do as you say.'

43　Then why have you not kept your agreement and obeyed my commandment?

44　And what about all the wicked things you did to my father, King David? May the Lord take revenge on you,

45　But may I receive God's rich blessings, and may one of David's descendants always sit upon this throne."

46　Then, at the king's command, Benaiah took Shime-i outside and killed him.

So Solomon's grip upon the kingdom became secure.

CHAPTER 3

Solomon made an alliance with Pharaoh, the king of Egypt, and married one of his daughters. He brought her to Jerusalem to live in the City of David until he could finish building his palace and the Temple and the wall around the city.

2 At that time the people of Israel sacrificed their offerings on altars in the hills, for the Temple of the Lord hadn't yet been built.

3 (Solomon loved the Lord and followed all of his father David's instructions except that he continued to sacrifice in the hills and to offer incense there.)

4 The most famous of the hilltop altars was at Gibeon and now the king went there and sacrificed one thousand burnt offerings!

5 The Lord appeared to him in a dream that night and told him to ask for anything he wanted, and it would be given to him!

6 Solomon replied, "You were wonderfully kind to my father David because he was honest and true and faithful to You, and obeyed Your commands. And You have continued Your kindness to him by giving him a son to succeed him.

7 O Lord my God, now You have made me the king instead of my father David, but I am as a little child who doesn't know his way around.

8 And here I am among Your own chosen people, a nation so great that there are almost too many people to count!

9 Give me an understanding mind so that I can govern Your people well and know the difference between what is right and what is wrong. For who by himself is able to carry such a heavy responsibility?"

10 The Lord was pleased with his reply and was glad that Solomon had asked for wisdom.

11 So He replied, "Because you have asked for wisdom in governing My people, and haven't asked

for a long life or riches for yourself, or the defeat of your enemies —

12 Yes, I'll give you what you asked for! I will give you a wiser mind than anyone else has ever had or ever will have!

13 And I will also give you what you didn't ask for — riches and honor! And no one in all the world will be as rich and famous as you for the rest of your life!

14 And I will give you a long life if you follow Me and obey My laws as your father David did.

15 Then Solomon woke up and realized it had been a dream. He returned to Jerusalem and went into the Tabernacle. And as he stood before the Ark of the Covenant of the Lord, he sacrificed burnt offerings and peace offerings. Then he invited all of his officials to a great banquet.

16 Soon afterwards two young prostitutes came to the king to have an argument settled.

17, 18 "Sir," one of them began, "we live in the same house, just the two of us, and recently I had a baby.

When it was three days old, this woman's baby was born too.

19 But her baby died during the night when she rolled over on it in her sleep and smothered it.

20 Then she got up in the night and took my son from beside me while I was asleep, and laid her dead child in my arms and took mine to sleep beside her.

21 And in the morning when I tried to feed my baby it was dead! But when it became light outside, I saw that it wasn't my son at all."

22 Then the other woman interrupted, "It cer-

tainly was her son, and the living child is mine."

"No," the first woman said, "the dead one is yours and the living one is mine." And so they argued back and forth before the king.

23 Then the king said, "Let's get the facts straight: both of you claim the living child, and each says that the dead child belongs to the other.

24 All right, bring me a sword." So a sword was brought to the king.

25 Then he said, "Divide the living child in two and give half to each of these women!"

26 Then the woman who really was the mother of the child, and who loved him very much, cried out, "Oh, no, sir! Give her the child — don't kill him!"

But the other woman said, "All right, it will be neither yours nor mine; divide it between us!"

27 Then the king said, "Give the baby to the woman who wants him to live, for she is the mother!"

28 Word of the king's decision spread quickly throughout the entire nation, and all the people were awed as they realized the great wisdom God had given him.

CHAPTER 4

Here is a list of King Solomon's cabinet members:
Azariah (son of Zadok) was the High Priest;

3   Elihoreph and Ahijah (sons of Shisha) were secretaries;

Jehoshaphat (son of Ahilud) was the official historian and in charge of the archives;

4 Benaiah (son of Jehoiada) was commander-in-chief of the army;

Zadok and Abiathar were priests;

5 Azariah (son of Nathan) was secretary of state;

Zabud (son of Nathan) was the king's personal priest and special friend;

6 Ahishar was manager of palace affairs;

Adoniram (son of Abda) was superintendent of public works.

7 There were also twelve officials of Solomon's court — one man from each tribe — responsible for requisitioning food from the people for the king's household. Each of them arranged provisions for one month of the year.

8 The names of these twelve officers were:

Ben-hur, whose area for this taxation was the hill country of Ephraim;

9 Ben-deker, whose area was Makaz, Shaalbim, Beth-shemesh, and Elon-bethhanan;

10 Ben-hesed, whose area was Arubboth, including Socoh and all the land of Hepher;

11 Ben-abinadab (who married Solomon's daughter, the princess Taphath), whose area was the highlands of Dor;

12 Baana (son of Ahilud), whose area was Taanach and Megiddo, all of Bethshean near Zarethan below Jezreel, and all the territory from Beth-shean to Abel-meholah and over to Jokmeam;

13 Ben-geber, whose area was Ramoth-gilead, including the villages of Jair (the son of Manasseh) in Gilead; and the region of Argob in Bashan, including sixty walled cities with bronze gates;

14 Ahinadab (the son of Iddo), whose area was Mahanaim;

15 Ahima-az (who married Princess Basemath, another of Solomon's daughters), whose area was Naphtali;

16 Baana (son of Hushai), whose areas were Asher and Bealoth;

17 Jehoshaphat (son of Paruah), whose area was Issachar;

18 Shime-i (son of Ela), whose area was Benjamin;

19 Geber (son of Uri), whose area was Gilead, including the territories of King Sihon of the Amorites and King Og of Bashan.

A general manager supervised these officials and their work.

20 Israel and Judah were a wealthy, populous, contented nation at this time.

21 King Solomon ruled the whole area from the Euphrates River to the land of the Philistines, and down to the borders of Egypt. The conquered peoples of those lands sent taxes to Solomon and continued to serve him throughout his lifetime.

22 The daily food requirements for the palace were 195 bushels of fine flour, 390 bushels of meal,

23 Ten oxen from the fattening pens, 20 pasture-fed cattle, 100 sheep, and, from time to time, deer,

gazelles, roebucks, and plump fowl.

24 His dominion extended over all the kingdoms west of the Euphrates River, from Tiphsah to Gaza. And there was peace throughout the land.

25 Throughout the lifetime of Solomon, all of Judah and Israel lived in peace and safety; and each family had its own home and garden.

26 Solomon owned forty thousand chariot horses and employed twelve thousand charioteers.

27 Each month the tax officials provided food for King Solomon and his court;

28 Also the barley and straw for the royal horses in the stables.

29 God gave Solomon great wisdom and understanding, and a mind with broad interests.

30 In fact, his wisdom excelled that of any of the wise men of the East, including those in Egypt.

31 He was wiser than Ethan the Ezrahite and Heman, Calcol, and Darda, the sons of Mahol; and he was famous among all the surrounding nations.

32 He was the author of 3,000 proverbs and wrote 1,005 songs.

33 He was a great naturalist, with interest in animals, birds, snakes, fish, and trees — from the great cedars of Lebanon down to the tiny hyssop which grows in cracks in the wall.

34 And kings from many lands sent their ambassadors to him for his advice.

CHAPTER 5

K ing Hiram of Tyre had always been a great admirer of David, so when he learned that David's

son Solomon was the new king of Israel, he sent ambassadors to extend congratulations and good wishes.

2, 3   Solomon replied with a proposal about the
Temple of the Lord he wanted to build. His father
David, Solomon pointed out to Hiram, had not been
able to build it because of the numerous wars going on,
and he had been waiting for the Lord to give him
peace.

4   "But now," Solomon said to Hiram, "the Lord
my God has given Israel peace on every side; I have
no foreign enemies or internal rebellions.

5   So I am planning to build a Temple for the
Lord my God, just as He instructed my father that I
should do. For the Lord told him, 'Your son, whom
I will place upon your throne, shall build Me a Temple.'

6   Now please assist me with this project. Send
your woodsmen to the mountains of Lebanon to cut
cedar timber for me, and I will send my men to work
beside them, and I will pay your men whatever wages
you ask; for as you know, no one in Israel can cut
timber like you Sidonians!"

7   Hiram was very pleased with the message from
Solomon. "Praise God for giving David a wise son to
be king of the great nation of Israel," he said.

8   Then he sent this reply to Solomon: "I have
received your message and I will do as you have
asked concerning the timber. I can supply both cedar
and cypress.

9   My men will bring the logs from the Lebanon
mountains to the Mediterranean Sea and build them
into rafts. We will float them along the coast to wherever you need them; then we will break the rafts

apart and deliver the timber to you. You can pay me with food for my household."

10   So Hiram produced for Solomon as much cedar and cypress timber as he desired,

11   And in return Solomon sent him an annual payment of 125,000 bushels of wheat for his household and 96 gallons of pure olive oil.

12   So the Lord gave great wisdom to Solomon just as He had promised. And Hiram and Solomon made a formal alliance of peace.

13   Then Solomon drafted thirty thousand laborers from all over Israel,

14   And rotated them to Lebanon, ten thousand a month, so that each man was a month in Lebanon and two months at home. Adoniram was the general superintendent of this labor camp.

15   Solomon also had seventy thousand additional laborers, eighty thousand stonecutters in the hill country,

16   And thirty-three hundred foremen.

17   The stonecutters quarried and shaped huge blocks of stone — a very expensive job — for the foundation of the Temple.

18   Men from Gebal helped Solomon's and Hiram's builders in cutting the timber and making the boards, and in preparing the stone for the Temple.

CHAPTER 6

It was in the spring of the fourth year of Solomon's reign that he began the actual construction of the Temple. (This was 480 years after the people of Israel left their slavery in Egypt.)

2   The Temple was ninety feet long, thirty feet wide, and forty-five feet high.

3   All along the front of the Temple was a porch thirty feet long and fifteen feet deep.

4   Narrow windows were used throughout.

5   An annex of rooms was built along the full length of both sides of the Temple against the outer walls.

6   These rooms were three stories high, the lower floor being 7½ feet wide, the second floor 9 feet wide, and the upper floor 10½ feet wide. The rooms were connected to the walls of the Temple by beams resting on blocks built out from the wall — so the beams were not inserted into the walls themselves.

7   The stones used in the construction of the Temple were prefinished at the quarry, so the entire structure was built without the sound of hammer, axe, or any other tool at the building site.

8   The bottom floor of the side rooms was entered from the right side of the Temple, and there were winding stairs going up to the second floor; another flight of stairs led from the second to the third.

9   After completing the Temple, Solomon paneled it all, including the beams and pillars, with cedar.

10   As already stated, there was an annex on each side of the building, attached to the Temple walls by cedar timbers. Each story of the annex was 7½ feet high.

11, 12   Then the Lord sent this message to Solomon concerning the Temple he was building: "If you do as I tell you to and follow all of My commandments and instructions, I will do what I told your father David I would do:

13 I will live among the people of Israel and never forsake them."

14 At last the Temple was finished.

15 The entire inside, from floor to ceiling, was paneled with cedar, and the floors were made of cypress boards.

16 The thirty-foot inner room at the far end of the Temple — the Most Holy Place — was also paneled from the floor to the ceiling with cedar boards.

17 The remainder of the Temple — other than the Most Holy Place — was sixty feet long.

18 Throughout the Temple the cedar paneling laid over the stone walls was carved with designs of rosebuds and open flowers.

19 The inner room was where the Ark of the Covenant of the Lord was placed.

20 This inner sanctuary was thirty feet long, thirty feet wide, and thirty feet high. Its walls and ceiling were overlaid with pure gold, and Solomon made a cedar-wood altar for this room.

21, 22 Then he overlaid the interior of the remainder of the Temple — including the cedar altar — with pure gold; and he made gold chains to protect the entrance to the Most Holy Place.

23-28 Within the inner sanctuary Solomon placed two statues of angels[1] made from olive wood, each fifteen feet high. They were placed so that their outspread wings reached from wall to wall, while their inner wings touched each other at the center of the room; each wing was 7½ feet long, so each angel measured fifteen feet from wing tip to wing tip. The

---

[1]Literally, "he made two cherubim."

two angels were identical in all dimensions, and each was overlaid with gold.

29 Figures of angels, palm trees, and open flowers were carved on all the walls of both rooms of the Temple,

30 And the floor of both rooms was overlaid with gold.

31 The doorway to the inner sanctuary was a five-sided opening,

32 And its two olive-wood doors were carved with cherubim, palm trees, and open flowers, all overlaid with gold.

33 Then he made square doorposts of olive wood for the entrance to the Temple.

34 There were two folding doors of cypress wood, and each door was hinged to fold back upon itself.

35 Angels, palm trees, and open flowers were carved on these doors and carefully overlaid with gold.

36 The wall of the inner court had three layers of hewn stone and one layer of cedar beams.

37 The foundation of the Temple was laid in the month of May in the fourth year of Solomon's reign,

38 And the entire building was completed in every detail in November of the eleventh year of his reign. So it took seven years to build.

CHAPTER 7

Then Solomon built his own palace, which took thirteen years to construct.

2 One of the rooms in the palace was called the Hall of the Forest of Lebanon. It was huge — measuring 150 feet long, 75 feet wide, and 45 feet high.

The great cedar ceiling beams rested upon four rows of cedar pillars.

3, 4 There were forty-five windows in the hall, set in three tiers, one tier above the other, five to a tier, facing each other from three walls.

5 Each of the doorways and windows had a square frame.

6 Another room was called the Hall of Pillars. It was seventy-five feet long and forty-five feet wide, with a porch in front covered by a canopy which was supported by pillars.

7 There was also the Throne Room or Judgment Hall, where Solomon sat to hear legal matters; it was paneled with cedar from the floor to the rafters.

8 His cedar-paneled living quarters surrounded a courtyard behind this hall. (He designed similar living quarters, the same size, in the palace which he built for Pharaoh's daughter — one of his wives.)

9 These buildings were constructed entirely from huge, expensive stones, cut to measure.

10 The foundation stones were twelve to fifteen feet across.

11 The huge stones in the walls were also cut to measure, and were topped with cedar beams.

12 The Great Court had three courses of hewn stone in its walls, topped with cedar beams, just like the inner court of the Temple and the porch of the palace.

13 King Solomon then asked for a man named Hiram to come from Tyre, for he was a skilled craftsman in bronze work.

14 He was half Jewish, being the son of a widow of the tribe of Naphtali, and his father had been a

foundry worker from Tyre. So he came to work for King Solomon.

15   He cast two hollow bronze pillars, each twenty-seven feet high and eighteen feet around, with four-inch-thick walls.

16-22   At the tops of the pillars he made two lily-shaped capitals of molten bronze, each 7½ feet high, and 6 feet wide. Each capital was decorated with seven sets of bronze, chain-designed lattices and four hundred pomegranates in two rows. Hiram set these pillars at the entrance of the Temple. The one on the south was named the Jachin Pillar, and the one on the north, the Boaz Pillar.[1]

23   Then Hiram cast a round bronze tank, 7½ feet high and 15 feet from brim to brim; 45 feet in circumference.

24   On the underside of the rim were two rows of ornaments an inch or two apart,[2] which were cast along with the tank.

25   It rested on twelve bronze[3] oxen standing tail to tail, three facing north, three west, three south, and three east.

26   The sides of the tank were four inches thick; its brim was shaped like a goblet, and it had a twelve thousand gallon capacity.

27-30   Then he made ten four-wheeled movable stands, each 6 feet square and 4½ feet high.

They were constructed with undercarriages braced with square[4] crosspieces. These crosspieces were decorated with carved lions, oxen, and angels.

[1]Jachin means "to establish," and Boaz means "strength."
[2]Literally, "ten in a cubit."
[3]Implied.
[4]Implied in verse 31.

Above and below the lions and oxen were wreath decorations. Each of these movable stands had four bronze wheels and bronze axles, and at each corner of the stands were supporting posts made of bronze and decorated with wreaths on each side.

31 The top of each stand was a round piece 1½ feet high. Its center was concave, 2¼ feet deep, decorated on the outside with wreaths. Its panels were square, not round.

32 The stands rode on four wheels which were connected to axles that had been cast as part of the stands. The wheels were twenty-seven inches high,

33 And were similar to chariot wheels. All the parts of the stands were cast from molten bronze, including the axles, spokes, rims, and hubs.

34 There were supports at each of the four corners of the stands, and these, too, were cast with the stands.

35 A nine-inch rim surrounded the top of each stand, banded with lugs. All was cast as one unit with the stand.

36 Cherubim, lions, and palm trees surrounded by wreaths were engraved on the borders of the band wherever there was room.

37 All ten stands were the same size and were made alike, for each was cast from the same mold.

38 Then he made ten brass vats, and placed them on the stands. Each vat was six feet square and contained 240 gallons of water.

39 Five of these vats were arranged on the left and five on the right-hand side of the room. The tank was in the southeast corner, on the right-hand side of the room.

40 Hiram also made the necessary pots, shovels,

and basins and at last completed the work in the Temple of the Lord which had been assigned to him by King Solomon.

41 Here is a list of the items he made:

> Two pillars;
>
> A capital at the top of each pillar;
>
> Latticework covering the bases of the capitals of each pillar;

42 Four hundred pomegranates in two rows on the latticework, to cover the bases of the two capitals;

43 Ten movable stands holding ten vats;

44 One large tank and twelve oxen supporting it;

45, 46 Pots;

> Shovels;
>
> Basins.

All these items were made of burnished bronze, and were cast at the plains of the Jordan River between Succoth and Zarethan.

47 The total weight of these pieces was not known because they were too heavy to weigh!

48 All the utensils and furniture used in the Temple were made of solid gold. This included the altar, the table where the Bread of the Presence of God was displayed,

49 The lampstands (five on the right-hand side and five on the left, in front of the Most Holy Place), the flowers, lamps, tongs,

50 Cups, snuffers, basins, spoons, firepans, the hinges of the doors to the Most Holy Place, and the main entrance doors of the Temple. Each of these was made of solid gold.

51   When the Temple was finally finished, Solomon took into the treasury of the Temple the silver, the gold, and all the vessels dedicated for that purpose by his father David.

CHAPTER 8

Then Solomon called a convocation at Jerusalem of all the leaders of Israel — the heads of the tribes and clans — to observe the transferring of the Ark of the Covenant of the Lord from the Tabernacle in Zion, the City of David, to the Temple.

2   This celebration occurred at the time of the Tabernacle Festival in the month of October.

3, 4   During the festivities the priests carried the Ark to the Temple, along with all the sacred vessels which had previously been in the Tabernacle.

5   King Solomon and all the people gathered before the Ark, sacrificing uncounted sheep and oxen.

6   Then the priests took the Ark into the inner sanctuary of the Temple — the Most Holy Place — and placed it under the wings of the angels.

7   The angels had been constructed in such a manner that their wings spread out over the spot where the Ark would be placed; so now their wings overshadowed the Ark and its carrying poles.

8   The poles were so long that they stuck out past the angels and could be seen from the next room, but not from the outer court; and they remain there to this day.

9   There was nothing in the Ark at that time except the two stone tablets which Moses had placed there at Mount Horeb at the time the Lord made His covenant with the people of Israel after they left Egypt.

10 *Look! As the priests are returning from the inner sanctuary, a bright cloud fills the Temple!*

11 *The priests have to go outside because the glory of the Lord is filling the entire building!*

12 Now King Solomon prayed this invocation:
"The Lord has said that He would live in the thick darkness;

13 But, O Lord, I have built You a lovely home on earth, a place for You to live forever."

14 Then the king turned around and faced the people as they stood before him, and blessed them.

15 "Blessed be the Lord God of Israel," he said, "who has done today what He promised my father David:

16 For He said to him, 'When I brought My people from Egypt, I didn't appoint a place for My Temple, but I appointed a man to be My people's leader.'

17 This man was my father, David. He wanted to build a Temple for the Lord God of Israel,

18 But the Lord told him not to. 'I am glad you want to do it,' He said,

19 'But your son is the one who shall build My Temple.'

20 And now the Lord has done what He promised; for I have followed my father as king of Israel, and now this Temple has been built for the Lord God of Israel.

21 And I have prepared a place in the Temple for the Ark which contains the covenant made by the Lord with our fathers, at the time that He brought them out of the land of Egypt."

22, 23 Then, as all the people watched, Solomon

stood before the altar of the Lord with his hands
spread out towards heaven and said, "O Lord God of
Israel, there is no god like You in heaven or earth,
for You are loving and kind and You keep Your
promises to Your people if they do their best to do
Your will.

24 Today You have fulfilled Your promise to my
father David, who was Your servant;

25 And now, O Lord God of Israel, fulfill Your
further promise to him: that if his descendants follow
Your ways and try to do Your will as he did, one of
them shall always sit upon the throne of Israel.

26 Yes, O God of Israel, fulfill this promise too.

27 But is it possible that God would really live on
earth? Why, even the skies and the highest heavens
cannot contain You, much less this Temple I have
built!

28 And yet, O Lord my God, You have heard
and answered my request:

29 Please watch over this Temple night and day
— this place You have promised to live in — and as
I face toward the Temple and pray, whether by night
or by day, please listen to me and answer my requests.

30 Listen to every plea of the people of Israel
whenever they face this place to pray; yes, hear in
heaven where You live, and when You hear, forgive.

31 If a man is accused of doing something wrong
and then, standing here before Your altar, swears that
he didn't do it,

32 Hear him in heaven and do what is right; judge
whether or not he did it.

33, 34 And when Your people sin and their enemies defeat them, hear them from heaven and forgive

them if they turn to You again and confess that You are their God. Bring them back again to this land which You have given to their fathers.

35, 36 And when the skies are shut up and there is no rain because of their sin, hear them from heaven and forgive them when they pray toward this place and confess Your name. And after You have punished them, help them to follow the good ways in which they should walk, and send rain upon the land which You have given Your people.

37 If there is a famine in the land caused by plant disease or locusts or caterpillers, or if Israel's enemies besiege one of her cities, or if the people are struck by an epidemic or plague — or whatever the problem is —

38 Then when the people realize their sin and pray toward this Temple,

39 Hear them from heaven and forgive and answer all who have made an honest confession; for You know each heart.

40 In this way they will always learn to reverence You as they continue to live in this land which You have given their fathers.

41, 42 And when foreigners hear of Your great name and come from distant lands to worship You (for they shall hear of Your great name and mighty miracles) and pray toward this Temple,

43 Hear them from heaven and answer their prayers. And all the nations of the earth will know and fear Your name just as Your own people Israel do; and all the earth will know that this is Your Temple.

44 When You send Your people out to battle

against their enemies and they pray to You, looking toward Your chosen city of Jerusalem and toward this Temple which I have built for Your name,

45   Hear their prayer and help them.

46   If they sin against You (and who doesn't?) and You become angry with them and let their enemies lead them away as captives to some foreign land, whether far or near,

47   And they come to their senses and turn to You and cry to You saying, 'We have sinned, we have done wrong';

48   If they honestly return to You and pray toward this land which You have given their fathers, and toward this city of Jerusalem which You have chosen, and toward this Temple, which I have built for Your name,

49   Hear their prayers and pleadings from heaven where You live, and come to their assistance.

50   Forgive Your people for all of their evil deeds, and make their captors merciful to them;

51   For they are Your people — Your inheritance that You brought out from the Egyptian furnace.

52   May Your eyes be open and Your ears listening to their pleas. O Lord, hear and answer them whenever they cry out to You,

53   For when You brought our fathers out of the land of Egypt, You told Your servant Moses that You had chosen Israel from among all the nations of the earth to be Your own special people."

54, 55   Solomon had been kneeling with his hands outstretched toward heaven. As he finished this prayer, he rose from before the altar of Jehovah and cried out this blessing upon all the people of Israel:

56 "Blessed be the Lord who has fulfilled His promise and given rest to His people Israel; not one word has failed of all the wonderful promises proclaimed by His servant Moses.

57 May the Lord our God be with us as He was with our fathers; may He never forsake us.

58 May He give us the desire to do His will in everything, and to obey all the commandments and instructions He has given our ancestors.

59 And may these words of my prayer be constantly before Him day and night, so that He helps me and all of Israel in accordance with our daily needs.

60 May people all over the earth know that the Lord is God, and that there is no other god at all.

61 O my people, may you live good and perfect lives before the Lord our God; may you always obey His laws and commandments, just as you are doing today."

62, 63 Then the king and all the people dedicated the Temple by sacrificing peace offerings to the Lord — a total of 22,000 oxen and 120,000 sheep and goats!

64 As a temporary measure the king sanctified the court in front of the Temple for the burnt offerings, grain offerings, and the fat of the peace offerings: for the bronze altar was too small to handle so much.

65 The celebration lasted for fourteen days, and a great crowd came from one end of the land to the other.

66 Afterwards Solomon sent the people home, happy for all the goodness that the Lord had shown to His servant David and to His people Israel. And they blessed the king.

CHAPTER 9

When Solomon had finished building the Temple and the palace and all the other buildings he had always wanted,

2, 3 The Lord appeared to him the second time (the first time had been at Gibeon) and said to him, "I have heard your prayer. I have hallowed this Temple which you have built and have put My name here forever. I will constantly watch over it and rejoice in it.

4 And if you live in honesty and truth as your father David did, always obeying Me,

5 Then I will cause your descendants to be the kings of Israel forever, just as I promised your father David when I told him, 'One of your sons shall always be upon the throne of Israel.'

6 However, if you or your children turn away from Me and worship other gods and do not obey My laws,

7 Then I will take away the people of Israel from this land which I have given them. I will take them from this Temple which I have hallowed for My name and I will cast them out of My sight; and Israel will become a joke to the nations and an example and proverb of sudden disaster.

8 This Temple will become a heap of ruins, and everyone passing by will be amazed and will whistle with astonishment, asking, 'Why has the Lord done such things to this land and this Temple?'

9 And the answer will be, 'The people of Israel abandoned the Lord their God who brought them out of the land of Egypt; they worshiped other gods in-

stead. That is why the Lord has brought this evil upon them.' "

10 At the end of the twenty years during which Solomon built the Temple and the palace,

11, 12 He gave twenty cities in the land of Galilee to King Hiram of Tyre as payment for all the cedar and cypress lumber and gold he had furnished for the construction of the palace and Temple. Hiram came from Tyre to see the cities, but he wasn't at all pleased with them.

13 "What sort of deal is this, my brother?" he asked. "These cities are a wasteland!" (And they are still known as "The Wasteland" today.)

14 For Hiram had sent gold to Solomon valued at $3,500,000!

15 Solomon had conscripted forced labor to build the Temple, his palace, Fort Millo, the wall of Jerusalem, and the cities of Hazor, Megiddo, and Gezer.

16 Gezer was the city the king of Egypt conquered and burned, killing the Israeli population; later he had given the city to his daughter as dowry — she was one of Solomon's wives.

17, 18 So now Solomon rebuilt Gezer along with Lower Beth-horon, Baalath, and Tamar, a desert city.

19 He also built cities for grain storage, cities in which to keep his chariots, cities for homes for his cavalry and chariot drivers, and resort cities near Jerusalem and in the Lebanon mountains and elsewhere throughout the land.

20, 21 Solomon conscripted his labor forces from those who survived in the nations he conquered — the Amorites, Hittites, Perizzites, Hivites, and Jebusites.

For the people of Israel had not been able to wipe them out completely at the time of the invasion and conquest of Israel, and they continue as slaves even today.

22 Solomon didn't conscript any Israelis for this work, although they became soldiers, officials, army officers, chariot commanders, and cavalrymen.

23 And there were 550 men of Israel who were overseers of the labor forces.

Miscellaneous Notes:

24 King Solomon moved Pharaoh's daughter from the City of David — the old sector of Jerusalem — to the new quarters he had built for her in the palace. Then he built Fort Millo.

* * * * *

25 After the Temple was completed, Solomon offered burnt offerings and peace offerings three times a year on the altar he had built. And he also burned incense upon it.

* * * * *

26 King Solomon had a shipyard in Ezion-geber near Eloth on the Red Sea in the land of Edom, where he built a fleet of ships.

* * * * *

27, 28 King Hiram supplied experienced sailors to accompany Solomon's crews. They used to run back and forth from Ophir, bringing gold to King Solomon, the total value of which was more than $12,000,000.

CHAPTER 10

When the queen of Sheba heard how wonderfully the Lord had blessed Solomon with wisdom,[1] she decided to test him with some hard questions.

2   She arrived in Jerusalem with a long train of camels carrying spices, gold, and jewels; and she told him all her problems.

3   Solomon answered all her questions; nothing was too difficult for him, for the Lord gave him the right answers every time.[2]

4   She soon realized that everything she had ever heard about his great wisdom was true. She also saw the beautiful palace he had built,

5   And when she saw the wonderful foods on his table, the great number of servants and aides who stood around in splendid uniforms, his cupbearers, and the many offerings he sacrificed by fire to the Lord — well, there was no more spirit in her!

6   She exclaimed to him, "Everything I heard in my own country about your wisdom and about the wonderful things going on here is all true.

7   I didn't believe it until I came, but now I have seen it for myself! And really! The half had not been told me! Your wisdom and prosperity are far greater than anything I've ever heard of!

8   Your people are happy and your palace aides are content — but how could it be otherwise, for they stand here day after day listening to your wisdom!

9   Blessed be the Lord your God who chose you

---

[1]Literally, "heard of the fame of Solomon concerning the name of the Lord."

[2]Literally, "there was nothing hidden from the king which he could not explain to her."

and set you on the throne of Israel. How the Lord must love Israel — for He gave you to them as their king! And you give your people a just, good government!"

10 Then she gave the king a gift of $3,500,000 in gold, along with a huge quantity of spices and precious gems; in fact, it was the largest single gift of spices King Solomon had ever received.

11 (And when King Hiram's ships brought gold to Solomon from Ophir, they also brought along a great supply of algum trees and gems.

12 Solomon used the algum wood to make pillars for the Temple and the palace, and for harps and harpsichords for his choirs. Never before or since has there been such a supply of beautiful wood.)

13 In exchange for the gifts from the queen of Sheba, King Solomon gave her everything she asked him for, besides the presents he had already planned. Then she and her servants returned to their own land.

14 Each year Solomon received gold worth about $20,000,000,

15 Besides sales taxes and profits from trade with the kings of Arabia and the other surrounding territories.

16, 17 Solomon had some of the gold beaten into two hundred pieces of armor (gold worth $6,000 went into each piece) and three hundred shields ($1,800 worth of gold in each). And he kept them in his palace in the Hall of the Forest of Lebanon.

18 He also made a huge ivory throne and overlaid it with pure gold.

19 It had six steps and a rounded back, with arm rests; and a lion standing on each side.

20 And there were two lions on each step — twelve in all. There was no other throne in all the world so splendid as that one.

21 All of King Solomon's cups were of solid gold, and in the Hall of the Forest of Lebanon his entire dining service was made of solid gold. (Silver wasn't used because it wasn't considered to be of much value!)

22 King Solomon's merchant fleet was in partnership with King Hiram's, and once every three years a great load of gold, silver, ivory, apes, and peacocks arrived at the Israeli ports.

23 So King Solomon was richer and wiser than all the kings of the earth.

24 Great men from many lands came to interview him and listen to his God-given wisdom.

25 They brought him annual tribute of silver and gold dishes, beautiful cloth, myrrh, spices, horses, and mules.

26 Solomon built up a great stable of horses with a vast number of chariots and cavalry — 1,400 chariots in all, and 12,000 cavalrymen who lived in the chariot cities and with the king at Jerusalem.

27 Silver was as common as stones in Jerusalem in those days, and cedar was of no greater value than the common sycamore!

28 Solomon's horses were brought to him from Egypt and southern Turkey, where his agents purchased them at wholesale prices.

29 An Egyptian chariot delivered to Jerusalem cost $400, and the horses were valued at $150 each. Many of these were then resold to the Hittite and Syrian kings.

CHAPTER 11

K ing Solomon married many other girls besides the Egyptian princess. Many of them came from nations where idols were worshiped[1] — Moab, Ammon, Edom, Sidon, and from the Hittites —

2   Even though the Lord had clearly instructed His people not to marry into those nations, because the women they married would get them started worshiping their gods. Yet Solomon did it anyway.

3   He had 700 wives and 300 concubines; and sure enough, they turned his heart away from the Lord,

4   Especially in his old age. They encouraged him to worship their gods instead of trusting completely in the Lord as his father David had done.

5   Solomon worshiped Ashtoreth, the goddess of the Sidonians, and Milcom, the horrible god of the Ammonites.

6   Thus Solomon did what was clearly wrong and refused to follow the Lord as his father David did.

7   He even built a temple on the Mount of Olives, across the valley from Jerusalem, for Chemosh, the depraved god of Moab, and another for Molech, the unutterably vile god of the Ammonites.

8   Solomon built temples for these foreign wives to use for burning incense and sacrificing to their gods.

9, 10   Jehovah was very angry with Solomon about this, for now Solomon was no longer interested in the Lord God of Israel who had appeared to him twice to warn him specifically against worshiping other gods. But he hadn't listened,

---

[1]Implied.

11   So now the Lord said to him, "Since you have not kept our agreement and have not obeyed My laws, I will tear the kingdom away from you and your family and give it to someone else.

12, 13   However, for the sake of your father David, I won't do this while you are still alive. I will take the kingdom away from your son. And even so I will let him be king of one tribe, for David's sake and for the sake of Jerusalem, my chosen city."

14   So the Lord caused Hadad the Edomite to grow in power. And Solomon became apprehensive, for Hadad was a member of the royal family of Edom.

15   Years before, when David had been in Edom with Joab to arrange for the burial of some Israeli soldiers who had died in battle, the Israeli army had killed nearly every male in the entire country.

16, 17, 18   It took six months to accomplish this, but they finally killed all except Hadad and a few royal officials who took him to Egypt (he was a very small child at the time). They slipped out of Midian and went to Paran, where others joined them and accompanied them to Egypt, and Pharaoh had given them homes and food.

19   Hadad became one of Pharaoh's closest friends, and he gave him a wife — the sister of Queen Tahpenes.

20   She presented him with a son, Genubath, who was brought up in Pharaoh's palace among Pharaoh's own sons.

21   When Hadad, there in Egypt, heard that David and Joab were both dead, he asked Pharaoh for permission to return to Edom.

22   "Why?" Pharaoh asked him. "What do you

lack here? How have we disappointed you?"

"Everything is wonderful," he replied, "but even so, I'd like to go back home."

23 Another of Solomon's enemies whom God raised to power was Rezon, one of the officials of King Hadadezer of Zobah who had deserted his post and fled the country.

24 He had become the leader of a gang of bandits — men who fled with him to Damascus (where he later became king) when David destroyed Zobah.

25 During Solomon's entire lifetime, Rezon and Hadad were his enemies, for they hated Israel intensely.

26 Another rebel leader was Jeroboam (the son of Nebat), who came from the city of Zeredah in Ephraim; his mother was Zeruah, a widow.

27 Here is the story back of his rebellion: Solomon was rebuilding Fort Millo, repairing the walls of this city his father had built. Jeroboam was very able, and when Solomon saw how industrious he was, he put him in charge of his labor battalions from the tribe of Joseph.

29 One day as Jeroboam was leaving Jerusalem, the prophet Ahijah from Shiloh (who had put on a new robe for the occasion) met him and called him aside to talk to him. And as the two of them were alone in the field,

30 Ahijah tore his new robe into twelve parts,

31 And said to Jeroboam, "Take ten of these pieces, for the Lord God of Israel says, 'I will tear the kingdom from the hand of Solomon and give ten of the tribes to you!

32 But I will leave him one tribe[2] for the sake of My servant David and for the sake of Jerusalem, which I have chosen above all the other cities of Israel.

33 For Solomon has forsaken Me and worships Ashtoreth, the goddess of the Sidonians; and Chemosh, the god of Moab; and Milcom, the god of the Ammonites. He has not followed My paths and has not done what I consider right; he has not kept My laws and instructions as his father David did.

34 I will not take the kingdom from him now, however; for the sake of My servant David, My chosen one who obeyed My commandments, I will let Solomon reign for the rest of his life.

35 But I will take away the kingdom from his son and give ten of the tribes to you.

36 His son shall have the other one so that the descendants of David will continue to reign in Jerusalem, the city I have chosen to be the place for My name to be enshrined.

37 And I will place you on the throne of Israel, and give you absolute power.

38 If you listen to what I tell you and walk in My path and do whatever I consider right, obeying My commandments as My servant David did, then I will bless you; and your descendants shall rule Israel forever. (I once made this same promise to David.

39 But because of Solomon's sin I will punish the descendants of David — though not forever.)' "

40 Solomon tried to kill Jeroboam, but he fled to King Shishak of Egypt and stayed there until the death of Solomon.

41 The rest of what Solomon did and said is writ-

[2] Of the twelve tribes, Judah and Benjamin were left to Solomon's son.

ten in the book *The Acts of Solomon.*

42   He ruled in Jerusalem for forty years,

43   And then died and was buried in the city of his father David; and his son Rehoboam reigned in his place.

CHAPTER 12

R ehoboam's inauguration was at Shechem, and all Israel came for the coronation ceremony.

2, 3, 4   Jeroboam, who was still in Egypt where he had fled from King Solomon, heard about the plans from his friends. They urged him to attend, so he joined the rest of Israel at Shechem, and was the ring-leader in getting the people to make certain demands upon Rehoboam.

"Your father was a hard master," they told Rehoboam. "We don't want you as our king unless you promise to treat us better than he did."

5   "Give me three days to think this over," Rehoboam replied. "Come back then for my answer." So the people left.

6   Rehoboam talked it over with the old men who had counseled his father Solomon.

"What do you think I should do?" he asked them.

7   And they replied, "If you give them a pleasant reply and agree to be good to them and serve them well, you can be their king forever."

8   But Rehoboam refused the old men's counsel and called in the young men with whom he had grown up.

9   "What do you think I should do?" he asked them.

10   And the young men replied, "Tell them, 'If you think my father was hard on you, well, I'll be harder!

11   Yes, my father was harsh, but I'll be even harsher! My father used whips on you, but I'll use scorpions!' "

12   So when Jeroboam and the people returned three days later,

13, 14   The new king answered them roughly. He ignored the old men's advice and followed that of the young men;

15   So the king refused the people's demands. (But the Lord's hand was in it — He caused the new king to do this in order to fulfill His promise to Jeroboam, made through Ahijah, the prophet from Shiloh.)

16, 17   When the people realized that the king meant what he said and was refusing to listen to them, they began shouting, "Down with David and all his relatives! Let's go home! Let Rehoboam be king of his own family!"

And they all deserted him except for the tribe of Judah, who remained loyal and accepted Rehoboam as their king.

18   When King Rehoboam sent Adoram (who was in charge of the draft) to conscript men from the other tribes, a great mob stoned him to death. But King Rehoboam escaped by chariot and fled to Jerusalem.

19   And Israel has been in rebellion against the dynasty of David to this day.

20   When the people of Israel learned of Jeroboam's return from Egypt, he was asked to come before an open meeting of all the people; and there he was

made king of Israel. Only the tribe of Judah[1] continued under the kingship of the family of David.

21 When King Rehoboam arrived in Jerusalem, he summoned his army — all the able-bodied men of Judah and Benjamin: 180,000 special troops — to force the rest of Israel to acknowledge him as their king.

22 But God sent this message to Shemaiah, the prophet:

23, 24 "Tell Rehoboam the son of Solomon, king of Judah, and all the people of Judah and Benjamin that they must not fight against their brothers, the people of Israel. Tell them to disband and go home, for what has happened to Rehoboam is according to My wish." So the army went home as the Lord had commanded.

25 Jeroboam now built the city of Shechem in the hill country of Ephraim, and it became his capital. Later he built Penuel.

26 Jeroboam thought, "Unless I'm careful, the people will want a descendant of David as their king.

27 When they go to Jerusalem to offer sacrifices at the Temple, they will become friendly with King Rehoboam; then they will kill me and ask him to be their king instead."

28 So on the advice of his counselors, the king had two gold calf-idols made and told the people, "It's too much trouble to go to Jerusalem to worship; from now on these will be your gods — they rescued you from your captivity in Egypt!"

29 One of these calf-idols was placed in Bethel and the other in Dan.

[1]Judah and Benjamin were sometimes (as in this instance) counted together as one tribe.

30   This was of course a great sin, for the people worshiped them.

31   He also made shrines on the hills and ordained priests from the rank and file of the people — even those who were not from the priest-tribe of Levi.

32, 33   Jeroboam also announced that the annual Tabernacle Festival would be held at Bethel on the first of November[2] (a date he decided upon himself), similar to the annual festival at Jerusalem; he himself offered sacrifices upon the altar to the calves at Bethel, and burned incense to them.   And it was there at Bethel that he ordained priests for the shrines on the hills.

CHAPTER 13

As Jeroboam approached the altar to burn incense to the golden calf-idol, a prophet of the Lord from Judah walked up to him.

2   Then, at the Lord's command, the prophet shouted, "O altar, the Lord says that a child named Josiah shall be born into the family line of David, and he shall sacrifice upon you the priests from the shrines on the hills who come here to burn incense; and men's bones shall be burned upon you."

3   Then he gave this proof that his message was from the Lord: "This altar will split apart, and the ashes on it will spill to the ground."

4   The king was very angry with the prophet for saying this. He shouted to his guards, "Arrest that man!" and shook his fist at him.   Instantly the king's

---

[2]Literally, "on the fifteenth day of the eighth month" of the Hebrew calendar. This was a month later than the annual celebration in Jerusalem, which God had ordained.

arm became paralyzed in that position; he couldn't pull it back again!

5　At the same moment a wide crack appeared in the altar and the ashes poured out, just as the prophet had said would happen. For this was the prophet's proof that God had been speaking through him.

6　"Oh, please, please," the king cried out to the prophet, "beg the Lord your God to restore my arm again."

So he prayed to the Lord, and the king's arm became normal again.

7　Then the king said to the prophet, "Come to the palace with me and rest awhile and have some food; and I'll give you a reward because you healed my arm."

8　But the prophet said to the king, "Even if you gave me half your palace, I wouldn't go into it; nor would I eat or drink even water in this place!

9　For the Lord has given me strict orders not to eat anything or drink any water while I'm here, and not to return to Judah by the road I came on."

10　So he went back another way.

11　As it happened, there was an old prophet living in Bethel, and his sons went home and told him what the prophet from Judah had done and what he had said to the king.

12　"Which way did he go?" the old prophet asked. So they told him.

13　"Quick, saddle the donkey," the old man said. And when they had saddled the donkey for him,

14　He rode after the prophet and found him sitting under an oak tree. "Are you the prophet who came from Judah?" he asked him.

"Yes," he replied, "I am."

15   Then the old man said to the prophet, "Come home with me and eat."

16, 17   "No," he replied, "I can't; for I am not allowed to eat anything or to drink any water at Bethel. The Lord strictly warned me against it; and He also told me not to return home by the same road I came on.

18   But the old man said, "I am a prophet too, just as you are; and an angel gave me a message from the Lord. I am to take you home with me and give you food and water." But the old man was lying to him.

19   So they went back together, and the prophet ate some food and drank some water at the old man's home.

20   Then, suddenly, while they were sitting at the table, a message from the Lord came to the old man,

21, 22   And he shouted at the prophet from Judah, "The Lord says that because you have been disobedient to His clear command, and have come here, and have eaten and drunk water in the place He told you not to, therefore your body shall not be buried in the grave of your fathers."

23   After finishing the meal, the old man saddled the prophet's donkey,

24, 25   And the prophet started off again. But as he was traveling along, a lion came out and killed him. His body lay there on the road, with the donkey and the lion standing beside it. Those who came by and saw the body lying in the road and the lion standing quietly beside it, reported it in Bethel where the old prophet lived.

26 When he heard what had happened he exclaimed, "It is the prophet who disobeyed the Lord's command; the Lord fulfilled His warning by causing the lion to kill him."

27 Then he said to his sons, "Saddle my donkey!" And they did.

28 He found the prophet's body lying in the road; and the donkey and lion were still standing there beside it, for the lion had not eaten the body nor attacked the donkey.

29 So the prophet laid the body upon the donkey and took it back to the city to mourn over it and bury it.

30 He laid the body in his own grave, exclaiming, "Alas, my brother!"

31 Afterwards he said to his sons, "When I die, bury me in the grave where the prophet is buried. Lay my bones beside his bones.

32 For the Lord told him to shout against the altar in Bethel, and his curse against the shrines in the cities of Samaria shall surely be fulfilled."

33 Despite the prophet's warning, Jeroboam did not turn away from his evil ways; instead, he made more priests than ever from the common people, to offer sacrifices to idols in the shrines on the hills. Anyone who wanted to could be a priest.

34 This was a great sin, and resulted in the destruction of Jeroboam's kingdom and the death of all of his family.

CHAPTER 14

Jeroboam's son Abijah now became very sick.

2 Jeroboam told his wife, "Disguise yourself so

that no one will recognize you as the queen, and go to Ahijah the prophet at Shiloh — the man who told me that I would become king.

3 Take him a gift of ten loaves of bread, some fig bars, and a jar of honey and ask him whether the boy will recover."

4 So his wife went to Ahijah's home at Shiloh. He was an old man now, and could no longer see.

5 But the Lord told him that the queen, pretending to be someone else, would come to ask about her son, for he was very sick. And the Lord told him what to tell her.

6 So when Ahijah heard her at the door, he called out, "Come in, wife of Jeroboam! Why are you pretending to be someone else?" Then he told her, "I have sad news for you.

7 Give your husband this message from the Lord God of Israel: 'I promoted you from the ranks of the common people and made you king of Israel.

8 I ripped the kingdom away from the family of David and gave it to you, but you have not obeyed My commandments as My servant David did. His heart's desire was always to obey Me and to do whatever I wanted him to.

9 But you have done more evil than all the other kings before you; you have made other gods and have made Me furious with your gold calves. And since you have refused to acknowledge me,

10 I will bring disaster upon your home and will destroy all of your sons — this boy who is sick and all those who are well.[1] I will sweep away your family

---

[1] Literally, "every male, both bond and free."

as a stable hand shovels out manure.

11 I vow that those of your family who die in the city shall be eaten by dogs, and those who die in the field shall be eaten by birds.' "

12 Then Ahijah said to Jeroboam's wife, "Go on home, and when you step into the city, the child will die.

13 All of Israel will mourn for him and bury him, but he is the only member of your family who will come to a quiet end. For this child is the only good thing which the Lord God of Israel sees in the entire family of Jeroboam.

14 And the Lord will raise up a king over Israel who will destroy the family of Jeroboam.

15 Then the Lord will shake Israel like a reed whipped about in a stream; He will uproot the people of Israel from this good land of their fathers and scatter them beyond the Euphrates River, for they have angered the Lord by worshiping idol-gods.

16 He will abandon Israel because Jeroboam sinned and made all of Israel sin along with him."

17 So Jeroboam's wife returned to Tirzah; and the child died just as she walked through the door of her home.

18 And there was mourning for him throughout the land, just as the Lord had predicted through Ahijah.

19 The rest of Jeroboam's activities — his wars and the other events of his reign — are recorded in *The Annals of the Kings of Israel.*

20 Jeroboam reigned twenty-two years, and when he died, his son Nadab took the throne.

21 Meanwhile, Rehoboam the son of Solomon was

king in Judah. He was forty-one years old when he began to reign, and he was on the throne seventeen years in Jerusalem, the city which, among all the cities of Israel, the Lord had chosen to live in. (Rehoboam's mother was Naamah, an Ammonite woman.)

22 During his reign the people of Judah, like those in Israel, did wrong and angered the Lord with their sin, for it was even worse than that of their ancestors.

23 They built shrines and obelisks and idols on every high hill and under every green tree.

24 There was homosexuality throughout the land, and the people of Judah became as depraved as the heathen nations which the Lord drove out to make room for His people.

25 In the fifth year of Rehoboam's reign, King Shishak of Egypt attacked and conquered Jerusalem.

26 He ransacked the Temple and the palace and stole everything, including all the gold shields Solomon had made.

27 Afterwards Rehoboam made bronze shields as substitutes, and the palace guards used these instead.

28 Whenever the king went to the Temple, the guards paraded before him and then took the shields back to the guard chamber.

29 The other events in Rehoboam's reign are written in *The Annals of the Kings of Judah*.

30 There was constant war between Rehoboam and Jeroboam.

31 When Rehoboam died — his mother was Naamah the Ammonitess — he was buried among his ancestors in Jerusalem, and his son Abijam took the throne.

CHAPTER 15

A bijam began his three-year reign as king of Judah in Jerusalem during the eighteenth year of Jeroboam's reign in Israel. (Abijam's mother was Maacah, the daughter of Abishalom.)

3 He was as great a sinner as his father was, and his heart was not right with God, as King David's was.

4 But despite Abijam's sin, the Lord remembered David's love[1] and did not end the line of David's royal descendants.

5 For David had obeyed God during his entire life except for the affair concerning Uriah the Hittite.

6 During Abijam's reign there was constant war between Israel and Judah.[2]

7 The rest of Abijam's history is recorded in *The Annals of the Kings of Judah.*

8 When he died he was buried in Jerusalem, and his son Asa reigned in his place.

9 Asa became king of Judah, in Jerusalem, in the twentieth year of the reign of Jeroboam over Israel,

10 And reigned forty-one years. (His grandmother was Maacah, the daughter of Abishalom.)

11 He pleased the Lord like his ancestor King David.

12 He executed the male prostitutes and removed all the idols his father had made.

13 He deposed his grandmother Maacah as queen-mother because she had made an idol — which he cut down and burned at Kidron Brook.

14 However, the shrines on the hills were not re-

---

[1]Literally, "for David's sake."
[2]Literally, "between Rehoboam and Jeroboam."

moved, for Asa did not realize that these were wrong.[3]

15 He made permanent exhibits in the Temple of the bronze shields his grandfather had dedicated,[4] along with the silver and gold vessels he himself had donated.

16 There was lifelong war between King Asa of Judah and King Baasha of Israel.

17 King Baasha built the fortress city of Ramah in an attempt to cut off all trade with Jerusalem.

18 Then Asa took all the silver and gold left in the Temple treasury and all the treasures of the palace, and gave them to his officials to take to Damascus, to King Ben-hadad of Syria, with this message:

19 "Let us be allies just as our fathers were. I am sending you a present of gold and silver. Now break your alliance with King Baasha of Israel so that he will leave me alone."

20 Ben-hadad agreed and sent his armies against some of the cities of Israel; and he destroyed Ijon, Dan, Abel-beth-maacah, all of Chinneroth, and all the cities in the land of Naphtali.

21 When Baasha received word of the attack, he discontinued building the city of Ramah and returned to Tirzah.

22 Then King Asa made a proclamation to all Judah, asking every able-bodied man to help demolish Ramah and haul away its stones and timbers. And King Asa used these materials to build the city of Geba in Benjamin and the city of Mizpah.

23 The rest of Asa's biography — his conquests

---

[3]Literally, "nevertheless, the heart of Asa was perfect toward Jehovah all his days."

[4]Literally, "the dedicated objects of his grandfather." See I Kings 14:27.

and deeds and the names of the cities he built — is found in *The Annals of the Kings of Judah*. In his old age his feet became diseased,

24   And when he died he was buried in the royal cemetery in Jerusalem. Then his son Jehoshaphat became the new king of Judah.

25   Meanwhile, over in Israel, Nadab the son of Jeroboam had become king. He reigned two years, beginning in the second year of the reign of King Asa of Judah.

26   But he was not a good king; like his father, he worshiped many idols and led all of Israel into sin.

27   Then Baasha (the son of Ahijah, from the tribe of Issachar) plotted against him and assassinated him while he was with the Israeli army laying siege to the Philistine city of Gibbethon.

28   So Baasha replaced Nadab as the king of Israel in Tirzah, during the third year of the reign of King Asa of Judah.

29   He immediately killed all of the descendants of King Jeroboam, so that not one of the royal family was left, just as the Lord had said would happen when He spoke through Ahijah, the prophet from Shiloh.

30   This was done because Jeroboam had angered the Lord God of Israel by sinning and leading the rest of Israel into sin.

31   Further details of Baasha's reign are recorded in *The Annals of the Kings of Israel*.

32, 33   There was continuous warfare between King Asa of Judah and King Baasha of Israel. Baasha reigned for twenty-four years,

34   But all that time he continually disobeyed the

Lord. He followed the evil paths of Jeroboam, for he led the people of Israel into the sin of worshiping idols.

CHAPTER 16

A message of condemnation from the Lord was delivered to King Baasha at this time by the prophet Jehu:

2 "I lifted you out of the dust," the message said, "to make you king of My people Israel; but you have walked in the evil paths of Jeroboam. You have made My people sin, and I am angry!

3 So now I will destroy you and your family, just as I did the descendants of Jeroboam.

4-7 Those of your family who die in the city will be eaten by dogs, and those who die in the fields will be eaten by the birds."

The message was sent to Baasha and his family because he had angered the Lord by all his evil deeds. He was as evil as Jeroboam despite the fact that the Lord had destroyed all of Jeroboam's descendants for their sins.

The rest of Baasha's biography — his deeds and conquests — are written in *The Annals of the Kings of Israel.*

8 Elah, Baasha's son, began reigning during the twenty-sixth year of the reign of King Asa of Judah, but he reigned only two years.

9 Then General Zimri, who had charge of half the royal chariot troops, plotted against him. One day King Elah was half drunk at the home of Arza, the superintendent of the palace, in the capital city of Tirzah.

10 Zimri simply walked in and struck him down

and killed him. (This occurred during the twenty-seventh year of the reign of King Asa of Judah.) Then Zimri declared himself to be the new king of Israel.

11 He immediately killed the entire royal family — leaving not a single male child. He even destroyed distant relatives and friends.

12 This destruction of the descendants of Baasha was in line with what the Lord had predicted through the prophet Jehu.

13 The tragedy occurred because of the sins of Baasha and his son Elah; for they had led Israel into worshiping idols and the Lord was very angry about it.

14 The rest of the history of Elah's reign is written in *The Annals of the Kings of Israel.*

15, 16 But Zimri lasted only seven days; for when the army of Israel, which was then engaged in attacking the Philistine city of Gibbethon, heard that Zimri had assassinated the king, they decided on General Omri, commander-in-chief of the army, as their new ruler.

17 So Omri led the army of Gibbethon to besiege Tirzah, Israel's capital.

18 When Zimri saw that the city had been taken, he went into the palace and burned it over him and died in the flames.

19 For he, too, had sinned like Jeroboam; he had worshiped idols and had led the people of Israel to sin with him.

20 The rest of the story of Zimri and his treason are written in *The Annals of the Kings of Israel.*

21 But now the kingdom of Israel was split in two; half the people were loyal to General Omri, and

the other half followed Tibni, the son of Ginath.

22   But General Omri won and Tibni was killed; so Omri reigned without opposition.

23   King Asa of Judah had been on the throne thirty-one years when Omri began his reign over Israel, which lasted twelve years, six of them in Tirzah.

24   Then Omri bought the hill now known as Samaria from its owner, Shemer, for $4,000 and built a city on it, calling it Samaria in honor of Shemer.

25   But Omri was worse than any of the kings before him;

26   He worshiped idols as Jeroboam had, and led Israel into this same sin. So God was very angry.

27   The rest of Omri's history is recorded in *The Annals of the Kings of Israel.*

28   When Omri died he was buried in Samaria, and his son Ahab became king in his place.

29   King Asa of Judah had been on the throne thirty-eight years when Ahab became the king of Israel; and Ahab reigned for twenty-two years.

30   But he was even more wicked than his father Omri; he was worse than any other king of Israel!

31   And as though that were not enough, he married Jezebel, the daughter of King Ethbaal of the Sidonians, and then began worshiping Baal.

32   First he built a temple and an altar for Baal in Samaria.

33   Then he made other idols and did more to anger the Lord God of Israel than any of the other kings of Israel before him.

34   (It was during his reign that Hiel, a man from Bethel, rebuilt Jericho. When he laid the foundations, his oldest son, Abiram, died; and when he finally com-

pleted it by setting up the gates, his youngest son, Segub, died. For this was the Lord's curse upon Jericho[1] as declared by Joshua, the son of Nun.)

CHAPTER 17

Then Elijah, the prophet[1] from Tishbe in Gilead, told King Ahab, "As surely as the Lord God of Israel lives — the God whom I worship and serve — there won't be any dew or rain for several years until I say the word!"

2 Then the Lord said to Elijah,

3 "Go to the east and hide by Cherith Brook at a place east of where it enters the Jordan River.

4 Drink from the brook and eat what the ravens bring you, for I have commanded them to feed you."

5 So he did as the Lord had told him to, and camped beside the brook.

6 The ravens brought him bread and meat each morning and evening, and he drank from the brook.

7 But after awhile the brook dried up, for there was no rainfall anywhere in the land.

8, 9 Then the Lord said to him, "Go and live in the village of Zarephath, near the city of Sidon. There is a widow there who will feed you. I have given her My instructions."

10 So he went to Zarephath. As he arrived at the gates of the city he saw a widow gathering sticks; and he asked her for a cup of water.

11 As she was going to get it, he called to her, "Bring me a bite of bread, too."

12 But she said, "I swear by the Lord your God

---

[1]See Joshua 6:26.
[1]Implied.

that I haven't a single piece of bread in the house. And I have only a handful of flour left and a little cooking oil in the bottom of the jar. I was just gathering a few sticks to cook this last meal, and then my son and I must die of starvation."

13 But Elijah said to her, "Don't be afraid! Go ahead and cook that 'last meal,' but bake me a little loaf of bread first; and afterwards there will still be enough food for you and your son.

14 For the Lord God of Israel says that there will always be plenty of flour and oil left in your containers until the time when the Lord sends rain, and the crops grow again!"

15 So she did as Elijah said, and she and Elijah and her son continued to eat from her supply of flour and oil as long as it was needed.

16 For no matter how much they used, there was always plenty left in the containers, just as the Lord had promised through Elijah!

17 But one day the woman's son became sick and died.

18 "O man of God," she cried, "what have you done to me? Have you come here to punish my sins by killing my son?"

19 "Give him to me," Elijah replied. And he took the boy's body from her and carried it upstairs to the guest room where he lived, and laid the body on his bed,

20 And then cried out to the Lord, "O Lord my God, why have You killed the son of this widow with whom I am staying?"

21 And he stretched himself upon the child three times, and cried out to the Lord, "O Lord my God,

please let this child's spirit return to him."

22 And the Lord heard Elijah's prayer; and the spirit of the child returned, and he became alive again!

23 Then Elijah took him downstairs and gave him to his mother. "See! He's alive!" he beamed.

24 "Now I know for sure that you are a prophet," she told him afterwards,[2] "and that whatever you say is from the Lord!"

CHAPTER 18

It was three years later that the Lord said to Elijah, "Go and tell King Ahab that I will soon send rain again!"

2 So Elijah went to tell him. Meanwhile the famine had become very severe in Samaria.

3, 4 The man in charge of Ahab's household affairs was Obadiah, who was a devoted follower of the Lord. Once when Queen Jezebel had tried to kill all of the Lord's prophets, Obadiah had hidden one hundred of them in two caves — fifty in each — and had fed them with bread and water.

5 That same day, while Elijah was on the way to see King Ahab,[1] the king said to Obadiah, "We must check every stream and brook to see if we can find enough grass to save at least some of my horses and mules. You go one way and I'll go the other, and we will search the entire land."

6 So they did, each going alone.

7 Suddenly Obadiah saw Elijah coming toward him! Obadiah recognized him at once and fell to the

---

[2]Implied.
[1]Implied.

ground before him. "Is it really you, my lord Elijah?" he asked.

8 "Yes, it is." Elijah replied. "Now go and tell the king I am here."

9 "Oh, sir," Obadiah protested, "what harm have I done to you that you are sending me to my death?

10 For I swear by God that the king has searched every nation and kingdom on earth from end to end to find you. And each time when he was told 'Elijah isn't here,' King Ahab forced the king of that nation to swear to the truth of his claim.

11 And now you say, 'Go and tell him Elijah is here'!

12 But as soon as I leave you, the Spirit of the Lord will carry you away, who knows where, and when Ahab comes and can't find you, he will kill me; yet I have been a true servant of the Lord all my life.

13 Has no one told you about the time when Queen Jezebel was trying to kill the Lord's prophets, and I hid a hundred of them in two caves and fed them with bread and water?

14 And now you say 'Go tell the king that Elijah is here'! Sir, if I do that, I'm dead!"

15 But Elijah said, "I swear by the Lord God of the armies of heaven, in whose presence I stand, that I will present myself to Ahab today."

16 So Obadiah went to tell Ahab that Elijah had come; and Ahab went out to meet him.

17 "So it's you, is it? — the man who brought this disaster upon Israel!" Ahab exclaimed when he saw him.

18 "You're talking about yourself," Elijah answered. "For you and your family have refused to

obey the Lord, and have worshiped Baal instead.

19 Now bring all the people of Israel to Mount Carmel, with all 450 prophets of Baal and the 400 prophets of Asherah who are supported by Jezebel."

20 So Ahab summoned all the people and the prophets to Mount Carmel.

21 Then Elijah talked to them, "How long are you going to waver between two opinions?" he asked the people. "If the Lord is God, *follow* him! But if Baal is God, then follow *him!*"

22 Then Elijah spoke again. "I am the only prophet of the Lord who is left," he told them, "but Baal has 450 prophets.

23 Now bring two young bulls. The prophets of Baal may choose whichever one they wish and cut it into pieces and lay it on the wood of their altar, but without putting any fire under the wood; and I will prepare the other young bull and lay it on the wood on the Lord's altar, with no fire under it.

24 Then pray to your god, and I will pray to the Lord; and the god who answers by sending fire to light the wood is the true God!" And all the people agreed to this test.

25 Then Elijah turned to the prophets of Baal. "You first," he said, "for there are many of you; choose one of the bulls and prepare it and call to your god; but don't put any fire under the wood."

26 So they prepared one of the young bulls and placed it on the altar; and they called to Baal all morning, shouting, "O Baal, hear us!" But there was no reply of any kind. Then they began to dance around the altar.

27 About noontime, Elijah began mocking them.

"You'll have to shout louder than that," he scoffed, "to catch the attention of your god! Perhaps he is talking to someone, or is out sitting on the toilet, or maybe he is away on a trip, or is asleep and needs to be wakened!"

28 So they shouted louder and, as was their custom, cut themselves with knives and swords until the blood gushed out.

29 They raved all afternoon until the time of the evening sacrifice, but there was no reply, no voice, no answer.

30 Then Elijah called to the people, "Come over here." And they all crowded around him as he repaired the altar of the Lord which had been torn down.

31 He took twelve stones, one to represent each of the tribes of Israel,[2]

32 And used the stones to rebuild the Lord's altar. Then he dug a trench about three feet wide[3] around the altar.

33 He piled wood upon the altar and cut the young bull into pieces and laid the pieces on the wood.

"Fill four barrels with water," he said, "and pour the water over the carcass and the wood." After they had done this he said,

34 "Do it again." And they did.

"Now, do it once more!" And they did;

35 And the water ran off the altar and filled the trench.

---

[2]Literally, "each of the tribes of the sons of Jacob to whom the Lord had said, 'Israel shall be your name.'"
[3]Literally, "as great as would contain two measures of seed."

36 At the customary time for offering the evening sacrifice, Elijah walked up to the altar and prayed, "O Lord God of Abraham, Isaac, and Israel, prove today that You are the God of Israel and that I am Your servant; prove that I have done all this at Your command.

37 O Lord, answer me! Answer me so these people will know that You are God and that You have brought them back to Yourself."

38 Then, suddenly, fire flashed down from heaven and burned up the young bull, the wood, the stones, the dust, and even evaporated all the water in the ditch!

39 And when the people saw it, they fell to their faces upon the ground shouting, "Jehovah is God! Jehovah is God!"

40 Then Elijah told them to grab the prophets of Baal. "Don't let a single one escape," he commanded.

So they seized them all, and Elijah took them to Kishon Brook and killed them there.

41 Then Elijah said to Ahab, "Go and enjoy a good meal! For I hear a mighty rainstorm coming!"

42 So Ahab prepared a feast. But Elijah climbed to the top of Mount Carmel and got down on his knees, with his face between his knees,

43 And said to his servant, "Go and look out toward the sea."

He did, but returned to Elijah and told him, "I didn't see anything."

Then Elijah told him, "Go again, and again, and again, seven times!"

44 Finally, the seventh time, his servant told him,

"I saw a little cloud about the size of a man's hand rising from the sea."

Then Elijah shouted, "Hurry to Ahab and tell him to get into his chariot and get down the mountain, or he'll be stopped by the rain!"

45 And sure enough, the sky was soon black with clouds, and a heavy wind brought a terrific rainstorm. Ahab left hastily for Jezreel,

46 And the Lord gave special strength to Elijah so that he was able to run ahead of Ahab's chariot to the entrance of the city!

CHAPTER 19

When Ahab told Queen Jezebel what Elijah had done, and that he had slaughtered the prophets of Baal,

2 She sent this message to Elijah: "You killed my prophets, and now I swear by the gods that I am going to kill you by this time tomorrow night."

3 So Elijah fled for his life; he went to Beersheba, a city of Judah, and left his servant there.

4 Then he went on alone into the wilderness, traveling all day, and sat down under a broom bush and prayed that he might die.

"I've had enough," he told the Lord, "Take away my life. I've got to die sometime, and it might as well be now."[1]

5 Then he lay down and slept beneath the broom bush. But as he was sleeping, an angel touched him and told him to get up and eat!

---

[1]Literally, "I am no better than my fathers."

6   He looked around and saw some bread baking on hot stones, and a jar of water! So he ate and drank and lay down again.

7   Then the angel of the Lord came again and touched him and said, "Get up and eat some more, for there is a long journey ahead of you."

8   So he got up and ate and drank, and the food gave him enough strength to travel forty days and forty nights to Mount Horeb, the mountain of God,

9   Where he lived in a cave. But the Lord said to him, "What are you doing here, Elijah?"

10   He replied, "I have worked very hard for the Lord God of the heavens; but the people of Israel have broken their covenant with You and torn down Your altars and killed Your prophets, and only I am left; and now they are trying to kill me, too."

11   "Go out and stand before Me on the mountain," the Lord told him. And as Elijah stood there the Lord passed by, and a mighty windstorm hit the mountain; it was such a terrible blast that the rocks were torn loose, but the Lord was not in the wind. After the wind, there was an earthquake, but the Lord was not in the earthquake.

12   And after the earthquake, there was a fire, but the Lord was not in the fire. And after the fire, there was the sound of a gentle whisper.

13   When Elijah heard it, he wrapped his face in his scarf and went out and stood at the entrance of the cave. And a voice said, "Why are you here, Elijah?"

14   He replied again, "I have been working very hard for the Lord God of the armies of heaven, but the people have broken their covenant and have torn

down Your altars; they have killed every one of Your prophets except me; and now they are trying to kill me, too."

15   Then the Lord told him, "Go back by the desert road to Damascus, and when you arrive, anoint Hazael to be king of Syria.

16   Then anoint Jehu (son of Himshi) to be king of Israel, and anoint Elisha (the son of Shaphat of Abel-meholah) to replace you as My prophet.

17   Anyone who escapes from Hazael shall be killed by Jehu, and those who escape Jehu shall be killed by Elisha!

18   And incidentally, there are 7,000 men in Israel who have never bowed to Baal nor kissed him!"

19   So Elijah went and found Elisha who was plowing a field with eleven other teams ahead of him; he was at the end of the line with the last team. Elijah went over to him and threw his coat across his shoulders and walked away again.[2]

20   Elisha left the oxen standing there and ran after Elijah and said to him, "First let me go and say goodbye to my father and mother, and then I'll go with you!"

Elijah replied, "Go on back! Why all the excitement?"

21   Elisha then returned to his oxen, killed them, and used wood from the plow to build a fire to roast their flesh. He passed around the meat to the other plowmen, and they all had a great feast. Then he went with Elijah as his assistant.

---

[2]Implied.

CHAPTER 20

King Ben-hadad of Syria now mobilized his army and, with thirty-two allied nations and their hordes of chariots and horses, besieged Samaria, the Israeli capital.

2, 3 He sent this message into the city to King Ahab of Israel: "Your silver and gold are mine, as are your prettiest wives and the best of your children!"

4 "All right, my lord," Ahab replied. "All that I have is yours!"

5, 6 Soon Ben-hadad's messengers returned again with another message: "You must not only give me your silver, gold, wives, and children, but about this time tomorrow I will send my men to search your palace and the homes of your people, and they will take away whatever they like!"

7 Then Ahab summoned his advisors. "Look what this man is doing," he complained to them. "He is stirring up trouble despite the fact that I have already told him he could have my wives and children and silver and gold, just as he demanded."

8 "Don't give him anything more," the elders advised.

9 So he told the messengers from Ben-hadad, "Tell my lord the king, 'I will give you everything you asked for the first time, but your men may not search the palace and the homes of the people.'"[1] So the messengers returned to Ben-hadad.

10 Then the Syrian king sent this message to Ahab: "May the gods do more to me than I am going

---

[1]Literally, "this thing I cannot do."

to do to you if I don't turn Samaria into handfuls of dust!"

11 The king of Israel retorted, "Don't count your chickens before they hatch!"

12 This reply of Ahab's reached Ben-hadad and the other kings as they were drinking in their tents.

"Prepare to attack!" Ben-hadad commanded his officers.

13 Then a prophet came to see King Ahab and gave him this message from the Lord: "Do you see all these enemy forces? I will deliver them all to you today. Then at last you will know that I am the Lord."

14 Ahab asked, "How will He do it?"

And the prophet replied, "The Lord says, 'By the troops from the provinces.' "

"Shall we attack first?" Ahab asked.

"Yes," the prophet answered.

15 So he mustered the troops from the provinces, 232 of them, then the rest of his army of 7,000 men.

16 About noontime, as Ben-hadad and the thirty-two allied kings were still drinking themselves drunk, the first of Ahab's troops marched out of the city.

17 As they approached, Ben-hadad's scouts reported to him, "Some troops are coming!"

18 "Take them alive," Ben-hadad commanded, "whether they have come for truce or for war."

19 By now Ahab's entire army had joined the attack.

20 Each one killed a Syrian soldier, and suddenly the entire Syrian army panicked and fled. The Israelis chased them, but King Ben-hadad and a few others escaped on horses.

21 However, the great bulk of the horses and char-

iots were captured, and most of the Syrian army was killed in a great slaughter.

22 Then the prophet approached King Ahab and said, "Get ready for another attack by the king of Syria."

23 For after their defeat, Ben-hadad's officers said to him, "The Israeli God is a god of the hills; that is why they won. But we can beat them easily on the plains.

24 Only this time replace the kings with generals!

25 Recruit another army like the one you lost; give us the same number of horses, chariots, and men, and we will fight against them in the plains; there's not a shadow of a doubt that we will beat them." So King Ben-hadad did as they suggested.

26 The following year he called up the Syrian army and marched out against Israel again, this time at Aphek.

27 Israel then mustered its army, set up supply lines, and moved into the battle; but the Israeli army looked like two little flocks of baby goats in comparison to the vast Syrian forces that filled the countryside!

28 Then a prophet went to the king of Israel with this message from the Lord: "Because the Syrians have declared, 'The Lord is a God of the hills and not of the plains,' I will help you defeat this vast army, and you shall know that I am indeed the Lord."

29 The two armies camped opposite each other for seven days, and on the seventh day the battle began. And the Israelis killed 100,000 Syrian infantrymen that first day.

30 The rest fled behind the walls of Aphek, but

the wall fell on them and killed another 27,000. Ben-hadad fled into the city and hid in the inner room of one of the houses.

31   "Sir," his officers said to him, "we have heard that the kings of Israel are very merciful. Let us wear sackcloth and put ropes on our heads and go out to King Ahab to see if he will let you live."

32   So they went to the king of Israel and begged, "Your servant Ben-hadad pleads, 'Let me live!' "

"Oh, is he still alive?" the king of Israel asked. "He is my brother!"

33   The men were quick to grab this straw of hope and hurried to clinch the matter by exclaiming, "Yes, your brother Ben-hadad!"

"Go and get him," the king of Israel told them. And when Ben-hadad arrived, he invited him up into his chariot!

34   Ben-hadad told him, "I will restore the cities my father took from your father, and you may establish trading posts in Damascus, as my father did in Samaria."

35   Meanwhile, the Lord instructed one of the prophets to say to another man, "Strike me with your sword!" But the man refused.

36   Then the prophet told him, "Because you have not obeyed the voice of the Lord, a lion shall kill you as soon as you leave me." And sure enough, as he turned to go a lion attacked and killed him.

37   Then the prophet turned to another man and said, "Strike me with your sword." And he did, wounding him.

38   The prophet waited for the king beside the

road, having placed a bandage over his eyes to disguise himself.

39 As the king passed by, the prophet called out to him, "Sir, I was in the battle, and a man brought me a prisoner and said, 'Keep this man; if he gets away, you must die,

40 Or else pay me $2,000!' But while I was busy doing something else, the prisoner disappeared!"

"Well, it's your own fault," the king replied. "You'll have to pay."

41 Then the prophet yanked off the bandage from his eyes, and the king recognized him as one of the prophets.

42 Then the prophet told him, "The Lord says, 'Because you have spared the man I said must die, now you must die in his place, and your people shall perish instead of his."

43 So the king of Israel went home to Samaria angry and sullen.

CHAPTER 21

Naboth, a man from Jezreel, had a vineyard on the outskirts of the city near King Ahab's palace.

2 One day the king talked to him about selling him this land. "I want it for a garden," the king explained, "because it's so convenient to the palace." He offered cash or, if Naboth preferred, a piece of better land in trade.

3 But Naboth replied, "Not on your life! That land has been in my family for generations."

4 So Ahab went back to the palace angry and sullen. He refused to eat and went to bed with his face to the wall!

5 "What in the world is the matter?" his wife, Jezebel, asked him. "Why aren't you eating? What has made you so upset and angry?"

6 "I asked Naboth to sell me his vineyard, or to trade it, and he refused!" Ahab told her.

7 "Are you the king of Israel or not?" Jezebel demanded. "Get up and eat and don't worry about it. I'll get you Naboth's vineyard!"

8 So she wrote letters in Ahab's name, sealed them with his seal, and addressed them to the civic leaders of Jezreel, where Naboth lived.

9 In her letter she commanded: "Call the citizens together for fasting and prayer.[1] Then summon Naboth,

10 And find two scoundrels who will accuse him of cursing God and the king. Then take him out and execute him."

11 The city fathers followed the queen's instructions.

12 They called the meeting and put Naboth on trial.

13 Then two men who had no conscience accused him of cursing God and the king; and he was dragged outside the city and stoned to death.

14 The city officials then sent word to Jezebel that Naboth was dead.

15 When Jezebel heard the news, she said to Ahab, "You know the vineyard Naboth wouldn't sell you? Well, you can have it now! He's dead!"

16 So Ahab went down to the vineyard to claim it.

---

[1]This inquisition was perhaps ostensibly to discover whose sins had caused the famine.

17   But the Lord said to Elijah,

18   "Go to Samaria to meet King Ahab. He will be at Naboth's vineyard, taking possession of it.

19   Give him this message from Me: 'Isn't killing Naboth bad enough? Must you rob him, too? Because you have done this, dogs shall lick your blood outside the city just as they licked the blood of Naboth!' "

20   "So my enemy has found me!" Ahab exclaimed to Elijah.

"Yes," Elijah answered, "I have come to place God's curse upon you because you have sold yourself to the devil.[2]

21   The Lord is going to bring great harm to you and sweep you away; He will not let a single one of your male descendants survive!

22   He is going to destroy your family as He did the family of King Jeroboam and the family of King Baasha, for you have made Him very angry and have led all of Israel into sin.

23   The Lord has also told me that the dogs of Jezreel shall tear apart the body of your wife, Jezebel.

24   The members of your family who die in the city shall be eaten by dogs and those who die in the country shall be eaten by vultures."

25   No one else was so completely sold out to the devil as Ahab, for his wife Jezebel encouraged him to do every sort of evil.

26   He was especially guilty because he worshiped idols just as the Amorites did — the people whom the Lord had chased out of the land to make room for the people of Israel.

---

[2]Literally, "I have found you because you have sold yourself to that which is evil in the sight of the Lord."

27 When Ahab heard these prophecies, he tore his clothing, put on rags, fasted, slept in sackcloth, and went about in deep humility.

28 Then another message came to Elijah:

29 "Do you see how Ahab has humbled himself before Me? Because he has done this, I will not do what I promised during his lifetime; it will happen to his sons; I will destroy his descendants."

CHAPTER 22

F or three years there was no war between Syria and Israel.

2 But during the third year, while King Jehoshaphat of Judah was visiting King Ahab of Israel,

3 Ahab said to his officials, "Do you realize that the Syrians are still occupying our city of Ramoth-gilead? And we're sitting here without doing a thing about it!"

4 Then he turned to Jehoshaphat and asked him, "Will you send your army with mine to recover Ramoth-gilead?"

And King Jehoshaphat of Judah replied, "Of course! You and I are brothers; my people are yours to command, and my horses are at your service.

5 But," he added, "we should ask the Lord first, to be sure of what He wants us to do."

6 So King Ahab summoned his 400 heathen[1] prophets and asked them, "Shall I attack Ramoth-gilead, or not?"

And they all said, "Yes, go ahead, for God

---

[1]Implied. These were evidently the 400 Asherah priests left alive by Elijah at Carmel, though the 450 prophets of Baal were slain. See I Kings 18:19 and 40.

will help you conquer it."

7   But Jehoshaphat asked, "Isn't there a prophet of the Lord here? I'd like to ask him, too."

8   "Well, there's one," King Ahab replied, "but I hate him, for he never prophesies anything good. He always has something gloomy to say. His name is Micaiah, the son of Imlah."

"Oh, come now!" Jehoshaphat replied, "Don't talk like that!"

9   So King Ahab called to one of his aides, "Go get Micaiah. Hurry!"

10   Meanwhile, all the prophets continued prophesying before the two kings, who were dressed in their royal robes and were sitting on thrones placed on the threshing floor near the city gate.

11   One of the prophets, Zedekiah (son of Chenaanah), made some iron horns and declared, "The Lord promises that you will push the Syrians around with these horns until they are destroyed."

12   And all the others agreed. "Go ahead and attack Ramoth-gilead," they said, "for the Lord will cause you to triumph!"

13   The messenger who went to get Micaiah told him what the other prophets were saying, and urged him to say the same thing.

14   But Micaiah told him, "This I vow, that I will say only what the Lord tells me to!"

15   When he arrived, the king asked him, "Micaiah, shall we attack Ramoth-gilead, or not?"

"Why, of course! Go right ahead!" Micaiah told him. "You will have a great victory, for the Lord will cause you to conquer!"

16   "How many times must I tell you to speak

only what the Lord tells you to?" the king demanded.

17   Then Micaiah told him, "I saw all Israel scattered upon the mountains as sheep without a shepherd. And the Lord said, 'Their king is dead; send them to their homes.' "

18   Turning to Jehoshaphat, Ahab complained, "Didn't I tell you this would happen? He *never* tells me anything good. It's *always* bad."

19   Then Micaiah said, "Listen to this further word from the Lord. I saw the Lord sitting on His throne, and the armies of heaven stood around Him.

20   Then the Lord said, 'Who will entice Ahab to go and die at Ramoth-gilead?' Various suggestions were made,

21   Until one angel approached the Lord and said, 'I'll do it!'

22   'How?' the Lord asked.

And he replied, 'I will go as a lying spirit in the mouths of all his prophets.'

And the Lord said, 'That will do it; you will succeed. Go ahead.'

23   Don't you see? The Lord has put a lying spirit in the mouths of all these prophets, but the fact of the matter is that the Lord has decreed disaster upon you."

24   Then Zedekiah (son of Chenaanah) walked over and slapped Micaiah on the face.

"When did the Spirit of the Lord leave me and speak to you?" he demanded.

25   And Micaiah replied, "You will have the answer to your question when you find yourself hiding in an inner room."

26   Then King Ahab ordered Micaiah's arrest.

"Take him to Amon, the mayor of the city, and to my son Joash.

27   Tell them, 'The king says to put this fellow in jail and feed him with bread and water — and only enough to keep him alive[2] — until I return in peace.' "

28   "If you return in peace," Micaiah replied, "it will prove that the Lord has not spoken through me." Then he turned to the people standing nearby and said, "Take note of what I've said."

29   So King Ahab of Israel and King Jehoshaphat of Judah led their armies to Ramoth-gilead.

30   Ahab said to Jehoshaphat, "You wear your royal robes, but I'll not wear mine!"

So Ahab went into the battle disguised in an ordinary soldier's uniform.

31   For the king of Syria had commanded his thirty-two chariot captains to fight no one except King Ahab himself.

32, 33   When they saw King Jehoshaphat in his royal robes, they thought, 'That's the man we're after.' So they wheeled around to attack him. But when Jehoshaphat shouted out to identify himself,[3] they turned back!

34   However, someone shot an arrow at random and it struck King Ahab between the joints of his armor.

"Take me out of the battle, for I am badly wounded," he groaned to his chariot driver.

35   The battle became more and more intense as the day wore on, and King Ahab went back in, propped up in his chariot with the blood from his

[2]Literally, "as though the city were under siege."
[3]Implied.

wound running down onto the floorboards. Finally, toward evening, he died.

36, 37   Just as the sun was going down the cry ran through his troops. "It's all over — return home! The king is dead!"

And his body was taken to Samaria and buried there.

38   When his chariot and armor were washed beside the pool of Samaria, where the prostitutes bathed, dogs came and licked the king's blood just as the Lord had said would happen.

39   The rest of Ahab's history — including the story of the ivory palace and the cities he built — is written in *The Annals of the Kings of Israel.*

40   So Ahab was buried among his ancestors, and Ahaziah his son became the new king of Israel.

*   *   *   *

41   Meanwhile, over in Judah, Jehoshaphat the son of Asa had become king during the fourth year of the reign of King Ahab of Israel.

42   Jehoshaphat was thirty-five years old when he ascended the throne, and he reigned in Jerusalem for twenty-five years. His mother was Azubah, the daughter of Shilhi.

43   He did as his father Asa had done, obeying the Lord in all but one thing: he did not destroy the shrines on the hills, so the people sacrificed and burned incense there.

44   He also made peace with Ahab, the king of Israel.

45   The rest of the deeds of Jehoshaphat and his

heroic achievements and his wars are described in
The Annals of the Kings of Judah.

46 He also closed all the houses of male prostitution that still continued from the days of his father Asa.

47 (There was no king in Edom at that time, only a deputy.)

48 King Jehoshaphat built great freighters to sail to Ophir for gold; but they never arrived, for they were wrecked at Ezion-geber.

49 Ahaziah, King Ahab's son and successor, had proposed to Jehoshaphat that his men go too, but Jehoshaphat had refused the offer.

50 When King Jehoshaphat died he was buried with his ancestors in Jerusalem, the city of his forefather David; and his son Jehoram took the throne.

51 It was during the seventeenth year of the reign of King Jehoshaphat of Judah that Ahaziah, Ahab's son, began to reign over Israel in Samaria; and he reigned two years.

52, 53 But he was not a good king, for he followed in the footsteps of his father and mother and of Jeroboam, who had led Israel into the sin of worshiping idols. So Ahaziah made the Lord God of Israel very angry.

II Kings

CHAPTER 1

After King Ahab's death the nation of Moab declared its independence and refused to pay tribute to Israel any longer.

*   *   *   *   *

2 Israel's new king, Ahaziah, had fallen off the upstairs porch of his palace at Samaria and was seriously injured. He sent messengers to the temple of the god Baal-zebub at Ekron to ask whether he would recover.

3 But an angel of the Lord told Elijah the prophet,[1] "Go and meet the messengers and ask them, 'Is it true that there is no God in Israel? Is that why you are going to Baal-zebub, the god of Ekron, to ask whether the king will get well?

4, 5 Because King Ahaziah has done this, the Lord says that he will never leave the bed he is lying on; he will surely die.' "

When Elijah told the messengers this, they returned immediately to the king.

"Why have you returned so soon?" he asked them.

6 "A man came up to us," they said, "and told us to go back to the king and tell him, 'The Lord wants to know why you are asking questions of Baal-

---

[1]Literally, "Elijah the Tishbite."

zebub, the god of Ekron. Is it because there is no God in Israel? Now, since you have done this, you will not leave the bed you are lying on; you will surely die.' "

7   "Who was this fellow?" the king demanded. "What did he look like?"

8   "He was a hairy man," they replied, "with a wide leather belt."

"It was Elijah the prophet!" the king exclaimed.

9   Then he sent an army captain with fifty soldiers to arrest him. They found him sitting on top of a hill.

The captain said to him, "O man of God, the king has commanded you to come along with us."

10   But Elijah replied, "If I am a man of God, let fire come down from heaven and destroy you and your fifty men!" Then lightning struck them and killed them all!

11   So the king sent another captain with fifty men to demand, "O man of God, the king says that you must come down right away."

12   Elijah replied, "If I am a man of God, let fire come down from heaven and destroy you and your fifty men." And again the fire from God burned them up.

13   Once more the king sent fifty men, but this time the captain fell to his knees before Elijah and pleaded with him, "O man of God, please spare my life and the lives of these, your fifty servants.

14   Have mercy on us! Don't destroy us as you did the others."

15   Then the angel of the Lord said to Elijah,

"Don't be afraid. Go with him." So Elijah went to the king.

16 "Why did you send messengers to Baal-zebub, the god of Ekron, to ask about your sickness?" Elijah demanded. "Is it because there is no god in Israel to ask? Because you have done this, you shall not leave this bed; you will surely die."

17 So Ahaziah died as the Lord had predicted through Elijah, and his brother Jehoram became the new king — for Ahaziah did not have a son to succeed him. This occurred in the second year of the reign of King Jehoram (son of Jehoshaphat) of Judah.

18 The rest of the history of Ahaziah's reign is recorded in *The Annals of the Kings of Israel.*

CHAPTER 2

Now the time came for the Lord to take Elijah to heaven — by means of a whirlwind! Elijah said to Elisha as they left Gilgal, "Stay here, for the Lord has told me to go to Bethel."

But Elisha replied, "I swear to God that I won't leave you!" So they went on together to Bethel.

3 There the young prophets of Bethel Seminary came out to meet them and asked Elisha, "Did you know that the Lord is going to take Elijah away from you today?"

"Quiet!" Elisha snapped. "Of course I know it."

4 Then Elijah said to Elisha, "Please stay here in Bethel, for the Lord has sent me to Jericho."

But Elisha replied again, "I swear to God that I won't leave you." So they went on together to Jericho.

5 Then the students at Jericho Seminary came to Elisha and asked him, "Do you know that the Lord is going to take away your master today?"

"Will you please be quiet?" he commanded. "Of course I know it!"

6, 7 Then Elijah said to Elisha, "Please stay here, for the Lord has sent me to the Jordan River."

But Elisha replied as before, "I swear to God that I won't leave you."

So they went on together and stood beside the Jordan River as fifty of the young prophets watched from a distance.

8 Then Elijah folded his cloak together and struck the water with it; and the river divided and they went across on dry ground!

9 When they arrived on the other side Elijah said to Elisha, "What wish shall I grant you before I am taken away?"

And Elisha replied, "Please grant me twice as much prophetic power as you have had."

10 "You have asked a hard thing," Elijah replied. "If you see me when I am taken from you, then you will get your request. But if not, then you won't."

11 As they were walking along, talking, suddenly a chariot of fire, drawn by horses of fire, appeared and drove between them, separating them, and Elijah was carried by a whirlwind into heaven.

12 Elisha saw it and cried out, "My father! My father! The Chariot of Israel and the charioteers!" As they disappeared from sight he tore his robe.

13, 14 Then he picked up Elijah's cloak and returned to the bank of the Jordan River, and struck the water with it.

"Where is the Lord God of Elijah?" he cried out. And the water parted and Elisha went across!

15 When the young prophets of Jericho saw what had happened, they exclaimed, "The spirit of Elijah rests upon Elisha!" And they went to meet him and greeted him respectfully.

16 "Sir," they said, "just say the word and fifty of our best athletes will search the wilderness for your master; perhaps the Spirit of the Lord has left him on some mountain or in some ravine."

"No," Elisha said, "don't bother."

17 But they kept urging until he was embarrassed, and finally said, "All right, go ahead." Then fifty men searched for three days, but didn't find him.

18 Elisha was still at Jericho when they returned. "Didn't I tell you not to go?" he growled.

19 Now a delegation of the city officials of Jericho visited Elisha. "We have a problem," they told him. "This city is located in beautiful natural surroundings, as you can see; but the water is bad, and causes our women to have miscarriages."[1]

20 "Well," he said, "bring me a new bowl filled with salt." So they brought it to him.

21 Then he went out to the city well and threw the salt in and declared, "The Lord has healed these waters. They shall no longer cause death or miscarriage."

22 And sure enough! The water was purified, just as Elisha had said.

23 From Jericho he went to Bethel. As he was walking along the road, some young boys from the city began mocking and making fun of him because of

---

[1]Implied in verse 21. Literally, "the land is unfruitful."

his bald head.

24   He turned around and cursed them in the name of the Lord; and two female bears came out of the woods and killed forty-two of them.

25   Then he went to Mount Carmel and finally returned to Samaria.

CHAPTER 3

A hab's son Jehoram began his reign over Israel during the eighteenth year of the reign of King Jehoshaphat[1] of Judah; and he reigned twelve years. His capital was Samaria.

2   He was a very evil man, but not as wicked as his father and mother had been, for he at least tore down the pillar to Baal that his father had made.

3   Nevertheless he still clung to the great sin of Jeroboam (the son of Nebat), who had led the people of Israel into the worship of idols.

4   King Mesha of Moab and his people were sheep ranchers. They paid Israel an annual tribute of 100,000 lambs and the wool of 100,000 rams;

5   But after Ahab's death, the king of Moab rebelled against Israel.

6, 7, 8   So King Jehoram mustered the Israeli army and sent this message to King Jehoshaphat of Judah:

"The king of Moab has rebelled against me. Will you help me fight him?"

"Of course I will," Jehoshaphat replied. "My people and horses are yours to command. What are your battle plans?"

---

[1]Chapter 1, verse 17, says King Jehoram was the king of Judah at this time. Possibly there was a co-regency.

"We'll attack from the wilderness of Edom," Jehoram replied.

9 So their two armies, now joined also by troops from Edom, moved along a roundabout route through the wilderness for seven days; but there was no water for the men or their pack animals.

10 "Oh, what shall we do?" the king of Israel cried out. "The Lord has brought us here to let the king of Moab defeat us."

11 But Jehoshaphat, the king of Judah, asked, "Isn't there a prophet of the Lord with us? If so, we can find out what to do!"

"Elisha is here," one of the king of Israel's officers replied. Then he added, "He was Elijah's assistant."

12 "Fine," Jehoshaphat said. "He's just the man we want."[2] So the kings of Israel, Judah, and Edom went to consult Elisha.

13 "I want no part of you," Elisha snarled at King Jehoram of Israel. "Go to the false prophets of your father and mother!"

But King Jehoram replied, "No! For it is the Lord who has called us here to be destroyed by the king of Moab!"

14 "I swear by the Lord God that I wouldn't bother with you except for the presence of King Jehoshaphat of Judah," Elisha replied.

15 "Now bring me someone to play the lute." And as the lute was played, the message of the Lord came to Elisha:

16 "The Lord says to fill this dry valley with trenches to hold the water He will send.

---

[2]Literally, "the word of the Lord is with him."

17 You won't see wind nor rain, but this valley will be filled with water, and you will have plenty for yourselves and for your animals!

18 But this is only the beginning, for the Lord will make you victorious over the army of Moab!

19 You will conquer the best of their cities — even those that are fortified — and ruin all the good land with stones."

20 And sure enough, the next day at about the time when the morning sacrifice was offered — look! Water! It was flowing from the direction of Edom; and soon there was water everywhere.

21 Meanwhile, when the people of Moab heard about the three armies marching against them, they mobilized every man who could fight, old and young, and stationed themselves along their frontier.

22 But early the next morning the sun looked red as it shone across the water!

23 "Blood!" they exclaimed. "The three armies have attacked and killed each other! Let's go and collect the loot!"

24 But when they arrived at the Israeli camp, the army of Israel rushed out and began killing them; and the army of Moab fled. Then the men of Israel moved forward into the land of Moab, destroying everything as they went.

25 They destroyed the cities, threw stones on every good piece of land, stopped up the wells, and felled the fruit trees; finally, only Fort Kir-hareseth was left, but even that finally fell to them.[3]

26 When the king of Moab saw that the battle had been lost, he led 700 of his swordsmen in a last

[3]Literally, "the slingers surrounded and conquered it."

desperate attempt to break through to the king of Edom; but he failed.

27 Then he took his oldest son, who was to have been the next king, and to the horror of the Israeli army, killed him and sacrificed him as a burnt offering upon the wall. So the army of Israel turned back in disgust to their own land.

CHAPTER 4

One day the wife of one of the seminary students came to Elisha to tell him of her husband's death. He was a man who had loved God, she said. But he had owed some money when he died, and now the creditor was demanding it back. If she didn't pay, he said he would take her two sons as his slaves.

2 "What shall I do?" Elisha asked, "How much food do you have in the house?"

"Nothing at all, except a jar of olive oil," she replied.

3 "Then borrow many pots and pans from your friends and neighbors!" he instructed.

4 "Go into your house with your sons and shut the door behind you. Then pour olive oil from your jar into the pots and pans, setting them aside as they are filled!"

5 So she did. Her sons brought the pots and pans to her, and she filled one after another!

6 Soon every container was full to the brim! "Bring me another jar," she said to her sons.

"There aren't any more!" they told her. And then the oil stopped flowing!

7 When she told the prophet what had hap-

pened, he said to her, "Go and sell the oil and pay your debt, and there will be enough money left for you and your sons to live on!"

8   One day Elisha went to Shunem. A prominent woman of the city invited him in to eat, and afterwards, whenever he passed that way, he stopped for dinner.

9   She said to her husband, "I'm sure this man who stops in from time to time is a holy prophet.

10   Let's make a little room for him on the roof; we can put in a bed, a table, a chair, and a lamp, and he will have a place to stay whenever he comes by."

11, 12   Once when he was resting in the room he said to his servant Gehazi, "Tell the woman I want to speak to her." When she came,

13   He said to Gehazi, "Tell her that we appreciate her kindness to us. Now ask her what we can do for her. Does she want me to put in a good word for her to the king or to the general of the army?"

"No," she replied, "I am perfectly content."

14   "What can we do for her?" he asked Gehazi afterwards.

He suggested, "She doesn't have a son, and her husband is an old man."

15, 16   "Call her back again," Elisha told him.

When she returned, he talked to her as she stood in the doorway. "Next year at about this time you shall have a son!"

"O man of God," she exclaimed, "don't lie to me like that!"

17   But it was true; the woman soon conceived

and had a baby boy the following year, just as Elisha had predicted.

18   One day when her child was older, he went out to visit his father, who was working with the reapers.

19   He complained about a headache, and soon was moaning in pain. His father said to one of the servants, "Carry him home to his mother."

20   So he took him home, and his mother held him on her lap; but around noontime he died.

21   She carried him up to the bed of the prophet and shut the door;

22   Then she sent a message to her husband: "Send one of the servants and a donkey so that I can hurry to the prophet and come right back."

23   "Why today?" he asked. "This isn't a religious holiday."

But she said, "It's important. I must go."

24   So she saddled the donkey and said to the servant, "Hurry! Don't slow down for my comfort unless I tell you to."

25   As she approached Mount Carmel, Elisha saw her in the distance and said to Gehazi, "Look, that woman from Shunem is coming.

26   Run and meet her and ask her what the trouble is. See if her husband is all right and if the child is well."

"Yes," she told Gehazi, "everything is fine."

27   But when she came to Elisha at the mountain she fell to the ground before him and caught hold of his feet. Gehazi began to push her away, but the prophet said, "Let her alone; something is deeply troubling her and the Lord hasn't told me what it is."

28   Then she said, "It was you who said I'd have a son. And I begged you not to lie to me!"

29   Then he said to Gehazi, "Quick, take my staff! Don't talk to anyone along the way. Hurry! Lay the staff upon the child's face."

30   But the boy's mother said, "I swear to God that I won't go home without you." So Elisha returned with her.

31   Gehazi went on ahead and laid the staff upon the child's face, but nothing happened. There was no sign of life. He returned to meet Elisha and told him, "The child is still dead."

32   When Elisha arrived, the child was indeed dead, lying there upon the prophet's bed.

33   He went in and shut the door behind him and prayed to the Lord.

34   Then he lay upon the child's body, placing his mouth upon the child's mouth, and his eyes upon the child's eyes, and his hands upon the child's hands. And the child's body began to grow warm again!

35   Then the prophet went down and walked back and forth in the house a few times; returning upstairs, he stretched himself again upon the child. This time the little boy sneezed seven times and opened his eyes!

36   Then the prophet summoned Gehazi. "Call her!" he said. And when she came in, he said, "Here's your son!"

37   She fell to the floor at his feet and then picked up her son and went out.

38   Elisha now returned to Gilgal, but there was a famine in the land. One day as he was teaching the young prophets, he said to Gehazi, "Make some stew for supper for these men."

39 One of the young men went out into the field to gather vegetables and came back with some wild gourds. He shredded them and put them into a kettle without realizing that they were poisonous.

40 But after the men had eaten a bite or two they cried out, "Oh, sir, there's poison in this stew!"

41 "Bring me some meal," Elisha said. He threw it into the kettle and said, "Now it's all right! Go ahead and eat!" And then it didn't harm them.

42 One day a man from Baal-shalishah brought Elisha a sack of fresh corn[1] and twenty individual loaves of barley bread made from the first grain of his harvest. Elisha told Gehazi to use it to feed the young prophets.

43 "What?" Gehazi exclaimed. "Feed one hundred men with only this?"

But Elisha said, "Go ahead, for the Lord says there will be plenty for all, and some will even be left over!"

44 And sure enough, there was, just as the Lord had said!

CHAPTER 5

The king of Syria had high admiration for Naaman, the commander-in-chief of his army, for he had led his troops to many glorious victories. So he was a great hero, but he was a leper.

2 Bands of Syrians had invaded the land of Israel and among their captives was a little girl who had been given to Naaman's wife as a maid.

3 One day the little girl said to her mistress, "I wish my master would go to see the prophet in Sa-

---

[1]Literally, "fresh grain."

maria. He would heal him of his leprosy!"

4 Naaman told the king what the little girl had said.

5 "Go and visit the prophet," the king told him. "I will send a letter of introduction for you to carry to the king of Israel."

So Naaman started out, taking gifts of $20,000 in silver, $60,000 in gold, and ten suits of clothing.

6 The letter to the king of Israel said: "The man bringing this letter is my servant Naaman; I want you to heal him of his leprosy."

7 When the king of Israel read it, he tore his clothes and said, "This man sends me a leper to heal! Am I God, that I can kill and give life? He is only trying to get an excuse to invade us again."

8 But when Elisha the prophet heard about the king of Israel's plight, he sent this message to him: "Why are you so upset? Send Naaman to me, and he will learn that there is a true prophet of God here in Israel."

9 So Naaman arrived with his horses and chariots and stood at the door of Elisha's home.

10 Elisha sent a messenger out to tell him to go and wash in the Jordan River seven times and he would be healed of every trace of his leprosy!

11 But Naaman was angry and stalked away. "Look," he said, "I thought at least he would come out and talk to me! I expected him to wave his hand over the leprosy and call upon the name of the Lord his God, and heal me!

12 Aren't the Abana River and Pharpar River of Damascus better than all the rivers of Israel put together? If it's rivers I need, I'll wash at home and

get rid of my leprosy." So he went away in a rage.

13 But his officers tried to reason with him and said, "If the prophet had told you to do some great thing, wouldn't you have done it? So you should certainly obey him when he says simply to go and wash and be cured!"

14 So Naaman went down to the Jordan River and dipped himself seven times, as the prophet had told him to. And his flesh became as healthy as a little child's, and he was healed!

15 Then he and his entire party went back to find the prophet; they stood humbly before him and Naaman said, "I know at last that there is no God in all the world except in Israel; now please accept my gifts."

16 But Elisha replied, "I swear by Jehovah my God that I will not accept them."

Naaman urged him to take them, but he absolutely refused.

17 "Well," Naaman said, "all right. But please give me two mule-loads of earth to take back with me, for from now on I will never again offer any burnt offerings or sacrifices to any other God except the Lord.[1]

18 However, may the Lord pardon me this one thing — when my master the king goes into the temple of the god Rimmon to worship there and leans on my arm, may the Lord pardon me when I bow too."

19 "All right," Elisha said. So Naaman started home again.

20 But Gehazi, Elisha's servant, said to himself, "My master shouldn't have let this fellow get away

---

[1]Thus even in a foreign land he could worship Jehovah on Israel's soil.

without taking his gifts. I will chase after him and get something from him."

21 So Gehazi caught up with him. When Naaman saw him coming, he jumped down from his chariot and ran to meet him.

"Is everything all right?" he asked.

22 "Yes," he said, "but my master has sent me to tell you that two young prophets from the hills of Ephraim have just arrived, and he would like $2,000 in silver and two suits to give to them."

23 "Take $4,000," Naaman insisted. He gave him two expensive robes, tied up the money in two bags, and gave them to two of his servants to carry back with Gehazi.

24 But when they arrived at the hill where Elisha lived,[2] Gehazi took the bags from the servants and sent the men back. Then he hid the money in his house.

25 When he went in to his master, Elisha asked him, "Where have you been, Gehazi?"

"I haven't been anywhere," he replied.

26 But Elisha asked him, "Don't you realize that I was there in thought when Naaman stepped down from his chariot to meet you? Is this the time to receive money and clothing and olive farms and vineyards and sheep and oxen and servants?

27 Because you have done this, Naaman's leprosy shall be upon you and upon your children and your children's children forever."

And Gehazi walked from the room a leper, his skin as white as snow.

---

[2]Implied.

CHAPTER 6

One day the seminary students came to Elisha and told him, "As you can see, our dormitory is too small. Tell us, as our president, whether we can build a new one down beside the Jordan River, where there are plenty of logs."

"All right," he told them, "go ahead."

3 "Please, sir, come with us," someone suggested. "I will," he said.

4 When they arrived at the Jordan, they began cutting down trees;

5 But as one of them was chopping, his axhead fell into the river. "Oh, sir," he cried, "it was borrowed!"

6 "Where did it fall?" the prophet asked. The youth showed him the place, and Elisha cut a stick and threw it into the water; and the axhead rose to the surface and floated!

7 "Grab it," Elisha said to him; and he did.

8 Once when the king of Syria was at war with Israel, he said to his officers, "We will mobilize our forces at _____," (naming the place).

9 Immediately Elisha warned the king of Israel, "Don't go near _____!" (naming the same place) for the Syrians are planning to mobilize their troops there!"

10 The king sent a scout to see if Elisha was right, and sure enough, he had saved him from disaster. This happened several times.

11 The king of Syria was puzzled. He called together his officers and demanded, "Which of you is

the traitor? Who has been informing the king of Israel about my plans?"

12 "It's not us, sir," one of the officers replied. "Elisha, the prophet, tells the king of Israel even the words you speak in the privacy of your bedroom!"

13 "Go and find out where he is, and we'll send troops to seize him," the king exclaimed.

And the report came back, "Elisha is at Dothan."

14 So one night the king of Syria sent a great army with many chariots and horses to surround the city.

15 When the prophet's servant got up early the next morning and went outside, there were troops, horses, and chariots everywhere.

"Alas, my master, what shall we do now?" he cried out to Elisha.

16 "Don't be afraid!" Elisha told him, "for our army is bigger than theirs!"

17 Then Elisha prayed, "Lord, open his eyes and let him see!" And the Lord opened the young man's eyes so that he could see horses of fire and chariots of fire everywhere upon the mountain!

18 As the Syrian army advanced upon them, Elisha prayed, "Lord, please make them blind." And He did.

19 Then Elisha went out and told them, "You've come the wrong way! This isn't the right city! Follow me and I will take you to the man you're looking for." And he led them to Samaria!

20 As soon as they arrived Elisha prayed, "Lord, now open their eyes and let them see." And the Lord did, and they discovered that they were in Samaria, the capital city of Israel!

21 When the king of Israel saw them, he shouted to Elisha, "Oh, sir, shall I kill them? Shall I kill them?"

22 "Of course not!" Elisha told him. "Do we kill prisoners of war? Give them food and drink and send them home again."

23 So the king made a great feast for them, and then sent them home to their king. And after that the Syrian raiders stayed away from the land of Israel.

24 Later on, however, King Ben-hadad of Syria mustered his entire army and besieged Samaria.

25 As a result there was a great famine in the city, and after a long while even a donkey's head sold for fifty dollars and a pint of dove's dung brought three dollars!

26-30 One day as the king of Israel was walking along the wall of the city, a woman called to him, "Help, my lord the king!"

"If the Lord doesn't help you, what can I do?" he retorted. "I have neither food nor wine to give you. However, what's the matter?"

She replied, "This woman proposed that we eat my son one day and her son the next. So we boiled my son and ate him, but the next day when I said, 'Kill your son so we can eat him,' she hid him."

When the king heard this he tore his clothes. (The people watching noticed through the rip he tore in them that he was wearing an inner robe made of sackcloth next to his flesh.)

31 "May God kill me if I don't execute Elisha this very day," the king vowed.

32 Elisha was sitting in his house at a meeting with the elders of Israel when the king sent a messenger to summon him. But before the messenger ar-

rived Elisha said to the elders, "This murderer has sent a man to kill me. When he arrives, shut the door and keep him out, for his master will soon follow him."

33   While Elisha was still saying this, the messenger arrived [followed by the king[1]].

"The Lord has caused this mess," the king stormed. "Why should I expect any help from Him?"

CHAPTER 7

Elisha replied, "The Lord says that by this time tomorrow two gallons of flour or four gallons of barley grain will be sold in the markets of Samaria for a dollar!"

2   The officer assisting the king said, "That couldn't happen if the Lord made windows in the sky!"

But Elisha replied, "You will see it happen, but you won't be able to buy any of it!"

3   Now there were four lepers sitting outside the city gates.

"Why sit here until we die?" they asked each other.

4   "We will starve if we stay here and we will starve if we go back into the city; so we might as well go out and surrender to the Syrian army. If they let us live, so much the better; but if they kill us, we would have died anyway."

5   So that evening they went out to the camp of the Syrians, but there was no one there!

6   (For the Lord had made the whole Syrian army hear the clatter of speeding chariots and a loud gal-

---

[1]Implied.

loping of horses and the sounds of a great army approaching. "The king of Israel has hired the Hittites and Egyptians to attack us," they cried out.

7   So they panicked and fled into the night, abandoning their tents, horses, donkeys, and everything else.)

8   When the lepers arrived at the edge of the camp they went into one tent after another, eating, drinking wine, and carrying out silver and gold and clothing and hiding it.

9   Finally they said to each other, "This isn't right. This is wonderful news, and we aren't sharing it with anyone! Even if we wait until morning, some terrible calamity will certainly fall upon us; come on, let's go back and tell the people at the palace."

10   So they went back to the city and told the watchmen what had happened — they had gone out to the Syrian camp and no one was there! The horses and donkeys were tethered and the tents were all in order, but there was not a soul around.

11   Then the watchmen shouted the news to those in the palace.

12   The king got out of bed and told his officers, "I know what has happened. The Syrians know we are starving, so they have left their camp and have hidden in the fields, thinking that we will be lured out of the city. Then they will attack us and make slaves of us and get in."

13   One of his officers replied, "We'd better send out scouts to see. Let them take five of the remaining horses — if something happens to the animals it won't be any greater loss than if they stay here and die with the rest of us!"

14　Four chariot-horses were found and the king sent out two charioteers to see where the Syrians had gone.

15　They followed a trail of clothing and equipment all the way to the Jordan River — thrown away by the Syrians in their haste. The scouts returned and told the king,

16　And the people of Samaria rushed out and plundered the camp of the Syrians. So it was true that two gallons of flour and four gallons of barley were sold that day for one dollar, just as the Lord had said!

17　The king appointed his special assistant to control the traffic at the gate, but he was knocked down and trampled and killed as the people rushed out. This is what Elisha had predicted on the previous day when the king had come to arrest him,

18　And the prophet had told the king that flour and barley would sell for so little on the following day.

19　The king's officer had replied, "That couldn't happen even if the Lord opened the windows of heaven!"

And the prophet had said, "You will see it happen, but you won't be able to buy any of it!"

20　And he couldn't, for the people trampled him to death at the gate!

CHAPTER 8

E lisha had told the woman whose son he had brought back to life, "Take your family and move to some other country, for the Lord has called down a famine on Israel that will last for seven years."

2   So the woman took her family and lived in the land of the Philistines for seven years.

3   After the famine ended, she returned to the land of Israel and went to see the king about getting back her house and land.

4   Just as she came in, the king was talking with Gehazi, Elisha's servant, and saying, "Tell me some stories of the great things Elisha has done."

5   And Gehazi was telling the king about the time when Elisha brought a little boy back to life. At that very moment, the mother of the boy walked in!

"Oh, sir!" Gehazi exclaimed, "Here is the woman now, and this is her son — the very one Elisha brought back to life!"

6   "Is this true?" the king asked her. And she told him that it was. So he directed one of his officials to see to it that everything she had owned was restored to her, plus the value of any crops that had been harvested during her absence.

7   Afterwards Elisha went to Damascus (the capital of Syria), where King Ben-hadad lay sick. Someone told the king that the prophet had come.

8, 9   When the king heard the news, he said to Hazael, "Take a present to the man of God and tell him to ask the Lord whether I will get well again."

So Hazael took forty camel-loads of the best produce of the land as presents for Elisha and said to him, "Your son Ben-hadad, the king of Syria, has sent me to ask you whether he will recover."

10   And Elisha replied, "Tell him, 'Yes.' But the Lord has shown me that he will surely die!"

11   Elisha stared at Hazael until he became embarrassed, and then Elisha started crying.

12 "What's the matter, sir?" Hazael asked him.

Elisha replied, "I know the terrible things you will do to the people of Israel: you will burn their forts, kill the young men, dash their babies against the rocks, and rip open the bellies of the pregnant women!"

13 "Am I a dog?" Hazael asked him. "I would *never* do that sort of thing."

But Elisha replied, "The Lord has shown me that you are going to be the king of Syria."

14 When Hazael went back, the king asked him, "What did he tell you?"

And Hazael replied, "He told me that you would recover."

15 But the next day Hazael took a blanket and dipped it in water and held it over the king's face until he smothered to death. And Hazael became king instead.

*   *   *   *   *

16 King Jehoram, the son of King Jehoshaphat of Judah, began his reign during the fifth year of the reign of King Joram of Israel, the son of Ahab.

17 Jehoram was thirty-two years old when he became king, and he reigned in Jerusalem for eight years.

18 But he was as wicked as Ahab and the other kings of Israel; he even married one of Ahab's daughters.

19 Nevertheless, because God had promised His servant David that He would watch over and guide his descendants, He did not destroy Judah.

20 During Jehoram's reign, the people in Edom revolted from Judah and appointed their own king.

21　King Jehoram[1] tried unsuccessfully to crush the rebellion: he crossed the Jordan River and attacked the city of Zair, but was quickly surrounded by the army of Edom. Under cover of night he broke through their ranks, but his army deserted him and fled.

22　So Edom has maintained its independence to this day. Libnah also rebelled at that time.

23　The rest of the history of King Joram is written in *The Annals of the Kings of Judah.*

24, 25　He died and was buried in the royal cemetery in the City of David — the old section of Jerusalem. Then his son Ahaziah[2] became the new king during the twelfth year of the reign of King Joram of Israel, the son of Ahab.

26　Ahaziah was twenty-two years old when he began to reign but he reigned only one year, in Jerusalem. His mother was Athaliah, the granddaughter of King Omri of Israel.

27　He was an evil king, just as all of King Ahab's descendants were — for he was related to Ahab by marriage.

28　He joined King Joram of Israel (son of Ahab) in his war against Hazael, the king of Syria, at Ramoth-gilead.

King Joram was wounded in the battle,

29　So he went to Jezreel to rest and recover from his wounds. While he was there, King Ahaziah of Judah (son of Jehoram) came to visit him.

---

[1]Literally, "Joram."

[2]Ahaziah is an alternate form of the name Jehoshaz.

CHAPTER 9

Meanwhile Elisha had summoned one of the young prophets. "Get ready to go to Ramoth-gilead," he told him. "Take this vial of oil with you,

2 And find Jehu (the son of Jehoshaphat, the son of Nimshi). Call him into a private room away from his friends,

3 And pour the oil over his head. Tell him that the Lord has anointed him to be the king of Israel; then run for your life!"

4 So the young prophet did as he was told. When he arrived in Ramoth-gilead,

5 He found Jehu sitting around with the other army officers.

"I have a message for you, sir," he said.

"For which one of us?" Jehu asked.

"For you," he replied.

6 So Jehu left the others and went into the house, and the young man poured the oil over his head and said, "The Lord God of Israel says, 'I anoint you king of the Lord's people, Israel.

7 You are to destroy the family of Ahab; you will avenge the murder of My prophets and of all My other people who were killed by Jezebel.

8 The entire family of Ahab must be wiped out — every male, no matter who.

9 I will destroy the family of Ahab as I destroyed the families of Jeroboam (son of Nebat) and of Baasha (son of Ahijah).

10 Dogs shall eat Ahab's wife Jezebel at Jezreel, and no one will bury her.' "

Then he opened the door and ran.

11 Jehu went back to his friends and one of them asked him, "What did that crazy fellow want? Is everything all right?"

"You know very well who he was and what he wanted," Jehu replied.

12 "No, we don't," they said. "Tell us."

So he told them what the man had said and that he had been anointed king of Israel!

13 They quickly carpeted the bare steps with their coats and blew a trumpet, shouting, "Jehu is king!"

14 That is how Jehu (son of Jehoshaphat, son of Nimshi) rebelled against King Joram. (King Joram had been with the army at Ramoth-gilead, defending Israel against the forces of King Hazael of Syria.

15 But he had returned to Jezreel to recover from his wounds.)

"Since you want me to be king," Jehu told the men who were with him, "don't let anyone escape to Jezreel to report what we have done."

16 Then Jehu jumped into a chariot and rode to Jezreel himself to find King Joram, who was lying there wounded. (King Ahaziah of Judah was there too, for he had gone to visit him.)

17 The watchman on the Tower of Jezreel saw Jehu and his company approaching and shouted, "Someone is coming."

"Send out a rider and find out if he is friend or foe," King Joram shouted back.

18 So a soldier rode out to meet Jehu. "The king wants to know whether you are friend or foe," he demanded. "Do you come in peace?"

Jehu replied, "What do you know about peace? Get behind me!"

The watchman called out to the king that the messenger had met them but was not returning.

19 So the king sent out a second rider. He rode up to them and demanded in the name of the king to know whether their intentions were friendly or not.

Jehu answered, "What do you know about friendliness? Get behind me!"

20 "He isn't returning either!" the watchman exclaimed. "It must be Jehu, for he is driving so furiously."

21 "Quick! Get my chariot ready!" King Joram commanded.

Then he and King Ahaziah of Judah rode out to meet Jehu. They met him at the field of Naboth,

22 And King Joram demanded, "Do you come as a friend, Jehu?"

Jehu replied, "How can there be friendship as long as the evils of your mother Jezebel are all around us?"

23 Then King Joram reined the chariot-horses around and fled, shouting to King Ahaziah, "There is treachery, Ahaziah! Treason!"

24 Then Jehu drew his bow with his full strength and shot Joram between the shoulders; and the arrow pierced his heart, and he sank down dead in his chariot.

25 Jehu said to Bidkar, his assistant, "Throw him into the field of Naboth, for once when you and I were riding along behind his father Ahab, the Lord revealed this prophecy to me:

26 'I will repay him here on Naboth's property for

the murder of Naboth and his sons.' So throw him out on Naboth's field, just as the Lord said."

27 Meanwhile, King Ahaziah of Judah had fled along the road to Beth-haggan. Jehu rode after him, shouting, "Shoot him, too."

So they shot him in his chariot at the place where the road climbs to Gur, near Ibleam. He was able to go on as far as Megiddo, but died there.

28 His officials took him by chariot to Jerusalem where they buried him in the royal cemetery.

29 (Ahaziah's reign over Judah had begun in the twelfth[1] year of the reign of King Joram of Israel.)

30 When Jezebel heard that Jehu had come to Jezreel, she painted her eyelids and fixed her hair and sat at a window.

31 When Jehu entered the gate of the palace, she shouted at him, "How are you today, you murderer! You son of a Zimri who murdered his master!"

32 He looked up and saw her at the window and shouted, "Who is on my side?" And two or three eunuchs looked out at him.

33 "Throw her down!" he yelled.

So they threw her out the window, and her blood spattered against the wall and on the horses; and she was trampled by the horses' hoofs.

34 Then Jehu went into the palace for lunch. Afterwards he said, "Someone go and bury this cursed woman, for she is the daughter of a king."

35 But when they went out to bury her, they found only her skull, her feet, and her hands.

36 When they returned and told him, he remarked, "That is just what the Lord said would hap-

---

[1]Implied in II Kings 8:25. Literally, "eleventh."

pen. He told Elijah the prophet that dogs would eat her flesh and that her body would be scattered like manure upon the field, so that no one could tell whose it was."

CHAPTER 10

Then Jehu wrote a letter to the city council of Samaria and to the guardians of Ahab's seventy sons — all of whom were living there.

2, 3 "Upon receipt of this letter, select the best one of Ahab's sons to be your king, and prepare to fight for his throne. For you have chariots and horses and a fortified city and an armory."

4 But they were too frightened to do it. "Two kings couldn't stand against this man! What can we do?" they said.

5 So the manager of palace affairs and the city manager, together with the city council and the guardians of Ahab's sons, sent him this message:

"Jehu, we are your servants and will do anything you tell us to. We have decided that you should be our king instead of one of Ahab's sons."

6 Jehu responded with this message: "If you are on my side and are going to obey me, bring the heads of your master's sons to me at Jezreel at about this time tomorrow."

(These seventy sons of King Ahab were living in the homes of the chief men of the city, where they had been raised since childhood.)

7 When the letter arrived, all seventy of them were murdered, and their heads were packed into baskets and presented to Jehu at Jezreel.

8 When a messenger told Jehu that the heads of

the king's sons had arrived, he said to pile them in two heaps at the entrance of the city gate, and to leave them there until the next morning.

9, 10   In the morning he went out and spoke to the crowd that had gathered around them. "You aren't to blame," he told them. "I conspired against my master and killed him, but I didn't kill his sons! The Lord has done that, for everything He says comes true. He declared through His servant Elijah that this would happen to Ahab's descendants."

11   Jehu then killed all the rest of the members of the family of Ahab who were in Jezreel, as well as all of his important officials, personal friends, and private chaplains. Finally, no one was left who had been close to him in any way.[1]

12   Then he set out for Samaria, and stayed overnight at a shepherd's inn along the way.

13   While he was there he met the brothers of King Ahaziah of Judah.

"Who are you?" he asked them.

And they replied, "We are brothers[2] of King Ahaziah. We are going to Samaria to visit the sons of King Ahab and of the Queen Mother, Jezebel."

14   "Grab them!" Jehu shouted to his men. And he took them out to the cistern and killed all forty-two of them.

15   As he left the inn, he met Jehonadab, the son of Rechab, who was coming to meet him. After they had greeted each other, Jehu said to him, "Are you as loyal to me as I am to you?"

"Yes," Jehonadab replied.

---

[1]Apparently Jehu in his zeal exceeded the Lord's command in this bloodbath, for he was blamed for it by the prophet Hosea (1:4).

[2]Literally, "kinsmen."

"Then give me your hand," Jehu said, and he helped him into the royal chariot.

16 "Now come along with me," Jehu said, "and see how much I have done for the Lord." So Jehonadab rode along with him.

17 When he arrived in Samaria he butchered all of Ahab's friends and relatives, just as Elijah, speaking for the Lord, had predicted. Then Jehu called a meeting of all the people of the city and said to them, "Ahab hardly worshiped Baal at all in comparison to the way I am going to!

18, 19 Summon all the prophets and priests of Baal, and call together all his worshipers. See to it that every one of them comes, for we worshipers of Baal are going to have a great celebration to praise him. Any of Baal's worshipers who don't come will be put to death." But Jehu's plan was to exterminate them.

20, 21 He sent messengers throughout all Israel summoning those who worshiped Baal; and they all came and filled the temple of Baal from one end to the other.

22 He instructed the head of the robing room, "Be sure that every worshiper wears one of the special robes."

23 Then Jehu and Jehonadab (son of Rechab) went into the temple to address the people: "Check to be sure that only those who worship Baal are here; don't let anyone in who worships the Lord!"

24 As the priests of Baal began offering sacrifices and burnt offerings, Jehu surrounded the building with eighty of his men and told them, "If you let anyone escape, you'll pay for it with your own life."

25 As soon as he had finished sacrificing the burnt

offering, Jehu went out and told his officers and men, "Go in and kill the whole bunch of them. Don't let a single one escape."

So they slaughtered them all and dragged their bodies outside. Then Jehu's men went into the inner temple,

26 Dragged out the pillar used for the worship of Baal, and burned it.

27 They wrecked the temple and converted it into a public toilet, which it still is today.

28 Thus Jehu destroyed every trace of Baal from Israel.

29 However, he didn't destroy the golden calves at Bethel and Dan — this was the great sin of Jeroboam (son of Nebat), for it resulted in all Israel sinning.

30 Afterwards the Lord said to Jehu, "You have done well in following My instructions to destroy the dynasty of Ahab. Because of this I will cause your son, your grandson, and your great-grandson to be the kings of Israel."

31 But Jehu didn't follow the Lord God of Israel with all his heart, for he continued to worship Jeroboam's gold calves that had been the cause of such great sin in Israel.

32, 33 At about that time the Lord began to whittle down the size of Israel. King Hazael conquered several sections of the country east of the Jordan River, as well as all of Gilead, Gad, and Reuben; he also conquered parts of Manasseh from the Aroer River in the valley of the Arnon as far as Gilead and Bashan.

34 The rest of Jehu's activities are recorded in *The Annals of the Kings of Israel.*

35 When Jehu died, he was buried in Samaria; and his son Jehoahaz became the new king.

36 In all, Jehu reigned as king of Israel, in Samaria, for twenty-eight years.

CHAPTER 11

When Athaliah, the mother of King Ahaziah of Judah, learned that her son was dead, she killed all of his children,

2, 3 Except for his year-old[1] son Joash. Joash was rescued by his Aunt Jehosheba, who was a sister of King Ahaziah (for she was a daughter of King Jehoram, Ahaziah's father). She stole him away from among the rest of the king's children who were waiting to be slain, and hid him and his nurse in a storeroom of the Temple.[2] They lived there for six years while Athaliah reigned as queen.

4 In the seventh year of Queen Athaliah's reign, Jehoiada the priest[1] summoned the officers of the palace guard and the queen's bodyguard. He met them in the Temple, swore them to secrecy, and showed them the king's son.

5 Then he gave them their instructions: "A third of those who are on duty on the Sabbath are to guard the palace.

6, 7, 8 The other two-thirds shall stand guard at the Temple; surround the king, weapons in hand, and kill anyone who tries to break through. Stay with the king at all times."

9 So the officers followed Jehoiada's instructions.

---

[1]Implied.
[2]This arrangement was practical because Jehosheba was the wife of Jehoiada the High Priest.

They brought to Jehoiada the men who were going off duty on the Sabbath and those who were coming on duty,

10 And he armed them from the supply of spears and shields in the Temple that had belonged to King David.

11 The guards, with weapons ready, stood across the front of the sanctuary, and surrounded the altar, which was near Joash's hideaway.

12 Then Jehoiada brought out the young prince and put the crown upon his head and gave him a copy of the Ten Commandments, and anointed him as king. Then everyone clapped and shouted, "Long live the king!"

13, 14 When Athaliah heard all the noise, she ran into the Temple and saw the new king standing beside the pillar, as was the custom at times of coronation, surrounded by her bodyguard and many trumpeters; and everyone was rejoicing and blowing trumpets.

"Treason! Treason!" she screamed, and began to tear her clothes.

15 "Get her out of here," shouted Jehoiada to the officers of the guard. "Don't kill her here in the Temple. But kill anyone who tries to come to her rescue."

16 So they dragged her to the palace stables and killed her there.

17 Jehoiada made a treaty between the Lord, the king, and the people, that they would be the Lord's people. He also made a contract between the king and the people.

18 Everyone went over to the temple of Baal and tore it down, breaking the altars and images and kill-

ing Mattan, the priest of Baal, in front of the altar. And Jehoiada set guards at the Temple of the Lord.

19 Then he and the officers and the guard and all the people led the king from the Temple, past the guardhouse, and into the palace. And he sat upon the king's throne.

20 So everyone was happy, and the city settled back into quietness after Athaliah's death.

21 Joash was seven years old when he became king.

CHAPTER 12

It was seven years after Jehu had become the king of Israel that Joash became king of Judah. He reigned in Jerusalem for forty years. (His mother was Zibiah, from Beer-sheba.)

2 All his life Joash did what was right because Jehoiada the High Priest instructed him.

3 Yet even so he didn't destroy the shrines on the hills — the people still sacrificed and burned incense there.

4, 5 One day King Joash said to Jehoiada, "The Temple building needs repairing. Whenever anyone brings a contribution to the Lord, whether it is a regular assessment or some special gift, use it to pay for whatever repairs are needed."

6 But in the twenty-third year of his reign the Temple was still in disrepair.

7 So Joash called for Jehoiada and the other priests and asked them, "Why haven't you done anything about the Temple? Now don't use any more money for your own needs; from now on it must all be spent on getting the Temple into good condition."

8   So the priests agreed to set up a special repair fund that would not go through their hands, lest it be diverted to care for their personal needs.

9   Jehoiada the priest bored a hole in the lid of a large chest and set it on the right-hand side of the altar at the Temple entrance. The doorkeepers put all of the peoples' contributions into it.

10   Whenever the chest became full, the king's financial secretary and the High Priest counted it, put it into bags,

11, 12   And gave it to the construction superintendents to pay the carpenters, stonemasons, quarrymen, timber dealers, and stone merchants, and to buy the other materials needed to repair the Temple of the Lord.

13, 14   It was not used to buy silver cups, gold snuffers, bowls, trumpets, or similar articles, but only for repairs to the building.

15   No accounting was required from the construction superintendents, for they were honest and faithful men.

16   However, the money that was contributed for guilt offerings and sin offerings was given to the priests for their own use. It was not put into the chest.

17   About this time, King Hazael of Syria went to war against Gath and captured it; then he moved on toward Jerusalem to attack it.

18   King Joash took all the sacred objects that his ancestors — Jehoshaphat, Jehoram, and Ahaziah, the kings of Judah — had dedicated, along with what he himself had dedicated, and all the gold in the treasuries of the Temple and the palace, and sent it to Hazael. So Hazael called off the attack.

19 The rest of the history of Joash is recorded in *The Annals of the Kings of Judah.*

20 But his officers plotted against him and assassinated him in his royal residence at Millo on the road to Silla.

21 The assassins were Jozachar, the son of Shimeath, and Jehozabad, the son of Shomer — both trusted aides.[1] He was buried in the royal cemetery in Jerusalem, and his son Amaziah became the new king.

CHAPTER 13

Jehoahaz (the son of Jehu) began a seventeen-year reign over Israel during the twenty-third year of the reign of King Joash of Judah.

2 But he was an evil king, and he followed the wicked paths of Jeroboam, who had caused Israel to sin.

3 So the Lord was very angry with Israel, and He continually allowed King Hazael of Syria and his son Ben-hadad to conquer them.

4 But Jehoahaz prayed for the Lord's help, and the Lord listened to him; for the Lord saw how terribly the king of Syria was oppressing Israel.

5 So the Lord raised up leaders among the Israelis to rescue them from the tyranny of the Syrians; and then Israel lived in safety again as they had in former days.

6 But they continued to sin, following the evil ways of Jeroboam; and they continued to worship the goddess Asherah at Samaria.

7 Finally the Lord reduced Jehoahaz's army to fifty mounted troops, ten chariots, and ten thousand

---

[1]Literally, "his servants."

infantry; for the king of Syria had destroyed the others as though they were dust beneath his feet.

8   The rest of the history of Jehoahaz is recorded in *The Annals of the Kings of Israel.*

9, 10   Jehoahaz died and was buried in Samaria, and his son Joash reigned in Samaria for sixteen years. He came to the throne in the thirty-seventh year of the reign of King Joash of Judah.

11   But he was an evil man, for, like Jeroboam, he encouraged the people to worship idols and led them into sin.

12   The rest of the history of the reign of Joash, including his wars against King Amaziah of Judah, are written in *The Annals of the Kings of Israel.*

13   Joash died and was buried in Samaria with the other kings of Israel; and Jeroboam II became the new king.

*   *   *   *   *

14   When Elisha was in his last illness, King Joash visited him and wept over him. "My father! My father! You are the strength of Israel!"[1] he cried.

15   Elisha told him, "Get a bow and some arrows," and he did.

16, 17   "Open that eastern window," he instructed. Then he told the king to put his hand upon the bow, and Elisha laid his own hands upon the king's hands. "Shoot!" Elisha commanded, and he did. Then Elisha proclaimed, "This is the Lord's arrow, full of victory over Syria; for you will completely conquer the Syrians at Aphek.

---

[1]Literally, "The chariots of Israel and its horsemen!"

18   Now pick up the other arrows and strike them against the floor."

So the king picked them up and struck the floor three times.

19   But the prophet was angry with him. "You should have struck the floor five or six times," he exclaimed, "for then you would have beaten Syria until they were entirely destroyed; now you will be victorious only three times."

20, 21   So Elisha died and was buried.

In those days bandit gangs of Moabites used to invade the land each spring. Once some men who were burying a friend spied these marauders so they hastily threw his body into the tomb of Elisha. And as soon as the body touched Elisha's bones, the dead man revived and jumped to his feet!

*   *   *   *   *

22   King Hazael of Syria had oppressed Israel during the entire reign of King Jehoahaz.

23   But the Lord was gracious to the people of Israel, and they were not totally destroyed. For God pitied them, and also He was honoring His contract with Abraham, Isaac, and Jacob. And this is still true.

24   Then King Hazael of Syria died, and his son Ben-hadad reigned in his place.

25   King Joash of Israel[2] (the son of Jehoahaz) was successful on three occasions in reconquering the cities that his father had lost to Ben-hadad.

---

[2]Implied.

CHAPTER 14

D uring the second year of the reign of King Joash of Israel, King Amaziah began his reign over Judah.

2 Amaziah was twenty-five years old at the time, and he reigned in Jerusalem for twenty-nine years. (His mother was Jeho-addin, a native of Jerusalem.)

3 He was a good king in the Lord's sight, though not quite like his ancestor David; but he was as good a king as his father Joash.

4 However, he didn't destroy the shrines on the hills, so the people still sacrificed and burned incense there.

5 As soon as he had a firm grip on the kingdom, he killed the men who had assassinated his father;

6 But he didn't kill their children, for the Lord had commanded through the law of Moses that fathers shall not be killed for their children, nor children for the sins of their fathers: everyone must pay the penalty for his own sins.

7 Once Amaziah killed ten thousand Edomites in Salt Valley; he also conquered Sela and changed its name to Jokthe-el, as it is called to this day.

8 One day he sent a message to King Joash of Israel (the son of Jehoahaz and the grandson of Jehu), daring him to mobilize his army and come out and fight.

9 But King Joash replied, "The thistle of Lebanon demanded of the mighty cedar tree, 'Give your daughter to be a wife for my son.' But just then a wild animal passed by and stepped on the thistle and trod it into the ground!

10 You have destroyed Edom and are very proud

about it; but my advice to you is, be content with your glory and stay home! Why provoke disaster for both yourself and Judah?"

11 But Amaziah refused to listen, so King Joash of Israel mustered his army. The battle began at Beth-shemesh, one of the cities of Judah,

12 And Judah was defeated and the army fled home.

13 King Amaziah was captured, and the army of Israel marched on Jerusalem and broke down its wall from the Gate of Ephraim to the Corner Gate, a distance of about six hundred feet.

14 King Joash took many hostages and all the gold and silver from the Temple and the palace treasury, also the gold cups. Then he returned to Samaria.

15 The rest of the history of Joash and his war with King Amaziah of Judah are recorded in *The Annals of the Kings of Israel*.

16 When Joash died, he was buried in Samaria with the other kings of Israel. And his son Jeroboam became the new king.

17 Amaziah lived fifteen years longer than Joash,

18 And the rest of his biography is recorded in *The Annals of the Kings of Judah*.

19 There was a plot against his life in Jerusalem, and he fled to Lachish; but his enemies sent assassins and killed him there.

20 His body was returned on horses, and he was buried in the royal cemetery, in the City of David section of Jerusalem.

21 Then his son Azariah[1] became the new king at the age of sixteen.

---

[1] Also known as "Uzziah."

22   After his father's death he built Elath and re-stored it to Judah.

23   Meanwhile, over in Israel, Jeroboam II had become king during the fifteenth year of the reign of King Amaziah of Judah. Jeroboam's reign lasted forty-one years.

24   But he was as evil as Jeroboam I (the son of Nebat), who had led Israel into the sin of worshiping idols.

25   Jeroboam II recovered the lost territories of Israel between Hamath and the Dead Sea, just as the Lord God of Israel had predicted through Jonah (son of Amittai) the prophet from Gath-hepher.

26   For the Lord saw the bitter plight of Israel — she had no one to help her.

27   And He had not said that He would blot out the name of Israel, so He used King Jeroboam II to save her.

28   The rest of Jeroboam's biography — all that he did, and his great power, and his wars, and how he recovered Damascus and Hamath (which had been captured by Judah) — is recorded in *The Annals of the Kings of Israel.*

29   When Jeroboam II died he was buried with the other kings of Israel, and his son Zechariah became the new king of Israel.

CHAPTER 15

New king of Judah: Azariah[1]
Name of his father: Amaziah, the former king

---

[1]Also called Uzziah.

Name of his mother: Jecoliah of Jerusalem

Length of his reign: 52 years, in Jerusalem

His age at the beginning of his reign: 16 years old

Reigning in Israel at this time: King Jeroboam, who had been the king there for 27 years

3 Azariah was a good king, and he pleased the Lord just as his father Amaziah had.

4 But like his predecessors, he didn't destroy the shrines on the hills where the people sacrificed and burned incense.

5 Because of this[2] the Lord struck him with leprosy, which lasted until the day of his death; so he lived in a house by himself. And his son Jotham was the acting king.

6 The rest of the history of Azariah is recorded in *The Annals of the Kings of Judah.*

7 When Azariah died, he was buried with his ancestors in the City of David, and his son Jotham became king.

*   *   *   *   *

8   New king of Israel: Zechariah

Name of his father: Jeroboam

Length of reign: 6 months

Reigning in Judah at that time: King Azariah, who had been the king there for 38 years

9 But Zechariah was an evil king in the Lord's opinion, just like his ancestors. Like Jeroboam I (the

[2]Implied.

son of Nebat), he encouraged Israel in the sin of worshiping idols.

10   Then Shallum (the son of Jabesh) conspired against him and assassinated him at Ibleam and took the crown himself.

11   The rest of the history of Zechariah's reign is found in *The Annals of the Kings of Israel.*

12   (So the Lord's statement to Jehu came true, that Jehu's son, grandson and great-grandson would be kings of Israel[3]).

*   *   *   *   *

13   New king of Israel: Shallum
           Father's name: Jabesh
           Length of reign: 1 month
           Reigning in Judah at that time: King Uzziah, who had been the king there for 39 years

14   One month after Shallum became king, Menahem (the son of Gadi) came to Samaria from Tirzah and assassinated him and took the throne.

15   Additional details about King Shallum and his conspiracy[4] are recorded in *The Annals of the Kings of Israel.*

16   Menahem destroyed the city of Tappuah and the surrounding countryside, for its citizens refused to accept him as their king; he killed the entire population and ripped open the pregnant women.

*   *   *   *   *

---

[3] See II Kings 10:30.
[4] See verse 10.

17   Name of new king of Israel: Menahem
         Length of reign: 10 years, in Samaria
         Concurrent with: King Azariah of Judah
           who had been the king there for 39
           years

18   But Menahem was an evil king. He worshiped idols, as King Jeroboam I had done so long before, and he led the people of Israel into grievous sin.

19, 20   Then King Pul of Assyria invaded the land; but King Menahem bought him off with a gift of $2,000,000, so he turned around and returned home. Menahem extorted the money from the rich, assessing each one $2,000 in the form of a special tax.

21   The rest of the history of King Menahem is written in *The Annals of the Kings of Israel.*

22   When he died, his son Pekahiah became the new king.

*   *   *   *   *

23   Name of new king of Israel: Pekahiah
         Father's name: King Menahem
         Length of reign: 3 years, in Samaria
         Concurrent with: King Azariah of Judah,
           who had been the king there for 50
           years

24   But Pekahiah was an evil king, and he continued the idol-worship begun by Jeroboam I (son of Nebat) who led Israel down that evil trail.

25   Then Pekah (son of Remaliah), the commanding general of his army, conspired against him with fifty men from Gilead, and assassinated him in the palace at Samaria (Argob and Arieh were also slain in the revolt). So Pekah became the new king.

26   The rest of the history of King Pekahiah is recorded in *The Annals of the Kings of Israel.*

*   *   *   *   *

27   New king of Israel: Pekah
                  Father's name: Remaliah
                  Length of reign: 20 years, in Samaria
                  Concurrent with: King Azariah of Judah,
                       who had been the king there for 52
                       years

28   Pekah, too, was an evil king, and he continued in the example of Jeroboam I (son of Nebat), who led all of Israel into the sin of worshiping idols.

29   It was during his reign that King Tiglath-pileser[5] led an attack against Israel. He captured the cities of Ijon, Abel-beth-ma-acah, Janoah, Kedesh, Hazor, Gilead, Galilee, and all the land of Naphtali; and he took the people away to Assyria as captives.

30   Then Hoshea (the son of Elah) plotted against Pekah and assisinated him; and he took the throne for himself.

*   *   *   *   *

         New king of Israel: Hoshea
         Concurrent with: Jotham (son of Uzziah) king of Judah, who had been the king there for 20 years

31   The rest of the history of Pekah's reign is recorded in *The Annals of the Kings of Israel.*

*   *   *   *   *

---

[5]Also called Pul, in verse 19 above.

32, 33   New king of Judah: Jotham

         Father's name: King Uzziah

         His age when he became king: 25 years old

         Duration of his reign: 16 years, in Jerusalem

         Mother's name: Jerusha (daughter of Zadok)

         Reigning in Israel at this time: Pekah (son of Remaliah), who had been the king there for 2 years

34, 35   Generally speaking, Jotham was a good king. Like his father Uzziah,[6] he followed the Lord. But he didn't destroy the shrines on the hills where the people sacrificed and burned incense. It was during King Jotham's reign that the upper gate of the Temple of the Lord was built.

36   The rest of Jotham's history is written in *The Annals of the Kings of Judah.*

37   In those days the Lord caused King Rezin of Syria and King Pekah of Israel to attack Judah.

38   When Jotham died he was buried with the other kings of Judah in the royal cemetery, in the City of David section of Jerusalem. Then his son Ahaz became the new king.

CHAPTER 16

New king of Judah: Ahaz

     Father's name: Jotham

Age: 20 years old

Duration of reign: 16 years, in Jerusalem

---

[6]Also called Azariah.

Character of his reign: evil
Reigning in Israel at this time: King Pekah
(son of Remaliah) who had been the
king there for 17 years

2 But he did not follow the Lord as his ancestor David had;

3 He was as wicked as the kings of Israel. He even killed his own son by offering him as a burnt sacrifice to the gods, following the heathen customs of the nations around Judah — nations which the Lord destroyed when the people of Israel entered the land.

4 He also sacrificed and burned incense at the shrines on the hills and at the numerous altars in the groves of trees.

5 Then King Rezin of Syria and King Pekah (son of Remaliah) of Israel declared war on Ahaz and besieged Jerusalem; but they did not conquer it.

6 However, at that time King Rezin of Syria recovered the city of Elath for Syria; he drove out the Jews and sent Syrians to live there, as they do to this day.

7 King Ahaz sent a messenger to King Tiglath-pileser of Assyria, begging him to help him fight the attacking armies of Syria and Israel.[1]

8 Ahaz took the silver and gold from the Temple and from the royal vaults and sent it as a payment to the Assyrian king.

9 So the Assyrians attacked Damascus, the capital of Syria. They took away the population of the city as captives, resettling them in Kir, and King Rezin of Syria was killed.

---

[1]Literally, "saying, 'I am your servant and your son. Come and rescue me.'"

10   King Ahaz now went to Damascus to meet with King Tiglath-pileser, and while he was there he noticed an unusual altar in a heathen temple.[2] He jotted down its dimensions and made a sketch and sent it back to Uriah the priest with a detailed description.

11, 12   Uriah built on just like it by following these directions and had it ready for the king, who, upon his return from Damascus, inaugurated it with an offering.

13   The king presented a burnt offering and a grain offering, poured a drink offering over it, and sprinkled the blood of peace offerings upon it.

14   Then he removed the old bronze altar from the front of the Temple (it had stood between the Temple entrance and the new altar), and placed it on the north side of the new altar.

15   He instructed Uriah the priest to use the new altar for the sacrifices of burnt offering, the evening grain offering, the king's burnt offering and grain offering, and the offerings of the people, including their drink offerings. The blood from the burnt offerings and sacrifices was also to be sprinkled over the new altar. So the old altar was used only for purposes of divination.

"The old bronze altar," he said, "will be only for my personal use."

16   Uriah the priest did as King Ahaz instructed him.

17   Then the king dismantled the wheeled stands in the Temple, removed their crosspieces and the water vats they supported, and removed the great tank

---

[2]Literally, "he saw the altar that was at Damascus."

from the backs of the bronze oxen and placed it upon the stone pavement.

18   In deference to the king of Assyria he also removed the festive passageway he had constructed between the palace and the Temple.[3]

19   The rest of the history of the reign of King Ahaz is recorded in *The Annals of the Kings of Judah.*

20   When Ahaz died he was buried in the royal cemetery, in the City of David sector of Jerusalem, and his son Hezekiah became the new king.

CHAPTER 17

New king of Israel: Hoshea
Father's name: Elah
Length of his reign: 9 years, in Samaria
Character of his reign: evil — but not as
        bad as some of the other kings of
        Israel
Reigning in Judah at this time: King Ahaz,
        who had been the king there for 12
        years

3   King Shalmaneser of Assyria attacked and defeated King Hoshea, so Israel had to pay heavy annual taxes to Assyria.

4   Then Hoshea conspired against the king of Assyria by asking King So of Egypt to help him shake free of Assyria's power, but this treachery was discovered. At the same time he refused to pay the annual tribute to Assyria. So the king of Assyria put him in prison and in chains for his rebellion.

5   Now the land of Israel was filled with Assyrian

---

[3]The Hebrew is unclear.

troops for three years besieging Samaria, the capital city of Israel.

6 Finally, in the ninth year of King Hoshea's reign, Samaria fell and the people of Israel were exiled to Assyria. They were placed in colonies in the city of Halah and along the banks of the Habor River in Gozan, and among the cities of the Medes.

7 This disaster came upon the nation of Israel because the people worshiped other gods, thus sinning against the Lord their God who had brought them safely out of their slavery in Egypt.

8 They had followed the evil customs of the nations which the Lord had cast out from before them.

9 The people of Israel had also secretly done many things that were wrong, and they had built altars to other gods throughout the land.[1]

10 They had placed obelisks and idols at the top of every hill and under every green tree;

11 And they had burned incense to the gods of the very nations which the Lord had cleared out of the land when Israel came in. So the people of Israel had done many evil things, and the Lord was very angry.

12 Yes, they worshiped idols, despite the Lord's specific and repeated warnings.

13 Again and again the Lord had sent prophets to warn both Israel and Judah to turn from their evil ways; He had warned them to obey His commandments which He had given to their ancestors through these prophets,

14 But Israel wouldn't listen. The people were

---

[1]Literally, "built them high places in all their cities."

as stubborn as their ancestors and refused to believe in the Lord their God.

15 They rejected His laws and the covenant He had made with their ancestors, and despised all His warnings. In their foolishness they worshiped heathen idols despite the Lord's stern warnings.

16 They defied all the commandments of the Lord their God and made two calves from molten gold. They made detestable, shameful idols and worshiped Baal and the sun, moon, and stars.

17 They even burned their own sons and daughters to death on the altars of Molech;[2] they consulted fortune-tellers and used magic and sold themselves to evil. So the Lord was very angry.

18 He swept them from His sight until only the tribe of Judah remained in the land.

19 But even Judah refused to obey the commandments of the Lord their God: they too walked in the same evil paths as Israel had.

20 So the Lord rejected all the descendants of Jacob.[3] He punished them by delivering them to their attackers until they were destroyed.

21 For Israel split off from the kingdom of David and chose Jeroboam I (the son of Nebat) as its king. Then Jeroboam drew Israel away from following the Lord. He made them sin a great sin,

22 And the people of Israel never quit doing the evil things that Jeroboam led them into,

23 Until the Lord finally swept them away, just as all His prophets had warned would happen. So

---

[2]Literally, "as offerings."
[3]Literally, "descendants of Israel."

Israel was carried off to the land of Assyria where they remain to this day.

24　And the king of Assyria transported colonies of people from Babylon, Cuthah, Avva, Hamath, and Sepharvaim and resettled them in the cities of Samaria, replacing the people of Israel. So the Assyrians took over Samaria and the other cities of Israel.

25　But since these Assyrian colonists did not worship the Lord when they first arrived, the Lord sent lions among them to kill some of them.

26　Then they sent a message to the king of Assyria: "We colonists here in Israel don't know the laws of the god of the land, and He has sent lions among us to destroy us because we have not worshiped him."

27, 28　The king of Assyria then decreed that one of the exiled priests from Samaria should return to Israel and teach the new residents the laws of the god of the land. So one of them returned to Bethel and taught the colonists from Babylon how to worship the Lord.

29　But these foreigners also worshiped their own gods. They placed them in the shrines on the hills near their cities.

30　Those from Babylon worshiped idols of their god Succoth-benoth; those from Cuth worshiped their god Nergal; and the men of Hamath worshiped Ashima.

31　The gods Nibhaz and Tartak were worshiped by the Avvites, and the people from Sephar even burned their own children on the altars of their gods Adrammelech and Anammelech.

32　They also worshiped the Lord, and they appointed from among themselves priests to sacrifice to the Lord on the hilltop altars.

33 But they continued to follow the religious customs of the nations from which they came.

34 And this is still going on among them today — they follow their former practices instead of truly worshiping the Lord or obeying the laws He gave to the descendants of Jacob (whose name was later changed to Israel).

35, 36 For the Lord had made a contract with them — that they were never to worship or make sacrifices to any heathen gods. They were to worship only the Lord who had brought them out of the land of Egypt with such tremendous miracles and power.

37 The descendants of Jacob were to obey all of God's laws and *never* worship other gods.

38 For God had said, *"You must never forget the covenant I made with you; never worship other gods.*

39 *You must worship only the Lord; He will save you from all your enemies."*

40 But Israel didn't listen, and the people continued to worship other gods.

41 These colonists from Babylon worshiped the Lord, yes — but they also worshiped their idols. And to this day their descendants do the same thing.

CHAPTER 18

New king of Judah: Hezekiah
Father's name: Ahaz
Length of his reign: 29 years, in Jerusalem
His age at the beginning of his reign: 25 years old
His mother's name: Abi (daughter of Zechariah)

Character of his reign: good (similar to that of his ancestor David.)

Reigning in Israel at this time: King Hoshea (son of Elah), who had been the king there for 3 years

4 He removed the shrines on the hills, broke down the obelisks, knocked down the shameful idols of Asherah, and broke up the bronze serpent that Moses had made, because the people of Israel had begun to worship it by burning incense to it; even though, as King Hezekiah[1] pointed out to them, it was merely a piece of bronze.

5 He trusted very strongly in the Lord God of Israel. In fact, none of the kings before or after him were as close to God as he was.

6 For he followed the Lord in everything, and carefully obeyed all of God's commands to Moses.

7 So the Lord was with him and prospered everything he did. Then he rebelled against the king of Assyria and refused to pay tribute any longer.

8 He also conquered the Philistines as far distant as Gaza and its suburbs, destroying cities both large and small.[2]

9 It was during the fourth year of his reign (which was the seventh year of the reign of King Hoshea in Israel) that King Shalmaneser of Assyria attacked Israel and began a siege on the city of Samaria.

10 Three years later (during the sixth year of the reign of King Hezekiah and the ninth year of the reign of King Hoshea of Israel) Samaria fell.

11 It was at that time that the king of Assyria

---

[1] Implied.
[2] Literally, "from the tower of the watchman to the fortified cities."

transported the Israelis to Assyria and put them in colonies in the city of Halath and along the banks of the Habor River in Gozan, and in the cities of the Medes.

12   For they had refused to listen to the Lord their God or to do what He wanted them to do. Instead, they had transgressed His covenant and disobeyed all the laws given to them by Moses the servant of the Lord.

13   Later, during the fourteenth year of the reign of King Hezekiah, King Sennacherib of Assyria besieged and captured all the fortified cities of Judah.

14   King Hezekiah sued for peace and sent this message to the king of Assyria at Lachish: "I have done wrong. I will pay whatever tribute you demand if you will only go away." The king of Assyria then demanded a settlement of $1,500,000.

15   To gather this amount, King Hezekiah used all the silver stored in the Temple and in the palace treasury.

16   He even stripped off the gold from the Temple doors, and from the doorposts he had overlaid with gold, and gave it all to the Assyrian king.

17   Nevertheless the king of Assyria sent his field marshal, his chief treasurer, and his chief of staff from Lachish with a great army; and they camped along the highway beside the field where cloth was bleached, near the conduit of the upper pool.

18   They demanded that King Hezekiah come out to speak to them, but instead he sent a truce delegation of the following men: Eliakam, his business manager; Shebnah, his secretary; and Joah, his royal historian.

19   Then the Assyrian general sent this message to

King Hezekiah: "The great King of Assyria says, 'No one can save you from my power!

20, 21　You need more than mere promises of help before rebelling against me. But which of your allies will give you more than words? Egypt? If you lean on Egypt, you will find her to be a stick that breaks beneath your weight and pierces your hand. The Egyptian Pharaoh is totally unreliable!

22　And if you say, "We're trusting the Lord to rescue us" — just remember that He is the very one whose hilltop altars you've destroyed. For you require everyone to worship at the altar in Jerusalem!'

23　I'll tell you what: Make a bet with my master, the king of Assyria! If you have two thousand men left who can ride horses, we'll furnish the horses!

24　And with an army as small as yours,[3] you are no threat to even the least lieutenant in charge of the smallest contingent in my master's army. Even if Egypt supplies you with horses and chariots, it will do no good.

25　And do you think we have come here on our own? No! The Lord sent us and told us, 'Go and destroy this nation!' "

26　Then Eliakim, Shebnah, and Joah said to them, "Please speak in Aramaic, for we understand it. Don't use Hebrew, for the people standing on the walls will hear you."

27　But the Assyrian general replied, "Has my master sent me to speak only to you and to your master? Hasn't he sent me to the people on the walls too? For they are doomed with you to eat their own excrement and drink their own urine!"

3Implied.

28 Then the Assyrian ambassador shouted in Hebrew to the people on the wall, "Listen to the great king of Assyria!

29 'Don't let King Hezekiah fool you. He will never be able to save you from my power.

30 Don't let him fool you into trusting in the Lord to rescue you.

31, 32 Don't listen to King Hezekiah. Surrender! You can live in peace here in your own land until I take you to another land just like this one — with plentiful crops, grain, wine, olive trees, and honey. All of this instead of death! Don't listen to King Hezekiah when he tries to persuade you that the Lord will deliver you.

33 Have any of the gods of the other nations ever delivered their people from the king of Assyria?

34 What happened to the gods of Hamath, Arpad, Sepharvaim, Hena, and Ivvah? Did they rescue Samaria?

35 What god has ever been able to save any nation from my power? So what makes you think the Lord can save Jerusalem?' "

36 But the people on the wall remained silent, for the king had instructed them to say nothing.

37 Then Eliakim (son of Hilkiah) the business manager, and Shebnah the king's secretary, and Joah (son of Asaph) the historian went to King Hezekiah with their clothes torn and told him what the Assyrian general had said.

CHAPTER 19

When King Hezekiah heard their report he tore his clothes and put on sackcloth and went into the

Temple to pray.

2 Then he told Eliakim, Shebnah, and some of the older priests to clothe themselves in sackcloth and to go to Isaiah (son of Amoz), the prophet, with this message:

3 "King Hezekiah says, 'This is a day of trouble, insult, and dishonor. It is as when a child is ready to be born, but the mother has no strength to deliver it.

4 Yet perhaps the Lord your God has heard the Assyrian general defying the living God, and will rebuke him. Oh, pray for the few of us who are left.' "

5, 6 Isaiah replied, "The Lord says, 'Tell your master not to be troubled by the sneers these Assyrians have made against Me.'

7 For the king of Assyria will receive bad news from home and will decide to return; and the Lord will see to it that he is killed when he arrives there."

8 Then the Assyrian general returned to his king at Libnah (for he received word that he had left Lachish).

9 Soon afterwards news reached the king that King Tirhakah of Ethiopia was coming to attack him. Before leaving to meet the attack, he sent back this message to King Hezekiah:

10 "Don't be fooled by that god you trust in. Don't believe it when he says that I won't conquer Jerusalem.

11 You know perfectly well what the kings of Assyria have done wherever they have gone; they have completely destroyed everything. Why would you be any different?

12 Have the gods of the other nations delivered them — such nations as Gozan, Haran, Rezeph, and

Eden in the land of Telassar? The former kings of Assyria destroyed them all!

13 What happened to the king of Hamoth and the king of Arpad? What happened to the kings of Sepharvaim, Hena, and Ivvah?"

14 Hezekiah took the letter from the messengers, read it, and went over to the Temple and spread it out before the Lord.

15 Then he prayed this prayer: "O Lord God of Israel, sitting on Your throne high above the angels,[1] You alone are the God of all the kingdoms of the earth. You created the heavens and the earth.

16 Bend low, O Lord, and listen. Open Your eyes, O Lord, and see. Listen to this man's defiance of the living God.

17 Lord, it is true that the kings of Assyria have destroyed all those nations,

18 And have burned their idol-gods. But they weren't gods at all; they were destroyed because they were only things that men had made of wood and stone.

19 O Lord our God, we plead with You to save us from his power; then all the kingdoms of the earth will know that You alone are God."

20 Then Isaiah sent this message to Hezekiah: "The Lord God of Israel says, 'I have heard you!

21 And this is My reply to King Sennacherib: The virgin daughter of Zion isn't afraid of you! The daughter of Jerusalem scorns and mocks at you.

22 Whom have you defied and blasphemed? And toward whom have you felt so cocky? It is the Holy One of Israel!

---

[1]Literally, "cherubim."

23 You have boasted, "My chariots have conquered the highest mountains, yes, the peaks of Lebanon. I have cut down the tallest cedars and choicest cypress tree and have conquered the farthest borders.

24 I have been refreshed at many conquered wells, and I destroyed the strength of Egypt just by walking by!"

25 Why haven't you realized long before this that it is I, the Lord, who lets you do these things? I decreed your conquest of all those fortified cities!

26 So of course the nations you conquered had no power against you! They were like grass shriveling beneath the hot sun, and like grain blighted before it is half-grown.

27 I know everything about you. I know all your plans and where you are going next; and I also know the evil things you have said about Me.

28 And because of your arrogance against Me I am going to put a hook in your nose and a bridle in your mouth and turn you back on the road by which you came.

29 And this is the proof that I will do as I have promised: This year My people will eat the volunteer wheat, and use it as seed for next year's crop; and in the third year they will have a bountiful harvest.

30 O My people Judah, those of you who have escaped the ravages of the siege shall become a great nation again; you shall be rooted deeply in the soil and bear fruit for God.

31 A remnant of My people shall become strong in Jerusalem. The Lord is eager to cause this to happen.

32 And My command concerning the king of Assyria is that he shall not enter this city. He shall not

stand before it with a shield, nor build a ramp against its wall, nor even shoot an arrow into it.

33 He shall return by the road he came,

34 For I will defend and save this city for the sake of My own name and for the sake of My servant David.' "

35 That very night the angel of the Lord killed 185,000 Assyrian troops, and dead bodies were seen all across the landscape in the morning.

36 Then King Sennacherib returned to Nineveh;

37 And as he was worshiping in the temple of his god Nisroch, his sons Adrammelech and Sharezer killed him. They escaped into eastern Turkey — the land of Ararat — and his son Esarhaddon became the new king.

CHAPTER 20

H ezekiah now became deathly sick, and Isaiah the prophet went to visit him.

"Set your affairs in order and prepare to die," Isaiah told him. "The Lord says you won't recover."

2 Hezekiah turned his face to the wall.

3 "O Lord," he pleaded, "remember how I've always tried to obey You and to please You in everything I do . . ." Then he broke down and cried.

4 So before Isaiah had left the courtyard, the Lord spoke to him again.

5 "Go back to Hezekiah, the leader of My people, and tell him that the Lord God of his ancestor David has heard his prayer and seen his tears. I will heal him, and three days from now he will be out of bed and at the Temple!

6 I will add fifteen years to his life and save him

and this city from the king of Assyria. And it will all be done for the glory of My own name and for the sake of My servant David."

7 Isaiah then instructed Hezekiah to boil some dried figs and to make a paste of them and spread it on the boil. And he recovered!

8 Meanwhile, King Hezekiah had said to Isaiah, "Do a miracle to prove to me that the Lord will heal me and that I will be able to go to the Temple again three days from now."

9 "All right, the Lord will give you a proof," Isaiah told him. "Do you want the shadow on the sundial to go forward ten points or backward ten points?"

10 "The shadow always moves forward," Hezekiah replied; "make it go backward."

11 So Isaiah asked the Lord to do this, and He caused the shadow to move ten points backward on the sundial of Ahaz![1]

12 At that time Merodach-baladan (the son of King Baladan of Babylon) sent ambassadors with greetings and a present to Hezekiah, for he had learned of his sickness.

13 Hezekiah welcomed them and showed them all his treasures — the silver, gold, spices, aromatic oils, the armory — everything.

14 Then Isaiah went to King Hezekiah and asked him, "What did these men want? Where are they from?"

"From far away in Babylon," Hezekiah replied.

15 "What have they seen in your palace?" Isaiah asked.

[1]Or, "on the steps of Ahaz." Egyptian sundials in this period were made in the form of miniature staircases, so that the shadow moved up and down the steps.

And Hezekiah replied, "Everything. I showed them all my treasures."

16 Then Isaiah said to Hezekiah, "Listen to the word of the Lord:

17 The time will come when everything in this palace shall be carried to Babylon. All the treasures of your ancestors will be taken — nothing shall be left.

18 Some of your own sons will be taken away and made into eunuchs who will serve in the palace of the king of Babylon."

19 "All right," Hezekiah replied, "if this is what the Lord wants, it is good." But he was really thinking, "At least there will be peace and security during the remainder of my own life!"

20 The rest of the history of Hezekiah and his great deeds — including the pool and conduit he made and how he brought water into the city — are recorded in *The Annals of the Kings of Judah.*

21 When Hezekiah died, his son Manasseh became the new king.

CHAPTER 21

New king of Judah: Manasseh
His age at beginning of his reign: 12 years
Length of his reign: 55 years, in Jerusalem
Name of his mother: Hephzibah
Character of his reign: evil. He did the same things the nations had done that were thrown out of the land to make room for the people of Israel

3, 4, 5 He rebuilt the hilltop shrines which his father Hezekiah had destroyed. He built altars for Baal and made a shameful Asherah idol, just as Ahab the king of Israel had done. Heathen altars to the sun god, moon god, and the gods of the stars were placed even in the Temple of the Lord — in the very city and building which the Lord had selected to honor His own name.

6 And he sacrificed one of his sons as a burnt offering on a heathen altar. He practiced black magic and used fortune-telling, and patronized mediums and wizards. So the Lord was very angry, for Manasseh was an evil man, in God's opinion.

7 Manasseh even set up a shameful Asherah-idol in the Temple — the very place which the Lord had spoken to David and Solomon about when He said, "I will place My name forever in this Temple, and in Jerusalem — the city I have chosen from among all the cities of the tribes of Israel.

8 If the people of Israel will only follow the instructions I gave them through Moses, I will never again expel them from this land of their fathers."

9 But the people did not listen to the Lord, and Manasseh enticed them to do even more evil than the surrounding nations had done, even though Jehovah had destroyed those nations for their evil ways when the people of Israel entered the land.

10 Then the Lord declared through the prophets,

11 "Because King Manasseh has done these evil things and is even more wicked than the Amorites who were in this land long ago, and because he has led the people of Judah into idolatry:

12 I will bring such evil upon Jerusalem and Judah

that the ears of those who hear about it will tingle with horror.

13   I will cause the kings of Israel to conquer Jerusalem, and I will wipe Jerusalem as a man wipes a dish and turns it upside down to dry.

14   Then I will reject even those few of My people who are left, and I will hand them over to their enemies.

15   For they have done great evil and have angered Me ever since I brought their ancestors from Egypt."

16   In addition to the idolatry which God hated and into which Manasseh led the people of Judah, he murdered great numbers of innocent people. And Jerusalem was filled from one end to the other with the bodies of his victims.

17   The rest of the history of Manasseh's sinful reign is recorded in *The Annals of the Kings of Judah.*

18   When he died he was buried in the garden of his palace at Uzza, and his son Amon became the new king.

*   *   *   *   *

19, 20   Name of the new king of Judah: Amon
          His age at the beginning of his reign: 22
              years old
          Length of his reign: 2 years, in Jerusalem
          His mother's name: Meshullemeth (daughter of Haruz, of Jotbah)
          Character of his reign: evil

21   He did all the evil things his father had done: he worshiped the same idols,

22 And turned his back on the Lord God of his ancestors. He refused to listen to God's instructions.

23 But his aides conspired against him and killed him in the palace.

24 Then a posse of civilians killed all the assassins and placed Amon's son Josiah upon the throne.

25 The rest of Amon's biography is recorded in *The Annals of the Kings of Judah.*

26 He was buried in a crypt in the garden of Uzza, and his son Josiah became the new king.

CHAPTER 22

New king of Judah: Josiah
His age at the beginning of his reign: 8 years old

Duration of his reign: 31 years in Jerusalem

Name of his mother: Jedidah (daughter of Adaiah of Bozkath)

Character of his reign: good; for he followed in the steps of his ancestor King David, obeying the Lord completely

3, 4 In the eighteenth year of his reign, King Josiah sent his secretary Shaphan (son of Azaliah, son of Meshullam) to the Temple to give instruction to Hilkiah, the high priest: "Collect the money given to the priests at the door of the Temple when the people come to worship.

5, 6 Give this money to the building superintendents so that they can hire carpenters and masons to repair the Temple, and to buy lumber and stone."

7 (The building superintendents were not required to keep account of their expenditures, for they were honest men.)

8 One day Hilkiah the high priest went to Shaphan, the secretary and exclaimed, "I have discovered a scroll in the Temple, with God's laws written on it!" He gave the scroll to Shaphan to read.

9, 10 When Shaphan reported to the king about the progress of the repairs at the Temple, he also mentioned the scroll found by Hilkiah. Then Shaphan read it to the king.

11 When the king heard what was written in it, he tore his clothes in terror.

12, 13 He commanded Hilkiah the priest, and Shaphan, and Asaiah, the king's assistant, and Ahikam (Shaphan's son), and Achbor (Michaiah's son) to ask the Lord, "What shall we do? For we have not been following the instructions of this book; You must be very angry with us, for neither we nor our ancestors have followed Your commands."

14 So Hilkiah the priest, and Ahikam, and Achbor, and Shaphan, and Asaiah went to the Mishneh section of Jerusalem to find Huldah the prophetess. (She was the wife of Shallum — son of Tikvah, son of Harhas — who was in charge of the palace tailor shop.)

15, 16 She gave them this message from the Lord God of Israel: "Tell the man who sent you to Me, that I am going to destroy this city and its people, just as I stated in that book you read.

17 For the people of Judah have thrown Me aside and have worshiped other gods and have made Me very angry; and My anger can't be stopped.

18, 19 But because you were sorry and concerned

and humbled yourself before the Lord when you read the book and its warnings that this land would be cursed and become desolate, and because you have torn your clothing and wept before Me in contrition, I will listen to your plea.

20 The death of this nation will not occur until after you die — you will not see the evil which I will bring upon this place."

So they took the message to the king.

CHAPTER 23

Then the king sent for the elders and other leaders of Judah and Jerusalem to go to the Temple with him. So all the priests and prophets and the people, small and great, of Jerusalem and Judah gathered there at the Temple so that the king could read to them the entire book of God's laws which had been discovered in the Temple.

3 He stood beside the pillar in front of the people, and he and they made a solemn promise to the Lord to obey Him at all times and to do everything the book commanded.

4 Then the king instructed Hilkiah the High Priest and the rest of the priests and the guards of the Temple to destroy all the equipment used in the worship of Baal, Asherah, and the sun, moon, and stars. The king had it all burned in the fields of the Kidron Valley outside Jerusalem, and he carried the ashes to Bethel.

5 He killed the heathen priests who had been appointed by the previous kings of Judah, for they had burned incense in the shrines on the hills through-

out Judah and even in Jerusalem. They had also offered incense to Baal and to the sun, moon, stars, and planets.

6   He removed the shameful idol of Asherah from the Temple and took it outside Jerusalem to Kidron Brook; there he burned it and beat it to dust and threw the dust on the graves of the common people.

7   He also tore down the houses of male prostitution around the Temple, where the women wove robes for the Asherah-idol.

8   He brought back to Jerusalem the priests of the Lord, who were living in other cities of Judah, and tore down all the shrines on the hills where they had burned incense, even those as far away as Geba and Beersheba. He also destroyed the shrines at the entrance of the palace of Joshua, the former mayor of Jerusalem, located on the left side as one enters the city gate.

9   However, these priests[1] did not serve at the altar of the Lord in Jerusalem, even though they ate with the other priests.

10   Then the king destroyed the altar of Topheth in the Valley of the Sons of Hinnom, so that no one could ever again use it to burn his son or daughter to death as a sacrifice to Molech.

11   He tore down the statues of horses and chariots located near the entrance of the Temple, next to the quarters of Nathan-melech the eunuch. These had been dedicated by former kings of Judah to the sun god.

12   Then he tore down the altars which the kings of Judah had built on the palace roof above the Ahaz Room. He also destroyed the altars which Manasseh had built in the two courts of the Temple; he

---

[1]Literally, "the priests of the high places."

smashed them to bits and scattered the pieces in Kidron Valley.

13   Next he removed the shrines on the hills east of Jerusalem and south of Destruction Mountain. (Solomon had built these shrines for Ashtoreth, the evil goddess of the Sidonians; and for Chemosh, the evil god of Moab; and for Milcom, the evil god of the Ammonites.)

14   He smashed the obelisks and cut down the shameful idols of Asherah; then he defiled these places by scattering human bones over them.

15   He also tore down the altar and shrine at Bethel which Jeroboam I had made when he led Israel into sin. He crushed the stones to dust and burned the shameful idol of Asherah.

16   As Josiah was looking around, he noticed several graves in the side of the mountain. He ordered his men to bring out the bones in them and to burn them there upon the altar at Bethel to defile it, just as the Lord's prophet had declared would happen to Jeroboam's altar.[2]

17   "What is that monument over there?" he asked.

And the men of the city told him, "It is the grave of the prophet who came from Judah and proclaimed that what you have just done would happen here at the altar at Bethel!"

18   So King Josiah replied, "Leave it alone. Don't disturb his bones."

So they didn't burn his bones or those of the prophet from Samaria.[3]

19   Josiah demolished the shrines on the hills in all

[2]See I Kings 13:20.
[3]See I Kings 13:31, 32.

of Samaria. They had been built by the various kings of Israel and had made the Lord very angry. But now he crushed them into dust, just as he had done at Bethel.

20   He executed the priests of the heathen shrines upon their own altars, and he burned human bones upon the altars to defile them. Finally he returned to Jerusalem.

21   The king then issued orders for his people to observe the Passover ceremonies as recorded by the Lord their God in *The Book of the Covenant.*

22   There had not been a Passover celebration like that since the days of the judges of Israel, and there was never another like it in all the years of the kings of Israel and Judah.

23   This Passover was in the eighteenth year of the reign of King Josiah, and it was celebrated in Jerusalem.

24   Josiah also exterminated the mediums and wizards, and every kind of idol worship, both in Jerusalem and throughout the land. For Josiah wanted to follow all the laws which were written in the book that Hilkiah the priest had found in the Temple.

25   There was no other king who so completely turned to the Lord and followed all the laws of Moses; and no king since the time of Josiah has approached his record of obedience.

26   But the Lord still did not hold back His great anger against Judah, caused by the evils of King Manasseh.

27   For the Lord had said, "I will destroy Judah just as I have destroyed Israel; and I will discard My

chosen city of Jerusalem and the Temple that I said was Mine."

28   The rest of the biography of Josiah is written in *The Annals of the Kings of Judah.*

29   In those days King Neco of Egypt attacked the king of Assyria at the Euphrates River, and King Josiah went to assist him; but King Neco killed Josiah at Megiddo when he saw him.

30   His officers took his body back in a chariot from Megiddo to Jerusalem and buried him in the grave he had selected. And his son Jehoahaz was chosen by the nation as its new king.

*   *   *   *   *

31, 32   New king of Judah: Jehoahaz

His age when he became king: 23 years old

Length of his reign: 3 months, in Jerusalem

His mother's name: Hamutal (the daughter of Jeremiah of Libnah)

Character of his reign: evil, like the other kings who had preceded him

33   Pharaoh-Neco jailed him at Riblah in Hamath to prevent his reigning in Jerusalem, and he levied a tax against Judah totaling $230,000.

34   The Egyptian king then chose Eliakim, another of Josiah's sons, to reign in Jerusalem; and he changed his name to Jehoiakim. Then he took King Jehoahaz to Egypt, where he died.

35   Jehoiakim taxed the people to get the money

that the Pharaoh had demanded.

*   *   *   *

36, 37   New king of Judah: Jehoiakim
           His age when he became king: 25 years
              old
           Length of his reign: 11 years, in Jerusalem
           His mother's name: Zebidah (daughter
              of Pedaiah of Rumah)
           Character of his reign: evil, like the other
              kings preceding him

CHAPTER 24

During the reign of King Jehoiakim, King Nebuchadnezzar of Babylon attacked Jerusalem. Jehoiakim surrendered and paid him tribute for three years, but then rebelled.

2   And the Lord sent bands of Chaldeans, Syrians, Moabites, and Ammonites against Judah in order to destroy the nation, just as the Lord had warned through His prophets that He would.

3, 4   It is clear that these disasters befell Judah at the direct command of the Lord. He had decided to wipe Judah out of His sight because of the many sins of Manasseh, for he had filled Jerusalem with blood, and the Lord would not pardon it.

5   The rest of the history of the life of Jehoiakim is recorded in *The Annals of the Kings of Judah.*

6   When he died, his son Jehoiachin became the new king.

7   (The Egyptian Pharaoh never returned after that, for the king of Babylon occupied the entire area claimed by Egypt — all of Judah from the Brook of

Egypt to the Euphrates River.)

*   *   *   *   *

8, 9   New king of Judah, Jehoiachin

His age at the beginning of his reign: 18 years old

Length of his reign: 3 months, in Jerusalem

Name of his mother: Nehushta, (daughter of Elnathan, a citizen of Jerusalem)

10   During his reign the armies of King Nebuchadnezzar of Babylon besieged the city of Jerusalem.

11   Nebuchadnezzar himself arrived during the siege,

12   And King Jehoiachin, all of his officials, and the queen mother surrendered to him. The surrender was accepted, and Jehoiachin was imprisoned in Babylon during the eighth year of Nebuchadnezzar's reign.

13   The Babylonians carried home all the treasures from the Temple and the royal palace; and they cut apart all the gold bowls which King Solomon of Israel had placed in the Temple at the Lord's directions.

14   King Nebuchadnezzar took ten thousand captives from Jerusalem, including all the princes and the best of the soldiers, craftsmen, and smiths. So only the poorest and least skilled people were left in the land.

15   Nebuchadnezzar took King Jehoiachin, his wives and officials, and the queen mother, to Babylon.

16   He also took seven thousand of the best troops and one thousand craftsmen and smiths, all of whom were strong and fit for war.

17   Then the king of Babylon appointed King Je-

hoiachin's great-uncle,[1] Mattaniah, to be the next king; and he changed his name to Zedekiah.

*   *   *   *   *

18, 19   New king of Judah: Zedekiah

His age when he became king: 21 years old

Length of his reign: 11 years, in Jerusalem

His mother's name: Hamutal (daughter of Jeremiah of Libnah)

Character of his reign: evil, like that of Jehoiakim

20   So the Lord finally, in His anger, destroyed the people of Jerusalem and Judah.

But now King Zedekiah rebelled against the king of Babylon.

CHAPTER 25

Then King Nebuchadnezzar of Babylon mobilized his entire army and laid siege to Jerusalem, arriving on March 25 of the ninth year of the reign of King Zedekiah of Judah.

2   The siege continued into the eleventh year of his reign.

3   The last food in the city was eaten on July 24,

4, 5   And that night the king and his troops made a hole in the inner wall and fled out toward the Arabah through a gate that lay between the double walls near the king's garden. The Babylonian troops surrounding the city took out after him and captured him in the plains of Jericho, and all his men scattered.

---

[1]Implied in 23:31 and 24:18.

6 He was taken to Riblah, where he was tried and sentenced before the king of Babylon.

7 He was forced to watch as his sons were killed before his eyes; then his eyes were put out and he was bound with chains and taken away to Babylon.

8 General Nebuzaradan, the captain of the royal bodyguard, arrived at Jerusalem from Babylon on July 22 of the nineteenth year of the reign of King Nebuchadnezzar.

9 He burned down the Temple, the palace, and all the other houses of any worth.

10 He then supervised the Babylonian army in tearing down the walls of Jerusalem.

11 The remainder of the people in the city and the Jewish deserters who had declared their allegiance to the king of Babylon were all taken as exiles to Babylon.

12 But the poorest of the people were left to farm the land.

13 The Babylonians broke up the bronze pillars of the Temple and the bronze tank and its bases and carried all the bronze to Babylon.

14, 15 They also took all the pots, shovels, firepans, snuffers, spoons, and other bronze instruments used for the sacrifices. The gold and silver bowls and all the rest of the gold and silver was melted down to bullion.

16 It was impossible to estimate the weight of the two pillars and the great tank and its bases — all made for the Temple by King Solomon — because they were so heavy.

17 Each pillar was 27 feet high, with an intricate

bronze network of pomegranates decorating the 4½-foot capitals at the tops of the pillars.

18   The general took Seraiah, the chief priest, his assistant Zephaniah, and the three Temple guards to Babylon as captives.

19   A commander of the army of Judah, the chief recruiting officer, five of the king's counselors, and sixty farmers, all of whom were discovered hiding in the city,

20   Were taken by General Nebuzaradan to the king of Babylon at Riblah,

21   Where they were put to the sword and died. So Judah was exiled from its land.

22   Then King Nebuchadnezzar appointed Gedaliah (the son of Ahikam and grandson of Shaphan) as governor over the people left in Judah.

23   When the Israeli guerrilla forces learned that the king of Babylon had appointed Gedaliah as governor, some of these underground leaders and their men joined him at Mizpah. These included Ishmael, the son of Nethaniah; Johanan, the son of Kareah; Seraiah, the son of Tanhumeth the Netophathite; and Ja-azaniah, son of Maachathite, and their men.

24   Gedaliah vowed that if they would give themselves up and submit to the Babylonians, they would be allowed to live in the land and would not be exiled.

25   But seven months later, Ishmael, who was a member of the royal line, went to Mizpah with ten men and killed Gedaliah and his court — both the Jews and the Babylonians.

26   Then all the men of Judah and the guerrilla leaders fled in panic to Egypt, for they were afraid of what the Babylonians would do to them.

27　King Jehoiachin was released from prison on the twenty-seventh day of the last month of the thirty-seventh year of his captivity. This occurred during the first year of the reign of King Evil-merodach of Babylon.

28　He treated Jehoiachin kindly and gave him preferential treatment over all the other kings who were being held as prisoners in Babylon.

29　Jehoiachin was given civilian clothing to replace his prison garb, and for as long as he lived, he ate regularly at the king's table.

30　The king also gave him a daily cash allowance for the rest of his life.

I Chronicles

CHAPTER 1

These are the earliest generations of mankind:[1]
    Adam,
    Seth,
    Enosh,
2   Kenan,
    Mahalalel,
    Jared,
3   Enoch,
    Methuselah,
    Lamech,
4   Noah,
    Shem, Ham, and **Japheth.**[2]

*   *   *   *   *

5 The sons of *Japheth*[3] were:

    Gomer, Magog, Madai, **Javan,** Tubal, Meshech, and Tiras.

6 The sons of *Gomer*:

    Ashkenaz, Diphath, and Togarmah.

7 The sons of *Javan*:

    Elishah, Tarshish, Kittim, and Rodanim.

---

[1]Implied.
[2]The names in bold face type are referred to in the following verse or verses. The use of bold type or italic type does not mean that these persons were more important; it is simply a way of easier identification of ancestors and descendants.
[3]Italic means that the name has previously appeared in bold face type.

8 The sons of *Ham*:

Cush, Misream, Canaan, and Put.

9 The sons of *Cush* were:

Seba, Havilah, Sabta, Raama, and Sabteca. The sons of Raama were Sheba and Dedan.

10 Another of the sons of *Cush* was Nimrod, who became a great hero.

11, 12 The clans named after the sons of *Misream* were:

the Ludim, the Anamim, the Lehabim, the Naphtuhim, the Pathrusim, the Caphtorim, and the Casluhim (the ancestors of the Philistines).

13-16 Among *Canaan's* sons were:

Sidon (his firstborn), and Heth.

Canaan was also the ancestor of the Jebusites, Amorites, Girgashites, Hivites, Arkites, Sinites, Arvadites, Zemarites, and Hamathites.

17 The sons of *Shem*:

Elam, Asshur, **Arpachshad,** Lud, Aram, Uz, Hul, Gether, and Meshech.

18 *Arpachshad's* son was **Shelah,** and *Shelah's* son was **Eber.**

19 *Eber* had two sons: Peleg (which means "Divided," for it was during his lifetime that the people of the earth were divided into different language groups), and Joktan.

20-23 The sons of Joktan:

Almodad, Sheleph, Hazarmaveth, Jerah, Hadoram, Uzal, Diklah, Ebal, Abimael, Sheba, Ophir, Havilah, and Jobab.

24 So the son[4] of *Shem* was Arpachshad, the son of Arpachshad was Shelah,

25 The son of Shelah was Eber,
The son of Eber was Peleg,
The son of Peleg was Reu,

26 The son of Reu was Serug,
The son of Serug was Nahor,
The son of Nahor was Terah,

27 The son of Terah was Abram (later known as Abraham).

28-31 Abraham's sons were **Isaac** and **Ishmael.**
The sons of *Ishmael*:
Nabaioth (the oldest), Kedar, Adbeel, Mibsam, Mishma, Dumah, Massa, Hadad, Tema, Jetur, Naphish, and Kedemah.

32 Abraham also had sons by his concubine Keturah:
Zimram, **Jokshan,** Medan, **Midian,** Ishbak, and Shuah.
Jokshan's sons were Sheba and Dedan.

33 The sons of *Midian*:
Ephah, Epher, Hanoch, Abida, and Eldaah. These were the descendants of Abraham by his concubine Keturah.

34 Abraham's son *Isaac* had two sons, **Esau** and Israel.

35 The sons of *Esau*:
Eliphaz, Reuel, Jeush, Jalam, and Korah.

36 The sons of *Eliphaz*:
Teman, Omar, Zephi, Gatam, Kenaz, Tim-

---

[4]Or, "descendant." The subsequent usage of the word "son" could also be interpreted "descendant."

na, and Amalek.

37 The sons of *Reuel*:

Nahath, Zerah, Shammah, and Mizzah.

38, 39 The sons of *Esau*[5] also included **Lotan, Shobal, Zibeon,** Anah, Dishon, **Ezer,** and **Dishan;** and Esau's daughter was named Timna.

Lotan's sons were Hori and Homam.

40 The sons of *Shobal*: Alian, Manahath, Ebal, Shephi, and Onam.

Zibeon's sons were Aiah and **Anah.**

41 *Anah's* son was **Dishon:**

The sons of *Dishon*: Hamran, Eshban, Ithran, and Cheran.

42 The sons of *Ezer*: Bilhan, Zaavan, and Jaakan.

Dishan's sons were Uz and Aran.

*   *   *   *   *

43 Here is a list of the names of the kings of Edom who reigned before the kingdom of Israel began:

Bela (the son of Beor), who lived in the city of Dinhabah.

44 When Bela died, Jobab the son of Zerah from Bozrah became the new king.

45 When Jobab died, Husham from the country of the Temanites became the king.

46 When Husham died, Hadad the son of Bedad — the one who destroyed the army of Midian in the fields of Moab — became king and ruled from the city of Avith.

47 When Hadad died, Samlah from the city of Masrekah came to the throne.

---

[5] Or, "Seir."

48 When Samlah died, Shaul from the river town of Rehoboth became the new king.

49 When Shaul died, Baal-hanan the son of Achbor became king.

50 When Baal-hanan died, Hadad became king and ruled from the city of Pai (his wife was Mehetabel, the daughter of Matred and granddaughter of Mezahab).

51 At the time of Hadad's death, the kings of Edom were:

> Chief Timna,
> Chief Aliah,
> Chief Jetheth,
52   Chief Oholibamah,
> Chief Elah,
> Chief Pinon,
53   Chief Kenaz,
> Chief Teman,
> Chief Mibzar,
54   Chief Magdi-el,
> Chief Iram.

CHAPTER 2

The sons of Israel were:
> Reuben,
> Simeon,
> Levi,
> Judah,
> Issachar,
> Zebulun,
> Dan,
> Joseph,
> Benjamin,

Naphtali,
Gad,
Asher.

3   Judah had three sons by Bath-shua, a girl from Canaan: **Er,** Onan, and Shelah. But the oldest son, *Er,* was so wicked that the Lord killed him.

4   Then Er's widow, Tamar, and her father-in-law, Judah, became the parents of twin sons, **Perez** and **Zerah.** So Judah had five sons.

5   The sons of *Perez* were **Hezron** and Hamul.

6   The sons of *Zerah* were:
Zimri, **Ethan,** Heman, Calcol, and Dara.

7   (Achan, the son of Carmi, was the man who robbed God and was such a troublemaker for his nation.)

8   *Ethan's* son was Azariah.

9   The sons of *Hezron* were Jerahmeel, Ram, and Chelubai.

10   Ram was the father of Amminadab, and Amminadab was the father of Nahshon, a leader of Israel.

11   Nahshon was the father of Salma, and Salma was the father of Boaz.

12   Boaz was the father of Obed, and Obed was the father of Jesse.

13   *Jesse's* first son was Eliab, his second was Abinadab, his third was Shimea,

14   His fourth was Nethanel, his fifth was Raddai,

15   His sixth was Ozem, and his seventh was David.

16   He also had two girls (by the same wife) named **Zeruiah** and **Abigail.**

Zeruiah's sons were Abishai, Joab, and Asahel.

17 *Abigail,* whose husband was Jether from the land of Ishmael, had a son named Amasa.

18 Caleb (the son of **Hezron**) had two wives, **Azubah** and Jerioth. These are the children of *Azubah:* Jesher, Shobab, and Ardon.

19 After Azubah's death, Caleb married Ephrath, who presented him with a son, **Hur.**

20 *Hur's* son was **Uri,** and *Uri's* son was Bezalel.

21 **Hezron** married Machir's daughter at the age of sixty, and she presented him with a son, **Segub.** (Machir was also the father of Gilead.)

22 *Segub* was the father of Jair, who ruled[1] twenty-three cities in the land of Gilead.

23 But Geshur and Aram wrested these cities from him and also took Kenath and its sixty surrounding villages.

24 Soon after his father *Hezron's* death, Caleb married Ephrathah, his father's widow, and she gave birth to Ashhur, the father of Tekoa.

25 These are the sons of **Jerahmeel** (the oldest son of *Hezron*):
Ram (the oldest), Bunah, Oren, Ozem, and Ahijah.

26 *Jerahmeel's* second wife Atarah was the mother of **Onam.**

27 The sons of *Ram:*
Maaz, Jamin, and Eker.

28 *Onam's* sons were **Shammai** and Jada.
Shammai's sons were **Nadab** and **Abishur.**

29 The sons of *Abishur* and his wife Abihail were Ahban and Molid.

---

[1] Literally, "had."

30 *Nadab's* sons were **Seled** and **Appa-im.** *Seled* died without children,

31 But *Appa-im* had a son named **Ishi;** *Ishi's* son was **Sheshan;** and *Sheshan's* son was Ahlai.

32 *Shammai's* brother Jada had two sons, **Jether** and **Jonathan.** *Jether* died without children,

33 But *Jonathan* had two sons named Peleth and Zaza.

34, 35 *Sheshan*[2] had no sons, although he had several daughters. He gave one of his daughters to be the wife of Jarha, his Egyptian servant. And they had a son whom they named **Attai.**

36 Attai's son was Nathan; Nathan's son was Zabad;

37 Zabad's son was Ephlal; Ephlal's son was Obed;

38 Obed's son was Jehu; Jehu's son was Azariah;

39 Azariah's son was Helez; Helez's son was Ele-asah;

40 Ele-asah's son was Sismai; Sismai's son was Shallum;

41 Shallum's son was Jekamiah; Jekamiah's son was Elishama.

42 The oldest son of **Caleb** (Jerahmeel's brother) was Mesha; he was the father of Ziph, who was father of Mareshah, who was the father of **Hebron.**

43 The sons of *Hebron:* Korah, Tappuah, **Rekem,** and **Shema.**

44 *Shema* was the father of Raham, who was the father of Jorke-am.

Rekem was the father of **Shammai.**

45 *Shammai's* son was Maon, the father of Bethzur.

---

[2]Apparently a different Sheshan than in verse 31.

46 *Caleb's* concubine Ephah bore him **Haran,** Moza, and Gazez; *Haran* had a son named Gazez.

47 The sons of Jahdai:

Regem, Jotham, Geshan, Pelet, Ephah, and Shaaph.

48, 49 Another of *Caleb's* concubines, Maacah, bore him Sheber, Tirhanah, Shaaph (the father of Madmannah), and Sheva (the father of Machbenah and of Gibe-a). *Caleb* also had a daughter, whose name was Achsah.

50 The sons of Hur (who was the oldest son of *Caleb*[3] and Ephrathah) were **Shobal** (the father of Kiriath-jearim),

51 **Salma** (the father of Bethlehem), and Hareph (the father of Beth-gader).

52 **Shobal's** sons included **Kiriath-jearim** and Haroeh, the ancestor of half of the Menuhoth tribe.

53 The families of *Kiriath-jearim* were the Ithrites, the Puthites, the Shumathites, and the Mishraites (from whom descended the Zorathites and Eshtaolites).

54 The descendants of Salma were his son Bethlehem, the Netophathites, Atroth-beth-joab, half the Manahathites, and the Zorites;

55 They also included the families of the writers living at Jabez — the Tirathites, Shime-athites, and Sucathites. All these are Kenites who descended from Hammath, the founder of the family of Rechab.

CHAPTER 3

K ing David's oldest son was Amnon, who was born to his wife, Ahino-am of Jezreel.

---

[3]Implied in 2:24.

The second was Daniel, whose mother was Abigail from Carmel.

2 The third was Absalom, the son of his wife Maacah, who was the daughter of King Talmai of Geshur.

The fourth was Adonijah, the son of Haggith.

3 The fifth was Shephatiah, the son of Abital.

The sixth was Ithream, the son of his wife Eglah.

4 These six were born to him in Hebron, where he reigned seven and one-half years. Then he moved the capital to Jerusalem, where he reigned another thirty-three years.

5 While he was in Jerusalem, his wife Bathsheba[1] (the daughter of Ammi-el) became the mother of his sons Shime-a, Shobab, Nathan, and **Solomon.**

6 David also had nine other sons: Ibhar, Elishama, Eliphelet,

7 Nogah, Nepheg, Japhia,

8 Elishama, Eliada, and Eliphelet.

9 (This list does not include the sons of his concubines.) David also had a daughter Tamar.

10-14 These are the descendants of King *Solomon:*
> Rehoboam,
> Abijah,
> Asa,
> Jehoshaphat,
> Joram,[2]
> Ahaziah,
> Joash,
> Amaziah,

---

[1]Literally, "Bath-shua."
[2]Or, "Jehoram."

> Azariah,[3]
> Jotham,
> Ahaz,
> Hezekiah,
> Manasseh,
> Amon,
> **Josiah.**

15 The sons of *Josiah* were:
> Johanan,[4]
> **Jehoiakim,**
> Zedekiah,
> Shallum.

16 The sons of *Jehoiakim*:[5]
> **Jeconiah,**
> Zedekiah.

17-18 These are the sons who were born to King *Jeconiah* during the years that he was under house arrest:

> She-altiel,
> Malchiram,
> **Pedaiah,**
> Shenazzar,
> Jekamiah,
> Hoshama,
> Nedabiah.

19, 20 *Pedaiah* was the father of **Zerubbabel** and Shime-i.

> *Zerubbabel's* children were:
> Meshullam,
> **Hananiah,**

---

[3]Or, "Uzziah."
[4]Or, "Jehoahaz" (see II Kings 23:30 f.).
[5]Also known as Jehoiachin or Coniah.

Hashubah,
Ohel,
Berechiah,
Hasadiah,
Jushab-hesed,
Shelomith (a daughter).

21 Hananiah's sons were Pelatiah and Jeshaiah;
Jeshaiah's son was Rephaiah;
Rephaiah's son was Arnan;
Arnan's son was Obadiah;
Obadiah's son was Shecaniah.

22 Shecaniah's son was Shemaiah;
Shemaiah had six sons, including Hattush, Igal,
Bariah, **Neariah,** and Shaphat.

23 *Neariah* had three sons:
Eli-o-enai,
Hizkiah,
Azrikam.

24 *Eli-o-enai* had seven sons:
Hodaviah,
Eliashib,
Pelaiah,
Akkub,
Johanan,
Delaiah,
Anani.

CHAPTER 4

These are the sons of Judah:
Perez,
Hezron,
Carmi,

Hur,
Shobal.

2 *Shobal's* son Re-aiah was the father of Jahath, the ancestor of Ahumai and Lahad. These were known as the Zorathite clans.

3-4 The descendants of Etam:

> Jezreel,
> Ishma,
> Idbash,
> Hazzelelponi (his daughter),
> Penuel (the ancestor of Gedor),
> Ezer (the ancestor of Hushah),
> The son of Hur, the oldest son of Ephrathah, who was the father of Bethlehem.

5 Ashhur, the father of Tekoa, had two wives — **Helah,** and **Naarah.**

6 *Naarah* bore him Ahuzzam, Hepher, Temeni, and Haahashtari;

7 And *Helah* bore him Zereth, Izhar, and Ethnan.

8 Koz was the father of Anub and Zobebah; he was also the ancestor of the clan named after Aharhel, the son of Harum.

9 Jabez was more distinguished than any of his brothers. His mother named him Jabez because she had such a hard time at his birth (Jabez means[1] "Distress").

10 He was the one who prayed to the God of Israel, "Oh, that You would wonderfully bless me and help me in my work; please be with me in all that

---

[1] A play on words. *Jabez* sounds like *ozeb*, the Hebrew word meaning "distress."

I do, and keep me from all evil and disaster!" And God granted him his request.

11, 12   The descendants of Recah were:

> Chelub (the brother of Shuhah), whose son was Mahir, the father of **Eshton;**
> *Eshton* was the father of Bethrapha, Paseah, and Tehinnah;
> *Tehinnah* was the father of Irnahash.

13   The sons of Kenaz were **Othni-el** and **Seraiah.** *Othni-el's* sons were Hathath and **Meonothai;**

14   *Meonothai* was the father of Ophrah;

Seraiah was the father of Joab, the ancestor of the inhabitants of Craftsman Valley (called that because many craftsmen lived there).

15   The sons of Caleb (the son of Jephunneh):

> Iru,
> **Elah,**
> Naam.

The sons of *Elah* included Kenaz.

16   Jehallelel's sons were:

> Ziph,
> Ziphah,
> **Tiri-a,**
> Asarel.

17   Ezrah's sons were:

> Jether,
> **Mered,**
> Epher,
> Jalon.

Mered married Bithi-ah, an Egyptian princess. She was the mother of Miriam, Shammai, and Ishbah — an ancestor of **Eshtemoa.**

18   *Eshtemoa's* wife was a Jewess; she was the

mother of Jered, Heber, and Jekuthiel, who were, respectively, the ancestors of the Gedorites, Socoites, and Zanoahites.

19 Hodiah's wife was the sister of Naham. One of her sons was the father of Keilah the Garmite, and another was the father of Eshtemoa the Maacathite.

20 The sons of Shimon:

Amnon,

Rinnah,

Ben-hanan,

Tilon.

The sons of Ishi:

Zoheth,

Ben-zoheth.

21-22 The sons of Shelah (the son of Judah):

Er (the father of Lecah),

Laadah (the father of Mareshah),

The families of the linen workers who worked at Beth-ashbea,

Jokim,

The clans of Cozeba,

Joash,

Saraph (who was a ruler in Moab before he returned to Lehem).

These names all come from very ancient records.

23 These clans were noted for their pottery, gardening, and planting; they all worked for the king:

24 The sons of Simeon:

Nemu-el,

Jamin,

Jarib,

Zerah,

Shaul.

25 *Shaul's* son was Shallum, his grandson was Mibsam, and his great-grandson was **Mishma.**

26 *Mishma's* sons included Hammu-el (the father of Zaccur and grandfather of **Shime-i).**

27 *Shime-i* had sixteen sons and six daughters, but none of his brothers had large families — they all had fewer children than was normal in Judah.

28 They lived at Beer-sheba, Moladah, Hazar-shual,

29 Bilhah, Ezem, Tolad,

30 Bethuel, Hormah, Ziklag,

31 Beth-marcaboth, Hazar-susim, Beth-biri, and Sha-araim. These cities were under their control until the time of David.

32, 33 Their descendants also lived in or near Etam, Ain, Rimmon, Tochen, and Ashan; some were as far away as Baal. (These facts are recorded in their genealogies.)

34-39 These are the names of some of the princes of wealthy clans who traveled to the east side of Gedor Valley in search of pasture for their flocks:

> Meshobab,
> Jamlech,
> Joshah,
> Joel,
> Jehu,
> Eli-o-enai,
> Ja-akobah,
> Jeshohaiah,
> Asaiah,
> Adi-el,
> Jesimi-el,
> Benaiah,

Ziza, (the son of Shiphi, son of Allon, son
of Jedaiah, son of Shimri, son of
Shemaiah).

40, 41 They found good pastures, and everything
was quiet and peaceful; but the land belonged to the
descendants of Ham. So during the reign of King Hezekiah of Judah these princes invaded the land and
struck down the tents and houses of the descendants
of Ham; they killed the inhabitants of the land and
took possession of it for themselves.

42 Later, five hundred of these invaders from the
tribe of Simeon went to Mount Seir. (Their leaders
were Pelatiah, Ne-ariah, Rephaiah, and Uzziel — all
sons of Ishi.)

43 There they destroyed the few surviving members of the tribe of Amalek. And they have lived
there ever since.

CHAPTER 5

The oldest son of Israel was Reuben, but since he
dishonored his father by sleeping with one of his
father's wives, his birthright was given to his half-
brother, Joseph. So the official genealogy doesn't
name Reuben as the oldest son.

2 Although Joseph received the birthright, yet
Judah was a powerful and influential tribe in Israel,
and from Judah came a Prince.

3 The sons of Reuben, Israel's oldest son, were:
Hanoch,
Pallu,
Hezron,
Carmi.

4 Joel's descendants were his son Shemaiah, his grandson Gog, and his great-grandson **Shime-i.**

5 *Shime-i's* son was Micah; his grandson was Re-aiah; and his great-grandson was **Baal.**

6 *Baal's* son was Beerah. He was a prince of the tribe of Reuben and was taken into captivity by King Tilgath-pilneser of Assyria.

7 His relatives became heads of clans and were included in the official genealogy:

Je-iel,

Zechariah,

8 Bela (the son of Azaz, grandson of Shema, and great-grandson of **Joel).**

These Reubenites[1] lived in Aroer and as far distant as Mount Nebo and Baal-meon.

9 Joel was a cattle man, and he pastured his animals eastward to the edge of the desert and to the Euphrates River, for there were many cattle in the land of Gilead.

10 During the reign of King Saul, the men of Reuben defeated the Hagrites in war and moved into their tents on the eastern edge of Gilead.

11 Across from them, in the land of Bashan, lived the descendants of Gad, who were spread as far as Salecah.

12 Joel was the greatest and was followed by Shapham, also Janai and Shaphat.

13 Their relatives, the heads of the seven clans, were Michael, Meshullam, Sheba, Jorai, Jacan, Zia, and Eber.

14 The descendants of Buz, in the order of their generations, were:

---

[1]Implied in 5:1.

Jahdo,
Jeshishai,
Michael,
Gilead,
Jaroah,
Huri,
Abihail.

15 Ahi, the son of Abdi-el and grandson of Guni, was the leader of the clan.

16 The clan lived in and around Gilead (in the land of Bashan) and throughout the entire pasture country of Sharon.

17 All were included in the official genealogy at the time of King Jotham of Judah and King Jeroboam of Israel.

18 There were 44,760 armed, trained, and brave troops in the army of Reuben, Gad, and the half-tribe of Manasseh.

19 They declared war on the Hagrites, the Jeturites, the Naphishites, and the Nodabites.

20 They cried out to God to help them, and He did, for they trusted in Him. So the Hagrites and all their allies were defeated.

21 The booty included 50,000 camels, 250,000 sheep, 2,000 donkeys, and 100,000 captives.

22 A great number of the enemy also died in the battle, for God was fighting against them. So the Reubenites lived in the territory of the Hagrites until the time of the exile.

23 The half-tribe of Manasseh spread through the land from Bashan to Baal-hermon, Senir, and Mount Hermon. They too were very numerous.

24 The chiefs of their clans were the following:

Epher,
Ishi,
Eliel,
Azri-el,
Jeremiah,
Hodaviah,
Jahdi-el.

Each of these men had a great reputation as a warrior and leader.

25 But they were not true to the God of their fathers; instead they worshiped the idols of the people whom God had destroyed.

26 So God caused King Pul of Assyria (also known as Tilgath-pilneser III) to invade the land and deport the men of Reuben, Gad, and the half-tribe of Manasseh. They took them to Halah, Habor, Hara, and the Gozan River, where they remain to this day.

CHAPTER 6

These are the names of the sons of Levi:
Gershom,
Kohath,
Merari.

2 *Kohath's* sons were:
Amram,
Izhar,
Hebron,
Uzziel.

3 *Amram's* descendants included:
Aaron,
Moses,
Miriam.

Aaron's sons were:

Nadab,
Abihu,
Eleazar,
Ithamar.

4-15   The oldest sons of the successive generations
of Aaron were as follows:[1]

Eleazar, the father of
Phinehas, the father of
Abishua, the father of
Bukki, the father of
Uzzi, the father of
Zerahiah, the father of
Meraioth, the father of
Amariah, the father of
Ahitub, the father of
Zadok, the father of
Ahima-az, the father of
Azariah, the father of
Johanan, the father of
Azariah (the high priest in Solomon's
          Temple at Jerusalem), the father of
Amariah, the father of
Ahitub, the father of
Zadok, the father of
Shallum, the father of
Hilkiah, the father of
Azariah, the father of
Seraiah, the father of
Jehozadak (who went into exile when the
          Lord sent the people of Judah and

---

[1]Implied.

Jerusalem into captivity near Nebuchadnezzar).

16 As previously stated,[2] the sons of Levi were:
Gershom,
Kohath,
Merari.

17 The sons of *Gershom* were:
Libni,
Shime-i.

18 The sons of *Kohath* were:
Amram,
Izhar,
Hebron,
Uzziel.

19, 20, 21 The sons of *Merari* were:
Mahli,
Mushi.

The subclans of the Levites were:
In the Gershom clan,
Libni,
Jahath,
Zimmah,
Joah,
Iddo,
Zerah,
Jeatherai.

22, 23, 24 In the Kohath clan:
Amminadab,
Korah,
Assir,
Elkanah,
Ebiasaph,

---

[2]Implied in 6:1.

> Assir,
> Tahath,
> Uriel,
> Uzziah,
> Shaul.

25, 26, 27   The subclan of *Elkanah* was further divided into the families of his sons:

> Amasai,
> Ahimoth,
> Elkanah,
> Zophai,
> Nahath,
> Eliab,
> Jeroham,
> Elkanah.

28   The families of the subclan of Samuel were headed by Samuel's sons:

> Joel, the oldest;
> Abijah, the second.

29, 30   The subclans of the clan of Merari were headed by his sons:

> Mahli,
> Libni,
> Shime-i,
> Uzzah,
> Shime-a,
> Haggiah,
> Asaiah.

31   King David appointed songleaders and choirs to praise God in the Tabernacle after he had placed the Ark in it.

32   Then, when Solomon built the Temple at Jerusalem, the choirs carried on their work there.

33-38   These are the names and ancestries[3] of choir leaders: Heman the Cantor was from the clan of Kohath; his genealogy was traced back through:

> Joel,
> Samuel,
> Elkanah III,
> Jeroham,
> Eliel,
> Toah,
> Zuph,
> Elkanah II,
> Mahath,
> Amasai,
> Elkanah I,
> Joel,
> Azariah,
> Zephaniah,
> Tahath,
> Assir,
> Ebiasaph,
> Korah,
> Izhar,
> Kohath,
> Levi,
> Israel.

39-43   Heman's assistant[4] was his colleague Asaph, whose genealogy was traced back through:

> Berechiah,
> Shime-a,
> Michael,
> Ba-aseiah,

---

[3]Implied.
[4]Literally, "brother," or "kinsman."

Malchijah,
Ethni,
Zerah,
Adaiah,
Ethan,
Zimmah,
Shime-i,
Jahath,
Gershom,
Levi.

44-47   Heman's second assistant was Ethan, a representative from the clan of Merari, who stood on his left. Merari's ancestry was traced back through:

Kishi,
Abdi,
Malluch,
Hashabiah,
Amaziah,
Hilkiah,
Amzi,
Bani,
Shemer,
Mahli,
Mushi,
Merari,
Levi.

48   Their relatives — all the other Levites — were appointed to various other tasks in the Tabernacle.

49   But only Aaron and his descendants were the priests. Their duties included sacrificing burnt offerings and incense, handling all the tasks relating to the inner sanctuary — the Holy of Holies — and the tasks relating to the annual Day of Atonement for Israel.

They saw to it that all the details commanded by Moses the servant of God were strictly followed.

50-53   The descendants of Aaron were:

      Eleazar,
      Phinehas,
      Abishua,
      Bukki,
      Uzzi,
      Zerahiah,
      Meraioth,
      Amariah,
      Ahitub,
      Zadok,
      Ahima-az.

*   *   *   *   *

54   This is a record of the cities and land assigned by lot to the descendants of Aaron, all of whom were members of the Kohath clan:

55, 56, 57   Hebron and its surrounding pasture-lands in Judah (although the fields and suburbs were given to Caleb the son of Jephunneh),

58, 59   And the following Cities of Refuge with their surrounding pasturelands:

      Libnah,
      Jattir,
      Eshtemoa,
      Hilen,
      Debir,
      Ashan,
      Beth-shemesh.

60   Thirteen other cities with surrounding pastures — including Geba, Alemeth, and Anathoth — were giv-

en to the priests by the tribe of Benjamin.

61   Lots were then drawn to assign land to the remaining descendants of Kohath, and they received ten cities in the territory of the half-tribe of Manasseh.

62   The subclans of the Gershom clan received by lot thirteen cities in the Bashan area from the tribes of Issachar, Asher, Naphtali, and Manasseh.

63   The subclans of Merari received by lot twelve cities from the tribes of Reuben, Gad, and Zebulun.

64, 65   Cities and pasturelands were also assigned by lot to the Levites (and then renamed) from the tribes of Judah, Simeon, and Benjamin.

66-69   The tribe of Ephraim gave these Cities of Refuge with the surrounding pasturelands to the subclans of Kohath:

> Shechem, in Mount Ephraim;
> Gezer;
> Jokme-am;
> Beth-horon;
> Aijalon;
> Gath-rimmon.

70   The following Cities of Refuge and their pasturelands were given to the subclans of the Kohathites by the half-tribe of Manasseh:

> Aner,
> Bile-am.

71   Cities of Refuge and pastureland given to the clan of Gershom by the half-tribe of Manasseh were:

> Golan, in Bashan;
> Ashtaroth.

72   The tribe of Issachar gave them Kedesh, Daberath,

73   Ramoth, and Anem, and the surrounding pastureland of each.

74   The tribe of Asher gave them Abdon, Mashal,

75   Hukok, and Rehob, with their pasturelands.

76   The tribe of Naphtali gave them Kedesh in Galilee, Hammon, and Kiriathaim with pasturelands.

77   The tribe of Zebulun gave Rimmono and Tabor to the Merari clan as Cities of Refuge.

78, 79   And across the Jordan River, opposite Jericho, the tribe of Reuben gave them Bezer (a desert town), Jahzah, Kedemoth and Mepha-ath, along with their pasturelands.

80   The tribe of Gad gave them Remoth in Gilead, Mahanaim,

81   Heshbon, and Jazer, each with their surrounding pasturelands.

CHAPTER 7

The sons of Issachar:
> **Tola,**
> Puah,
> Jashub,
> Shimron.

2   The sons of *Tola,* each of whom was the head of a subclan:
> **Uzzi,**
> Rephaiah,
> Jeri-el,
> Jahmai,
> Ibsam,
> Shemuel.

At the time of King David, the total number of men of war from these families totaled 22,600.

3 *Uzzi's* son was Izrahiah among whose five sons were Michael, Obadiah, Joel, and Isshiah, all chiefs of subclans.

4 Their descendants, at the time of King David, numbered 36,000 troops; for all five of them had several wives and many sons.

5 The total number of men available for military service from all the clans of the tribe of Isssachar numbered 87,000 stouthearted warriors, all included in the official genealogy.

6 The sons of Benjamin were:

Bela,

Becher,

Jedia-el.

7 The sons of *Bela*:

Ezbon,

Uzzi,

Uzziel,

Jerimoth,

Iri.

These five mighty warriors were chiefs of subclans and were the leaders of 22,034 troops (all of whom were recorded in the official genealogies).

8 The sons of *Becher* were:

Zemirah,

Joash,

Eliezer,

Eli-o-enai,

Omri,

Jeremoth,

Abijah,

Anathoth,

Alemeth.

9   At the time of David there were 22,200 mighty warriors among their descendants; and they were led by their clan chiefs.

10   The son of *Jedia-el* was **Bilhan.**

The sons of *Bilhan* were:

> Jeush,
> Benjamin,
> Ehud,
> Chenaanah,
> Zethan,
> Tarshish,
> Ahishahar.

11   They were the chiefs of the subclans of *Jedia-el,* and their descendants included 17,200 warriors at the time of King David.

12   The sons of Ir were Shuppim and Huppim. Hushim was one of the sons of Aher.

13   The sons of Naphtali (descendants of Jacob's wife[1] Bilhah) were:

> Jahzi-el,
> Guni,
> Jezer,
> Shallum.

14   The sons of Manasseh, born to his Aramaean concubine, were Asri-el and **Machir** (who became the father of Gilead).

15   It was Machir who found wives for Huppim and Shuppim.[2] Machir's sister was Maacah. Another descendant was Zelophehad, who had only[3] daughters.

16   Machir's wife, also named Maacah, bore him

---

[1]Implied.
[2]See verse 12.
[3]Implied. See Numbers 26:33.

a son whom she named Peresh; his brother's name was Sheresh, and he had sons named Ulam and Rakem.

17 Ulam's son was Bedan. So these were the sons of Gilead, the grandsons of Machir, and the great-grandsons of Manasseh.

18 Hammolecheth, Machir's sister, bore Ishhod, Abiezer, and Mahlah.

19 The sons of Shemida were Ahian, Shechem, Likhi, and Aniam.

20, 21 The sons of Ephraim:
Shuthelah,
Bered,
Tahath,
Eleadah,
Tahath,
Zabad,
Shuthelah,
Ezer,
Ele-ad.

Ele-ad and *Ezer* attempted to rustle cattle at Gath, but they were killed by the local farmers.

22 Their father Ephraim mourned for them a long time, and his brothers tried to comfort him.

23 Afterwards, his wife conceived and bore a son whom he called Beriah (meaning "a tragedy") because of what had happened.

24 Ephraim's daughter's name was Sheerah. She built Lower and Upper Beth-horon and Uzzen-sheerah.

25, 26, 27 This is Ephraim's line of descent:
Rephah, the father of
Resheph, the father of
Telah, the father of

Tahan, the father of
Ladan, the father of
Ammihud, the father of
Elishama, the father of
Nun, the father of
Joshua.

28 They lived in an area bounded on one side by Bethel and its surrounding towns, on the east by Naaran, on the west by Gezer and its villages, and finally by Shechem and its surrounding villages as far as Ayyah and its towns.

29 The tribe of Manasseh, descendants of Joseph the son of Israel, controlled the following cities and their surrounding areas: Beth-shean, Taanach, Megiddo, and Dor.

30 The children of Asher:
Imnah,
Ishvah,
Ishvi,
Beriah,
Serah (their sister).

31 The sons of *Beriah* were:
Heber,
Malchi-el (the father of Birzaith).

32 *Heber's* children were:
Japhlet,
Shomer,
Hotham,
Shua (their sister).

33 *Japhlet's* sons were:
Pasach,
Bimhal,
Ashvath.

34 His brother *Shomer's*[4] sons were:
Rohgah,
Jehubbah,
Aram.

35 The sons of his brother *Hotham*[5] were:
Zophah,
Imna,
Shelesh,
Amal.

36 The sons of *Zophah* were:
Suah,
Harnepher,
Shual,
Beri,
Imrah,

37 Bezer,
Hod,
Shamma,
Shilshah,
Ithran,
Be-era.

38 The sons of *Ithran*[6] were:
Jephunneh,
Pispa,
Ara.

39 The sons of Ulla were:
Arah,
Hanniel,
Rizia.

40 These descendants of Asher were heads of subclans and were all skilled warriors and chiefs.

---

[4]Or, "Shemer."
[5]Literally, "Helem."
[6]Literally, "Jether."

Their descendants in the official genealogy numbered 36,000 men of war.

CHAPTER 8

Т^{he} sons of Benjamin, according to age, were:
> **Bela,** the first,
> Ashbel, the second,
> Aharah, the third,
> Nohah, the fourth,
> Rapha, the fifth.

3, 4, 5   The sons of *Bela* were:
> Addar,
> Gera,
> Abihud,
> Abishua,
> Naaman,
> Ahoah,
> Gera,
> Shephuphan,
> Huram.

6, 7   The sons of Ehud, chiefs of the subclans living at Geba, were captured in war and exiled to Manahath. They were:
> Naaman,
> Ahijah,
> Gera, (also called Heglam), the father of Uzza and Ahihud.

8, 9, 10   Shaharaim divorced his wives **Hushim** and Baara, but he had children in the land of Moab by Hodesh, his new wife:
> Jobab,
> Zibia,

> Mesha,
> Malcam,
> Jeuz,
> Sachia,
> Mirmah.

These sons all became chiefs of subclans.

11　His wife *Hushim* had borne him Abitub and **Elpaal.**

12　The sons of *Elpaal* were:

> Eber,
> Misham,
> Shemed (who built Ono and Lod and their
> surrounding villages).

13　His other sons were **Beriah** and Shema, chiefs of subclans living in Aijalon; they chased out the inhabitants of Gath.

14　*Elpaal's* sons also included:

> Ahio,
> **Shashak,**
> Jeremoth.

15, 16　The sons of *Beriah* were:

> Zebadiah,
> Arad,
> Eder,
> Michael,
> Ishpah,
> Joha.

17, 18　The sons of *Elpaal* also included:

> Zebadiah,
> Meshullam,
> Hizki,
> Heber,
> Ishmerai,

Izliah,
Jobab.

19, 20, 21   The sons of Shime-i were:
Jakim,
Zichri,
Zabdi,
Eli-enai,
Zille-thai,
Eliel,
Adaiah,
Beraiah,
Shimrath.

22-25   The sons of *Shashak* were:
Ishpan,
Eber,
Eliel,
Abdon,
Zichri,
Hanan,
Hananiah,
Elam,
Anthothijah,
Iphdeiah,
Penuel.

26, 27   The sons of Jeroham were:
Shamsherai
Shehariah,
Athaliah,
Jaareshiah,
Elijah,
Zichri.

28   These were the chiefs of the subclans living at Jerusalem.

29   Je-iel, the father of Gibeon, lived at Gibeon; and his wife's name was Maacah.

30, 31   His oldest son was named Abdon, followed by:

> Zur,
> Kish,
> Baal,
> Nadab,
> Gedor,
> Ahio,
> Zecher,

32   Mikloth who was the father of Shimeah. All of these families lived together near Jerusalem.

33   Ner was the father of Kish, and Kish was the father of Saul;

> Saul's sons included:
> **Jonathan,**
> Malchishua,
> Abinadab,
> Eshbaal.

34   The son of *Jonathan* was Mephibosheth;[1]
The son of Mephibosheth[1] was Micah.

35   The sons of Micah:

> Pithon,
> Melech,
> Tarea,
> Ahaz.

36   Ahaz was the father of Jehoaddah,
Jehoaddah was the father of:

> Alemeth,
> Azmaveth,

---

[1]Or, "Merib-baal."

Zimri.

Zimri's son was Moza.

37 Moza was the father of Bine-a, whose sons were:

Raphah,
Eleasah,
Azel.

38 Azel had six sons:

Azrikam,
Bocheru,
Ishmael,
She-ariah,
Obadiah,
Hanan.

39 Azel's brother Eshek had three sons:

Ulam, the first,
Jeush, the second,
Eliphelet, the third.

40 *Ulam's* sons were prominent warriors who were expert marksmen with their bows. These men had 150 sons and grandsons, and they were all from the tribe of Benjamin.

CHAPTER 9

The family tree of every person in Israel was carefully recorded in *The Annals of the Kings of Israel.*

Judah was exiled to Babylon because the people worshiped idols.

2 The first to return and live again in their former cities were families from the tribes of Israel, and also the priests, the Levites, and the Temple assistants.

3 Then some families from the tribes of Judah,

Benjamin, Ephraim, and Manasseh arrived in Jerusalem:

4 One family was that of Uthai (the son of Ammihud, son of Omri, son of Imri, son of Bani) of the clan of Perez (son of Judah).

5 The Shilonites were another family to return, including Asaiah (Shilon's oldest son) and his sons;

6 There were also the sons of Zerah, including Jeuel and his relatives: 690 in all.

7, 8 Among the members of the tribe of Benjamin who returned were these:

> Sallu (the son of Meshullam, the son of Hodaviah, the son of Hassenuah);
>
> Ibneiah (the son of Jeroham);
>
> Elah (the son of Uzzi, the son of Michri);
>
> Meshullam, (the son of Shephatiah, the son of Reuel, the son of Ibnijah).

9 These men were all chiefs of subclans. A total of 956 Benjaminites returned.

10 The priests who returned were:

> Jedaiah,
>
> Jehoiarib,
>
> Jachin,

11 Azariah (the son of Hilkiah, son of Meshullam, son of Zadok, son of Meraioth, son of Ahitub).

He was the chief custodian of the Temple.

12 Another of the returning priests was Adaiah (son of Jeroham, son of Pashhur, son of Malchijah).

> Another priest was Maasai (son of Adi-el, son of Jahzerah, son of Meshullam, son of Meshillemith, son of Immer).

13 In all, 1,760 priests returned.

14 Among the Levites who returned was Shemaiah (son of Hasshub, son of Azrikam, son of Hashabiah, who was a descendant of Merari).

15, 16 Other Levites who returned included:

Bakbakkar,

Heresh,

Galal,

Mattaniah (the son of Mica, who was the son of Zichri, who was the son of Asaph).

Obadiah (the son of Shemaiah, son of Galal, son of Jeduthun).

Berechiah (the son of Asa, son of Elkanah, who lived in the area of the Netophathites).

17, 18 The gatekeepers were Shallum (the chief gatekeeper), Akkub, Talmon, and Ahiman — all Levites. They are still responsible for the eastern royal gate.

19 Shallum's ancestry went back through Kore and Ebiasaph to Korah. He and his close relatives the Korahites were in charge of the sacrifices and the protection of the sanctuary, just as their ancestors had supervised and guarded the Tabernacle.

20 Phinehas, the son of Eleazar, was the first director of this division in ancient times. And the Lord was with him.

21 At that time Zechariah, the son of Meshelemiah, had been responsible for the protection of the entrance to the Tabernacle.

22 There were 212 doorkeepers in those days. They were chosen from their villages on the basis of

their genealogies, and they were appointed by David and Samuel because of their reliability.

23 They and their descendants were in charge of the Lord's Tabernacle.

24 They were assigned to each of the four sides: east, west, north, and south.

25 And their relatives in the villages were assigned to them from time to time, for seven days at a time.

26 The four head gatekeepers, all Levites, were in an office of great trust, for they were responsible for the rooms and treasuries in the Tabernacle of God.

27 Because of their important positions they lived near the Tabernacle, and they opened the gates each morning.

28 Some of them were assigned to care for the various vessels used in the sacrifices and worship; they checked them in and out to avoid loss.

29 Others were responsible for the furniture, the items in the sanctuary, and the supplies such as fine flour, wine, incense, and spices.

30 Other priests prepared the spices and incense.

31 And Mattithiah (a Levite and the oldest son of Shallum the Korahite) was entrusted with making the flat cakes for grain offerings.

32 Some members of the Kohath clan were in charge of the preparation of the special bread[1] each sabbath.

33, 34 The cantors were all prominent Levites. They lived in Jerusalem at the Temple and were on duty at all hours. They were free from other responsibilities and were selected by their genealogies.

---

[1]Literally, "showbread."

*   *   *   *   *

35, 36, 37   Jeiel (whose wife was Maacah) lived in Gibeon. He had many[2] sons, including:

> Gibeon,
> Abdon (the oldest),
> Zur,
> Kish,
> Baal,
> **Ner,**
> Nadab,
> Gedor,
> Ahio,
> Zechariah,
> Mikloth.

38   Mikloth lived with his son Shime-am in Jerusalem near his relatives.

39   Ner was the father of Kish,
Kish was the father of Saul,
Saul was the father of Jonathan, Malchishua, Abinadab, and Eshbaal.

40   Jonathan was the father of Mephibosheth;[3]
Mephibosheth[3] was the father of Micah;

41   Micah was the father of Pithon, Melech, Tahre-a, and Ahaz;

42   Ahaz was the father of Jarah;
Jarah was the father of Alemeth, Azmaveth, and Zimri;
Zimri was the father of Moza.

43   Moza was the father of Bine-a, Rephaiah, Ele-asah, and Azel.

44   Azel had six sons:

---

[2]Implied.
[3]Or, "Merib-baal."

Azrikam, Bocheru, Ishmael, She-ariah, Obadiah, Hanan.

CHAPTER 10[1]

The Philistines attacked and defeated the Israeli troops, who turned and fled and were slaughtered on the slopes of Mount Gilboa.

2 They caught up with Saul and his three sons, Jonathan, Abinadab, and Malchishua, and killed them all.

3 Saul had been hard pressed with heavy fighting all around him, when the Philistine archers shot and wounded him.

4 He cried out to his bodyguard, "Quick, kill me with your sword before these uncircumcised heathen capture and torture me." But the man was afraid to do it, so Saul took his own sword and fell against its point; and it pierced his body.

5 Then his bodyguard, seeing that Saul was dead, killed himself in the same way.

6 So Saul and his three sons died together; the entire family was wiped out in one day.

7 When the Israelis in the valley below the mountain heard that their troops had been routed and that Saul and his sons were dead, they abandoned their cities and fled. And the Philistines came and lived in them.

8 When the Philistines went back the next day to strip the bodies of the men killed in action and to gather the booty from the battlefield, they found the bodies of Saul and his sons.

---

[1]The remainder of I Chronicles deals with events preceding chapter 9.

9 So they stripped off Saul's armor and cut off his head; then they displayed them throughout the nation and celebrated the wonderful news before their idols.

10 They fastened his armor to the walls of the Temple of the Gods and nailed his head to the wall of Dagon's temple.

11 But when the people of Jabesh-gilead heard what the Philistines had done to Saul,

12 Their heroic warriors went out to the battle-field[2] and brought back his body and the bodies of his three sons. Then they buried them beneath the oak tree at Jabesh and mourned and fasted for seven days.

13 Saul died for his disobedience to the Lord and because he had consulted a medium,[3]

14 And did not ask the Lord for guidance. So the Lord killed him and gave the kingdom to David, the son of Jesse.

CHAPTER 11

Then the leaders of Israel went to David at Hebron and told him, "We are your relatives,[1]

2 And even when Saul was king, you were the one who led our armies to battle and brought them safely back again. And the Lord your God has told you, 'You shall be the shepherd of My people Israel. You shall be their king.'"

3 So David made a contract with them before the Lord, and they anointed him as king of Israel, just as the Lord had told Samuel.

---

[2]Implied.
[3]See I Samuel 28.
[1]Literally, "your bone and flesh."

4   Then David and the leaders went to Jerusalem (or Jebus, as it used to be called) where the Jebusites — the original inhabitants of the land — lived.

5, 6   But the people of Jebus refused to let them enter the city. So David captured the fortress of Zion, later called the City of David, and said to his men, "The first man to kill a Jebusite shall be made commander-in-chief!" Joab, the son of Zeruiah, was the first, so he became the general of David's army.

7   David lived in the fortress and that is why that area of Jerusalem is called the City of David.

8   He extended the city out around the fortress while Joab rebuilt the rest of Jerusalem.

9   And David became more and more famous and powerful, for the Lord of the heavens was with him.

10   These are the names of some of the bravest of David's warriors (who also encouraged the leaders of Israel to make David their king, as the Lord had said would happen):

11   Jashobeam (the son of a man from Hachmon) was the leader of The Top Three — the three greatest heroes among David's men. He once killed 300 men with his spear.

12   The second of The Top Three was Eleazar, the son of Dodo, a member of the subclan of Ahoh.

13   He was with David in the battle against the Philistines at Pas-dammim. The Israeli army was in a barley field and had begun to run away,

14   But he held his ground in the middle of the field, and recovered it and slaughtered the Philistines; and the Lord saved them with a great victory.

15   Another time, three of The Thirty[2] went to

---

[2]"The Thirty" were the highest-ranking officers in the army.

David while he was hiding in the cave of Adullam. The Philistines were camped in the Valley of Rephaim,

16 And David was in the stronghold at the time; an outpost of the Philistines had occupied Bethlehem.

17 David wanted a drink from the Bethlehem well beside the gate, and when he mentioned this to his men,

18, 19 These three broke through to the Philistine camp, drew some water from the well, and brought it back to David. But he refused to drink it! Instead he poured it out as an offering to the Lord and said, "God forbid that I should drink it! It is the very blood of these men who risked their lives to get it."

20 Abishai, Joab's brother, was commander of The Thirty. He had gained his place among The Thirty by killing 300 men at one time with his spear.

21 He was the chief and the most famous of The Thirty, but he was not as great as The Three.

22 Benaiah, whose father was a mighty warrior from Kabzeel, killed the two famous giants[3] from Moab. He also killed a lion in a slippery pit when there was snow on the ground.

23 Once he killed an Egyptian who was seven and one-half feet tall, whose spear was as thick as a weaver's beam. But Benaiah went up to him with only a club in his hand and pulled the spear away from him and used it to kill him.

24, 25 He was nearly as great as The Three, and he was very famous among The Thirty. David made him captain of his bodyguard.

---

[3]Literally, "ariels." The meaning of the term is uncertain.

26-47   Other famous warriors among David's men
were:

Asahel (Joab's brother);
Elhanan, the son of Dodo from Bethle-
    hem;
Shammoth from Harod;
Helez from Pelon;
Ira (son of Ikkesh) from Tekoa;
Abi-ezer from Anathoth;
Sibbecai from Hushath;
Ilai from Ahoh;
Maharai from Netophah;
Heled (son of Baanah) from Netophah;
Ithai (son of Ribai) a Benjaminite from
    Gibe-ah;
Benaiah from Pirathon;
Hurai from near the brooks of Gaash;
Abiel from Arbath;
Azmaveth from Baharum;
Eliahba from Sha-albon;
The sons[4] of Hashem from Gizon;
Jonathan (son of Shagee) from Harar;
Ahiam (son of Sacher) from Harar;
Eliphal (son of Ur);
Hepher from Mecherath;
Ahijah from Pelon;
Hezro from Carmel;
Naarai (son of Ezbai);
Joel (brother of Nathan);
Mibhar (son of Hagri);
Zelek from Ammon;

---

[4]Implied in II Samuel 23:30.

Naharai from Be-eroth — he was General Joab's armorbearer;

Ira from Ithra;

Gareb from Ithra;

Uriah the Hittite;

Zabad (son of Ahlai);

Adina (son of Shiza) from the tribe of Reuben — he was among the thirty-one leaders of the tribe of Reuben;

Hanan (son of Maacah);

Joshaphat from Mithna;

Uzzia from Ashterath;

Shama and Je-iel (sons of Hotham) from Aroer;

Jedia-el (son of Shimri);

Joha (his brother) from Tiza;

Eliel from Mahavi;

Jeribai and Joshaviah (sons of Elna-am);

Ithmah from Moab;

Eliel;

Obed;

Ja-asiel from Mezoba.

CHAPTER 12

These are the names of the famous warriors who joined David at Ziklag while he was hiding from King Saul.[1]

2 All of them were expert archers and slingers, and they could use their left hands as readily as their right! Like King Saul, they were all of the tribe of Benjamin.

---

[1]Literally, "the son of Kish."

3-7 Their chief was Ahi-ezer, son of Shemaah from Gibe-ah. The others were:

His brother Joash;
Jezi-el and Pelet, sons of Azmaveth;
Beracah;
Jehu from Anathoth;
Ishmaiah from Gibeon (a brave warrior rated as high or higher than The Thirty;
Jeremiah;
Jahaziel;
Johanan;
Jozabad from Gederah;
Eluzai;
Jerimoth;
Bealiah;
Shemariah;
Shephatiah from Haruph;
Elkanah,
Isshiah,
Azarel,
Jo-ezer,
Jashobe-am — all Korahites;
Jo-elah and Zebadiah (sons of Jeroham from Gedor).

8 Great and brave warriors from the tribe of Gad also went to David in the wilderness. They were experts with both shield and spear and were "lion-faced men, swift as deer upon the mountains."

9-13 Ezer was the chief,
Obadiah was second in command;
Eliab was third in command;
Mishmannah was fourth in command;

Jeremiah was fifth in command;
Attai was sixth in command;
Eliel was seventh in command;
Johanan was eighth in command;
Elzabad was ninth in command;
Jeremiah was tenth in command;
Machbannai was eleventh in command.

14 These men were army officers; the weakest was worth a hundred normal troops, and the greatest was worth a thousand!

15 They crossed the Jordan River during its seasonal flooding and conquered the lowlands on both the east and west banks.

16 Others came to David from Benjamin and Judah.

17 David went out to meet them and said, "If you have come to help me, we are friends; but if you have come to betray me to my enemies when I am innocent, then may the God of our fathers see and judge you."

18 Then the Holy Spirit came upon them, and Amasai, a leader of The Thirty, replied,

"We are yours, David;
We are on your side, son of Jesse.
Peace, peace be unto you,
And peace to all who aid you;
For your God is with you."

So David let them join him, and he made them captains of his army.

19 Some men from Manasseh deserted the Israeli army and joined David just as he was going into battle with the Philistines against King Saul. But as it turned out, the Philistine generals refused to let David and

his men go with them. After much discussion they sent them back, for they were afraid that David and his men would imperil them by deserting to King Saul.

20 Here is a list of the men from Manasseh who deserted to David as he was enroute to Ziklag:

> Adnah,
> Jozabad,
> Jedia-el,
> Michael,
> Jozabad,
> Elihu,
> Zillethai.

Each was a high-ranking officer of Manasseh's troops.

21 They were brave and able warriors, and they assisted David when he fought against the Amalek raiders at Ziklag.[2]

22 More men joined David almost every day until he had a tremendous army — the army of God.

23 Here is the registry of recruits who joined David at Hebron. They were all anxious to see David become king instead of Saul, just as the Lord had said would happen.

24-37 From Judah, 6,800 troops armed with shields and spears.

From the tribe of Simeon, 7,100 outstanding warriors.

From the Levites, 4,600.

From the priests — descendants of Aaron — there were 3,700 troops under the command of Zadok, a young man of unusual courage, and Jehoi-

---

[2]Implied.

ada. (He and twenty-two members of his family were officers of the fighting priests.)

From the tribe of Benjamin, the same tribe Saul was from, there were 3,000. (Most of that tribe retained its allegiance to Saul.)

From the tribe of Ephraim, 20,800 mighty warriors, each famous in his respective clan.

From the half-tribe of Manasseh, 18,000 were sent for the express purpose of helping David become king.

From the tribe of Issachar there were 200 leaders of the tribe with their relatives — all men who understood the temper of the times and knew the best course for Israel to take.

From the tribe of Zebulun there were 50,000 trained warriors; they were fully armed and totally loyal to David.

From Naphtali there were 1,000 officers and 37,000 troops equipped with shields and spears.

From the tribe of Dan there were 28,600 troops, all of them prepared for war.

From the tribe of Asher, there were 40,000 trained and ready troops.

From the other side of the Jordan River — where the tribes of Reuben and Gad and the half-tribe of Manasseh lived — there were 120,000 troops equipped with every kind of weapon.

38 All these men came in battle array to Hebron with the single purpose of making David the king of Israel. In fact, all of Israel was ready for this change.

39 They feasted and drank with David for three days, for preparations had been made for their arrival.

40 People from nearby and from as far away as Issachar, Zebulun, and Naphtali brought food on donkeys, camels, mules, and oxen. Vast supplies of flour, fig cakes, raisins, wine, oil, cattle, and sheep were brought to the celebration, for joy had spread throughout the land.

CHAPTER 13

After David had consulted with all of his army officers,

2 He addressed the assembled men of Israel as follows: "Since you think that I should be your king, and since the Lord our God has given His approval, let us send messages to our brothers throughout the land of Israel, including the priests and Levites, inviting them to come and join us.

3 And let us bring back the Ark of our God, for we have been neglecting it ever since Saul became king."

4 There was unanimous consent, for everyone agreed with him.

5 So David summoned the people of Israel from all across the nation[1] so that they could be present when the Ark of God was brought from Kiriath-jearim.

---

[1]Literally, "from Shihor — the Brook of Egypt — to the entrance of Hamath."

6 Then David and all Israel went to Baalah (i.e., Kiriath-jearim) in Judah to bring back the Ark of the Lord God enthroned above the angels.[2]

7 It was taken from the house of Abinadab on a new cart. Uzza and Ahio drove the oxen.

8 Then David and all the people danced before the Lord with great enthusiasm, accompanied by singing and by zithers, harps, tambourines, cymbals, and trumpets.

9 But as they arrived at the threshing-floor of Chidon, the oxen stumbled and Uzza reached out his hand to steady the Ark.

10 Then the anger of the Lord blazed out against Uzza, and killed him because he had touched the Ark. And so he died there before God.

11 David was angry at the Lord for what He had done to Uzza, and he named the place "The Outbreak Against Uzza." And it is still called that today.

12 Now David was afraid of God and asked, "How shall I ever get the Ark of God home?"

13 Finally he decided to take it to the home of Obed-edom the Gittite instead of bringing it to the City of David.

14 The Ark remained there with the family of Obed-edom for three months, and the Lord blessed him and his family.

CHAPTER 14

K ing Hiram of Tyre sent masons and carpenters to help build David's palace and he supplied him with much cedar lumber.

---

[2]Literally, "above the cherubim."

2   David now realized why the Lord had made him king and why He had made his kingdom so great; it was for a special reason — to give joy to God's people!

3   After David moved to Jerusalem, he married additional wives and became the father of many sons and daughters.

4-7   These are the names of the sons born to him in Jerusalem:

> Shammua,
> Shobab,
> Nathan,
> Solomon,
> Ibhar,
> Elishu-a,
> Elpelet,
> Nogah,
> Nepheg,
> Japhia,
> Elishama,
> Beeliada,
> Eliphelet.

8   When the Philistines heard that David was Israel's new king, they mobilized their forces to capture him. But David learned that they were on the way, so he called together his army.

9   The Philistines were raiding the Valley of Rephaim,

10   And David asked the Lord, "If I go out and fight them, will You give me the victory?"

And the Lord replied, "Yes, I will."

11   So he attacked them at Baal-perazim and wiped them out. He exulted, "God has used me to sweep

away my enemies like water bursting through a dam!" That is why the place has been known as Baal-perazim ever since (meaning, "The Place of Breaking Through").

12 After the battle the Israelis picked up many idols left by the Philistines; but David ordered them burned.

13 Later the Philistines raided the valley again,

14 And again David asked God what to do. The Lord replied, "Go around by the mulberry trees and attack from there.

15 When you hear a sound like marching in the tops of the mulberry trees, that is your signal to attack, for God will go before you and destroy the enemy."

16 So David did as the Lord commanded him; and he cut down the army of the Philistines all the way from Gibeon to Gezer.

17 David's fame spread everywhere, and the Lord caused all the nations to fear him.

CHAPTER 15

David now built several palaces for himself in Jerusalem, and he also built a new Tabernacle to house the Ark of God,

2 And issued these instructions: [When we transfer the Ark to its new home[1]], no one except the Levites may carry it, for God has chosen them for this purpose; they are to minister to Him forever."

3 Then David summoned all Israel to Jerusalem to

---

[1]Implied.

celebrate the bringing of the Ark into the new Tabernacle.

4-10 These were the priests and Levites present:

> 120 from the clan of Kohath; with Uriel as their leader;
>
> 220 from the clan of Merari; with Asaiah as their leader;
>
> 130 from the clan of Gershom; with Joel as their leader;
>
> 200 from the subclan of Elizaphan; with Shemaiah as their leader;
>
> 80 from the subclan of Hebron; with Eliel as their leader;
>
> 112 from the subclan of Uzziel; with Amminadab as their leader.

11 Then David called for Zadok and Abiathar, the High Priests, and for the Levite leaders: Uriel, Asaiah, Joel, Shemaiah, Eliel, and Amminadab.

12 "You are the leaders of the clans of the Levites," he told them. "Now sanctify yourselves with all your brothers so that you may bring the Ark of Jehovah, the God of Israel, to the place I have prepared for it.

13 The Lord destroyed us before because we handled the matter improperly — you were not carrying it."

14 So the priests and the Levites underwent the ceremonies of sanctification in preparation for bringing home the Ark of Jehovah, the God of Israel.

15 Then the Levites carried the Ark on their shoulders with its carrying poles, just as the Lord had instructed Moses.

16 King David also ordered the Levite leaders to

organize the singers into an orchestra; and they played loudly and joyously upon psaltries, harps, and cymbals.

17 Heman (son of Joel), Asaph (son of Berechiah), and Ethan (son of Kushaiah) from the clan of Merari were the heads of the musicians.

18 The following men were chosen as their assistants:

> Zechariah,
> Ja-aziel,
> Shemiramoth,
> Jehiel,
> Unni,
> Eliab,
> Benaiah,
> Ma-asseiah,
> Mattithiah,
> Eliphelehu,
> Mikneiah,
> Obed-edom and Je-iel, the door keepers.

19 Heman, Asaph, and Ethan were chosen to sound the bronze cymbals;

20 And Zechariah, Azi-el, Shemiramoth, Jehiel, Unni, Eliab, Ma-aseiah, and Benaiah comprised an octet accompanied by harps.[2]

21 Mattithiah, Eliphelehu, Mikneiah, Obed-edom, Je-iel, and Azaziah were the harpists.[3]

22 The song leader was Chenaniah, the chief of the Levites, who was selected for his skill.

23 Berechiah and Elkanah were guards for the Ark.

---

[2]Literally, "set to Alamoth." The meaning of the term is uncertain.
[3]Literally, "were to lead with zithers (or harps) set to the Sheminith." The meaning is uncertain.

24   Shebaniah, Joshaphat, Nethanel, Amasai, Zechariah, Benaiah, and Eliezer — all of whom were priests — formed a bugle corps to march at the head of the procession. And Obed-edom and Jehiah guarded the Ark.

25   Then David and the elders of Israel and the high officers of the army went with great joy to the home of Obed-edom to take the Ark to Jerusalem.

26   And because God didn't destroy the Levites who were carrying the Ark, they sacrificed seven bulls and seven lambs.

27   David, the Levites carrying the Ark, the singers, and Chenaniah the song leader were all dressed in linen robes. David also wore a linen ephod.

28   So the leaders of Israel took the Ark to Jerusalem with shouts of joy, the blowing of horns and trumpets, the crashing of cymbals, and loud playing on the harps and zithers.

29   (But as the Ark arrived in Jerusalem, David's wife Michal, the daughter of King Saul, felt a deep disgust for David as she watched from the window and saw him dancing like a madman.)

CHAPTER 16

So the Ark of God was brought into the Tabernacle. David had prepared for it, and the leaders of Israel sacrificed burnt offerings and peace offerings before God.

2   At the conclusion of these offerings David blessed the people in the name of the Lord;

3   Then he gave every person present[1] (men and

---

[1] Literally, "to each Israelite."

women alike) a loaf of bread, some wine, and a cake of raisins.

4 He appointed certain of the Levites to minister before the Ark by giving constant praise and thanks to the Lord God of Israel and by asking for His blessings upon His people. These are the names of those given this assignment:

5 Asaph, the leader of this detail, sounded the cymbals. His associates were Zechariah, Je-iel, Shemiramoth, Jehiel, Mattithiah, Eliab, Benaiah, Obed-edom, and Je-iel; they played the harps and zithers.

6 The priests Benaiah and Jahaziel played their trumpets regularly before the Ark.

7 At that time David began the custom of using choirs in the Tabernacle to sing thanksgiving to the Lord. Asaph was the director of this choral group of priests.

8 "Oh, give thanks to the Lord and pray to
    Him," they sang.
  "Tell the peoples of the world
  About His mighty doings.

9 Sing to Him; yes, sing His praises
  And tell of His marvelous works.

10 Glory in His holy name;
  Let all rejoice who seek the Lord.

11 Seek the Lord; yes, seek His strength
  And seek His face untiringly.

12, 13 O descendants of His servant Abraham,
  O chosen sons of Jacob,
  Remember His mighty miracles
  And His marvelous miracles
  And His authority:

14 He is the Lord our God!

His authority is seen throughout the earth.

15 Remember His covenant forever —
The words He commanded
To a thousand generations:

16 His agreement with Abraham,
And His oath to Isaac,

17 And His confirmation to Jacob.
He promised Israel
With an everlasting promise:

18 'I will give you the land of Canaan
As your inheritance.'

19 When Israel was few in number — oh, so
few —
And merely strangers in the Promised
Land;

20 When they wandered from country to
country,
From one kingdom to another —

21 God didn't let anyone harm them.
Even kings were killed who sought to hurt
them.

22 'Don't harm My chosen people,' He declared.
'These are My prophets — touch them
not.'

23 Sing to the Lord, O earth,
Declare each day that He is the One who
saves!

24 Show His glory to the nations!
Tell everyone about His miracles.

25 For the Lord is great, and should be highly praised;
He is to be held in awe above all gods.

26   The other so-called gods are demons,
But the Lord made the heavens.

27   Majesty and honor march before Him,
Strength and gladness walk beside Him.

28   O people of all nations of the earth,
Ascribe great strength and glory to His name!

29   Yes, ascribe to the Lord
The glory due His name!
Bring an offering and come before Him;
Worship the Lord when clothed with holiness!

30   Tremble before Him, all the earth!
The world stands unmoved.

31   Let the heavens be glad, the earth rejoice;
Let all the nations say, 'It is the Lord who reigns.'

32   Let the vast seas roar,
Let the countryside and everything in it rejoice!

33   Let the trees in the woods sing for joy before the Lord,
For He comes to judge the earth.

34   Oh, give thanks to the Lord, for He is good;
His love and His kindness go on forever.

35   Cry out to Him, 'Oh, save us, God of our salvation;
Bring us safely back from among the nations.
Then we will thank Your holy name,
And triumph in Your praise.'

36　　　　Blessed be Jehovah, God of Israel,
　　　　　Forever and forevermore."
And all the people shouted "Amen!" and praised the Lord.

37　David arranged for Asaph and his fellow Levites to minister regularly at the Tabernacle,[2] doing each day whatever needed to be done.

38　This group included Obed-edom (the son of Jeduthun), Hosah and sixty-eight of their colleagues as guards.

39　Meanwhile the old Tabernacle of the Lord on the hill of Gibeon continued to be active. David left Zadok the priest and his fellow-priests to minister to the Lord there.

40　They sacrificed burnt offerings to the Lord each morning and evening upon the altar set aside for that purpose, just as the Lord had commanded Israel.

41　David also appointed Heman, Jeduthun, and several others who were chosen by name to give thanks to the Lord for His constant love and mercy.

42　They used their trumpets and cymbals to accompany the singers with loud praises to God. And Jeduthun's sons were appointed as guards.

43　At last the celebration ended and the people returned to their homes, and David returned to bless his own household.

CHAPTER 17

After David had been living in his new palace for some time he said to Nathan the prophet, "Look! I'm living here in a cedar-paneled home while the Ark of the Covenant of God is out there in a tent!"

---

[2]Literally, "before the Ark of the Covenant of the Lord."

2 And Nathan replied, "Carry out your plan in every detail, for it is the will of the Lord."

3 But that same night God said to Nathan,

4 "Go and give My servant David this message: 'You are not to build My Temple!

5 I've gone from tent to tent as My home from the time I brought Israel out of Egypt.

6 In all that time I never suggested to any of the leaders of Israel — the shepherds I appointed to care for My people — that they should build me a cedar-lined Temple.'

7 Tell My servant David, 'The Lord of heaven says to you, I took you from being a shepherd and made you the king of My people.

8 And I have been with you everywhere you've gone; I have destroyed your enemies, and I will make your name as great as the greatest of the earth.

9 And I will give a permanent home to My people Israel, and will plant them in their land. They will not be disturbed again; the wicked nations won't conquer them as they did before,

10 When the judges ruled them. I will subdue all of your enemies. And I now declare that I will cause your descendants to be kings of Israel just as you are.

11 When your time here on earth is over and you die, I will place one of your sons upon your throne; and I will make his kingdom strong.

12 He is the one who shall build Me a Temple, and I will establish his royal line of descent forever.

13 I will be his father, and he shall be My son; I will never remove My mercy and love from him as I did from Saul.

14 I will place him over My people and over the kingdom of Israel forever — and his descendants will always be kings.' "

15 So Nathan told King David everything the Lord had said.

16 Then King David went in and sat before the Lord and said, "Who am I, O Lord God, and what is my family that You have given me all this?

17 For all the great things You have already done for me are nothing in comparison to what You have promised to do in the future! For now, O Lord God, You are speaking of future generations of my children being kings too! You speak as though I were someone very great.

18 What else can I say? You know that I am but a dog, yet You have decided to honor me!

19 O Lord, You have given me these wonderful promises just because You want to be kind to me, because of Your own great heart.

20 O Lord, there is no one like You — there is no other God. In fact, we have never even heard of another god like You!

21 And what other nation in all the earth is like Israel? You have made a unique nation and have redeemed it from Egypt so that the people could be Your people. And You made a great name for Yourself when You did glorious miracles in driving out the nations from before Your people.

22 You have declared that Your people Israel belong to You forever, and You have become their God.

23 And now I accept Your promise, Lord, that I and my children will always rule this nation.

24 And may this bring eternal honor to Your name as everyone realizes that You always do what You say. They will exclaim, 'The Lord of heaven is indeed the God of Israel!' And Israel shall always be ruled by my children and their posterity!

25 Now I have the courage to pray to You, for You have revealed this to me.

26 God Himself has promised this good thing to me!

27 May this blessing rest upon my children forever, for when You grant a blessing, Lord, it is an eternal blessing!"

CHAPTER 18

D avid finally subdued the Philistines and conquered Gath and its surrounding towns.

2 He also conquered Moab and required its people to send him a large sum of money every year.

3 He conquered the dominion of King Hadadezer of Zobah (as far as Hamath) at the time Hadadezer went to tighten his grip along the Euphrates River.

4 David captured a thousand of his chariots, seven thousand cavalry, and twenty thousand troops. He crippled all the chariot teams except a hundred that he kept for his own use.

5 When the Syrians arrived from Damascus to help King Hadadezer, David killed twenty-two thousand of them;

6 Then he placed a garrison of his troops in Damascus, the Syrian capital. So the Syrians, too, were forced to send him large amounts of money every

year. And the Lord gave David victory everywhere he went.

7 He brought the gold shields of King Hadadezer's officers to Jerusalem,

8 As well as a great amount of bronze from Hadadezer's cities of Tibhath and Cun. (King Solomon later melted the bronze and used it for the Temple. He molded it into the bronze tank, the pillars, and the instruments used in offering sacrifices on the altar.)

9 When King Tou of Hamath learned that King David had destroyed Hadadezer's army,

10 He sent his son Hadoram to greet and congratulate King David on his success and to present him with many gifts of gold, silver, and bronze, seeking an alliance. For Hadadezer and Tou had been enemies and there had been many wars between them.

11 King David dedicated these gifts to the Lord, as he did the silver and gold he took from the nations of Edom, Moab, Ammon, Amalek, and the Philistines.

12 Abishai (son of Zeruiah) then destroyed eighteen thousand Edomites in the Valley of Salt.

13 He put garrisons in Edom and forced the Edomites to pay large sums of money annually to David. This is just another example of how the Lord gave David victory after victory.

14 David reigned over all of Israel and was a just ruler.

15 Joab (son of Zeruiah) was commander-in-chief of the army; Jehoshaphat (son of Ahilud) was the historian;

16 Zadok (son of Ahitub) and Ahimelech (son of Abiathar) were the head priests;

Shavsha was the king's special assistant;[1]

17 Benaiah (son of Jehoiada) was in charge of the king's bodyguard — the Cherethites and Pelethites — and David's sons were his chief aides.

CHAPTER 19

When King Nahash of Ammon died, his son Hanun became the new king.

2, 3 Then David declared, "I am going to show friendship to Hanun because of all the kind things his father did for me." So David sent a message of sympathy to Hanun for the death of his father. But when David's ambassadors arrived, King Hanun's counselors warned him, "Don't fool yourself that David has sent these men to honor your father! They are here to spy out the land so that they can come in and conquer it!"

4 So King Hanun insulted King David's ambassadors by shaving their beards and cutting their robes off at the middle to expose their buttocks; then he sent them back to David in shame.

5 When David heard what had happened, he sent a message to his embarrassed emissaries, telling them to stay at Jericho until their beards had grown out again.

6 When King Hanun realized his mistake he sent $2,000,000[1] to enlist mercenary troops, chariots, and cavalry from Mesopotamia, Aram-maacah, and Zobah.

7 He hired thirty-two thousand chariots, as well as the support of the king of Maacah and his entire army. These forces camped at Medeba where they

---

[1]Literally, "secretary" or "scribe."
[1]Literally, "a thousand talents of silver," approximately 800,000 pounds sterling at current value.

were joined by the troops King Hanun had recruited from his cities.

8   When David learned of this, he sent Joab and the mightiest warriors of Israel.

9   The army of Ammon went out to meet them and began the battle at the gates of the city of Medeba. Meanwhile, the mercenary forces were out in the field.

10   When Joab realized that the enemy forces were both in front and behind him, he divided his army and sent one group to engage the Syrians.

11   The other group, under the command of his brother Abishai, moved against the Ammonites.

12   "If the Syrians are too strong for me, come and help me," Joab told his brother; "and if the Ammonites are too strong for you, I'll come and help you.

13   Be courageous and let us act like men to save our people and the cities of our God. And may the Lord do what is best."

14   So Joab and his troops attacked the Syrians, and the Syrians turned and fled.

15   When the Ammonites, under attack by Abishai's troops, saw that the Syrians were retreating, they fled into the city. Then Joab returned to Jerusalem.

16   After their defeat, the Syrians summoned additional troops from east of the Euphrates River, led personally by Shophach, King Hadadezer's commander-in-chief.

17, 18   When this news reached David, he mobilized all Israel, crossed the Jordan River, and engaged the enemy troops in battle. But the Syrians again fled from David; and he killed seven thousand charioteers

and forty thousand of their troops. He also killed Shophach, the commander-in-chief of the Syrian army.

19 Then King Hadadezer's troops surrendered to
King David and became his subjects. And never again
did the Syrians aid the Ammonites in their battles.

CHAPTER 20

The following spring (spring was the season when
wars usually began) Joab led the Israeli army in
successful attacks against the cities and villages of the
people of Ammon. After destroying them, he laid
siege to Rabbah and conquered it. Meanwhile, David
had stayed in Jerusalem.

2 When David arrived on the scene, he removed
the crown from the head of King Milcom[1] of Rabbah
and placed it upon his own head. It was made of
gold inlaid with gems and weighed seventy-five
pounds! David also took great amounts of plunder
from the city.

3 He drove the people from the city and set
them to work with saws, iron picks, and axes,[2] as
was his custom and all the conquered Ammonite peoples. Then David and all his army returned to Jerusalem.

4 The next war was against the Philistines again,
at Gezer. But Sibbecai, a man from Hushath, killed
one of the sons of the giant, Sippai, and so the Philistines surrendered.

5 During another war with the Philistines, Elhanan (the son of Jair) killed Lahmi, the brother of

---

[1]Implied; see I Kings 11:5.
[2]Literally, "he conducted them to the saw." Whether this means that
he made them labor with saws or that he sawed them to pieces is
uncertain.

Goliath the giant; the handle of his spear was like a weaver's beam!

6, 7 During another battle, at Gath, a giant with six fingers on each hand and six toes on each foot (his father was also a giant) defied and taunted Israel; but he was killed by David's nephew Jonathan, the son of David's brother Shimea.

8 These giants were descendants of the giants of Gath, and they were killed by David and his soldiers.

CHAPTER 21

Then Satan brought disaster upon Israel, for he made David decide to take a census.

2 "Take a complete census throughout the land[1] and bring me the totals," he told Joab and the other leaders.

3 But Joab objected. "If the Lord were to multiply His people a hundred times, would they not all be yours? So why are you asking us to do this? Why must you cause Israel to sin?"

4 But the king won the argument, and Joab did as he was told; he traveled all through Israel and returned to Jerusalem.

5 The total population figure which he gave came to 1,100,000 men of military age in Israel and 470,000 in Judah.

6 But he didn't include the tribes of Levi and Benjamin in his figures because he was so distressed at what the king had made him do.

7 And God, too, was displeased with the census and punished Israel for it.

---

[1]Literally, "from Beer-sheba to Dan."

8 But David said to God, "I am the one who has sinned. Please forgive me, for I realize now how wrong I was to do this."

9 Then the Lord said to Gad, David's personal prophet,

10, 11 "Go and tell David, 'The Lord has offered you three choices. Which will you choose?

12 You may have three years of famine, or three months of destruction by the enemies of Israel, or three days of deadly plague as the angel of the Lord brings destruction to the land. Think it over and let me know what answer to return to the One who sent me.' "

13 "This is a terrible decision to make," David replied, "but let me fall into the hands of the Lord rather than into the power of men, for God's mercies are very great."

14 So the Lord sent a plague upon Israel and 70,-000 men died as a result.

15 During the plague God sent an angel to destroy Jerusalem; but then He felt such compassion that He changed His mind and commanded the destroying angel, "Stop! It is enough!" (The angel of the Lord was standing at the time by the threshing-floor of Ornan the Jebusite.)

16 When David saw the angel of the Lord standing between heaven and earth with his sword drawn, pointing toward Jerusalem, he and the elders of Israel clothed themselves in sackcloth and fell to the ground before the Lord.

17 And David said to God, "I am the one who sinned by ordering the census. But what have these sheep done? O Lord my God, destroy me and my family, but do not destroy Your people."

18   Then the angel of the Lord told Gad to instruct David to build an altar to the Lord at the threshing-floor of Ornan the Jebusite.

19, 20   So David went to see Ornan, who was threshing wheat at the time. Ornan saw the angel as he turned, and his four sons ran and hid.

21   Then Ornan saw the king approaching. So he left the threshing-floor and bowed to the ground before King David.

22   David said to Ornan, "Let me buy this threshing-floor from you at its full price; then I will build an altar to the Lord and the plague will stop."

23   "Take it, my lord, and use it as you wish," Ornan said to David. "Take the oxen, too, for burnt offerings; use the threshing instruments for wood for the fire and use the wheat for the grain offering. I give it all to you."

24   "No," the king replied, "I will buy it for the full price; I cannot take what is yours and give it to the Lord. I will not offer a burnt offering that has cost me nothing!"

25   So David paid Ornan $4,300 in gold,[2]

26   And built an altar to the Lord there, and sacrificed burnt offerings and peace offerings upon it; and he called out to the Lord, who answered by sending down fire from heaven to burn up the offering on the altar.

27   Then the Lord commanded the angel to put back his sword into its sheath;

28   And when David saw that the Lord had answered his plea, he sacrificed to Him again.

29   The Tabernacle and altar made by Moses in

---

[2]Literally, "six hundred shekels of gold by weight."

the wilderness were on the hill of Gibeon,

30   But David didn't have time to go there to plead before the Lord, for he was terrified by the drawn sword of the angel of Jehovah.

CHAPTER 22

Then David said, "Right here at Ornan's threshing-floor is the place where I'll build the Temple of the Lord and construct the altar for Israel's burnt offering!"

2   David now drafted all the resident aliens in Israel to prepare blocks of squared stone for the Temple.

3   They also manufactured iron into the great quantity of nails needed for the doors in the gates and for the clamps; and they smelted so much bronze that it was too much to weigh.

4   The men of Tyre and Sidon brought great rafts of cedar logs to David.

5   "Solomon my son is young and tender," David said, "and the Temple of the Lord must be a marvelous structure, famous and glorious throughout the world; so I will begin the preparations for it now." So David collected the construction materials before his death.

6   He now commanded his son Solomon to build a Temple for the Lord God of Israel.

7   "I wanted to build it myself," David told him,

8   "But the Lord said not to do it. 'You have killed too many men in great wars,' He told me. 'You have reddened the ground before Me with blood: so you are not to build My Temple.

9   But I will give you a son,' He told me, 'who

will be a man of peace, for I will give him peace with his enemies in the surrounding lands. His name shall be Solomon (meaning "Peaceful"), and I will give peace and quietness to Israel during his reign.

10 He shall build My Temple, and he shall be as My own son and I will be his father; and I will cause his sons and his descendants to reign over every generation of Israel.'

11 So now, my son, may the Lord be with you and prosper you as you do what He told you to do and build the Temple of the Lord.

12 And may the Lord give you the good judgment to follow all His laws when He makes you king of Israel.

13 For if you carefully obey the rules and regulations which He gave to Israel through Moses, you will prosper. Be strong and courageous, fearless and enthusiastic!

14 By hard work I have collected $3,000,000,000 worth of gold bullion, $2,000,000 worth of silver,[1] and so much iron and bronze that I haven't even weighed it; I have also gathered timber and stone for the walls. This is at least a beginning, something with which to start.

15 And you have many skilled stonemasons and carpenters and craftsmen of every kind.

16 They are expert gold and silver smiths and bronze and iron workers. So get to work, and may the Lord be with you!"

17 Then David ordered all the leaders of Israel to assist his son in this project.

---

[1] Literally, "a hundred thousand talents of gold" and "a million talents of silver."

18 "The Lord your God is with you," he declared. "He has given you peace with the surrounding nations, for I have conquered them in the name of the Lord and for His people.

19 Now try with every fiber of your being to obey the Lord your God, and you will soon be bringing the Ark and the other holy articles of worship into the Temple of the Lord!"

CHAPTER 23

By this time David was an old, old man, so he stepped down from the throne and appointed his son Solomon as the new king of Israel.

2 He summoned all the political and religious leaders of Israel for the coronation ceremony.

3 At this time a census was taken of the men of the tribe of Levi who were thirty years or older. The total came to 38,000.

4, 5 "Twenty-four thousand of them will supervise the work at the Temple," David instructed, "Six thousand are to be bailiffs and judges, four thousand will be temple guards, and four thousand will praise the Lord with the musical instruments I have made."

6 Then David divided them into three main divisions named after the sons of Levi — the **Gershom** division, the **Kohath** division and the **Merari** division.

7 Subdivisions of the *Gershom* corps were named after his sons **Ladan** and **Shime-i.**

8, 9 These subdivisions were still further divided into six groups named after the sons of *Ladan*:

Jehiel the leader, Zetham, Joel; and the

> sons of *Shime-i*[1] — Shelomoth, Haziel, and Haran.

10, 11 The subclans of *Shime-i* were named after his four sons:

> Jahath was greatest, Zizah[2] was next, and Jeush and Beriah were combined into a single subclan because neither had many sons.

12 The division of Kohath was subdivided into four groups named after his sons **Amram, Izhar, Hebron,** and **Uzziel.**

13 *Amram* was the ancestor of Aaron and Moses.[3] Aaron and his sons were set apart for the holy service of sacrificing the people's offerings to the Lord. He served the Lord constantly and pronounced blessings in His name at all times.

14, 15 As for Moses, the man of God, his sons **Gershom** and **Eliezer** were included with the tribe of Levi.

16 *Gershom's* sons were led by Shebuel,

17 And *Eliezer's* only son, Rehabiah, was the leader of his clan, for he had many children.

18 The sons of *Izhar* were led by Shelomith.

19 The sons of *Hebron* were led by Jeriah. Amariah was second in command, Jahaziel was third, and Jekameam was fourth.

20 The sons of *Uzziel* were led by Micah, and Isshiah was the second in command.

21 The sons of *Merari* were **Mahli** and **Mushi.** The sons of *Mahli* were **Eleazar** and **Kish.**

---

[1]Probably not the same Shime-i as in verse 7.
[2]Or "Zina."
[3]Literally, "the sons of Amram: Aaron and Moses."

22   *Eleazar* died without any sons, and his daughters were married to their cousins, the sons of *Kish*.

23   *Mushi's* sons were Mahli, Eder, and Jeremoth.

24   In the census, all the men of Levi who were twenty years old or older were classified under the names of these clans and subclans; and they were all assigned to the ministry at the Temple.

25   For David said, "The Lord God of Israel has given us peace, and He will always live in Jerusalem.

26   Now the Levites will no longer need to carry the Tabernacle and its instruments from place to place."

27   (This census of the tribe of Levi was one of the last things David did before his death.)

28   The work of the Levites was to assist the priests — the descendants of Aaron — in the sacrifices at the Temple; they also did the custodial work and helped perform the ceremonies of purification.

29   They provided the Bread of the Presence, the flour for the grain offerings, and the wafers made without yeast (either fried or mixed with olive oil); they also checked all the weights and measures.

30   Each morning and evening they stood before the Lord to sing thanks and praise to Him.

31   They assisted in the special sacrifices of burnt offerings, the sabbath sacrifices, the new moon celebrations, and at all the festivals. There were always as many Levites present as were required for the occasion.

32   And they took care of the Tabernacle and the Temple and assisted the priests in whatever way they were needed.

CHAPTER 24

The priests (the descendants of Aaron) were placed into two divisions named after Aaron's sons, **Eleazar** and **Ithamar.**

Nadab and Abihu were also sons of Aaron, but they died before their father did and had no children; so only Eleazar and Ithamar were left to carry on.

3 David consulted with Zadok, who represented the Eleazar clan, and with Ahimelech, who represented the Ithamar clan; then he divided Aaron's descendants into many groups to serve at various times.

4 *Eleazar's* descendants were divided into sixteen groups and *Ithamar's* into eight (for there was more leadership ability among the descendants of Eleazar).

5 All tasks were assigned to the various groups by coin-toss[1] so that there would be no preference, for there were many famous men and high officials of the Temple in each division.

6 Shemaiah, a Levite and the son of Nethanel, acted as recording secretary and wrote down the names and assignments in the presence of the king and of these leaders: Zadok the priest, Ahimelech the son of Abiathar, and the heads of the priests and Levites. Two groups from the division of Eleazar and one from the division of Ithamar were assigned to each task.

7-18 The work was assigned (by coin-toss) in this order:

> First, the group led by Jehoiarib;
> Second, the group led by Jedaiah;
> Third, the group led by Harim;

---

[1]Literally, "by lot."

> Fourth, the group led by Se-orim;
> Fifth, the group led by Malchijah;
> Sixth, the group led by Mijamin;
> Seventh, the group led by Hakkoz;
> Eighth, the group led by Ahijah;
> Ninth, the group led by Jeshua;
> Tenth, the group led by Shecaniah;
> Eleventh, the group led by Eliashib;
> Twelfth, the group led by Jakim;
> Thirteenth, the group led by Huppah;
> Fourteenth, the group led by Jeshebe-ab;
> Fifteenth, the group led by Bilgah;
> Sixteenth, the group led by Immer;
> Seventeenth, the group led by Hezir;
> Eighteenth, the group led by Happizzez;
> Nineteenth, the group led by Pethahiah;
> Twentieth, the group led by Jehezkel;
> Twenty-first, the group led by Jachin;
> Twenty-second, the group led by Gamul;
> Twenty-third, the group led by Delaiah;
> Twenty-fourth, the group led by Maaziah.

19   Each group carried out the Temple duties as **originally** assigned by God through their ancestor Aaron.

20   **These were** the other descendants of Levi: Amram; his descendant Shuba-el; and Shuba-el's descendant Jehdeiah;

21   The Rehabiah group, led by his oldest son Isshiah;

22   The Izhar group, consisting of **Shelamoth and** his descendant Jahath.

23   The Hebron group:

> Jeriah, Hebron's oldest son;

Amariah, his second son;
Jahaziel, his third son;
Jekameam, his fourth son.

24, 25   The Uzziel group was led by his son Micah and his grandsons Shamir and Isshiah, and by Isshiah's son Zechariah.

26, 27   The Merari group was led by his sons: **Mahli** and **Mushi.**

(Ja-aziah's group, led by his son Beno, included his brothers Shoham, Zaccur, and Ibri.)

28   *Mahli's* descendants were Eleazar, who had no sons,

29   And Kish, among whose sons was Jerahmeel.

30   The sons of *Mushi* were Mahli, Eder, and Jerimoth. These were the descendants of Levi in their various clans.

31   Like the descendants of Aaron, they were assigned to their duties by coin-toss without distinction as to age or rank. It was done in the presence of King David, Zadok, Ahimelech, and the leaders of the priests and the Levites.

CHAPTER 25

D avid and the officials of the Tabernacle then appointed men to prophesy to the accompaniment of zithers, harps, and cymbals. These men were from the groups of Asaph, Heman, and Jeduthun. Here is a list of their names and their work:

2   Under the leadership of Asaph, the king's private prophet, were his sons Zaccur, Joseph, Nethaniah, and Asharelah.

3   Under Jeduthun, who led in giving thanks and

praising the Lord (while accompanied by the zither), were his six sons: Gedaliah, Zeri, Jeshaiah, Shime-i, Hashabiah, and Mattithiah.

4, 5 Under the direction of Heman, the king's private chaplain, were his sons: Bukkiah, Mattaniah, Uzziel, Shebuel, Jerimoth, Hananiah, Hanani, Eliathah, Geddalti, Romamti-ezer, Joshbekashah, Mallothi, Hothir, and Mahazi-oth. (For God had honored him with fourteen sons and three daughters.)

6, 7 Their music ministry included the playing of cymbals, harps, and zithers; all were under the direction of their father as they performed this ministry in the Tabernacle.

Asaph, Jeduthun, and Heman reported directly to the king. They and their families were all trained in singing praises to the Lord; each one — 288 of them in all — was a master musician.

8 The singers were appointed to their particular term of service by coin-toss, without regard to age or reputation.

9-31 The first toss indicated Joseph of the Asaph clan;

The second, Gedaliah, along with twelve of his sons and brothers;

The third, Zaccur and twelve of his sons and brothers;

The fourth, Izri and twelve of his sons and brothers;

Fifth, Nethaniah and twelve of his sons and brothers;

Sixth, Bukkiah and twelve of his sons and brothers;

Seventh, Jesharelah and twelve of his sons

and brothers;

Eighth, Jeshaiah and twelve of his sons and brothers;

Ninth, Mattaniah, and twelve of his sons and brothers;

Tenth, Shime-i and twelve of his sons and brothers;

Eleventh, Azarel and twelve of his sons and brothers;

Twelfth, Hashabiah and twelve of his sons and brothers;

Thirteenth, Shuba-el and twelve of his sons and brothers;

Fourteenth, Mattithiah and twelve of his sons and brothers;

Fifteenth, Jeremoth and twelve of his sons and brothers;

Sixteenth, Hananiah and twelve of his sons and brothers;

Seventeenth, Joshbekasha and twelve of his sons and brothers;

Eighteenth, Hanani and twelve of his sons and brothers;

Nineteenth, Mallothi and twelve of his sons and brothers;

Twentieth, Eliathah and twelve of his sons and brothers;

Twenty-first, Hothir and twelve of his sons and brothers;

Twenty-second, Giddalti and twelve of his sons and brothers;

Twenty-third, Mahazi-oth and twelve of his sons and brothers;

Twenty-fourth, Romamti-ezer and twelve
of his sons and brothers.

CHAPTER 26

The temple guards were from the Asaph division of
the Korah clan. The captain of the guard was
Meshelemiah, the son of Kore.

2, 3 His sergeants were his sons:
Zechariah (the oldest),
Jedia-el (the second),
Zebadiah (the third),
Jathni-el (the fourth),
Elam (the fifth),
Jeho-hanan (the sixth),
Elie-ho-enai (the seventh).

4, 5 The sons of Obed-edom were also appointed
as temple guards:
Shemaiah (the oldest),
Jehozabad (the second),
Joah (the third),
Sacar (the fourth),
Nethanel (the fifth),
Ammi-el (the sixth),
Issachar (the seventh),
Pe-ullethai (the eighth).

What a blessing God gave him with all those
sons!

6, 7 Shemaiah's sons were all outstanding men,
and had positions of great authority in their clan.
Their names were:
Othni,
Repha-el,

Obed,

Elzabad.

Their brave brothers, Elihu and Semachiah, were also very able men.

8   All of these sons and grandsons of Obed-edom — all sixty-two of them — were outstanding men who were particularly well qualified for their work.

9   Meshelemiah's eighteen sons and brothers, too, were real leaders.

10   Hosah, one of the Merari group, appointed Shimri as the leader among his sons, though he was not the oldest.

11   The names of some of his other sons were:

Hilkiah, the second;

Tebaliah, the third;

Zechariah, the fourth.

Hosah's sons and brothers numbered thirteen in all.

12   The divisions of the temple guards were named after the leaders. Like the other Levites, they were responsible to minister at the Temple.

13   They were assigned guard duty at the various gates without regard to the reputation of their families, for it was all done by coin-toss.

14, 15   The responsibility of the east gate went to Shelemiah and his group; of the north gate to his son Zechariah, a man of unusual wisdom; of the south gate to Obed-edom and his group (his sons were given charge of the storehouses);

16   Of the west gate and the Shallecheth Gate on the upper road, to Shuppim and Hosah.

17   Six guards were assigned daily to the east gate, four to the north gate, four to the south gate, and two to each of the storehouses.

18 Six guards were assigned each day to the west gate, four to the upper road, and two to the nearby areas.

19 The Temple guards were chosen from the clans of Korah and Merari.

20, 21, 22 Other Levites, led by Ahijah, were given the care of the gifts brought to the Lord and placed in the Temple treasury. These men of the Ladan sub-clan from the clan of Gershom included Zetham and Joel, the sons of Jehieli.

23, 24 Shebuel, son of Gershom and grandson of Moses, was the chief officer of the treasury. He was in charge of the divisions named after Amram, Iz-har, Hebron, and Uzziel.

25 The line of descendants from Eliezer went through Rehabiah, Jesha-iah, Joram, Zichri, and Shelo-moth.

26 Shelomoth and his brothers were appointed to care for the gifts given to the Lord by King David and the other leaders of the nation such as the officers and generals of the army.

27 For these men dedicated their war loot to sup-port the operating expenses of the Temple.

28 Shelomoth and his brothers were also respon-sible for the care of the items dedicated to the Lord by Samuel the prophet, Saul the son of Kish, Abner the son of Ner, Joab the son of Zeruiah, and anyone else of distinction[1] who brought gifts to the Lord.

29 Chenaniah and his sons (from the subclan of Izhar) were appointed public administrators and judges.

30 Hashabiah and 1,700 of his clansmen from He-

---

[1]Implied.

bron, all outstanding men, were placed in charge of the territory of Israel west of the Jordan River; they were responsible for the religious affairs and public administration of that area.

31, 32   Twenty-seven hundred outstanding men of the clan of the Hebronites, under the supervision of Jerijah were appointed to control the religious and public affairs of the tribes of Reuben, Gad, and the half-tribe of Manasseh. These men, all of whom had excellent qualifications, were appointed on the basis of their ancestry and ability at Jazer in Gilead in the fortieth year of King David's reign.

CHAPTER 27

The Israeli army was divided into twelve regiments, each with 24,000 troops, including officers and administrative staff. These units were called up for active duty one month each year. Here is the list of the units and their regimental commanders:

2, 3   The commander of the First Division was Jashobeam. He had charge of 24,000 troops who were on duty the first month of each year.

4   The commander of the Second Division was Dodai (a descendant of Ahohi). He had charge of 24,000 troops who were on duty the second month of each year. Mikloth was his executive officer.

5, 6   The commander of the Third Division was Benaiah. His 24,000 men were on duty the third month of each year. (He was the son of Jehoiada the High Priest, and was the chief of the thirty highest-ranking officers in David's army.) His son Ammizabad succeeded him as division commander.

7 The commander of the Fourth Division was Asahel (the brother of Joab), who was later replaced by his son Zebadiah. He had 24,000 men on duty the fourth month of each year.

8 The commander of the Fifth Division was Shamuth from Izrah, with 24,000 men on duty the fifth month of each year.

9 The commander of the Sixth Division was Ira, the son of Ikkesh from Tekoa; he had 24,000 men on duty the sixth month of each year.

10 The commander of the Seventh Division was Helez from Pelona in Ephraim, with 24,000 men on duty the seventh month of each year.

11 The commander of the Eighth Division was Sibbecai of the Hushite subclan from Zerah, who had 24,000 men on duty the eighth month of each year.

12 The commander of the Ninth Division was Abi-ezer (from Anathoth in the tribe of Benjamin), who commanded 24,000 troops during the ninth month of each year.

13 The commander of the Tenth Division was Maharai from Netophah in Zerah, with 24,000 men on duty the tenth month of each year.

14 The commander of the Eleventh Division was Benaiah from Pirathon in Ephraim, with 24,000 men on duty during the eleventh month of each year.

15 The commander of the Twelfth Division was Heldai from Netophah in the area of Othni-el, who commanded 24,000 men on duty during the twelfth month of each year.

16-22 The top political officers of the tribes of Israel were as follows:

Over Reuben, Eliezer (son of Zichri);

Over Simeon, Shephatiah (son of Maacah);

Over Levi, Hashabiah (son of Kemuel);

Over the descendants of Aaron, Zadok;

Over Judah, Elihu (a brother of King David);

Over Issachar, Omri (son of Michael);

Over Zebulun, Ishmaiah (son of Obadiah);

Over Naphtali, Jeremoth (son of Azriel);

Over Ephraim, Hoshea (son of Azaziah);

Over the half-tribe of Manasseh, Joel (son of Pedaiah);

Over the other half of Manasseh, in Gilead, Iddo (son of Zechariah);

Over Benjamin, Ja-asiel (son of Abner);

Over Dan, Azarel (son of Jeroham).

23 When David took his census he didn't include the twenty-year-olds, or those younger, for the Lord had promised a population explosion for His people.[1]

24 Joab began the census, but he never finished it, for the anger of God broke out upon Israel; the final total was never put into the annals of King David.

25 Azmaveth (son of Adi-el) was the chief financial officer in charge of the palace treasuries, and Jonathan (son of Uzziah) was chief of the regional treasuries throughout the cities, villages, and fortresses of Israel.

26 Ezri (son of Chelub) was manager of the laborers on the king's estates.

---

[1]Literally, "the Lord had said He would increase Israel like to the stars of heaven."

27 And Shime-i from Ramath had the oversight of the king's vineyards; and Zabdi from Shiphma was responsible for his wine production and storage.

28 Baal-hanan from Gedera was responsible for the king's olive yards and sycamore trees in the lowlands bordering Philistine territory, while Joash had charge of the supplies of olive oil.

29 Shitrai from Sharon was in charge of the cattle on the Plains of Sharon, and Shaphat (son of Adlai) had charge of those in the valleys.

30 Obil, from the territory of Ishmael, had charge of the camels, and Jehdeiah from Meronoth had charge of the donkeys.

31 The sheep were under the care of Jaziz the Hagrite. These men were King David's overseers.

32 The attendant to the king's sons was Jonathan, David's uncle, a wise counselor and an educated man.[2] Jehiel (the son of Hachmoni) was their tutor.

33 Ahithophel was the king's official counselor and Hushai the Archite was his personal advisor.

34 Ahithophel was assisted by Jehoiada (the son of Benaiah) and by Abiathar. Joab was commander-in-chief of the Israeli army.

CHAPTER 28

David now summoned all of his officials to Jerusalem — the political leaders, the commanders of the twelve army divisions, the other army officers, those in charge of his property and livestock and all the other men of authority in his kingdom.

---

[2]Literally, "a scribe."

2   He rose and stood before them and addressed them as follows:

"My brothers and my people! It was my desire to build a Temple in which the Ark of the Covenant of the Lord could rest — a place for our God to live in.[1] I have now collected everything that is necessary for the building,

3   But God has told me, 'You are not to build My Temple, for you are a warrior and have shed much blood.'

4   Nevertheless, the Lord God of Israel has chosen me from among all my father's family to begin a dynasty that will rule Israel forever; He has chosen the tribe of Judah, and from among the families of Judah, my father's family; and from among his sons, the Lord took pleasure in me and has made me king over all Israel.

5   And from among my sons — the Lord has given me many children — He has chosen Solomon to succeed me on the throne of His Kingdom of Israel.

6   He has told me, 'Your son Solomon shall build My Temple; for I have chosen him as My son and I will be his father.

7   And if he continues to obey My commandments and instructions as he has until now, I will make his kingdom last forever.' "

8   Then David turned to Solomon and said:[2]

"Here before the leaders of Israel, the people of God, and in the sight of our God, I am instructing you to search out every commandment of the Lord so

---

[1]Literally, "a footstool."
[2]Implied.

that you may continue to rule this good land and leave it to your children to rule forever.

9 Solomon, my son, get to know the God of your fathers. Worship and serve Him with a clean heart and a willing mind, for the Lord sees every heart and understands and knows every thought. If you seek Him, you will find Him; but if you forsake Him, He will permanently throw you aside.

10 So be very careful, for the Lord has chosen you to build His holy Temple. Be strong and do as He commands."

11 Then David gave Solomon the blueprint of the Temple and its surroundings — the treasuries, the upstairs rooms, the inside rooms, and the sanctuary for the place of mercy.

12 He also gave Solomon his plans for the outer court, the outside rooms, the Temple storage areas, and the treasuries for the gifts dedicated by famous persons. For the Holy Spirit had given David all these plans.[3]

13 The king also passed on to Solomon the instructions concerning the work of the various groups of priests and Levites; and he gave specifications for each item in the Temple which was to be used for worship and sacrifice.

14 David weighed out enough gold and silver to make these various items,

15 As well as the specific amount of gold needed for the lampstands and lamps. He also weighed out enough silver for the silver candlesticks and lamps, each according to its use.

---

[3]Or, "and the other plans he had in mind." The word in the Hebrew for "spirit" can be interpreted either way.

16 He weighed out the gold for the table on which the Bread of the Presence would be placed and for the other gold tables, and he weighed the silver for the silver tables.

17 Then he weighed out the gold for the solid gold hooks used in handling the sacrificial meat and for the basins, cups, and bowls of gold and silver.

18 Finally, he weighed out the refined gold for the altar of incense and for the gold angels whose wings were stretched over the Ark of the Covenant of the Lord.

19 "Every part of this blueprint," David told Solomon, "was given to me in writing from the hand of the Lord."

20 Then he continued, "Be strong and courageous and get to work. Don't be frightened by the size of the task, for the Lord my God is with you; He will not forsake you. He will see to it that everything is finished correctly.

21 And these various groups of priests and Levites will serve in the Temple. Others with skills of every kind will volunteer, and the army and the entire nation are at your command."

CHAPTER 29

Then King David turned to the entire assembly and said: "My son Solomon, whom God has chosen to be the next king of Israel, is still young and inexperienced, and the work ahead of him is enormous; for the Temple he will build is not just another building — it is for the Lord God Himself!

2 Using every resource at my command, I have

gathered as much as I could for building it — enough gold, silver, bronze, iron, wood, and great quantities of onyx, other precious stones, costly jewels, and marble.

3   And now, because of my devotion to the Temple of God, I am giving all of my own private treasures to aid in the construction. This is in addition to the building materials I have already collected.

4, 5   These personal contributions consist of $85,000,000 worth of gold from Ophir and $20,000,000 worth of purest silver to be used for overlaying the walls of the buildings. This will be used for the articles made of gold and silver and for the artistic decorations. Now then, who will follow my example? Who will give himself and all that he has to the Lord?"

6, 7   Then the clan leaders, the heads of the tribes, the army officers, and the administrative officers of the king pledged $145,000,000 in gold; $50,000 in foreign currency, $30,000,000 in silver; 800 tons of bronze; and 4,600 tons of iron.

8   They also contributed great amounts of jewelry, which were deposited at the Temple treasury with Jehiel (a descendant of Gershom).

9   Everyone was excited and happy for this opportunity of service, and King David was moved with deep joy.

10   While still in the presence of the whole assembly, David expressed his praises to the Lord: "O Lord God of our father Israel, praise Your name for ever and ever!

11   Yours is the mighty power and glory and victory and majesty. Everything in the heavens and earth

is Yours, O Lord, and this is Your kingdom. We adore You as being in control of everything.

12 Riches and honor come from You alone, and You are the ruler of all mankind; Your hand controls power and might, and it is at Your discretion that men are made great and given strength.

13 O our God, we thank You and praise Your glorious name,

14 But who am I and who are my people that we should be permitted to give anything to You? Everything we have has come from You, and we only give You what is Yours already!

15 For we are here for but a moment, strangers in the land as our fathers were before us; our days on earth are like a shadow, gone so soon, without a trace.

16 O Lord our God, all of this material that we have gathered to build a Temple for Your holy name comes from You! It all belongs to You!

17 I know, my God, that You test men to see if they are good; for You enjoy good men. I have done all this with good motives, and I have watched Your people offer their gifts willingly and joyously.

18 O Lord God of our fathers: Abraham, Isaac, and Israel! Make Your people always want to obey You, and see to it that their love for You never changes.

19 Give my son Solomon a good heart toward God, so that he will want to obey You in the smallest detail, and will look forward eagerly to finishing the building of Your Temple, for which I have made all of these preparations."

20 Then David said to all the people, "Give praise to the Lord your God!" And they did, bowing low be-

fore the Lord and the king.

21 The next day they brought a thousand young bulls, a thousand rams, and a thousand lambs as burnt offerings to the Lord; they also offered drink offerings and many other sacrifices on behalf of all Israel.

22 Then they feasted and drank before the Lord with great joy.

And again[1] they crowned King David's son Solomon as their king. They anointed him before the Lord as their leader, and they anointed Zadok as their priest.

23 So God appointed Solomon to take the throne of his father David; and he prospered greatly, and all Israel obeyed him.

24 The national leaders, the army officers, and his brothers all pledged their allegiance to King Solomon.

25 And the Lord gave him great popularity with all the people of Israel, and he amassed even greater wealth and honor than his father.

26, 27 David was king of the land of Israel for forty years; seven of them during his reign in Hebron and thirty-three in Jerusalem.

28 He died at an old age, wealthy and honored; and his son Solomon reigned in his place.

29 Detailed biographies of King David have been written in the history of Samuel the prophet, the history written by Nathan the prophet, and in the history written by the prophet Gad.

30 These accounts tell of his reign and of his might and all that happened to him and to Israel and to the kings of the nearby nations.

---

[1]Or, "and they installed him as co-regent" (with King David).

II Chronicles

CHAPTER 1

K ing David's son Solomon was now the undisputed ruler of Israel, for the Lord his God had made him a powerful monarch.

2, 3 He summoned all the army officers and judges to Gibeon[1] as well as all the political and religious leaders of Israel. He led them up to the hill to the old[2] Tabernacle constructed by Moses, the Lord's assistant, while he was in the wilderness.

4 (There was a later Tabernacle in Jerusalem, built by King David for the Ark of God when he removed it from Kiriath-jearim.)

5, 6 The bronze altar made by Bezalel (son of Uri, son of Hur) still stood in front of the old Tabernacle, and now Solomon and those he had invited assembled themselves before it, as he sacrificed upon it 1,000 burnt offerings to the Lord.

7 That night God appeared to Solomon and told him, "Ask Me for anything, and I will give it to you!"

8 Solomon replied, "O God, You have been so kind and good to my father David, and now You have given me the kingdom —

9 This is all I want! For You have fulfilled

---

[1] Implied.
[2] Moses had built the Tabernacle 500 years before the reign of King Solomon.

Your promise to David my father and have made me king over a nation as full of people as the earth is full of dust!

10 Now give me wisdom and knowledge to rule them properly, for who is able to govern by himself such a great nation as this one of Yours?"

11 God replied, "Because your greatest desire is to help your people, and you haven't asked for personal wealth and honor, and you haven't asked Me to curse your enemies, and you haven't asked for a long life, but for wisdom and knowledge to properly guide My people —

12 Yes, I am giving you the wisdom and knowledge you asked for! And I am also giving you such riches, wealth, and honor as no other king has ever had before you! And there will never again be so great a king in all the world!"

13 Solomon then left the Tabernacle, returned down the hill, and went back to Jerusalem to rule Israel.

14 He built up a huge force of 1,400 chariots and recruited 12,000 cavalry to guard the cities where the chariots were garaged, though some, of course, were stationed at Jerusalem near the king.

15 During Solomon's reign, silver and gold were as plentiful in Jerusalem as rocks on the road! And expensive cedar lumber was used like common sycamore!

16 Solomon sent horse-traders to Egypt to purchase entire herds at wholesale prices.

17 At that time Egyptian chariots sold for $400 each and horses for $100, delivered at Jerusalem. Many of these were then resold to the kings of the Hittites and Syria.

CHAPTER 2

Solomon now decided that the time had come to build a Temple for the Lord and a palace for himself.

2 This required a force of 70,000 laborers, 80,000 stonecutters in the hills, and 3,600 foremen.

3 Solomon sent an ambassador to King Hiram at Tyre, requesting shipments of cedar lumber such as Hiram had supplied to David when he was building his palace.

4 "I am about to build a Temple for the Lord my God," Solomon told Hiram. "It will be a place where I can burn incense and sweet spices before God, and display the special sacrificial bread,[1] and sacrifice burnt offerings each morning and evening, and on the Sabbaths, and at the new moon celebration and other regular festivals of the Lord our God. For God wants Israel always to celebrate these special occasions.

5 It is going to be a wonderful Temple because He is a great God, greater than any other.

6 But who can ever build Him a worthy home? Not even the highest heaven would be beautiful enough! And who am I to be allowed to build a Temple for God? But it will be a place to worship[2] Him.

7 So send me skilled craftsmen — goldsmiths and silversmiths, brass and iron workers; and send me weavers to make purple, crimson, and blue cloth; and skilled engravers to work beside the craftsmen of Judah and Jerusalem who were selected by my father David.

---

[1]Literally, "The Bread of the Presence."
[2]Literally, "a place to burn incense before Him."

8　Also send me cedar trees, fir trees, and algum trees from the Forests of Lebanon, for your men are without equal as lumbermen, and I will send my men to help them.

9　An immense amount of lumber will be needed, for the Temple I am going to build will be huge and incredibly beautiful.

10　As to the financial arrangements, I will pay your men 20,000 sacks of crushed wheat, 20,000 barrels of barley, 20,000 barrels of wine, and 20,000 barrels of olive oil."

11　King Hiram replied to King Solomon: "It is because the Lord loves His people that He has made you their king!

12　Blessed be the Lord God of Israel who made the heavens and the earth and who has given to David such a wise, intelligent, and understanding son to build God's Temple, and a royal palace for himself.

13　I am sending you a master craftsman — my famous Huramabi! He is a brilliant man,

14　The son of a Jewish woman from Dan in Israel; his father is from here in Tyre. He is a skillful goldsmith and silversmith, and also does exquisite work with brass and iron, and knows all about stonework, carpentry, and weaving; and he is an expert in the dying of purple and blue linen and crimson cloth. He is an engraver besides, and an inventor! He will work with your craftsmen and those appointed by my lord David, your father.

15　So send along the wheat, barley, olive oil, and wine you mentioned,

16　And we will begin cutting wood from the Lebanon mountains, as much as you need, and bring it to you in log floats across the sea to Joppa, and from there you can take them inland to Jerusalem."

17 Solomon now took a census of all foreigners in the country (just as his father David had done) and found that there were 153,600 of them.

18 He indentured 70,000 as common laborers, 80,000 as loggers and 3,600 as foremen.

CHAPTER 3

Finally the actual construction of the Temple began. Its location was in Jerusalem at the top of Mount Moriah, where the Lord had appeared to Solomon's father, King David; and where the threshing-floor of Ornan the Jebusite had been. David had selected it as the site for the Temple.

2 The actual construction began on the seventeenth day of April in the fourth year of King Solomon's reign.

3 The foundation was ninety feet long and thirty feet wide.

4 A covered porch ran along the entire thirty-foot width of the house, with the inner walls and ceiling overlaid with pure gold! The roof was 180 feet high.

5 The main part of the Temple was paneled with cypress wood, plated with pure gold, and engraved with palm trees and chains.

6 Beautiful jewels were inlaid into the walls to add to the beauty; the gold, by the way, was of the best, from Parvaim.

7 All the walls, beams, doors, and thresholds throughout the Temple were plated with gold, with angels engraved on the walls.

8   Within the Temple, at one end, was the most sacred room — the Holy of Holies — thirty feet square. This too was overlaid with the finest gold, valued at $18,000,000.

9   Twenty-six-ounce gold nails were used. The upper rooms were also plated with gold.

10   Within the innermost room, the Holy of Holies, Solomon placed two sculptured statues of angels, and plated them with gold.

11, 12, 13   They stood on the floor facing the outer room, with wings stretched wingtip to wingtip across the room, from wall to wall.[1]

14   Across the entrance to this room he placed a veil of blue and crimson fine-spun linen, decorated with angels.

15   At the front of the Temple were two pillars 52½ feet high, topped by a 7½-foot capital flaring out to the roof.

16   He made chains[2] and placed them on top of the pillars, with 100 pomegranates attached to the chains.

17   Then he set up the pillars at the front of the Temple, one on the right and the other on the left. And he gave them names: Jachin (the one on the right), and Boaz (the one on the left).

CHAPTER 4

H e also made a bronze altar thirty feet long, thirty feet wide, and fifteen feet high.

2   Then he forged a huge round tank fifteen feet

---

[1]Literally, "one wing of a cherub, five cubits long."
[2]Literally, "chains in the Holy of Holies, and . . ."

across from rim to rim. The rim stood 7½ feet above the floor, and was forty-five feet around.

3　This tank was set on the backs of two rows of metal oxen. The tank and oxen were cast as one piece.

4　There were twelve of these oxen standing tail to tail, three facing north, three west, three south, and three east.

5　The walls of the tank were five inches thick, flaring out like the cup of a lily. It held 3,000 barrels of water.

6　He also constructed ten vats for water to wash the offerings, five to the right of the huge tank and five to the left. The priests used the tank, and not the vats, for their own washing.

7　Carefully following God's instructions, he then cast ten gold lampstands and placed them in the Temple, five against each wall;

8　He also built ten tables and placed five against each wall on the right and left. And he molded 100 solid gold bowls.

9　Then he constructed a court for the priests, also the public court, and overlaid the doors of these courts with bronze.

10　The huge tank was in the southeast corner of the outer room of the Temple.

11　Huramabi also made the necessary pots, shovels, and basins for use in connection with the sacrifices. So at last he completed the work assigned to him by King Solomon:

12　　　The construction of the two pillars,
　　　　The two flared capitals on the tops of the
　　　　　　pillars,

The two sets of chains on the capitals,

13   The 400 pomegranates hanging from the two sets of chains on the capitals,

14   The bases for the vats, and the vats themselves,

15   The huge tank and the twelve oxen under it.

16   The pots, shovels, and fleshhooks.

This skillful craftsman, Huramabi, made all of the above-mentioned items for King Solomon, using polished bronze.

17, 18   The king did the casting at the claybanks of the Jordan valley between Succoth and Zeredah. Great quantities of bronze were used, too heavy to weigh.

19   But in the Temple only gold was used. For Solomon commanded that all of the utensils, the altar, and the table for the Bread of the Presence must be made of gold;

20   Also the lamps and lampstands,

21   The floral decorations, tongs,

22   Lamp snuffers, basins, spoons, and firepans — all were made of pure gold. Even the doorway of the Temple, the main door, and the inner doors to the Holy of Holies were of gold.

CHAPTER 5

So the Temple was finally finished. Then Solomon brought in the gifts dedicated to the Lord by his father, King David. They were stored in the Temple treasuries.

2   Solomon now summoned to Jerusalem all of

the leaders of Israel — the heads of the tribes and clans — for the ceremony of transferring the Ark from the [Tabernacle in the[1]] City of David, also known as Zion, [to its new home in the Temple[1]].

3   This celebration took place in October at the annual Festival of Tabernacles.

4, 5   As the leaders of Israel watched, the Levites lifted the Ark and carried it out of the Tabernacle, along with all the other sacred vessels.

6   King Solomon and the others sacrificed sheep and oxen before the Ark in such numbers that no one tried to keep count!

7, 8   Then the priests carried the Ark into the inner room of the Temple — the Holy of Holies — and placed it beneath the angels' wings; their wings spread over the Ark and its carrying poles.

9   These carrying poles were so long that their ends could be seen from the outer room, but not from the outside doorway. The Ark is still there at the time of this writing.

10   Nothing was in the Ark except the two stone tablets which Moses had put there at Mount Horeb, when the Lord made a covenant with the people of Israel as they were leaving Egypt.

11, 12   When the priests had undergone the purification rites for themselves, they all took part in the ceremonies without regard to their normal duties. And how the Levites were praising the Lord as the priests came out of the Holy of Holies! The singers were Asaph, Heman, Jeduthun and all their sons and brothers, dressed in finespun linen robes and standing at the east side of the altar. The choir was accompanied

---

[1]Implied.

by 120 priests who were trumpeters, while others played the cymbals, lyres, and harps.

13, 14   The band and chorus united as one to praise and thank the Lord; their selections were interspersed with trumpet obbligatos, the clashing of cymbals, and the loud playing of other musical instruments — all praising and thanking the Lord. Their theme was "He is so good! His lovingkindness lasts forever!" And at that moment the glory of the Lord, coming as a bright cloud, filled the Temple so that the priests could not continue their work.

CHAPTER 6

This is the prayer prayed by Solomon on that occasion:

> "The Lord has said that He would live in the thick darkness,

2   But I have made a Temple for You, O Lord, to live in forever!"

3   Then the king turned around to the people and they stood to receive his blessing:

4   "Blessed be the Lord God of Israel," he said to them, "— the God who talked personally to my father David and has now fulfilled the promise He made to him. For He told him,

5, 6   'I have never before, since bringing My people from the land of Egypt, chosen a city anywhere in Israel as the location of My Temple where My name will be glorified; and never before have I chosen a king for My people Israel. But now I have chosen Jerusalem as that city, and David as that king.'

7   My father David wanted to build this Temple,

8　But the Lord said not to. It was good to have the desire, the Lord told him,

9　But he was not the one to build it: his son was chosen for that task.

10　And now the Lord has done what He promised, for I have become king in my father's place, and I have built the Temple for the Name of the Lord God of Israel,

11　And placed the Ark there. And in the Ark is the Covenant between the Lord and His people Israel."

12, 13　As he spoke, Solomon was standing before the people on a platform in the center of the outer court, in front of the altar of the Lord. The platform was made of bronze, 7½ feet square and 4½ feet high. Now, as all the people watched, he knelt down, reached out his arms toward heaven, and prayed this prayer:

14　"O Lord God of Israel, there is no God like You in all of heaven and earth. You are the God who keeps His kind promises to all those who obey You, and who are anxious to do Your will.

15　And You have kept Your promise to my father David,[1] as is evident today.

16　And now, O God of Israel, carry out Your further promise to him that 'Your descendants shall always reign over Israel if they will obey My laws as you have.'

17　Yes, Lord God of Israel, please fulfill this promise too.

18　But will God really live upon the earth with men? Why, even the heaven and the heaven of heav-

---

[1]Literally, "David Your servant."

ens cannot contain You — how much less this Temple which I have built!

19 How I pray that You will heed my prayers, O Lord my God! Listen to my prayer that I am praying to You now!

20, 21 Look down with favor day and night upon this Temple — upon this place where You have said that You would put Your name. May You always hear and answer the prayers I will pray to You as I face toward this place. Listen to my prayers and to those of Your people Israel when they pray toward this Temple; yes, hear us from heaven, and when You hear, forgive.

22 Whenever someone commits a crime, and is required to swear to his innocence before this altar,

23 Then hear from heaven and punish him if he is lying, or else declare him innocent.

24 If Your people Israel are destroyed before their enemies because they have sinned against You, and if they turn to You and call themselves Your people, and pray to You here in this Temple,

25 Then listen to them from heaven and forgive their sins and give them back this land You gave to their fathers.

26 When the skies are shut and there is no rain because of our sins, and then we pray toward this Temple and claim You as our God, and turn from our sins because You have punished us,

27 Then listen from heaven and forgive the sins of Your people, and teach them what is right; and send rain upon this land which You have given to Your people as their own property.

28 If there is a famine in the land, or plagues,

or crop disease, or attacks of locusts or caterpillars, or if Your people's enemies are in the land besieging our cities — whatever the trouble is —

29   Listen to every individual's prayer concerning his private sorrow, as well as all the public prayers.

30   Hear from heaven where You live, and forgive, and give each one whatever he deserves, for You know the hearts of all mankind.

31   Then they will reverence You forever, and will continually walk where You tell them to go.[2]

32   And when foreigners hear of Your power, and come from distant lands to worship Your great name, and to pray toward this Temple,

33   Hear them from heaven where You live, and do what they request of You. Then all the peoples of the earth will hear of Your fame and will reverence You, just as Your people Israel do; and they too will know that this Temple I have built is truly Yours.

34   If Your people go out at Your command to fight their enemies, and they pray toward this city of Jerusalem which You have chosen, and this Temple which I have built for Your name,

35   Then hear their prayers from heaven and give them success.

36   If they sin against You (and who has never sinned?) and You become angry with them, and You let their enemies defeat them and take them away as captives to some foreign nation near or far,

37, 38   And if in that land of exile they turn to You again, and face toward this land You gave their fathers, and this city and Your Temple I have built,

---

[2]Or, "as long as they are living in this land which You gave to our fathers."

and plead with You with all their hearts to forgive them,

39 Then hear from heaven where You live and help them and forgive Your people who have sinned against You.

40 Yes, O my God, be wide awake and attentive to all the prayers made to You in this place.

41 And now, O Lord God, arise and enter this resting place of Yours where the Ark of Your strength has been placed. Let Your priests, O Lord God, be clothed with salvation, and let Your saints rejoice in Your kind deeds.

42 O Lord God, do not ignore me — do not turn Your face away from me, Your anointed one. Oh, remember Your love for David and Your kindness to him."

CHAPTER 7

As Solomon finished praying, fire flashed down from heaven and burned up the sacrifices! And the glory of the Lord filled the Temple, so that the priests couldn't enter!

3 All the people had been watching and now they fell flat on the pavement, and worshiped and thanked the Lord. "How good He is!" they exclaimed. "He is always so loving and kind."

4, 5 Then the king and all the people dedicated the Temple by sacrificing burnt offerings to the Lord. King Solomon's contribution for this purpose was 22,-000 oxen and 120,000 sheep.

6 The priests were standing at their posts of duty, and the Levites were playing their thanksgiving song, "His Lovingkindness Is Forever," using the musi-

cal instruments that King David himself had made and had used to praise the Lord. Then, when the priests blew the trumpets, all the people stood again.

7 Solomon consecrated the inner court of the Temple for use that day as a place of sacrifice, for there were too many sacrifices for the bronze altar to accommodate.

8 For the next seven days, they celebrated the Tabernacle Festival, with large crowds coming in from all over Israel; they arrived from as far away as Hamath at one end of the country to the brook of Egypt at the other.

9 A final religious service was held on the eighth day.

10 Then, on October 7, he sent the people home, joyful and happy because the Lord had been so good to David and Solomon and to His people Israel.

11 So Solomon finished building the Temple as well as his own palace. He completed what he had planned to do.

12 One night the Lord appeared to Solomon and told him, "I have heard Your prayer and have chosen this Temple as the place where I want you to sacrifice to Me.

13 If I shut up the heavens so that there is no rain, or if I command the locust swarms to eat up all of your crops, or if I send an epidemic among you,

14 Then if My people will humble themselves and pray, and search for Me, and turn from their wicked ways, I will hear them from heaven and forgive their sins and heal their land.

15 I will listen, wide awake, to every prayer made in this place.

16 For I have chosen this Temple and sanctified it to be My home forever; My eyes and My heart shall always be here.

17 As for yourself, if you follow Me as your father David did,

18 Then I will see to it that you and your descendants will always be the kings of Israel;

19 But if you don't follow Me, if you refuse the laws I have given you, and worship idols,

20 Then I will destroy My people from this land of Mine which I have given them, and this Temple shall be destroyed even though I have sanctified it for Myself. Instead, I will make it a public horror and disgrace.

21 Instead of its being famous, all who pass by will be incredulous. 'Why has the Lord done such a terrible thing to this land and to this Temple?' they will ask.

22 And the answer will be, 'Because His people abandoned the Lord God of their fathers, the God who brought them out of the land of Egypt, and they worshiped other gods instead. That is why He has done all this to them.'

CHAPTER 8

It was now twenty years since Solomon had become king, and the great building projects of the Lord's Temple and his own royal palace were completed.

2 He now turned his energies to rebuilding the cities which King Hiram of Tyre had given to him, and he relocated some of the people of Israel into them.

3   It was at this time, too, that Solomon fought against the city of Hamath-zobah and conquered it.

4   He built Tadmor in the desert, and built cities in Hamath as supply centers.

5   He fortified the cities of upper Beth-horon and lower Beth-horon, both being supply centers, building their walls and installing barred gates.

6   He also built Baalath and other supply centers at this time, and constructed cities where his chariots and horses were kept. He built to his heart's desire in Jerusalem and Lebanon and throughout the entire realm.

7, 8   He began the practice that still continues of conscripting as slave laborers the Hittites, Amorites, Perizzites, Hivites, and Jebusites — the descendants of those nations which the Israelis had not completely wiped out.

9   However, he didn't make slaves of any of the Israeli citizens, but used them as soldiers, officers, charioteers, and cavalrymen;

10   Also, two hundred fifty of them were government officials who administered all public affairs.

11   Solomon now moved his wife (she was Pharaoh's daughter) from the City of David sector of Jerusalem to the new palace he had built for her. For he said, "She must not live in King David's palace, for the Ark of the Lord was there and it is holy ground."

12   Then Solomon sacrificed burnt offerings to the Lord on the altar he had built in front of the porch of the Temple.

13   The number of sacrifices differed from day to day in accordance with the instructions Moses had given; there were extra sacrifices on the Sabbaths, on

new moon festivals, and at the three annual festivals — the Passover celebration, the Festival of Weeks, and the Festival of Tabernacles.

14 In assigning the priests to their posts of duty he followed the organizational chart prepared by his father David; he also assigned the Levites to their work of praise and of helping the priests in each day's duties; and he assigned the gatekeepers to their gates.

15 Solomon did not deviate in any way from David's instructions concerning these matters and concerning the treasury personnel.

16 Thus Solomon successfully completed the construction of the Temple.

17, 18 Then he went to the seaport towns of Ezion-geber and Eloth, in Edom, to launch a fleet presented to him by King Hiram. These ships, with King Hiram's experienced crews working alongside Solomon's men, went to Ophir and brought back $13,-000,000 worth of gold to him!

CHAPTER 9

When the Queen of Sheba heard of Solomon's fabled wisdom, she came to Jerusalem to test him with hard questions. A very great retinue of aides and servants accompanied her, including camel-loads of spices, gold, and jewels.

2 And Solomon answered all her problems. Nothing was hidden from him; he could explain everything to her.

3 When she discovered how wise he really was, and how breathtaking the beauty of his palace,

4 And how wonderful the food at his tables, and

how many servants and aides he had, and when she saw their spectacular uniforms and his stewards in full regalia, and saw the size of the men in his bodyguard, she could scarcely believe it!

5 Finally she exclaimed to the king, "Everything I heard about you in my own country is true!

6 I didn't believe it until I got here and saw it with my own eyes. Your wisdom is far greater than I could ever have imagined.

7 What a privilege for these men of yours to stand here and listen to you talk!

8 Blessed be the Lord your God! How He must love Israel to give them a just king like you! He wants them to be a great, strong nation forever."

9 She gave the king a gift of over a million dollars in gold, and great quantities of spices of incomparable quality, and many, many jewels.

10 King Hiram's and King Solomon's crews brought gold from Ophir, also sandalwood and jewels.

11 The king used the sandalwood to make terraced steps for the Temple and the palace, and to construct harps and lyres for the choir. Never before had there been such beautiful instruments in all the land of Judah.

12 King Solomon gave the Queen of Sheba gifts of the same value as she had brought to him, plus everything else she asked for! Then she and her retinue returned to their own land.

13, 14 Solomon received a billion dollars worth of gold each year from the kings of Arabia and many other lands that paid annual tribute to him. In addition, there was a trade balance from the exports of his merchants.

15 He used some of the gold to make 200 large shields, each worth $280,000,

16 And 300 smaller shields, each worth $140,-000. The king placed these in the Forest of Lebanon Room in his palace.

17 He also made a huge ivory throne overlaid with pure gold.

18 It had six gold steps and a footstool of gold; also gold armrests, each flanked by a gold lion.

19 Gold lions also stood at each side of each step. No other throne in all the world could be compared with it!

20 All of King Solomon's cups were solid gold, as were all the furnishings in the Forest of Lebanon Room. Silver was too cheap to count for much in those days!

21 Every three years the king sent his ships to Tarshish, using sailors supplied by King Hiram, to bring back gold, silver, ivory, apes, and peacocks.

22 So King Solomon was richer and wiser than any other king in all the earth.

23 Kings from every nation came to visit him, and to hear the wisdom God had put into his heart.

24 Each brought him annual tribute of silver and gold bowls, clothing, armor, spices, horses, and mules.

25 In addition, Solomon had 4,000 stalls of horses and chariots, and 12,000 cavalrymen stationed in the chariot cities, as well as in Jerusalem to protect the king.

26 He ruled over all kings and kingdoms from the Euphrates River to the land of the Philistines and as far away as the border of Egypt.

27 He made silver become as plentiful in Jerusalem as stones in the road! And cedar was used as

though it were common sycamore.

28   Horses were brought to him from Egypt and other countries.

29   The rest of Solomon's biography is written in the history of Nathan the prophet and in the prophecy of Ahijah the Shilonite, and also in the visions of Iddo the seer concerning Jeroboam the son of Nebat.

30   So Solomon reigned in Jerusalem over all of Israel for forty years.

31   Then he died and was buried in Jerusalem, and his son Rehoboam became the new king.

CHAPTER 10

All the leaders of Israel came to Shechem for Rehoboam's coronation.

2, 3   Meanwhile, friends of Jeroboam (son of Nebat) sent word to him of Solomon's death. He was in Egypt at the time, where he had gone to escape from King Solomon. He now quickly returned, and was present at the coronation, and led the people's demands on Rehoboam:

4   "Your father was a hard master," they said. "Be easier on us than he was, and we will let you be our king!"

5   Rehoboam told them to return in three days for his decision.

6   He discussed their demand with the old men who had counseled his father Solomon. "What shall I tell them?" he asked.

7   "If you want to be their king," they replied, "you will have to give them a favorable reply and treat them with kindness."

8, 9   But he rejected their advice and asked the opinion of the young men who had grown up with him. "What do you fellows think I should do?" he asked. "Shall I be easier on them than my father was?"

10   "No!" they replied. "Tell them, 'If you think my father was hard on you, just wait and see what I'll be like!' Tell them, 'My little finger is thicker than my father's loins!

11   I am going to be tougher on you, not easier! My father used whips on you, but I'll use scorpions!' "

12   So when Jeroboam and the people returned in three days to hear King Rehoboam's decision,

13   He spoke roughly to them; for he refused the advice of the old men,

14   And followed the counsel of the younger ones. "My father gave you heavy burdens but I will give you heavier!" he told them. "My father punished you with whips, but I will punish you with scorpions!"

15   So the king turned down the people's demands. (God caused him to do it in order to fulfill His prediction[1] spoken to Jeroboam by Ahijah, the Shilonite.)

16   When the people realized what the king was saying they turned around and deserted him. "Forget David and his dynasty!" they shouted angrily. "We'll get someone else to be our king. Let Rehoboam rule his own tribe of Judah! Let's go home!" So they did.

17   The people of the tribe of Judah, however, remained loyal to Rehoboam.

18   Afterwards, when King Rehoboam sent Hadoram to draft forced labor from the other tribes of Israel, the people stoned him to death. When this news

---

[1]See I Kings 11:30, 31.

reached King Rehoboam he jumped into his chariot and fled to Jerusalem.

19   And Israel has refused to be ruled by a descendant of David to this day.

CHAPTER 11

U pon arrival at Jerusalem, Rehoboam mobilized the armies of Judah and Benjamin, 180,000 strong, and declared war against the rest of Israel in an attempt to reunite the kingdom.

2   But the Lord told Shemaiah the prophet,

3   "Go and say to King Rehoboam of Judah, Solomon's son, and to the people of Judah and of Benjamin:

4   'The Lord says, Do not fight against your brothers. Go home, for I am behind their rebellion.'" So they obeyed the Lord and refused to fight against Jeroboam.

5-10   Rehoboam stayed in Jerusalem and fortified these cities of Judah with walls and gates to protect himself:

> Bethlehem, Etam, Tekoa,
> Beth-zur, Soco, Adullam,
> Gath, Mareshah, Ziph,
> Adoraim, Lachish, Azekah,
> Zorah, Aijalon, and Hebron.

11   He also rebuilt and strengthened the forts, and manned them with companies of soldiers under their officers, and stored them with food, olive oil, and wine.

12   Shields and spears were placed in armories in every city as a further safety measure. For only Ju-

dah and Benjamin remained loyal to him.

13, 14   However, the priests and Levites from the other tribes now abandoned their homes and moved to Judah and Jerusalem, for King Jeroboam had fired them, telling them to stop being priests of the Lord.

15   He had appointed other priests instead who encouraged the people to worship idols instead of God, and to sacrifice to carved statues of goats and calves which he placed on the hills.

16   Laymen, too, from all over Israel began moving to Jerusalem where they could freely worship the Lord God of their fathers, and sacrifice to Him.

17   This strengthened the kingdom of Judah, so King Rehoboam survived for three years without difficulty; for during those years there was an earnest effort to obey the Lord as King David and King Solomon had done.[1]

18   Rehoboam married his cousin[2] Mahalath. She was the daughter of David's son Jerimoth and of Abihail, the daughter of David's brother Eliab.

19   Three sons were born from this marriage — Jeush, Shemariah, and Zaham.

20   Later he married Maacah, the daughter of Absalom. The children she bore him were Abijah, Attai, Ziza, and Shelomith.

21   He loved Maacah more than any of his other wives and concubines (he had eighteen wives and sixty concubines — with twenty-eight sons and sixty daughters).

22   Maacah's son Abijah was his favorite, and he intended to make him the next king.

---

[1]Literally, "they walked in the way of David and Solomon."
[2]Implied.

23 He very wisely scattered his other sons in the fortified cities throughout the land of Judah and Benjamin, and gave them large allowances and arranged for them to have several wives apiece.

CHAPTER 12

But just when Rehoboam was at the height of his popularity and power he abandoned the Lord, and the people followed him in this sin.

2 As a result, King Shishak of Egypt attacked Jerusalem in the fifth year of King Rehoboam's reign,

3 With twelve hundred chariots, sixty thousand cavalrymen and an unnumbered host of infantrymen — Egyptians, Libyans, Sukkiim, and Ethiopians.

4 He quickly conquered Judah's fortified cities and soon arrived at Jerusalem.

5 The prophet Shemaiah now met with Rehoboam and the Judean leaders from every part of the nation (they had fled to Jerusalem for safety), and told them, "The Lord says, 'You have forsaken Me, so I have forsaken you and abandoned you to Shishak.'"

6 Then the king and the leaders of Israel confessed their sins and exclaimed, "The Lord is right in doing this to us!"

7 And when the Lord saw them humble themselves He sent Shemaiah to tell them, "Because you have humbled yourselves, I will not completely destroy you; some will escape. I will not use Shishak to pour out My anger upon Jerusalem.

8 But you must pay annual tribute to him. Then you will realize how much better it is to serve Me than to serve him!"

9 So King Shishak of Egypt conquered Jerusalem and took away all the treasures of the Temple and of the palace, also all of Solomon's gold shields.

10 King Rehoboam replaced them with bronze shields and committed them to the care of the captain of his bodyguard.

11 Whenever the king went to the Temple, the guards would carry them, and afterwards return them to the armory.

12 When the king humbled himself, the Lord's anger was turned aside and He didn't send total destruction; in fact, even after Shishak's invasion, the economy of Judah remained strong.

13 King Rehoboam reigned seventeen years in Jerusalem, the city God had chosen as His residence after considering all the other cities of Israel. He had become king at the age of forty-one; and his mother's name was Naamah the Ammonitess.

14 But he was an evil king, for he never did decide really to please the Lord.

15 The complete biography of Rehoboam is recorded in the histories written by Shemaiah the prophet and by Iddo the seer, and in *The Genealogical Register*.

There were continual wars between Rehoboam and Jeroboam.

16 When Rehoboam died he was buried in Jerusalem, and his son Abijah became the new king.

CHAPTER 13

A bijah became the new king of Judah, in Jerusalem, in the eighteenth year of the reign of King Jeroboam of Israel. He lasted three years. His mother's name was Micaiah (daughter of Uriel of Gibeah).

Early in his reign war broke out between Judah and Israel.

3 Judah, led by King Abijah, fielded 400,000 seasoned warriors against twice as many Israeli troops — strong, courageous men led by King Jeroboam.

4 When the army of Judah arrived at Mount Zemaraim, in the hill country of Ephraim, King Abijah shouted to King Jeroboam and the Israeli army:

5 "Listen! Don't you realize that the Lord God of Israel swore that David's descendants would always be the kings of Israel?

6 Your King Jeroboam is a mere servant of David's son, and was a traitor to his master.

7 Then a whole gang of worthless rebels joined him, defying Solomon's son Rehoboam, for he was young and frightened and couldn't stand up to them.

8 Do you really think you can defeat the kingdom of the Lord that is led by a descendant of David? Your army is twice as large as mine, but you are cursed with those gold calves you have with you, that Jeroboam made for you — he calls them your gods!

9 And you have driven away the priests of the Lord and the Levites, and have appointed heathen priests instead. Just like the people of other lands, you accept as priests anybody who comes along with a young bullock and seven rams for consecration. Anyone at all can be a priest of these no-gods of yours!

10 But as for us, the Lord is our God and we have not forsaken Him. Only the descendants of Aaron are our priests, and the Levites alone may help them in their work.

11 They burn sacrifices to the Lord every morning and evening — burnt offerings and sweet incense; and they place the Bread of the Presence upon the holy table. The golden lampstand is lighted every night, for we are careful to follow the instructions of the Lord our God; but you have forsaken Him.

12 So you see, God is with us; He is our leader. His priests, trumpeting as they go, will lead us into battle against you. O people of Israel, do not fight against the Lord God of your fathers, for you will not succeed!"

13, 14 Meanwhile, Jeroboam had secretly sent part of his army around behind the men of Judah to ambush them; so Judah was surrounded, with the enemy before and behind them. Then they cried out to the Lord for mercy, and the priests blew the trumpets.

15, 16 The men of Judah began to shout. And as they shouted, God used King Abijah and the men of Judah to turn the tide of battle against King Jeroboam and the army of Israel,

17 And they slaughtered 500,000 elite troops of Israel that day.

18, 19 So Judah, depending upon the Lord God of their fathers, defeated Israel, and chased King Jeroboam's troops, and captured some of his cities — Bethel, Jeshanah, Ephron, and their suburbs.

20 King Jeroboam of Israel never regained his power during Abijah's lifetime, and eventually the Lord struck him and he died.

21 Meanwhile, King Abijah of Judah became very strong. He married fourteen wives and had twenty-two sons and sixteen daughters.

22 His complete biography and speeches are recorded in the prophet Iddo's *History of Judah.*

CHAPTER 14

King Abijah was buried in Jerusalem. Then his son Asa became the new king of Judah, and there was peace in the land for the first ten years of his reign.

2 For Asa was careful to obey the Lord his God.

3 He demolished the heathen altars on the hills, and broke down the obelisks, and chopped down the shameful Asherim-idols,

4 And demanded that the entire nation obey the commandments of the Lord God of their ancestors.

5 Also, he removed the sun-images from the hills, and the incense altars from every one of Judah's cities. That is why God gave his kingdom peace.

6 This made it possible for him to build walled cities throughout Judah.

7 "Now is the time to do it, while the Lord is blessing us with peace because of our obedience to Him," he told his people. "Let us build and fortify cities now, with walls, towers, gates, and bars." So they went ahead with these projects very successfully.

8 King Asa's Judean army was 300,000 strong, equipped with light shields and spears. His army of Benjaminites numbered 280,000, armed with large shields and bows. Both armies were composed of well-trained, brave men.

9, 10 But now he was attacked by an army of 1,000,000 troops from Ethiopia with 300 chariots, under the leadership of General Zerah. They advanced to the city of Mareshah, in the valley of Zephathah, and King Asa sent his troops to meet them there.

11 "O Lord," he cried out to God, "no one else can help us! Here we are, powerless against this mighty army. Oh, help us, Lord our God! For we trust in You alone to rescue us, and in Your name we attack this vast horde. Don't let mere men defeat You!"

12 Then the Lord defeated the Ethiopians, and Asa and the army of Judah triumphed as the Ethiopians fled.

13 They chased them as far as Gerar, and the entire Ethiopian army was wiped out so that not one man remained; for the Lord and His army destroyed them all. Then the army of Judah carried off vast quantities of plunder.

14 While they were at Gerar they attacked all the cities in that area, and terror from the Lord came upon the residents. As a result, additional vast quantities of plunder were collected from these cities too.

15 They not only plundered the cities, but destroyed the cattle tents and captured great herds of sheep and camels before finally returning to Jerusalem.

CHAPTER 15

Then the Spirit of God came upon Azariah (son of Oded),

2 And he went out to meet King Asa as he was returning from the battle. "Listen to me, Asa! Listen, armies of Judah and Benjamin!" he shouted. "The Lord will stay with you as long as you stay with Him! Whenever you look for Him, you will find Him. But if you forsake Him, He will forsake you.

3 For a long time now, over in Israel, the people

haven't worshiped the true God, and have not had a true priest to teach them. They have lived without God's laws.

4 But whenever they have turned again to the Lord God of Israel in their distress, and searched for Him, He has helped them.

5 In their times of rebellion against God there was no peace. Problems troubled the nation on every hand. Crime was on the increase everywhere.

6 There were external wars, and internal fighting of city against city, for God was plaguing them with all sorts of trouble.

7 But you men of Judah, keep up the good work and don't get discouraged, for you will be rewarded."

8 When King Asa heard this message from God, he took courage and destroyed all the idols in the land of Judah and Benjamin, and in the cities he had captured in the hill country of Ephraim, and he rebuilt the altar of the Lord in front of the Temple.

9 Then he summoned all the people of Judah and Benjamin, and the immigrants from Israel (for many had come from the territories of Ephraim, Manasseh, and Simeon, in Israel, when they saw that the Lord God was with King Asa).

10 They all came to Jerusalem in June of the fifteenth year of King Asa's reign,

11 And sacrificed to the Lord seven hundred oxen and seven thousand sheep — it was part of the plunder they had captured in the battle.

12 Then they entered into a contract to worship only the Lord God of their fathers,

13 And agreed that anyone who refused to do this

must die — whether old or young, man or woman.

14 They shouted out their oath of loyalty to God with trumpets blaring and horns sounding.

15 All were happy for this covenant with God, for they had entered into it with all their hearts and wills, and wanted Him above everything else, and they found Him! And He gave them peace throughout the nation.

16 King Asa even removed his mother Maacah from being the queen mother because she made an Asherah-idol; he cut down the idol and crushed and burned it at Kidron Brook.

17 Over in Israel the idol-temples were not removed. But here in Judah and Benjamin the heart of King Asa was perfect before God throughout his lifetime.

18 He brought back into the Temple the silver and gold bowls which he and his father had dedicated to the Lord.

19 So there was no more war until the thirty-fifth year of King Asa's reign.

CHAPTER 16

In the thirty-sixth year of King Asa's reign, King Baasha of Israel declared war on him and built the fortress[1] of Ramah in order to control the road to Judah.

2 Asa's response was to take the silver and gold from the Temple and from the palace, and to send it to King Ben-hadad of Syria, at Damascus, with this message:

---

[1]Literally, "high places."

3 "Let us renew the mutual security pact that there was between your father and my father. See, here is silver and gold to induce you to break your alliance with King Baasha of Israel, so that he will leave me alone."

4 Ben-hadad agreed to King Asa's request and mobilized his armies to attack Israel. They destroyed the cities of Ijon, Dan, Abel-maim and all of the supply centers in Naphtali.

5 As soon as King Baasha of Israel heard what was happening, he discontinued building Ramah and gave up his plan to attack Judah.

6 Then King Asa and the people of Judah went out to Ramah and carried away the building stones and timbers and used them to build Geba and Mizpah instead.

7 About that time the prophet Hanani came to King Asa and told him, "Because you have put your trust in the king of Syria instead of in the Lord your God, the army of the king of Syria has escaped from you.

8 Don't you remember what happened to the Ethiopians and Libyans and their vast army, with all of their chariots and cavalrymen? But you relied then on the Lord, and He delivered them all into your hand.

9 For the eyes of the Lord search back and forth across the whole earth, looking for people whose hearts are perfect toward Him, so that He can show His great power in helping them. What a fool you have been! From now on you shall have wars."

10 Asa was so angry with the prophet for saying this that he threw him into jail. And Asa oppressed all the people at that time.

11 The rest of the biography of Asa is written in *The Annals of the Kings of Israel and Judah.*

12 In the thirty-ninth year of his reign, Asa became seriously diseased in his feet but he didn't go to the Lord with the problem, but to the doctors.

13, 14 So he died in the forty-first year of his reign, and was buried in his own vault that he had hewn out for himself in Jerusalem. He was laid on a bed perfumed with sweet spices and ointments, and his people made a very great burning of incense for him at his funeral.

CHAPTER 17

Then his son Jehoshaphat became the king and mobilized for war against Israel.

2 He placed garrisons in all of the fortified cities of Judah, in various other places throughout the country, and in the cities of Ephraim that his father had conquered.

3 The Lord was with Jehoshaphat because he followed in the good footsteps of his father's early years, and did not worship idols.

4 He obeyed the commandments of his father's God — quite unlike the people across the border in the land of Israel.

5 So the Lord strengthened his position as king of Judah. All the people of Judah cooperated by paying their taxes, so he became very wealthy as well as being very popular.

6 He boldly followed the paths of God — even knocking down the heathen altars on the hills, and destroying the Asherim idols.

7, 8, 9   In the third year of his reign he began a nationwide religious education program. He sent out top government officials as teachers in all the cities of Judah. These men included Ben-hail, Obadiah, Zechariah, Nethanel, and Micaiah. He also used the Levites for this purpose, including Shemaiah, Nethaniah, Zebadiah, Asahel, Shemiramoth, Jehonathan, Adonijah, Tobijah, and Tobadonijah; also the priests, Elishama and Jehoram. They took copies of *The Book of the Law of the Lord* to all the cities of Judah, to teach the Scriptures to the people.

10   Then the fear of the Lord fell upon all the surrounding kingdoms so that none of them declared war on King Jehoshaphat.

11   Even some of the Philistines brought him presents and annual tribute, and the Arabs donated 7,700 rams and 7,700 male goats.

12   So Jehoshaphat became very strong, and built fortresses and supply cities throughout Judah.

13   His public works program was also extensive, and he had a huge army stationed at Jerusalem, his capital.

14, 15   Three hundred thousand Judean troops were there under General Adnah. Next in command was Jeho-hanan with an army of 280,000 men.

16   Next was Amasiah (son of Zichri), a man of unusual piety, with 200,000 troops.

17   Benjamin supplied 200,000 men equipped with bows and shields under the command of Eliada, a great general.

18   His second in command was Jehozabad, with 180,000 trained men.

19   These were the troops in Jerusalem in addi-

tion to those placed by the king in the fortified cities throughout the nation.

CHAPTER 18

But rich, popular King Jehoshaphat of Judah made a marriage alliance [for his son[1]] with [the daughter of[1]] King Ahab of Israel.

2 A few years later he went down to Samaria to visit King Ahab, and King Ahab gave a great party for him and his aides, butchering great numbers of sheep and oxen for the feast. Then he asked King Jehoshaphat to join forces with him against Ramoth-gilead.

3, 4, 5 "Why, of course!" King Jehoshaphat replied. "I'm with you all the way. My troops are at your command! However, let's check with the Lord first." So King Ahab summoned 400 of his heathen prophets and asked them, "Shall we go to war with Ramoth-gilead or not?"

And they replied, "Go ahead, for God will give you a great victory!"

6, 7 But Jehoshaphat wasn't satisfied. "Isn't there some prophet of the Lord around here too?" he asked. "I'd like to ask him the same question."

"Well," Ahab told him, "there is one, but I hate him, for he never prophesies anything but evil! His name is Micaiah (son of Imlah)."

"Oh, come now, don't talk like that!" Jehoshaphat exclaimed. "Let's hear what he has to say."

8 So the king of Israel called one of his aides. "Quick! Go and get Micaiah (son of Imlah)," he ordered.

---

[1]Implied in 21:6.

9 The two kings were sitting on thrones in full regalia at an open place near the Samaria gate, and all the "prophets" were prophesying before them.

10 One of them, Zedekiah (son of Chenaanah), made some iron horns for the occasion and proclaimed, "The Lord says you will gore the Syrians to death with these!"

11 And all the others agreed. "Yes," they chorused, "go up to Ramoth-gilead and prosper, for the Lord will cause you to conquer."

12 The man who went to get Micaiah told him what was happening, and what all the prophets were saying — that the war would end in triumph for the king. "I hope you will agree with them and give the king a favorable reading," the man ventured.

13 But Micaiah replied, "I vow by God that whatever God says is what I will say."

14 When he arrived before the king, the king asked him, "Micaiah, shall we go to war against Ramoth-gilead or not?"

And Micaiah replied, "Sure, go ahead! It will be a glorious victory!"

15 "Look here," the king said sharply, "how many times must I tell you to speak nothing except what the Lord tells you to?"

16 Then Micaiah told him, "In my vision I saw all Israel scattered upon the mountain as sheep without a shepherd. And the Lord said, 'Their master has been killed. Send them home.' "

17 "Didn't I tell you?" the king of Israel exclaimed to Jehoshaphat. "He does it every time. He *never* prophesies *anything* but evil against me."

18 "Listen to what else the Lord has told me,"

Micaiah continued. "I saw Him upon His throne surrounded by vast throngs of angels.

19, 20 And the Lord said, 'Who can get King Ahab to go to battle against Ramoth-gilead and be killed there?'

There were many suggestions, but finally a spirit stepped forward before the Lord and said, 'I can do it!'

'How?' the Lord asked him.

21 He replied, 'I will be a lying spirit in the mouth of all of the king's prophets!'

'It will work,' the Lord said; 'go and do it.'

22 So you see, the Lord has put a lying spirit in the mouth of these prophets of yours, when actually He has determined just the opposite of what they are telling you!"

23 Then Zedekiah (son of Chenaanah) walked up to Micaiah and slapped him across the face. "You liar!" he yelled. "When did the Spirit of the Lord leave me and enter you?"

24 "You'll find out soon enough," Micaiah replied, "— when you are hiding in an inner room!"

25 "Arrest this man and take him back to Governor Amon and to my son Joash," the king of Israel ordered.

26 "Tell them, 'The king says to put this fellow in prison and feed him with bread and water until I return safely from the battle!' "

27 Micaiah replied, "If you return safely, the Lord has not spoken through me." Then, turning to those around them, he remarked, "Take note of what I have said."

28 So the king of Israel and the king of Judah led

their armies to Ramoth-gilead.

29   The king of Israel said to Jehoshaphat, "I'll disguise myself so that no one will recognize me; but you put on your royal robes!" So that is what they did.

30   Now the king of Syria had issued these instructions to his charioteers: "Ignore everyone but the king of Israel!"

31   So when the Syrian charioteers saw King Jehoshaphat of Judah in his royal robes, they went for him, supposing that he was the man they were after. But Jehoshaphat cried out to the Lord to save him, and the Lord made the charioteers see their mistake and leave him.

32   For as soon as they realized he was not the king of Israel, they stopped chasing him.

33   But one of the Syrian soldiers shot an arrow haphazardly at the Israeli troops, and it struck the king of Israel at the opening where the lower armor and the breastplate meet. "Get me out of here," he groaned to the driver of his chariot, "for I am badly wounded."

34   The battle grew hotter and hotter all that day, and King Ahab went back in, propped up in his chariot, to fight the Syrians, but just as the sun sank into the western skies, he died.

CHAPTER 19

A s King Jehoshaphat of Judah returned home, uninjured,

2   The prophet Jehu (son of Hanani) went out to meet him. "Should you be helping the wicked, and

loving those who hate the Lord?" he asked him. "Because of what you have done, God's wrath is upon you.

3 But there are some good things about you, in that you got rid of the shame-idols throughout the land, and you have tried to be faithful to God."

4 So Jehoshaphat made no more trips to Israel after that, but remained quietly at Jerusalem. Later he went out again among the people, traveling from Beer-sheba to the hill country of Ephraim to encourage them to worship the God of their ancestors.

5 He appointed judges throughout the nation in all the larger cities,

6 And instructed them: "Watch your step — I have not appointed you — God has; and He will stand beside you and help you give justice in each case that comes before you.

7 Be very much afraid to give any other decision than what God tells you to. For there must be no injustice among God's judges, no partiality, no taking of bribes."

8 Jehoshaphat set up courts in Jerusalem, too, with the Levites and priests and clan leaders and judges.

9 These were his instructions to them: "You are to act always in the fear of God, with honest hearts.

10 Whenever a case is referred to you by the judges out in the provinces, whether murder cases or other violations of the laws and ordinances of God, you are to clarify the evidence for them and help them to decide justly, lest the wrath of God come down upon you and them; if you do this, you will discharge your responsibility."

11　Then he appointed Amariah, the High Priest, to be the court of final appeal in cases involving violation of sacred affairs; and Zebadiah (son of Ishmael), a ruler in Judah, as the court of final appeal in all civil cases; with the Levites as their assistants. "Be fearless in your stand for truth and honesty. And may God use you to defend the innocent," was his final word to them.

CHAPTER 20

L ater on, the armies of the kings of Moab, Ammon, and of the Meunites declared war on Jehoshaphat and the people of Judah.

2　Word reached Jehoshaphat that "a vast army is marching against you from beyond the Salt Sea, from Syria. It is already at Hazazon-tamar" (also called Engedi).

3　Jehoshaphat was badly shaken by this news and determined to beg for help from the Lord; so he announced that all the people of Judah should go without food for a time, in penitence and intercession before God.

4　People from all across the nation came to Jerusalem to plead unitedly with Him.

5　Jehoshaphat stood among them as they gathered at the new court of the Temple, and prayed this prayer:

6　"O Lord God of our fathers — the only God in all the heavens, the ruler of all the kingdoms of the earth — You are so powerful, so mighty. Who can stand against You?

7　O our God, didn't You drive out the heathen who lived in this land when Your people arrived?

And didn't You give this land forever to the descendants of Your friend Abraham?

8 Your people settled here and built this Temple for You,

9 Truly believing that in a time like this — whenever we are faced with any calamity such as war, disease, or famine — we can stand here before this Temple and before You — for You are here in this Temple — and cry out to You to save us; and that You will hear us and rescue us.

10 And now see what the armies of Ammon, Moab, and Mount Seir are doing. You wouldn't let our ancestors invade those nations when Israel left Egypt, so we went around and didn't destroy them.

11 Now see how they reward us! For they have come to throw us out of Your land which You have given us.

12 O our God, won't You stop them? We have no way to protect ourselves against this mighty army. We don't know what to do; but we are looking to You."

13 As the people from every part of Judah stood before the Lord with their little ones, wives, and children,

14 The Spirit of the Lord came upon one of the men standing there — Jahaziel (son of Zechariah, son of Benaiah, son of Jeiel, son of Mattaniah the Levite, who was one of the sons of Asaph).

15 "Listen to me, all you people of Judah and Jerusalem, and you, O king Jehoshaphat!" he exclaimed. "The Lord says, 'Don't be afraid! Don't be paralyzed by this mighty army! For the battle is not yours, but God's!

16 Tomorrow, go down and attack them! You will find them coming up the slopes of Ziz at the end of the valley that opens into the wilderness of Jeruel.

17 But you will not need to fight! Take your places; stand quietly and see the incredible rescue operation God will perform for you, O people of Judah and Jerusalem! Don't be afraid or discouraged! Go out there tomorrow, for the Lord is with you!' "

18 Then King Jehoshaphat fell to the ground with his face to the earth, and all the people of Judah and the people of Jerusalem did the same, worshiping the Lord.

19 Then the Levites of the Kohath clan and the Korah clan stood to praise the Lord God of Israel with songs of praise that rang out strong and clear.

20 Early the next morning the army of Judah went out into the wilderness of Tekoa. On the way Jehoshaphat stopped and called them to attention. "Listen to me, O people of Judah and Jerusalem," he said. "Believe in the Lord your God, and you shall have success! Believe His prophets, and everything will be all right!"

21 After consultation with the leaders of the people, he determined that there should be a choir leading the march, clothed in sanctified garments and singing the song "His Lovingkindness Is Forever" as they walked along praising and thanking the Lord!

22 And at the moment they began to sing and to praise, the Lord caused the armies of Ammon, Moab, and Mount Seir to begin fighting among themselves, and they destroyed each other!

23 For the Ammonites and Moabites turned against their allies from Mount Seir and killed every one of them. And when they had finished that job,

they turned against each other!

24 So, when the army of Judah arrived at the watchtower that looks out over the wilderness, as far as they could look there were dead bodies lying on the ground — not a single one of the enemy had escaped.

25 King Jehoshaphat and his people went out to plunder the bodies and came away loaded with money, garments, and jewels stripped from the corpses — so much that it took them three days to cart it all away!

26 On the fourth day they gathered in the Valley of Blessing, as it is called today, and how they praised the Lord!

27 Then they returned to Jerusalem, with Jehoshaphat leading them, full of joy that the Lord had given them this marvelous rescue from their enemies.

28 They marched into Jerusalem accompanied by a band of harps, lyres, and trumpets and proceeded to the Temple.

29 And as had happened before, when the surrounding kingdoms heard that the Lord Himself had fought against the enemies of Israel, the fear of God fell upon them.

30 So Jehoshaphat's kingdom was quiet, for his God had given him rest.

31 A thumbnail sketch of King Jehoshaphat: He became king of Judah when he was thirty-five years old, and reigned twenty-five years, in Jerusalem. His mother's name was Azubah, the daughter of Shilhi.

32 He was a good king, just as his father Asa was. He continually tried to follow the Lord,

33 With the exception that he did not destroy the

idol shrines on the hills, nor had the people as yet really decided to follow the God of their ancestors.

34 The details of Jehoshaphat's reign from first to last are written in the history of Jehu the son of Hanani, which is inserted in *The Annals of the Kings of Israel.*

35 But at the close of his life, Jehoshaphat, king of Judah, went into partnership with Ahaziah, king of Israel, who was a very wicked man.

36 They made ships in Ezion-geber to sail to Tarshish.

37 Then Eliezer, son of Dodavahu from Mareshah, prophesied against Jehoshaphat, telling him, "Because you have allied yourself with King Ahaziah, the Lord has destroyed your work." So the ships met disaster and never arrived at Tarshish.

CHAPTER 21

When Jehoshaphat died, he was buried in the cemetery of the kings in Jerusalem, and his son Jehoram became the new ruler of Judah.

2 His brothers — other sons of Jehoshaphat — were Azariah, Jehiel, Zechariah, Azariah, Michael, and Shephatiah.

3, 4 Their father had given each of them valuable gifts of money and jewels, also the ownership of some of the fortified cities of Judah. However, he gave the kingship to Jehoram because he was the oldest. But when Jehoram had become solidly established as king, he killed all of his brothers and many other leaders of Israel.

5 He was thirty-two years old when he began to reign, and he reigned eight years, in Jerusalem.

6 But he was as wicked as the kings who were over in Israel. Yes, as wicked as Ahab, for Jehoram had married one of the daughters of Ahab, and his whole life was one constant binge of doing evil.

7 However, the Lord was unwilling to end the dynasty of David, for He had made a covenant with David always to have one of his descendants upon the throne.

8 At that time the king of Edom revolted, declaring his independence of Judah.

9 Jehoram attacked him with his full army and with all of his chariots, marching by night, and almost[1] managed to subdue him.

10 But to this day Edom has been successful in throwing off the yoke of Judah. Libnah revolted too, because Jehoram had turned away from the Lord God of his fathers.

11 What's more, Jehoram constructed idol shrines in the mountains of Judah, and led the people of Jerusalem in worshiping idols; in fact, he compelled his people to worship them.

12 Then Elijah the prophet wrote him this letter: "The Lord God of your ancestor David says that because you have not followed in the good ways of your father Jehoshaphat, nor the good ways of King Asa,

13 But you have been as evil as the kings over in Israel, and have made the people of Jerusalem and Judah worship idols just as in the times of King Ahab, and because you have killed your brothers who were better than you,

14 Now the Lord will destroy your nation with

---

[1]Literally, "Jehoram . . . struck down the Edomites . . . Nevertheless Edom . . . revolted . . ."

a great plague. You, your children, your wives, and all that you have will be struck down.

15 You will be stricken with an intestinal disease and your bowels will rot away."

16 Then the Lord stirred up the Philistines and the Arabs living next to the Ethiopians to attack Jehoram.

17 They marched against Judah, broke across the border, and carried away everything of value in the king's palace, including his sons and his wives; only his youngest son, Jehoahaz, escaped.

18 It was after this that Jehovah struck him down with the incurable bowel disease.

19 In the process of time, at the end of two years, his intestines came out and he died in terrible suffering. (The customary pomp and ceremony was omitted at his funeral.)

20 He was thirty-two years old when he began to reign and he reigned in Jerusalem eight years, and died unmourned. He was buried in Jerusalem, but not in the royal cemetery.

CHAPTER 22

Then the people of Jerusalem chose Ahaziah,[1] his youngest son, as their new king, (for the marauding bands of Arabs had killed his older sons).

2 Ahaziah was twenty-two years old[2] when he began to reign, and he reigned one year, in Jerusalem. His mother's name was Athaliah, granddaughter of Omri.

---

[1] Also called "Jehoahaz."
[2] Literally, "forty-two years old"; but see II Kings 8:26.

3　He, too, walked in the evil ways of Ahab, for his mother encouraged him in doing wrong.

4　Yes, he was as evil as Ahab, for Ahab's family became his advisors after his father's death, and they led him on to ruin.

5　Following their evil advice, Ahaziah made an alliance with King Jehoram of Israel (the son of Ahab), who was at war with King Hazael of Syria at Ramoth-gilead. Ahaziah led his army there to join the battle. King Jehoram of Israel was wounded,

6　And returned to Jezreel to recover. Ahaziah went to visit him,

7　But this turned out to be a fatal mistake; for God had decided to punish Ahaziah for his alliance with Jehoram. It was during this visit that Ahaziah went out with Jehoram to challenge Jehu, (son of Nimshi), whom the Lord had appointed to end the dynasty of Ahab.

8　While Jehu was hunting down and killing the family and friends of Ahab, he met King Ahaziah's nephews, the princes of Judah, and killed them.

9　As he and his men were searching for Ahaziah, they found him hiding in the city of Samaria, and brought him to Jehu, who killed him. Even so, Ahaziah was given a royal burial because he was the grandson of King Jehoshaphat — a man who enthusiastically served the Lord. None of his sons, however, except for Joash, lived to succeed him as king,

10　For their grandmother Athaliah killed them when she heard the news of her son Ahaziah's death.

11　Joash was rescued by his aunt Jehoshabeath, who was King Ahaziah's sister[3], and was hidden away

---

[3]Literally, "the king's daughter," i.e., King Jehoram's daughter, verse 11.

in a storage room in the Temple. She was a daughter of King Jehoram, and the wife of Jehoiada the priest.

12 Joash remained hidden in the Temple for six years while Athaliah reigned as queen. He was cared for by his nurse and by his aunt and uncle.

CHAPTER 23

In the seventh year of the reign of Queen Athaliah, Jehoiada the priest got up his courage and took some of the army officers into his confidence: Azariah (son of Jeroham), Ishmael (son of Jehohanan), Azariah (son of Obed), Maaseiah (son of Adaiah), and Elishaphat (son of Zichri).

2, 3 These men traveled out across the nation secretly, to tell the Levites and clan leaders about his plans and to summon them to Jerusalem. On arrival they swore allegiance to the young king, who was still in hiding at the Temple. "At last the time has come for the king's son to reign!" Jehoiada exclaimed. "The Lord's promise — that a descendant of King David shall be our king — will be true again.

4 This is how we'll proceed: A third of you priests and Levites who come off duty on the Sabbath will stay at the entrance as guards.

5, 6 Another third will go over to the palace, and a third will be at the Lower Gate. Everyone else must stay in the outer courts of the Temple, as required by God's laws. For only the priests and Levites on duty may enter the Temple itself, for they are sanctified.

7 You Levites, form a bodyguard for the king, weapons in hand, and kill any unauthorized person entering the Temple. Stay right beside the king."

8 So all the arrangements were made. Each of the three leaders led a third of the priests arriving for duty that Sabbath, and a third of those whose week's work was done and were going off duty — for Jehoiada the chief priest didn't release them to go home.

9 Then Jehoiada issued spears and shields to all the army officers. These had once belonged to King David and were stored in the Temple.

10 These officers, fully armed, formed a line from one side to the other in front of the Temple and around the altar in the outer court.

11 Then they brought out the little prince and placed the crown upon his head and handed him a copy of the Law of God, and proclaimed him king.

A great shout went up, "Long live the king!" as Jehoiada and his sons anointed him.

12 When Queen Athaliah heard all the noise and commotion, and the shouts of praise to the king, she rushed over to the Temple to see what was going on — and there stood the king by his pillar at the entrance, with the army officers and the trumpeters surrounding him, and people from all over the land rejoicing and blowing trumpets, and the singers singing, accompanied by an orchestra leading the people in a great psalm of praise.

Athaliah ripped her clothes and screamed, "Treason! Treason!"

13, 14 "Take her out and kill her," Jehoiada the priest shouted to the army officers. "Don't do it here at the Temple. And kill anyone who tries to help her."

15, 16, 17 So the crowd opened up for them to take her out and they killed her at the palace stables.

Then Jehoiada made a solemn contract that he and the king and the people would be the Lord's. And all the people rushed over to the Temple of Baal and knocked it down, and broke up the altars and knocked down the idols, and killed Mattan the priest of Baal before his altar.

18   Jehoiada now appointed the Levite priests as guards, and to sacrifice the burnt offering to the Lord as prescribed in the law of Moses. He made the identical assignments of the Levite clans that King David had. They sang with joy as they worked.

19   The guards at the Temple gates kept out everything that was not consecrated and all unauthorized personnel.

20   Then the army officers, nobles, governors, and all the people escorted the king from the Temple, wending their way from the Upper Gate to the palace, and seated the king upon his throne.

21   So all the people of the land rejoiced, and the city was quiet and peaceful because Queen Athaliah was dead.

CHAPTER 24

Joash was seven years old when he became king, and he reigned forty years, in Jerusalem. His mother's name was Zibiah, from Beer-sheba.

2   Joash tried hard to please the Lord all during the lifetime of Jehoiada the priest.

3   Jehoiada arranged two marriages for him, and he had sons and daughters.

4   Later on, Joash decided to repair and recondition the Temple.

5   He summoned the priests and Levites and gave

them these instructions: "Go to all the cities of Judah and collect offerings for the building fund, so that we can maintain the Temple in good repair. Get at it right away. Don't delay." But the Levites took their time.

6 So the king called for Jehoiada, the High Priest, and asked him, "Why haven't you demanded that the Levites go out and collect the Temple taxes from the cities of Judah, and from Jerusalem? The tax law enacted by Moses the servant of the Lord must be enforced so that the Temple can be repaired."

7, 8 (The followers of wicked Athaliah had ravaged the Temple, and everything dedicated to the worship of God had been removed to the temple of Baalam.) So now the king instructed that a chest be made and set outside the Temple gate.

9 Then a proclamation was sent to all the cities of Judah and throughout Jerusalem telling the people to bring to the Lord the tax that Moses the servant of God had assessed upon Israel.

10 And all the leaders and the people were glad, and brought the money and placed it in the chest until it was full.

11 Then the Levites carried the chest to the king's accounting office where the recording secretary and the representative of the High Priest counted the money, and took the chest back to the Temple again. This went on day after day, and money continued to pour in.

12 The king and Jehoiada gave the money to the building superintendents, who hired masons and carpenters to restore the Temple; and to foundrymen who made articles of iron and brass.

13 So the work went forward, and finally the Temple was in even better condition than before.

14 When all was finished, the remaining money was brought to the king and Jehoiada, and it was agreed to use it for making the gold and silver spoons and bowls used for incense, and for making the instruments used in the sacrifices and offerings.

Burnt offerings were sacrificed continually during the lifetime of Jehoiada the priest.

15 He lived to a very old age, finally dying at 130.

16 He was buried in the City of David among the kings, because he had done so much good for Israel, for God, and for the Temple.

17, 18 But after his death the leaders of Judah came to King Joash and induced him to abandon the Temple of the God of their ancestors, and to worship shame-idols instead! So the wrath of God came down upon Judah and Jerusalem again.

19 God sent prophets to bring them back to the Lord, but the people wouldn't listen.

20 Then the Spirit of God came upon Zechariah, Jehoiada's son. He called a meeting of all the people. Standing before them upon a platform he said to them, "God wants to know why you are disobeying His commandments. For when you do, everything you try fails. You have forsaken the Lord, and now He has forsaken you."

21 Then the leaders plotted to kill Zechariah, and finally King Joash himself ordered him executed in the court of the Temple.

22 That was how King Joash repaid Jehoiada for his love and loyalty — by killing his son. Zechariah's last words as he died were "Lord, see what they are

doing and pay them back."

23 A few months later the Syrian army arrived and conquered Judah and Jerusalem, killing all the leaders of the nation and sending back great quantities of booty to the king of Damascus.

24 It was a great triumph for the tiny Syrian army, but the Lord let the great army of Judah be conquered by them because they had forsaken the Lord God of their ancestors. In that way God executed judgment upon Joash.

25 When the Syrians left — leaving Joash severely wounded — his own officials decided to kill him for murdering the son of Jehoiada the priest. They assassinated him as he lay in bed, and buried him in the City of David, but not in the cemetery of the kings.

26 The conspirators were Zabad, whose mother was Shime-ath, a woman from Ammon; and Jehozabad, whose mother was Shimrith, a woman from Moab.

27 If you want to read about the sons of Joash, and the curses laid upon Joash, and about the restoration of the Temple, see *The Annals of the Kings.*

When Joash died, his son Amaziah became the new king.

CHAPTER 25

A maziah was twenty-five years old when he became king, and he reigned twenty-nine years, in Jerusalem. His mother's name was Jeho-addan, a native of Jerusalem.

2 He did what was right, but sometimes resented it!

3 When he was well established as the new king,

he executed the men who had assassinated his father.

4 However, he didn't kill their children but followed the command of the Lord written in the law of Moses, that the fathers shall not die for the children's sins, nor the children for the father's sins. No, everyone must pay for his own sins.

5, 6 Another thing Amaziah did was to organize the army, assigning leaders to each clan from Judah and Benjamin. Then he took a census and found that he had an army of 300,000 men twenty years old and older, all trained and highly skilled in the use of spear and sword. He also paid $200,000 to hire 100,000 experienced mercenaries from Israel.

7 But a prophet arrived with this message from the Lord: "Sir, do not hire troops from Israel, for the Lord is not with them.

8 If you let them go with your troops to battle, you will be defeated no matter how well you fight; for God has power to help or to frustrate."

9 "But the money!" Amaziah whined. "What shall I do about that?"

And the prophet replied, "The Lord is able to give you much more than this!"

10 So Amaziah sent them home again to Ephraim; which made them very angry and insulted.

11 Then Amaziah took courage and led his army to the Valley of Salt, and there killed 10,000 men from Seir.

12 Another 10,000 were taken alive to the top of a cliff and thrown over, so that they were crushed upon the rocks below.

13 Meanwhile, the army of Israel that had been sent home raided several of the cities of Judah in the

vicinity of Bethhoron, toward Samaria, killing 3,000 people and carrying off great quantities of booty.

14 When King Amaziah returned from this slaughter of the Edomites, he brought with him idols taken from the people of Seir, and set them up as gods, and bowed before them, and burned incense to them!

15 This made the Lord very angry and He sent a prophet to demand, "Why have you worshiped gods who couldn't even save their own people from you?"

16 "Since when have I asked your advice?" the king retorted. "Be quiet now, before I have you killed."

The prophet left with this parting warning: "I know that God has determined to destroy you because you have worshiped these idols, and have not accepted my counsel."

17 King Amaziah of Judah now took the advice of his counselors and declared war on King Joash of Israel (son of Jehoahaz, grandson of Jehu).

18 King Joash replied with this parable: "Out in the Lebanon mountains a thistle demanded of a cedar tree, 'Give your daughter in marriage to my son.' Just then a wild animal came by and stepped on the thistle, crushing it!

19 You are very proud about your conquest of Edom, but my advice is to stay home and don't meddle with me, lest you and all Judah get badly hurt."

20 But Amaziah wouldn't listen, for God was arranging to destroy him for worshiping the gods of Edom.

21 The armies met at Beth-shemesh, in Judah,

22   And Judah was defeated, and its army fled home.

23   King Joash of Israel captured the defeated King Amaziah of Judah and took him as a prisoner to Jerusalem. Then King Joash ordered 200 yards of the walls of Jerusalem dismantled, from the gate of Ephraim to the Corner Gate.

24   He carried off all the treasures and golden bowls from the Temple, as well as the treasures from the palace; and he took hostages, including Obed-edom, and returned to Samaria.

25   However, King Amaziah of Judah lived on for fifteen years after the death of King Joash of Israel.

26   The complete biography of King Amaziah is written in *The Annals of the Kings of Judah and Israel.*

27   This account includes a report of Amaziah's turning away from God, and how his people conspired against him in Jerusalem, and how he fled to Lachish — but they went after him and killed him there.

28   And they brought him back on horses to Jerusalem and buried him in the royal cemetery.

CHAPTER 26

The people of Judah now crowned sixteen-year-old Uzziah as their new king.

2   After his father's death, he rebuilt the city of Eloth and restored it to Judah.

3   In all, he reigned fifty-two years, in Jerusalem. His mother's name was Jecoliah, from Jerusalem.

4   He followed in the footsteps of his father Amaziah, and was, in general, a good king so far as the Lord's opinion of him was concerned.

5 While Zechariah was alive Uzziah was always eager to please God. Zechariah was a man who had special revelations from God. And as long as the king followed the paths of God, he prospered, for God blessed him.

6 He declared war on the Philistines and captured the city of Gath and broke down its walls, also those of Jabneh and Ashdod. Then he built new cities in the Ashdod area and in other parts of the Philistine country.

7 God helped him not only with his wars against the Philistines but also in his battles with the Arabs of Gurbaal and in his wars with the Meunites.

8 The Ammonites paid annual tribute to him, and his fame spread even to Egypt, for he was very powerful.

9 He built fortified towers in Jerusalem at the Corner Gate, and the Valley Gate, and at the turning of the wall.

10 He also constructed forts in the Negeb, and made many water reservoirs, for he had great herds of cattle out in the valleys and on the plains. He was a man who loved the soil and had many farms and vineyards, both on the hillsides and in the fertile valleys.

11 He organized his army into regiments to which men were drafted under quotas set by Jeiel, the secretary of the army, and his assistant, Maaseiah. The commander-in-chief was General Hananiah.

12 Twenty-six hundred brave clan leaders commanded these regiments.

13 The army consisted of 307,500 men, all elite troops.

14 Uzziah issued to them shields, spears, helmets,

coats of mail, bows, and slingstones.

15   And he produced engines of war manufactured in Jerusalem, invented by brilliant men to shoot arrows and huge stones from the towers and battlements. So he became very famous, for the Lord helped him wonderfully until he was very powerful.

16   But at that point he became proud — and corrupt. He sinned against the Lord his God by entering the forbidden sanctuary of the Temple and personally burning incense upon the altar.

17, 18   Azariah the High Priest went in after him with eighty other priests, all brave men, and demanded that he get out.

"It is not for you, Uzziah, to burn incense," they declared. "That is the work of the priests alone, the sons of Aaron who are consecrated to this work. Get out, for you have trespassed, and the Lord is not going to honor you for this!"

19   Uzziah was furious, and refused to set down the incense burner he was holding. But look! Suddenly — leprosy appeared in his forehead!

20   When Azariah and the others saw it, they rushed him out; in fact, he himself was as anxious to get out as they were to get him out, because the Lord had struck him.

21   So King Uzziah was a leper until the day of his death and lived in isolation, cut off from his people and from the Temple. His son Jotham became vice-regent, in charge of the king's affairs and of the judging of the people of the land.

22   The other details of Uzziah's reign from first to last are recorded by the prophet Isaiah (son of Amoz).

23 When Uzziah died, he was buried in the royal cemetery even though he was a leper, and his son Jotham became the new king.

CHAPTER 27

Jotham was twenty-five years old at the time he became king, and he reigned sixteen years, in Jerusalem. His mother was Jerushah, daughter of Zadok.

2 He followed the generally good example of his father Uzziah — who had, however, sinned by invading the Temple — but even so his people became very corrupt.

3 He built the Upper Gate of the Temple, also did extensive rebuilding of the walls on the hill where the Temple was situated.

4 And he built cities in the hill country of Judah, and erected fortresses and towers on the wooded hills.

5 His war against the Ammonites was successful, so that for the next three years he received from them an annual tribute of $200,000 in silver, 10,000 sacks of wheat, and 10,000 sacks of barley.

6 King Jotham became powerful because he was careful to follow the path of the Lord his God.

7 The remainder of his history, including his wars and other activities, are written in *The Annals of the Kings of Israel and Judah.*

8 In summary, then, he was twenty-five years old when he began to reign and he reigned sixteen years, in Jerusalem.

9 When he died, he was buried in Jerusalem, and his son Ahaz became the new king.

CHAPTER 28

A haz was twenty years old when he became king and he reigned sixteen years, in Jerusalem. But he was an evil king, unlike his ancestor King David.

2 For he followed the example of the kings over in Israel and worshiped the idols of Baal.

3 He even went out to the Valley of Hinnom, and it was not just to burn incense to the idols, for he even sacrificed his own children in the fire, just like the heathen nations that were thrown out of the land by the Lord to make room for Israel.

4 Yes, he sacrificed and burned incense at the idol shrines on the hills and under every green tree.

5 That is why the Lord God allowed the king of Syria to defeat him and deport large numbers of his people to Damascus. The armies from Israel also slaughtered great numbers of his troops.

6 On a single day, Pekah, the son of Remaliah, killed 120,000 of his bravest soldiers because they had turned away from the Lord God of their fathers.

7 Then Zichri, a great warrior from Ephraim, killed the king's son Maaseiah, and the king's administrator Azrikam, and the king's second-in-command Elkanah.

8 The armies from Israel also captured 200,000 Judean women and children, and tremendous amounts of booty which they took to Samaria.

9 But Oded, a prophet of the Lord, was there in Samaria and he went out to meet the returning army. "Look!" he exclaimed, "The Lord God of your fathers was angry with Judah and let you capture them, but you have butchered them without mercy, and all heaven is disturbed.

10   And now are you going to make slaves of these people from Judah and Jerusalem? What about your own sins against the Lord your God?

11   Listen to me and return these relatives of yours to their homes, for now the fierce anger of the Lord is upon *you*."

12   Some of the top leaders of Ephraim also added their opposition. These men were Azariah the son of Johanan, Berechiah the son of Meshillemoth, Jehizkiah the son of Shallum, and Amasa the son of Hadlai.

13   "You must not bring the captives here!" they declared. "If you do, the Lord will be angry, and this sin will be added to our many others. We are in enough trouble with God as it is."

14   So the army officers turned over the captives and booty to the political leaders to decide what to do.

15   Then the four men already mentioned distributed captured stores of clothing to the women and children who needed it, and gave them shoes, food, and wine, and put those who were sick and old on donkeys, and took them back to their families in Jericho, the City of Palm Trees. Then their escorts returned to Samaria.

16   About that time King Ahaz of Judah asked the king of Assyria to be his ally in his war against the armies of Edom. For Edom was invading Judah and capturing many people as slaves.

17, 18   Meanwhile, the Philistines had invaded the lowland cities and the Negeb and had already captured Bethshemesh, Aijalon, Gederoth, Soco, Timnah, and Gimzo with their surrounding villages, and were living there.

19   For the Lord brought Judah very low on ac-

count of the evil deeds of King Ahaz of Israel,[1] for he had destroyed the spiritual fiber of Judah and had been faithless to the Lord.

20   But when Tilgath-pilneser, king of Assyria, arrived, he caused trouble for King Ahaz instead of helping him.

21   So even though Ahaz had given him the Temple gold and the palace treasures, it did no good.

22   In this time of deep trial, King Ahaz collapsed spiritually.

23   He sacrificed to the gods of the people of Damascus who had defeated him, for he felt that since these gods had helped the kings of Syria, they would help him too if he sacrificed to them. But instead, they were his ruin, and that of all his people.

24   The king took the gold bowls from the Temple and slashed them to pieces, and nailed the door of the Temple shut so that no one could worship there, and made altars to the heathen gods in every corner of Jerusalem.

25   And he did the same in every city of Judah, thus angering the Lord God of his fathers.

26   The other details of his life and activities are recorded in *The Annals of the Kings of Judah and Israel.*

27   When King Ahaz died, he was buried in Jerusalem but not in the royal tombs, and his son Hezekiah became the new king.

CHAPTER 29

Hezekiah was twenty-five years old when he became the king of Judah, and he reigned twenty-

---

[1]King Ahaz ruled two tribes of Israel — Judah and Benjamin — and so is referred to here in this unusual way as a king of Israel.

nine years, in Jerusalem. His mother's name was Abijah, the daughter of Zechariah.

2 His reign was a good one in the Lord's opinion, just as his ancestor David's had been.

3 In the very first month of the first year of his reign, he reopened the doors of the Temple and repaired them.

4, 5 He summoned the priests and Levites to meet him at the open space east of the Temple, and addressed them thus:

"Listen to me, you Levites. Sanctify yourselves and sanctify the Temple of the Lord God of your ancestors — clean all the debris from the holy place.

6 For our fathers have committed a deep sin before the Lord our God; they abandoned the Lord and His Temple and turned their backs on it.

7 The doors have been shut tight, the perpetual flame has been put out, and the incense and burnt offerings have not been offered.

8 Therefore the wrath of the Lord has been upon Judah and Jerusalem. He has caused us to be objects of horror, amazement, and contempt, as you see us today.

9 Our fathers have been killed in war, and our sons and daughters and wives are in captivity because of this.

10 But now I want to make a covenant with the Lord God of Israel so that His fierce anger will turn away from us.

11 My children, don't neglect your duties any longer, for the Lord has chosen you to minister to Him and to burn incense."

12 Then the Levites went into action:

> From the Kohath clan, Mahath (son of Amasai) and Joel (son of Azariah);
>
> From the Merari clan, Kish (son of Abdi) and Azariah (son of Jehallelel);
>
> From the Gershon clan, Joah (son of Zimmah) and Eden (son of Joah).

13
> From the Elizaphan clan, Shimri and Jeuel;
>
> From the Asaph clan, Zechariah and Mattaniah;

14
> From the Hemanite clan, Jehuel and Shimei;
>
> From the Jeduthun clan, Shemaiah and Uzziel.

15 They in turn summoned their fellow Levites and sanctified themselves, and began to clean up and sanctify the Temple, as the king (who was speaking for the Lord) had commanded them.

16 The priests cleaned up the inner room of the Temple, and brought out into the court all the filth and decay they found there. The Levites then carted it out to the brook Kidron.

17 This all began on the first day of April, and by the eighth day they had reached the outer court, which took eight days to clean up, so the entire job was completed in sixteen days.

18 Then they went back to the palace and reported to King Hezekiah, "We have completed the cleansing of the Temple and of the altar of burnt offerings and of its accessories, also the table of the Bread of the Presence and its equipment.

19 What's more, we have recovered and sanctified all the utensils thrown away by King Ahaz when he

closed the Temple. They are beside the altar of the Lord."

20 Early the next morning, King Hezekiah went to the Temple with the city officials,

21 Taking seven young bulls, seven rams, seven lambs, and seven male goats for a sin offering for the nation and for the Temple.

He instructed the priests, the sons of Aaron, to sacrifice them on the altar of the Lord.

22 So they killed the young bulls, and the priests took the blood and sprinkled it on the altar, and they killed the rams and sprinkled their blood upon the altar, and did the same with the lambs.

23 The male goats for the sin offering were then brought before the king and his officials, who laid their hands upon them.

24 Then the priests killed the animals and made a sin offering with their blood upon the altar, to make atonement for all Israel as the king had commanded — for the king had specified that the burnt offering and sin offering must be sacrificed for the entire nation.

25, 26 He organized Levites at the Temple into an orchestral group, using cymbals, psalteries, and harps. This was in accordance with the directions of David and the prophets Gad and Nathan — who had received their instructions from the Lord. The priests formed a trumpet corps.

27 Then Hezekiah ordered the burnt offering to be placed upon the altar, and as the sacrifice began, the instruments of music began to play the songs of the Lord, accompanied by the trumpets.

28 Throughout the entire ceremony everyone wor-

shiped the Lord as the singers sang and the trumpets blew.

29 Afterwards the king and his aides bowed low before the Lord in worship.

30 Then King Hezekiah ordered the Levites to sing before the Lord some of the psalms of David and of the prophet Asaph, which they gladly did, and bowed their heads and worshiped.

31 "The consecration ceremony is now ended," Hezekiah said. "Now bring your sacrifices and thank offerings." So the people from every part of the nation brought their sacrifices and thank offerings, and those who wished to, brought burnt offerings too.

32, 33 In all, there were 70 young bulls for burnt offerings, 100 rams, and 200 lambs. In addition 600 oxen and 3,000 sheep were brought as holy gifts.

34 But there were too few priests to prepare the burnt offerings, so their brothers the Levites helped them until the work was finished — and until more priests had reported to work — for the Levites were much more ready to sanctify themselves than the priests were.

35 There was an abundance of burnt offerings, and the usual drink offering with each, and many peace offerings. So it was that the Temple was restored to service, and the sacrifices offered again.

36 And Hezekiah and all the people were very happy because of what God had accomplished so quickly.

CHAPTER 30

King Hezekiah now sent letters throughout all of Israel, Judah, Ephraim, and Manasseh, inviting everyone to come to the Temple at Jerusalem for the annual Passover celebration.

2, 3 The king, his aides, and all the assembly of Jerusalem had voted to celebrate the Passover in May this time, rather than at the normal time in April, because not enough priests were sanctified at the earlier date, and there wasn't enough time to get notices out.

4 The king and his advisors were in complete agreement in this matter,

5 So they sent a Passover proclamation throughout Israel, from Dan to Beer-sheba, inviting everyone. They had not kept it in great numbers as prescribed.[1]

6 "Come back to the Lord God of Abraham, Isaac, and Israel," the king's letter said, "so that He will return to us who have escaped from the power of the kings of Assyria.

7 Do not be like your fathers and brothers who sinned against the Lord God of their fathers and were destroyed.

8 Do not be stubborn, as they were, but yield yourselves to the Lord and come to His Temple which He has sanctified forever, and worship the Lord your God so that His fierce anger will turn away from you.

9 For if you turn to the Lord again, your brothers and your children will be treated mercifully by their captors, and they will be able to return to this land. For the Lord your God is full of kindness and mercy and will not continue to turn away His face from you if you return to Him."

10 So the messengers went from city to city throughout Ephraim and Manasseh and as far as Zebu-

---

[1]Or, "The Passover had not been celebrated by the northern tribe of Israel for a long time; only a faithful few had been doing it in the proper way."

lun. But for the most part they were received with laughter and scorn!

11 However, some from the tribes of Asher, Manasseh, and Zebulun turned to God and came to Jerusalem.

12 But in Judah the entire nation felt a strong, God-given desire to obey the Lord's direction as commanded by the king and his officers.

13 And so it was that a very large crowd assembled at Jerusalem in the month of May for the Passover celebration.

14 They set to work and destroyed the heathen altars in Jerusalem, and knocked down all the incense altars, and threw them into Kidron Brook.

15 On the first day of May the people killed their Passover lambs. Then the priests and Levites became ashamed of themselves for not taking a more active part, so they sanctified themselves and brought burnt offerings into the Temple.

16 They stood at their posts as instructed by the law of Moses the man of God; and the priests sprinkled the blood received from the Levites.

17, 18, 19 Since many of the people arriving from Ephraim, Manasseh, Issachar, and Zebulun were ceremonially impure because they had not undergone the purification rites, the Levites killed their Passover lambs for them, to sanctify them. Then King Hezekiah prayed for them and they were permitted to eat the Passover anyway, even though this was contrary to God's rules. But Hezekiah said, "May the good Lord pardon every one who determines to follow the Lord God of his fathers, even though he is not properly sanctified for the ceremony."

20 And the Lord listened to Hezekiah's prayer and did not destroy them.

21 So the people of Israel celebrated the Passover at Jerusalem for seven days with great joy.

Meanwhile the Levites and priests praised the Lord with music and cymbals day after day.

22 (King Hezekiah spoke very appreciatively to the Levites of their excellent music.) So, for seven days the observance continued, and peace offerings were sacrificed, and the people confessed their sins to the Lord God of their fathers.

23 The enthusiasm continued, so it was unanimously decided to continue the observance for another seven days.

24 King Hezekiah gave the people 1,000 young bulls for offerings, and 7,000 sheep; and the princes donated 1,000 young bulls and 10,000 sheep. And at this time another large group of priests stepped forward and sanctified themselves.

25 Then the people of Judah, together with the priests, the Levites, the foreign residents, and the visitors from Israel, were filled with deep joy.

26 For Jerusalem hadn't seen a celebration like this one since the days of King David's son Solomon.

27 Then the priests and Levites stood and blessed the people, and the Lord heard their prayers from His holy Temple in heaven.

CHAPTER 31

Afterwards a massive campaign against idol worship was begun. Those who were at Jerusalem for the Passover went out to the cities of Judah, Benjamin,

Ephraim, and Manasseh and tore down the idol altars, the obelisks, shame-images, and other heathen centers of worship. Then the people who had come to the Passover from the northern tribes returned again to their own homes.

2　Hezekiah now organized the priests and Levites into service corps to offer the burnt offerings and peace offerings, and to worship and give thanks and praise to the Lord.

3　He also made a personal contribution of animals for the daily morning and evening burnt offerings, as well as for the weekly Sabbath and monthly new moon festivals, and for the other annual feasts as required in the law of God.

4　In addition, he required the people in Jerusalem to bring their tithes to the priests and Levites, so that they wouldn't need other employment but could apply themselves fully to their duties as required in the law of God.

5, 6　The people responded immediately and generously with the first of their crops and grain, new wine, olive oil, money, and everything else — a tithe of all they owned, as required by law to be given to the Lord their God. Everything was laid out in great piles. The people who had moved to Judah from the northern tribes and the people of Judah living in the provinces also brought in the tithes of their cattle and sheep, and brought a tithe of the dedicated things to give to the Lord and piled them up in great heaps.

7, 8　The first of these tithes arrived in June, and the piles continued to grow until October. When Hezekiah and his officials came and saw these huge piles, how they blessed the Lord and praised His people!

9 "Where did all this come from?" Hezekiah asked the priests and Levites.

10 And Azariah the High Priest from the clan of Zadok replied, "These are tithes! We have been eating from these stores of food for many weeks, but all this is left over, for the Lord has blessed His people."

11 Hezekiah decided to prepare storerooms in the Temple.

12 All the dedicated supplies were brought into the Lord's house. Conaniah, the Levite, was put in charge, assisted by his brother Shimei and the following aides:

13   Jehiel, Azaziah, Nahath,
         Asahel, Jerimoth, Jozabad, Eliel,
         Ismachiah, Mahath, Benaiah.

These appointments were made by King Hezekiah and Azariah the High Priest.

14, 15 Kore (son of Imnah, the Levite), who was the gatekeeper at the East Gate, was put in charge of distributing the offerings to the priests. His faithful assistants were Eden, Miniamin, Jeshua, Shemaiah, Amariah, and Shecaniah. They distributed the gifts to the clans of priests in their cities, dividing it to young and old alike.

16 However, the priests on duty at the Temple and their families[1] were supplied directly from there, so they were not included in this distribution.

17, 18 The priests were listed in the genealogical register by clans, and the Levites twenty years old and older were listed under the names of their work corps. A regular food allotment was given to all families of properly registered priests, for they had no other source

---

[1]Literally, "males from three years old and upward."

of income because their time and energies were devoted to the service of the Temple.

19   One of the priests was appointed in each of the cities of the priests to issue food and other supplies to all priests in the area, and to all registered Levites.

20   In this way King Hezekiah handled the distribution throughout all Judah, doing what was just and fair in the sight of the Lord his God.

21   He worked very hard to encourage respect for the Temple, the law, and godly living, and was very successful.

CHAPTER 32

Some time later, after this good work of King Hezekiah, King Sennacherib of Assyria invaded Judah and laid siege to the fortified cities, planning to place them under tribute.

2   When it was clear that Sennacherib was intending to attack Jerusalem,

3   Hezekiah summoned his princes and officers for a council of war, and it was decided to plug the springs outside the city.

4   They organized a huge work crew to block them, and to cut off the brook running through the fields. "Why should the king of Assyria come and find water?" they asked.

5   Then Hezekiah further strengthened his defenses by repairing the wall wherever it was broken down and by adding to the fortifications, and constructing a second wall outside it. He also reinforced Fort Millo in the City of David, and manufactured large numbers of weapons and shields.

6   He recruited an army and appointed officers

and summoned them to the plains before the city, and encouraged them with this address:

7 "Be strong, be brave, and do not be afraid of the king of Assyria or his mighty army, for there is Someone with us who is far greater than he is!

8 He has a great army, but they are all mere men, while we have the Lord our God to fight our battles for us!" This greatly encouraged them.

9 Then King Sennacherib of Assyria, while still besieging the city of Lachish, sent ambassadors with this message to King Hezekiah and the citizens of Jerusalem:

10 "King Sennacherib of Assyria asks, 'Do you think you can survive my siege of Jerusalem?

11 King Hezekiah is trying to persuade you to commit suicide by staying there — to die by famine and thirst — while he promises that "the Lord our God will deliver us from the king of Assyria"!

12 Don't you realize that Hezekiah is the very person who destroyed all the idols, and commanded Judah and Jerusalem to use only the one altar at the Temple, and to burn incense upon it alone?

13 Don't you realize that I and the other kings of Assyria before me have never yet failed to conquer a nation we attacked? The gods of those nations weren't able to do a thing to save their lands!

14 Name just one time when anyone, anywhere, was able to resist us successfully. What makes you think your God can do any better?

15 Don't let Hezekiah fool you! Don't believe him. I say it again — no god of any nation has ever yet been able to rescue his people from me or my ancestors; how much less your God!' "

16 Thus the ambassador mocked the Lord God and His servant Hezekiah, heaping up insults.

17 King Sennacherib also sent letters scorning the Lord God of Israel. "The gods of all the other nations failed to save their people from my hand, and the God of Hezekiah will fail, too," he wrote.

18 The messengers who brought the letters shouted threats in the Jewish language to the people gathered on the walls of the city, trying to frighten and dishearten them.

19 These messengers talked about the God of Jerusalem just as though He were one of the heathen gods — a handmade idol!

20 Then King Hezekiah and Isaiah the prophet (son of Amoz) cried out in prayer to God in heaven,

21 And the Lord sent an angel who destroyed the Assyrian army with all its officers and generals! So Sennacherib returned home in deep shame to his own land. And when he arrived at the temple of his god, some of his own sons killed him there.

22 That is how the Lord saved Hezekiah and the people of Jerusalem. And now there was peace at last throughout his realm.

23 From then on King Hezekiah became immensely respected among the surrounding nations, and many gifts for the Lord arrived at Jerusalem, with valuable presents for King Hezekiah, too.

24 But about that time Hezekiah became deathly sick, and he prayed to the Lord, and the Lord replied with a miracle.

25 However, Hezekiah didn't respond with true thanksgiving and praise, for he had become proud,

and so the anger of God was upon him and upon Judah and Jerusalem.

26 But finally Hezekiah and the residents of Jerusalem humbled themselves, so the wrath of the Lord did not fall upon them during Hezekiah's lifetime.

27 So Hezekiah became very wealthy and was highly honored. He had to construct special treasury buildings for his silver, gold, precious stones, and spices, and for his shields and gold bowls.

28, 29 He also built many storehouses for his grain, new wine, and olive oil, with many stalls for his animals, and folds for the great flocks of sheep and goats he purchased; and he acquired many towns, for God had given him great wealth.

30 He dammed up the Upper Spring of Gihon and brought the water down through an aqueduct to the west side of the City of David sector in Jerusalem. He prospered in everything he did.

31 However, when ambassadors arrived from Babylon to find out about the miracle of his being healed, God left him to himself in order to test him and to see what he was really like.

32 The rest of the story of Hezekiah and all of the good things he did are written in *The Book of Isaiah* (the prophet, the son of Amoz), and in *The Annals of the Kings of Judah and Israel.*

33 When Hezekiah died he was buried in the royal hillside cemetery among the other kings, and all Judah and Jerusalem honored him at his death. Then his son Manasseh became the new king.

CHAPTER 33

Manasseh was only twelve years old when he be- came king, and he reigned fifty-five years, in Je- rusalem.

2 But it was an evil reign, for he encouraged his people to worship the idols of the heathen nations de- stroyed by the Lord when the people of Israel entered the land.

3 He rebuilt the heathen altars his father Heze- kiah had destroyed — the altars of Baal, and of the shame-images, and of the sun, moon, and stars.

4, 5 He even constructed heathen altars in both courts of the Temple of the Lord, for worshiping the sun, moon and stars — in the very place where the Lord had said that He would be honored forever.

6 And Manasseh sacrificed his own children as burnt offerings in the Valley of Hinnom. He consulted spirit-mediums, too, and fortune-tellers and sorcerers, and encouraged every sort of evil, making the Lord very angry.

7 Think of it! He placed an idol in the very Temple of God, where God had told David and his son Solomon, "I will be honored here in this Temple, and in Jerusalem — the city I have chosen to be hon- ored forever above all the other cities of Israel.

8 And if you will only obey My commands — all the laws and instructions given to you by Moses — I won't ever again exile Israel from this land which I gave your ancestors."

9 But Manasseh encouraged the people of Judah and Jerusalem to do even more evil than the nations the Lord destroyed when Israel entered the land.

10 Warnings from the Lord were ignored by both Manasseh and his people.

11 So God sent the Assyrian armies, and they seized him with hooks and bound him with bronze chains and carted him away to Babylon.

12 Then at last he came to his senses and cried out humbly to God for help.

13 And the Lord listened, and answered his plea by returning him to Jerusalem and to his kingdom! At that point Manasseh finally realized that the Lord was really God!

14 It was after this that he rebuilt the outer wall of the City of David and the wall from west of the Spring of Gihon in the Kidron Valley, and then to the Fish Gate, and around Citadel Hill, where it was built very high. And he stationed his army generals in all of the fortified cities of Judah.

15 He also removed the foreign gods from the hills and took his idol from the Temple and tore down the altars he had built on the mountain where the Temple stood, and the altars that were in Jerusalem, and dumped them outside the city.

16 Then he rebuilt the altar of the Lord and offered sacrifices upon it — peace offerings and thanksgiving offerings — and demanded that the people of Judah worship the Lord God of Israel.

17 However, the people still sacrificed upon the altars on the hills, but only to the Lord their God.

18 The rest of Manasseh's deeds, and his prayer to God, and God's reply through the prophets — this is all written in *The Annals of the Kings of Israel*.

19 His prayer, and the way God answered, and a frank account of his sins and errors, including a list

of the locations where he built idols on the hills and set up shame-idols and graven images (this of course was before the great change in his attitude) is recorded in *The Annals of the Prophets.*

20, 21 When Manasseh died he was buried beneath his own palace, and his son Amon became the new king. Amon was twenty-two years old when he began to reign in Jerusalem, but he lasted for only two years.

22 It was an evil reign like the early years of his father Manasseh; for Amon sacrificed to all the idols just as his father had.

23 But he didn't change as his father did; instead he sinned more and more.

24 At last his own officers assassinated him in his palace.

25 But some public-spirited citizens killed all of those who assassinated him, and declared his son Josiah to be the new king.

CHAPTER 34

Josiah was only eight years old when he became king. He reigned thirty-one years, in Jerusalem.

2 His was a good reign, as he carefully followed the good example of his ancestor King David.

3 For when he was sixteen years old, in the eighth year of his reign, he began to search for the God of his ancestor David; and four years later he began to clean up Judah and Jerusalem, destroying the heathen altars and the shame-idols on the hills.

4 He went out personally to watch as the altars of Baal were knocked apart, the obelisks above the al-

tars chopped down, and the shame-idols ground into dust and scattered over the graves of those who had sacrificed to them.

5 Then he burned the bones of the heathen priests upon their own altars, feeling that this action would clear the people of Judah and Jerusalem from the guilt of their sin of idol-worship.

6 Then he went to the cities of Manasseh, Ephraim, and Simeon, even to distant Naphtali, and did the same thing there.

7 He broke down the heathen altars, ground to powder the shame-idols, and chopped down the obelisks. He did this everywhere throughout the whole land of Israel before returning to Jerusalem.

8 During the eighteenth year of his reign, after he had purged the land and cleaned up the situation at the Temple, he appointed Shaphan (son of Azaliah) and Maaseiah, governor of Jerusalem, and Joah (son of Joahaz), the city treasurer, to repair the Temple.

9 They set up a collection system for gifts for the Temple. The money was collected at the Temple gates by the Levites on guard duty there. Gifts were brought by the people coming from Manasseh, Ephraim, and other parts of the remnant of Israel, as well as from the people of Jerusalem. The money was taken to Hilkiah the High Priest for accounting,

10, 11 And then used by the Levites to pay the carpenters and stonemasons, and to purchase building materials — stone building blocks, timber, lumber, and beams. He now rebuilt what earlier kings of Judah had torn down.

12 The workmen were energetic under the leadership of Jahath and Obadiah, Levites of the subclan of

Merari. Zechariah and Meshullam, of the subclan of Kohath, were the building superintendents. The Levites who were skilled musicians played background music while the work progressed.

13   Other Levites superintended the unskilled laborers who carried in the materials to the workmen. Still others assisted as accountants, supervisors, and carriers.

14   One day when Hilkiah, the High Priest, was at the Temple recording the money collected at the gates, he found an old scroll which turned out to be the laws of God as given to Moses!

15, 16   "Look!" Hilkiah exclaimed to Shaphan, the king's secretary, "See what I have found in the Temple! These are the laws of God!" Hilkiah gave the scroll to Shaphan, and Shaphan took it to the king, along with his report that there was good progress being made in the reconstruction of the Temple.

17   "The money chests have been opened and counted, and the money has been put into the hand of the overseers and workmen," he said to the king.

18   Then he mentioned the scroll, and how Hilkiah had discovered it. So he read it to the king.

19   When the king heard what these laws required of God's people, he ripped his clothing in despair,

20   And summoned Hilkiah, Ahikam (son of Shaphan), Abdon (son of Micah), Shaphan the treasurer, and Asaiah, the king's personal aide.

21   "Go to the Temple and plead with the Lord for me!" the king told them. "Pray for all the remnant of Israel and Judah! For this scroll says that the reason the Lord's great anger has been poured out upon us is that our ancestors have not obeyed these

laws that are written here."

22 So the men went to Huldah the prophetess, the wife of Shallum (son of Tokhath, son of Hasrah). (Shallum was the king's tailor, living in the second ward.) When they told her of the king's trouble,

23 She replied, "The Lord God of Israel says, Tell the man who sent you,

24 'Yes, the Lord will destroy this city and its people. All the curses written in the scroll will come true.

25 For My people have forsaken Me and have worshiped heathen gods, and I am very angry with them for their deeds. Therefore, My unquenchable wrath is poured out upon this place.'

26 But the Lord also says this to the king of Judah who sent you to ask Me about this. Tell him, The Lord God of Israel says,

27 'Because you are sorry and have humbled yourself before God when you heard My words against this city and its people, and have ripped your clothing in despair and wept before Me — I have heard you, says the Lord,

28 And I will not send the promised evil upon this city and its people until after your death.' " So they brought back to the king this word from the Lord.

29 Then the king summoned all the elders of Judah and Jerualem,

30 And the priests and Levites and all the people great and small, to accompany him to the Temple. There the king read the scroll to them — the covenant of God that was found in the Temple.

31 As the king stood before them, he made a pledge to the Lord to follow His commandments with

all his heart and soul, and to do what was written in the scroll.

32 And he required everyone in Jerusalem and Benjamin to subscribe to this pact with God, and all of them did.

33 So Josiah removed all idols from the areas occupied by the Jews, and required all of them to worship Jehovah their God. And throughout the remainder of his lifetime they continued serving Jehovah, the God of their ancestors.

CHAPTER 35

Then Josiah announced that the Passover would be celebrated on the first day of April, in Jerusalem. The Passover lambs were slain that evening.

2 He also reestablished the priests in their duties, and encouraged them to begin their work at the Temple again.

3 He issued this order to the sanctified Levites, the religious teachers in Israel: "Since the Ark is now in Solomon's Temple and you don't need to carry it back and forth upon your shoulders, spend your time ministering to the Lord and to His people.

4, 5 Form yourselves into the traditional service corps of your ancestors, as first organized by King David of Israel and by his son Solomon. Each corps will assist particular clans of the people who bring in their offerings to the Temple.

6 Kill the Passover lambs and sanctify yourselves and prepare to assist the people who come. Follow all of the instructions of the Lord through Moses."

7 Then the king contributed 30,000 lambs and

young goats for the people's Passover offerings, and 3,000 young bulls.

8   The king's officials made willing contributions to the priests and Levites. Hilkiah, Zechariah, and Jehiel, the overseers of the Temple, gave the priests 2,600 sheep and goats, and 300 oxen as Passover offerings.

9   The Levite leaders — Conaniah, Shemaiah, and Nethanel, and his brothers Hashabiah, Jeiel, and Jozabad — gave 5,000 sheep and goats and 500 oxen to the Levites for their Passover offerings.

10   When everything was organized, and the priests were standing in their places, and the Levites were formed into service corps as the king had instructed,

11   Then the Levites killed the Passover lambs and presented the blood to the priests, who sprinkled it upon the altar as the Levites removed the skins.

12   They piled up the carcasses for each tribe to present its own burnt sacrifices to the Lord, as it is written in the law of Moses. They did the same with the oxen.

13   Then, as directed by the laws of Moses, they roasted the Passover lambs and boiled the holy offerings in pots, kettles, and pans, and hurried them out to the people to eat.

14   Afterwards the Levites prepared a meal for themselves and for the priests, for they had been busy from morning till night offering the fat of the burnt offerings.

15   The singers (the sons of Asaph) were in their places, following directions issued centuries earlier by King David, Asaph, Heman, and Jeduthun the king's prophet. The gatekeepers guarded the gates, and didn't

need to leave their posts of duty, for their meals were brought to them by their Levite brothers.

16   The entire Passover ceremony was completed in that one day. All the burnt offerings were sacrificed upon the altar of the Lord, as Josiah had instructed.

17   Everyone present in Jerusalem took part in the Passover observance, and this was followed by the Feast of Unleavened Bread for the next seven days.

18   Never since the time of Samuel the prophet had there been such a Passover — not one of the kings of Israel could vie with King Josiah in this respect, involving so many of the priests, Levites, and people from Jerusalem and from all parts of Judah, and from over in Israel.

19   This all happened in the eighteenth year of the reign of Josiah.

20   Afterwards King Neco of Egypt led his army [against the Assyrians[1]] at Carchemish on the Euphrates River, and Josiah declared war on him.

21   But King Neco sent ambassadors to Josiah with this message: "I don't want a fight with you, O king of Judah! I have come only to fight the King of Assyria![2] Leave me alone! God has told me to hurry! Don't meddle with God or He will destroy you, for He is with me."

22   But Josiah refused to turn back. Instead he led his army into the battle at the Valley of Megiddo. (He laid aside his royal robes so that the enemy wouldn't recognize him.) Josiah refused to believe that Neco's message was from God.

23   The enemy archers struck King Josiah with

1Implied. See II Kings 23:29.
2Implied. Literally, "the power with which I am at war."

their arrows and fatally wounded him. "Take me out of the battle," he exclaimed to his aides.

24, 25　So they lifted him out of his chariot and placed him in his second chariot and brought him back to Jeruslem where he died. He was buried there, in the royal cemetery. And all Judah and Jerusalem, including even Jeremiah the prophet, mourned for him, as did the Temple choirs. To this day they still sing sad songs about his death, for these songs of sorrow were recorded among the official lamentations.

26　The other activities of Josiah, and his good deeds, and how he followed the laws of the Lord,

27　All are written in *The Annals of the Kings of Israel and Judah.*

CHAPTER 36

Josiah's son Jehoahaz was selected as the new king.
2　He was twenty-three years old when he began to reign, but lasted only three months.

3　Then he was deposed by the king of Egypt, who demanded an annual tribute from Judah of $250,-000.

4　The king of Egypt now appointed Eliakim, the brother of Jehoahaz, as the new king of Judah. (Eliakim's name was changed to Jehoiakim). Jehoahaz was taken to Egypt as a prisoner.

5　Jehoiakim was twenty-five years old when he became king, and he reigned eleven years, in Jerusalem; but his reign was an evil one.

6　Finally Nebuchadnezzar king of Babylon conquered Jerusalem, and took away the king in chains to Babylon.

7　Nebuchadnezzar also took some of the golden

bowls and other items from the Temple, placing them in his own temple in Babylon.

8   The rest of the deeds of Jehoiakim, and all the evil he did, are written in *The Annals of the Kings of Judah;* and his son Jehoiachin became the new king.

9   Jehoiachin was eight years old when he ascended the throne. But he lasted only three months and ten days, and it was an evil reign as far as the Lord was concerned.

10   The following spring he was summoned to Babylon by King Nebuchadnezzar. Many treasures from the Temple were taken away to Babylon at that time, and King Nebuchadnezzar appointed Jehoiachin's brother Zedekiah as the new king of Judah and Jerusalem.

11   Zedekiah was twenty-one years old when he became king and he reigned eleven years, in Jerusalem.

12   His reign, too, was evil so far as the Lord was concerned, for he refused to take the counsel of Jeremiah the prophet, who gave him messages from the Lord.

13   He rebelled against King Nebuchadnezzar, even though he had taken an oath of loyalty. Zedekiah was a hard and stubborn man so far as obeying the Lord God of Israel was concerned, for he refused to follow Him.

14   All the important people of the nation, including the High Priests, worshiped the heathen idols of the surrounding nations, thus polluting the Temple of the Lord in Jerusalem.

15   Jehovah the God of their fathers sent His prophets again and again to warn them, for He had compassion on His people and on His Temple.

16 But the people mocked these messengers of God and despised their words, scoffing at the prophets until the anger of the Lord could no longer be restrained, and there was no longer any remedy.

17 Then the Lord brought the king of Babylon against them and killed their young men, even going after them right into the Temple, and had no pity upon them, killing even young girls and old men. The Lord used the king of Babylon to destroy them completely.

18 He also took home with him all the items, great and small, used in the Temple, and treasures from both the Temple and the palace, and took with him all the royal princes.

19 Then his army burned the Temple and broke down the walls of Jerusalem and burned all the palaces and destroyed all the valuable Temple utensils.

20 Those who survived were taken away to Babylon as slaves to the king and his sons until the kingdom of Persia conquered Babylon.

21 Thus the word of the Lord spoken through Jeremiah came true, that the land must rest for seventy years to make up for the years when the people refused to observe the Sabbath.

22, 23 But in the first year of King Cyrus of Persia, the Lord stirred up the spirit of Cyrus to make this proclamation throughout his kingdom, putting it into writing:

"All the kingdoms of the earth have been given to me by the Lord God of heaven, and He has instructed me to build Him a Temple in Jerusalem, in the land of Judah. All among you who are the Lord's people, return to Israel for this task, and the Lord be with you."

This also fulfilled the prediction of Jeremiah the prophet.

Ezra

CHAPTER 1

During the first year of the reign of King Cyrus of Persia, the Lord fulfilled Jeremiah's prophecy[1] by giving King Cyrus the desire to send this proclamation throughout his empire (he also put it into the permanent records of the realm):

2 "Cyrus, King of Persia, hereby announces that Jehovah, the God of heaven who gave me my vast empire, has now given me the responsibility of building Him a Temple in Jerusalem, in the land of Judah.

3 All Jews throughout the kingdom may now return to Jerusalem to rebuild this Temple of Jehovah, who is the God of Israel and of Jerusalem. May His blessings rest upon you.

4 Those Jews[2] who do not go should contribute toward the expenses of those who do, and also supply them with clothing, transportation, supplies for the journey, and a freewill offering for the Temple."

5 Then God gave a great desire to the leaders of the tribes of Judah and Benjamin, and to the priests and Levites, to return to Jerusalem at once to rebuild the Temple.

6 And all the Jewish exiles[2] who chose to remain in Persia gave them whatever assistance they could,

---

[1]Jeremiah had predicted (in Jeremiah 25:12 and 29:10) that the Jews would remain in captivity to the Babylonians for 70 years.

[2]Implied.

as well as gifts for the Temple.

7   King Cyrus himself donated the gold bowls and other valuable items which King Nebuchadnezzar had taken from the Temple at Jerusalem and had placed in the temple of his own gods.

8   He instructed Mithredath, the treasurer of Persia, to present these gifts to Shesh-bazzar, the leader of the exiles returning to Judah.

9, 10   The items Cyrus donated included:

    1,000 gold trays,
    1,000 silver trays,
    29 censers,
    30 bowls of solid gold,
    2,410 silver bowls (of various designs),
    1,000 miscellaneous items.

11   In all there were 5,469 gold and silver items turned over to Shesh-bazzar to take back to Jerusalem.

CHAPTER 2

Here is the list of the Jewish exiles who now returned to Jerusalem and to the other cities of Judah, from which their parents[1] had been deported to Babylon by King Nebuchadnezzar.

2   The leaders were:

    Zerubbabel,
    Jeshua,
    Nehemiah,
    Seraiah,
    Re-el-aiah,
    Mordecai,
    Bilshan,

---

[1]Implied.

Mispar,
Bigvai,
Rehum,
Baanah.

Here is a census of those who returned (listed by sub-clans):

3-35   From the subclan of Parosh, 2,172;
From the subclan of Shephatiah, 372;
From the subclan of Arah, 775;
From the subclan of Pahath-moab (the descendants of Jeshua and Joab), 2,812;
From the subclan of Elam, 1,254;
From the subclan of Zattu, 945;
From the subclan of Zaccai, 760;
From the subclan of Bani, 642;
From the subclan of Bebai, 623;
From the subclan of Azgad, 1,222;
From the subclan of Adonikam, 666;
From the subclan of Bigvai, 2,056;
From the subclan of Adin, 454;
From the subclan of Ater (the descendants of Hezekiah), 98;
From the subclan of Bezai, 323;
From the subclan of Jorah, 112;
From the subclan of Hashum, 223;
From the subclan of Gibbar, 95;
From the subclan of Bethlehem, 123;
From the subclan of Netophah, 56;
From the subclan of Anathoth, 128;
From the subclan of Azmaveth, 42;
From the subclans of Kiriatharim, Chephirah, and Be-eroth, 743;

From the subclans of Ramah and Geba, 621;

From the subclan of Michmas, 122;

From the subclans of Bethel and Ai, 223;

From the subclan of Nebo, 52;

From the subclan of Magbish, 156;

From the subclan of Elam, 1,254;

From the subclan of Harim, 320;

From the subclans of Lod, Hadid, and Ono, 725;

From the subclan of Jericho, 345;

From the subclan of Senaah, 3,630;

36-39 Here are the statistics concerning the returning priests:

From the families of Jedaiah of the subclan of Jeshua, 973;

From the subclan of Immer, 1,052;

From the subclan of Pashhur, 1,247;

From the subclan of Harim, 1,017;

40, 41, 42 Here are the statistics concerning the Levites who returned:

From the families of Jeshua and Kedmi-el of the subclan of Hodaviah, 74;

The choir members from the clan of Asaph, 128;

From the descendants of the gatekeepers (the families of Shallum, Ater, Talmon, Akkub, Hatita, and Shobai), 139;

43-54 The following families of the Temple assistants were represented:

Ziha, Hasupha, Tabbaoth,

Keros, Siaha, Padon,

> Lebanah, Hagabah, Akkub,
> Hagab, Shamlai, Hanan,
> Giddel, Gahar, Re-aiah,
> Rezin, Nekoda, Gazzam,
> Uzza, Paseah, Besai,
> Asnah, Me-unim, Nephisim,
> Bakbuk, Hakupha, Harhur,
> Bazluth, Mehida, Harsha,
> Barkos, Sisera, Temah,
> Neziah, Hatipha.

55, 56, 57 Those who made the trip also included the descendants of King Solomon's officials:

> Sotai, Hassophereth, Peruda,
> Jaalah, Darkon, Giddel,
> Shephatiah, Hattil, Pochereth-hazzebaim,
> Ami.

58 The Temple assistants and the descendants of Solomon's officers numbered 392.

59 Another group returned to Jerusalem at this time from the Persian cities of Tel-melah, Tel-harsha, Cherub, Addan, and Immer. However, they had lost their genealogies and could not prove that they were really Israelites.

60 This group included the subclans of Delaiah, Tobiah, and Nekoda — a total of 652.

61 Three subclans of priests — Habaiah, Hakkoz, and Barzillai (he married one of the daughters of Barzillai the Gileadite and took her family name) — also returned to Jerusalem.

62, 63 But they too had lost their genealogies, so the leaders refused to allow them to continue as priests; they would not even allow them to eat the priests' share of food from the sacrifices until the

Urim and Thummim could be consulted, to find out from God whether they actually were descendants of priests or not.

64, 65   So a total of 42,360 persons returned to Judah; in addition to 7,337 slaves and 200 choir members, both men and women.

66, 67   They took with them 736 horses, 245 mules, 435 camels, and 6,720 donkeys.

68   Some of the leaders were able to give generously toward the rebuilding of the Temple,

69   And each gave as much as he could. The total value of their gifts amounted to $300,000 of gold, $170,000 of silver, and 100 robes for the priests.

70   So the priests and Levites and some of the common people settled in Jerusalem and its nearby villages; and the singers, the gatekeepers, the Temple workers, and the rest of the people returned to the other cities of Judah from which they had come.

CHAPTER 3

During the month of September everyone who had returned to Judah came to Jerusalem from their homes in the other towns. Then Jeshua (son of Jozadak) with his fellow priests, and Zerubbabel (son of She-alti-el) and his clan, rebuilt the altar of the God of Israel; and sacrificed burnt offerings upon it, as instructed in the laws of Moses, the man of God.

3   The altar was rebuilt on its old site, and it was used immediately to sacrifice morning and evening burnt offerings to the Lord; for the people were fearful of attack.

4   And they celebrated the Feast of Tabernacles

as prescribed in the laws of Moses, sacrificing the burnt offerings specified for each day of the feast.

5 They also offered the special sacrifices required for the Sabbaths, the new-moon celebrations, and the other regular annual feasts of the Lord. Voluntary offerings of the people were also sacrificed.

6 It was on the fifteenth day of September[1] that the priests began sacrificing the burnt offerings to the Lord. (This was before they began building the foundation of the Temple.)

7 Then they hired masons and carpenters, and bought cedar logs from the people of Tyre and Sidon, paying for them with food, wine, and olive oil. The logs were brought down from the Lebanon mountains and floated along the coast of the Mediterranean Sea to Joppa; for King Cyrus had included this provision in his grant.

8 The actual construction of the Temple began in June of the second year of their arrival at Jerusalem. The work force was made up of all those who had returned, and they were under the direction of Zerubbabel (son of She-alti-el), Jeshua (son of Jozadak), and their fellow priests and the Levites. The Levites who were twenty years old or older were appointed to supervise the workmen.

9 The supervision of the entire project was given to Jeshua, Kadmi-el, Henadad, and their sons and relatives, all of whom were Levites.

10 When the builders completed the foundation of the Temple, the priests put on their priestly robes and blew their trumpets; and the descendants of Asaph

---

[1]Literally, "the first day of the seventh month" of the Hebrew calendar.

crashed their cymbals to praise the Lord in the manner ordained by King David.

11　They sang rounds of praise and thanks to God, singing this song: "He is good, and His love and mercy toward Israel will last forever." Then all the people gave a great shout, praising God because the foundation of the Temple had been laid.

12　But many of the priests and Levites and other leaders — the old men who remembered Solomon's beautiful Temple — wept aloud, while others were shouting for joy!

13　So the shouting and the weeping mingled together in a loud commotion that could be heard from far away!

CHAPTER 4

When the enemies of Judah and Benjamin heard that the exiles had returned and were rebuilding the Temple,

2　They approached Zerubbabel and the other leaders and suggested, "Let us work with you, for we are just as interested in your God as you are; we have sacrificed to Him ever since King Esar-haddon of Assyria brought us here."

3　But Zerubbabel and Jeshua and the other Jewish leaders replied, "No, you may have no part in this work. The Temple of the God of Israel must be built by the Israelis, just as King Cyrus has commanded."

4, 5　Then the local residents tried to discourage and frighten them by sending agents to tell lies about them to King Cyrus. This went on during his entire reign and lasted until King Darius took the throne.

6　And afterwards, when King Ahasu-erus began

to reign, they wrote him a letter of accusation against the people of Judah and Jerusalem,

7 And did the same thing during the reign of Ar-ta-xerxes. Bishlam, Mithredath, and Tabe-el and their associates wrote a letter to him in the Aramaic language, and it was translated to him.

8, 9 Others who participated were Governor Rehum, Shimshai (a scribe), several judges and other local leaders, the Persians, the Babylonians, the men of Erech and Susa,

10 And men from several other nations. (They had been taken from their own lands by the great and noble Osnappar and relocated in Jerusalem, Samaria, and throughout the neighboring lands west of the Euphrates River.)

11 Here is the text of the letter they sent to King Ar-ta-xerxes:

"Sir: Greetings from your loyal subjects west of the Euphrates River.

12 Please be informed that the Jews sent to Jerusalem from Babylon are rebuilding this historically rebellious and evil city; they have already rebuilt its walls and have repaired the foundations of the Temple.

13 But we wish you to know that if this city is rebuilt, it will be much to your disadvantage, for the Jews will then refuse to pay their taxes to you.

14 Since we are grateful to you as our patron, and we do not want to see you taken advantage of and dishonored in this way, we have decided to send you this information.

15 We suggest that you search the ancient records to discover what a rebellious city this has been in the

past; in fact, it was destroyed because of its long history of sedition against the kings and countries who attempted to control it.

16   We wish to declare that if this city is rebuilt and the walls finished, you might as well forget about this part of your empire beyond the Euphrates, for it will be lost to you."

17   Then the king made this reply to Governor Rehum and Shimshai the scribe, and to their companions living in Samaria and throughout the area west of the Euphrates River:

18   "Gentlemen: Greetings! The letter you sent has been translated and read to me.

19   I have ordered a search made of the records and have indeed found that Jerusalem has in times past been a hotbed of insurrection against many kings; in fact, rebellion and sedition are normal there!

20   I find, moreover, that there have been some very great kings in Jerusalem who have ruled the entire land beyond the Euphrates River and have received vast tribute, custom, and toll.

21   Therefore, I command that these men must stop building the Temple until I have investigated the matter more thoroughly.

22   Do not delay, for we must not permit the situation to get out of control!"

23   When this letter from King Ar-ta-xerxes was read to Rehum and Shimshai, they hurried to Jerusalem and forced the Jews to stop building.

24   So the work ended until the second year of the reign of King Darius of Persia.

CHAPTER 5

Βut there were prophets in Jerusalem and Judah at
that time — Haggai, and Zechariah (the son of
Iddo) — who brought messages from the God of Israel to Zerubbabel (son of She-alti-el) and Jeshua (son
of Jozadak), encouraging them to begin building
again! So they did and the prophets helped them.

3   But Tattenai, the governor of the lands west
of the Euphrates, and Shethar-bozenai, and their companions soon arrived in Jerusalem and demanded,
"Who gave you permission to rebuild this Temple and
finish these walls?"

4   They also asked for a list of the names of all
the men who were working on the Temple.

5   But because the Lord was overseeing the entire situation, our enemies did not force us to stop
building, but let us continue while King Darius looked
into the matter and returned his decision.

6   Following is the letter which Governor Tattenai,
Shethar-bozenai, and the other officials sent to King
Darius:

7   "To King Darius:
     Greetings!

8   We wish to inform you that we went to the
construction site of the Temple of the great God of Judah. It is being built with huge stones, and timber is
being laid in the city walls. The work is going forward with great energy and success.

9   We asked the leaders, 'Who has given you permission to do this?'

10   And we demanded their names so that we
could notify you.

11 Their answer was, 'We are the servants of the God of heaven and earth and we are rebuilding the Temple that was constructed here many centuries ago by a great king of Israel.

12 But afterwards our ancestors angered the God of heaven, and He abandoned them and let King Nebuchadnezzar destroy this Temple and exile the people to Babylonia.'

13 But they insist that King Cyrus of Babylon, during the first year of his reign, issued a decree that the Temple should be rebuilt,

14 And they say King Cyrus returned the gold and silver bowls which Nebuchadnezzar had taken from the Temple in Jerusalem and had placed in the temple of Babylon. They say these items were delivered into the safekeeping of a man named Shesh-bazzar, whom King Cyrus appointed as governor of Judah.

15 The king instructed him to return the bowls to Jerusalem and to let the Temple of God be built there as before.

16 So Shesh-bazzar came and laid the foundations of the Temple at Jerusalem; and the people have been working on it ever since, though it is not yet completed.

17 We request that you search in the royal library of Babylon to discover whether King Cyrus ever made such a decree; and then let us know your pleasure in this matter."

CHAPTER 6

So King Darius issued orders that a search be made in the Babylonian archives, where documents were stored.

2   Eventually the record was found in the palace at Ecbatana, in the province of Media. This is what it said:

3   "In this first year of the reign of King Cyrus, a decree has been sent out concerning the Temple of God at Jerusalem where the Jews offer sacrifices. It is to be rebuilt, and the foundations are to be strongly laid. The height will be ninety feet and the width will be ninety feet.

4   There will be three layers of huge stones in the foundation, topped with a layer of new timber. All expenses will be paid by the king.

5   And the gold and silver bowls which were taken from the Temple of God by Nebuchadnezzar shall be taken back to Jerusalem and put into the Temple as they were before."

6   So King Darius sent this message[1] to Governor Shethar-bozenai, and the other officials west of the Euphrates:

"Do not disturb the construction of the Temple. Let it be rebuilt on its former site,

7   And don't molest the governor of Judah and the other leaders in their work.

8   Moreover, I decree that you are to pay the full construction costs without delay from my taxes collected in your territory.

9   Give the priests in Jerusalem young bulls, rams, and lambs for burnt offerings to the God of heav-

[1]Implied.

en; and give them wheat, wine, salt, and olive oil each day without fail.

10 Then they will be able to offer acceptable sacrifices to the God of heaven, and to pray for me and my sons.

11 Anyone who attempts to change this message in any way shall have the beams pulled from his house and built into a gallows on which he will be hanged;[2] and his house shall be reduced to a pile of rubble.

12 The God who has chosen the city of Jerusalem will destroy any king and any nation that alters this commandment and destroys this Temple. I, Darius, have issued this decree; let it be obeyed with all diligence."

13 Governor Tattenai, Shethar-bozenai, and their companions complied at once with the command of King Darius.

14 So the Jewish leaders continued in their work; and they were greatly encouraged by the preaching of the prophets Haggai and Zechariah (son of Iddo).

The Temple was finally finished, as had been commanded by God and decreed by Cyrus, Darius, and Ar-ta-xerxes, the kings of Persia.

15 The completion date was February 18[3] in the sixth year of the reign of King Darius.

16 The Temple was then dedicated with great joy by the priests, the Levites, and all the people.

17 During the dedication celebration 100 young bulls, 200 rams, and 400 lambs were sacrificed; and twelve male goats were presented as a sin offering for the twelve tribes of Israel.

---

[2]Literally, "impaled."
[3]Literally, "the third day of the month of Adar."

18 Then the priests and Levites were divided into their various service corps, to do the work of God as instructed in the laws of Moses.

19 The Passover was celebrated on the first day of April.[4]

20 For by that time many of the priests and Levites had consecrated themselves.

21, 22 And some of the heathen people who had been relocated in Judah turned from their immoral customs and joined the Israelis in worshiping the Lord God. They, with the entire nation, ate the Passover feast and celebrated the Feast of Unleavened Bread for seven days. There was great joy throughout the land because the Lord had caused the king of Assyria to be generous to Israel and to assist in the construction of the Temple.

CHAPTER 7

Here is the genealogy of Ezra, who traveled from Babylon to Jerusalem[1] during the reign of King Ar-ta-xerxes of Persia;

> Ezra was the son of Seriah;
> Seriah was the son of Azariah;
> Azariah was the son of Hilkiah;

2   Hilkiah was the son of Shallum;
> Shallum was the son of Zadok;
> Zadok was the son of Ahitub;

3   Ahitub was the son of Amariah;
> Amariah was the son of Meraioth;

4   Meraioth was the son of Zerahiah;

---

[4]Literally, "the fourteenth day of the first month" of the Hebrew calendar.
[1]Implied.

Zerahiah was the son of Uzzi;
Uzzi was the son of Bukki;

5　　Bukki was the son of Abishu-a;
Abishu-a was the son of Phinehas;
Phinehas was the son of Eleazar;
Eleazar was the son of Aaron, the chief priest.

6 As a Jewish religious leader, Ezra was well versed in Jehovah's laws which Moses had given to the people of Israel. He asked to be allowed to return to Jerusalem, and the king granted his request; for the Lord his God was blessing him.

7, 8, 9 Many ordinary people as well as priests, Levites, singers, gatekeepers, and Temple workers traveled with him. They left Babylon in the middle of March in the seventh year of the reign of Ar-ta-xerxes and arrived at Jerusalem in the month of August; for the Lord gave them a good trip.

10 This was because Ezra had determined to study and obey the laws of the Lord and to become a Bible teacher, teaching those laws to the people of Israel.

11 King Ar-ta-xerxes presented this letter to Ezra the priest, the student of God's commands:

12 "From: Ar-ta-xerxes, the king of kings.

To: Ezra, the priest, the teacher of the laws of the God of heaven.

13 I decree that any Jew in my realm, including the priests and Levites, may return to Jerusalem with you.

14 I and my Council of Seven hereby instruct you to take a copy of God's laws to Judah and Jerusalem

and to send back a report of the religious progress being made there.

15 We also commission you to take with you to Jerusalem the silver and gold which we are presenting as an offering to the God of Israel.

16 Moreover, you are to collect voluntary Temple offerings of silver and gold from the Jews and their priests in all of the provinces of Babylon;

17 These funds are to be used primarily for the purchase of oxen, rams, lambs, grain offerings, and drink offerings, all of which will be offered upon the altar of your Temple when you arrive in Jerusalem.

18 The money that is left over may be used in whatever way you and your brothers feel is the will of your God.

19 And take with you the gold bowls and other items we are giving you for the Temple of your God at Jerusalem.

20 If you run short of money for the construction of the Temple or for any similar needs, you may requisition funds from the royal treasury.

21 I, Ar-ta-xerxes the king, send this decree to all the treasurers in the provinces west of the Euphrates River: 'You are to give Ezra whatever he requests of you (for he is a priest and teacher of the laws of the God of heaven),

22 Up to $200,000 in silver; 1,225 bushels of wheat; 990 gallons of wine; any amount of salt;

23 And whatever else the God of heaven demands for His Temple; for why should we risk God's wrath against the king and his sons?

24 I also decree that no priest, Levite, choir member, gatekeeper, Temple attendant, or other worker

in the Temple shall be required to pay taxes of any kind.'

25   And you, Ezra, are to use the wisdom God has given you to select and appoint judges and other officials to govern all the people west of the Euphrates River; if they are not familiar with the laws of your God, you are to teach them.

26   Anyone refusing to obey the law of your God and the law of the king shall be punished immediately by death, banishment, confiscation of goods, or imprisonment."

27   Well, praise the Lord God of our ancestors, who made the king want to beautify the Temple of the Lord in Jerusalem!

28   And praise God for demonstrating such lovingkindness to me[2] by honoring me before the king and his Council of Seven and before all of his mighty princes! I was given great status because the Lord my God was with me; and I persuaded some of the leaders of Israel to return with me to Jerusalem.

CHAPTER 8

These are the names and genealogies of the leaders who accompanied me from Babylon during the reign of King Ar-ta-xerxes:

2-14   From the clan of Phinehas — Gershom;
         From the clan of Ithamar — Daniel;
         From the subclan of David of the clan of
              Shecaniah — Hattush;
         From the clan of Parosh — Zechariah, and
              150 other men;

---

[2]The speaker, as in the remainder of the book, is Ezra.

From the clan of Pahath-moab — Eli-e-hoenai (son of Zerahiah), and 200 other men;

From the clan of Shecaniah — the son of Jahaziel, and 300 other men;

From the clan of Adin — Ebed (son of Jonathan), and 50 other men;

From the clan of Elam — Jeshaiah (son of Athaliah), and 70 other men;

From the clan of Shephatiah — Zebadiah (son of Michael), and 80 other men;

From the clan of Joab — Obadiah (son of Jehiel), and 218 other men;

From the clan of Bani — Shelomith (son of Josiphiah), and 160 other men;

From the clan of Bebai — Zechariah (son of Bebai), and 28 other men;

From the clan of Azgad — Johanan (son of Hakkatan), and 110 other men;

From the clan of Adonikam — Eliphelet, Jeuel, Shemaiah, and 60 other men (they arrived at a later time);

From the clan of Bigvai — Uthai, Zaccur, and 70 other men.

15 We assembled at the Ahava River and camped there for three days while I went over the lists of the people and the priests who had arrived; and I found that not one Levite had volunteered!

16 So I sent for Eliezer, Ari-el, Shemaiah, Elnathan, Jarib, Elnathan, Nathan, Zechariah, and Meshullam: the Levite leaders; I also sent for Joiarib and Elnathan, who were very wise men.

17 I sent them to Iddo, the leader of the Jews at Casiphia, to ask him and his brothers and the Temple attendants to send us priests for the Temple of God at Jerusalem.

18 And God was good! He sent us an outstanding man named Sherebiah, along with eighteen of his sons and brothers; he was a very astute man and a descendant of Mahli, the son of Levi and grandson of Israel.

19 God also sent Hashabiah; and Jeshaiah (the son of Merari), with twenty of his sons and brothers;

20 And 220 Temple attendants. (The Temple attendants were assistants to the Levites — a job classification of Temple employees first instituted by King David.) These 220 men were all listed by name.

21 Then I declared a fast while we were at the Ahava River so that we would humble ourselves before our God; and we prayed that He would give us a good journey and protect us, our children, and our goods as we traveled.

22 For I was ashamed to ask the king for soldiers and cavalry to accompany us and protect us from the enemies along the way. After all, we had told the king that our God would protect all those who worshiped Him, and that disaster could come only to those who had forsaken Him!

23 So we fasted and begged God to take care of us. And He did.

24 I appointed twelve leaders of the priests — Sherebiah, Hashabiah, and ten other priests —

25 To be in charge of transporting the silver, gold, the golden bowls, and the other items which the king and his council and the leaders and people of Israel

had presented to the Temple of God.

26, 27   I weighed the money as I gave it to them and found it to total $1,300,000 in silver; $200,000 in silver utensils; $3,000,000 in gold; and twenty gold bowls worth a total of $5,000. There were also two beautiful pieces of brass which were as precious as gold.

28   I consecrated these men to the Lord, and then consecrated the treasures — the equipment and money and bowls which had been given as freewill offerings to the Lord God of our fathers.

29   "Guard these treasures well!" I told them; "present them without a penny lost to the priests and the Levite leaders and the elders of Israel at Jerusalem, where they are to be placed in the treasury of the Temple."

30   So the priests and the Levites accepted the responsibility of taking it to God's Temple in Jerusalem.

31   We broke camp at the Ahava River at the end of March[1] and started off to Jerusalem; and God protected us and saved us from enemies and bandits along the way.

32   So at last we arrived safely at Jerusalem.

33   On the fourth day after our arrival the silver, gold, and other valuables were weighed in the Temple by Meremoth (the son of Uriah the priest), Eleazar (son of Phinehas), Jozabad (son of Jeshua), and Noadiah (son of Binnui) — all of whom were Levites.

34   A receipt was given for each item, and the weight of the gold and silver was noted.

35   Then everyone in our party sacrificed burnt offerings to the God of Israel — twelve oxen for the

---

[1]Or, "the twelfth day of the first month" of the Hebrew calendar.

nation of Israel; ninety-six rams; seventy-seven lambs; and twelve goats as a sin offering.

36 The king's decrees were delivered to his lieutenants and the governors of all the provinces west of the Euphrates River, and of course they then cooperated in the rebuilding of the Temple of God.

CHAPTER 9

But then the Jewish leaders came to tell me that many of the Jewish people and even some of the priests and Levites had taken up the horrible customs of the heathen people who lived in the land — the Canaanites, Hittites, Perizzites, Jebusites, Ammonites, Moabites, Egyptians, and Amorites:

2 The men of Israel had married girls from these heathen nations, and had taken them as wives for their sons. So the holy people of God were being polluted by these mixed marriages; and the political leaders were some of the worst offenders.

3 When I heard this, I tore my clothing and pulled hair from my head and beard and sat down utterly baffled.

4 Then many who feared the God of Israel because of this sin of His people came and sat with me until the time of the evening burnt offering.

5 Finally I stood before the Lord in great embarrassment; then I fell to my knees and lifted my hands to the Lord,

6 And cried out, "O my God, I am ashamed; I blush to lift up my face to You, for our sins are piled higher than our heads and our guilt is as boundless as the heavens.

7 Our whole history has been one of sin; that is why we and our kings and our priests were slain by the heathen kings — we were captured, robbed, and disgraced, just as we are today.

8 But now we have been given a moment of peace, for You have permitted a few of us to return to Jerusalem from our exile. You have given us a moment of joy and new life in our slavery.

9 For we were slaves, but in Your love and mercy You did not abandon us to slavery; instead You caused the kings of Persia to be favorable to us. They have even given us their assistance in rebuilding the Temple of our God and in giving us Jerusalem as a walled city in Judah.

10 And now, O God, what can we say after all of this? For once again we have abandoned You and broken Your laws!

11 The prophets warned us that the land we would possess was totally defiled by the horrible practices of the people living there. From one end to the other it is filled with corruption.

12 You told us not to let our daughters marry their sons, and not to let our sons marry their daughters, and not to help those nations in any way. You warned us that only if we followed this rule could we become a prosperous nation and forever leave that prosperity to our children as an inheritance.

13 And now, even after our punishment in exile because of our wickedness (and we have been punished far less than we deserved), and even though You have let some of us return,

14 We have broken Your commandments again and intermarried with people who do these awful

things. Surely Your anger will destroy us now until not even this little remnant escapes.

15 O Lord God of Israel, You are a just God; what hope can we have if You give us justice as we stand here before You in our wickedness?"

CHAPTER 10

A s I lay on the ground in front of the Temple, weeping and praying and making this confession, a large crowd of men, women, and children gathered around and cried with me.

2 Then Shecaniah (the son of Jehiel of the clan of Elam) said to me, "We acknowledge our sin against our God, for we have married these heathen women. But there is hope for Israel in spite of this.

3 For we agree before our God to divorce our heathen wives and to send them away with our children; we will follow your commands, and the commands of the others who fear our God. We will obey the laws of God.

4 Take courage and tell us how to proceed in setting things straight, and we will fully cooperate."

5 So I stood up and demanded that the leaders of the priests and the Levites and all the people of Israel swear that they would do as Shecaniah had said; and they all agreed.

6 Then I went into the room of Jeho-hanan in the Temple and refused all food and drink; for I was mourning because of the sin of the returned exiles.

7, 8 Then a proclamation was made throughout Judah and Jerusalem that everyone should appear at Jerusalem within three days and that the leaders and elders had decided that anyone who refused to come would be disinherited and excommunicated from Israel.

9   Within three days, on the fifth day of December,[1] all the men of Judah and Benjamin had arrived and were sitting in the open space before the Temple; and they were trembling because of the seriousness of the matter and because of the heavy rainfall.

10   Then I, Ezra the priest, arose and addressed them: "You have sinned, for you have married heathen women; now we are even more deeply under God's condemnation than we were before.

11   Confess your sin to the Lord God of your fathers and do what He demands: separate yourselves from the heathen people about you and from these women."

12   Then all the men spoke up and said, "We will do what you have said.

13   But this isn't something that can be done in a day or two, for there are many of us involved in this sinful affair. And it is raining so hard that we can't stay out here much longer.

14   Let our leaders arrange trials for us. Everyone who has a heathen wife will come at the scheduled time with the elders and judges of his city; then each case will be decided and the situation will be cleared up and the fierce wrath of our God will be turned away from us."

15   Only Jonathan (son of Asahel), Jahzeiah (son of Tikvah), Meshullam, and Shabbethai the Levite opposed this course of action.

---

[1] Literally, "the twentieth day of the ninth month" of the Hebrew calendar.

16-19 So this was the plan that was followed: Some of the clan leaders and I were designated as judges; we began our work on December 15, and finished by March 15.

Following is the list of priests who had married heathen wives (they vowed to divorce their wives and acknowledged their guilt by offering rams as sacrifices):

> Ma-aseiah,
> Eliezer,
> Jarib,
> Gedaliah;

20 The sons of Immer:
> Hanani,
> Zebadiah;

21 The sons of Harim:
> Ma-aseiah,
> Elijah,
> Shemaiah,
> Jehiel,
> Uzziah;

22 The sons of Pashhur:
> Eli-o-enai,
> Ma-aseiah,
> Ishmael,
> Nethanel,
> Jozabad,
> Elasah.

23 The Levites who were guilty:
> Jozabad,
> Shime-i,
> Kelaiah (also called Kelita),
> Petha-haiah,

Judah,
Eliezer.

24 Of the singers, there was Eliashib;
Of the gatekeepers, Shallum, Telem, and Uri.

25 Here is the list of ordinary citizens who were declared guilty:

From the clan of Parosh:
Ramiah,
Izziah,
Malchijah,
Mijamin,
Eleazar,
Hashabiah,
Benaiah;

26 From the clan of Elam:
Mattaniah,
Zechariah,
Jehiel,
Abdi,
Jeremoth,
Elijah;

27 From the clan of Zattu:
Eli-o-enai,
Eliashib,
Mattaniah,
Jeremoth,
Zabad,
Aziza;

28 From the clan of Bebai:
Jeho-hanan,
Hananiah,
Zabbai,
Athlai;

29   From the clan of Bani:
> Meshullam,
> Malluch,
> Adaiah,
> Jashub,
> Sheal,
> Jeremoth;

30   From the clan of Pahath-moab:
> Adna,
> Chelal,
> Benaiah,
> Ma-aseiah,
> Mattaniah,
> Bezalel,
> Binnui,
> Manasseh;

31, 32   From the clan of Harim:
> Eliezer,
> Isshijah,
> Malchijah,
> Shemaiah,
> Shime-on.
> Benjamin,
> Malluch,
> Shemariah;

33   From the clan of Hashum:
> Mattenai,
> Matattah,
> Zabad,
> Eliphelet,
> Jeremai,
> Manasseh,
> Shime-i;

34-42   From the clan of Bani:
> Ma-adai,
> Amram,
> Uel,
> Banaiah,
> Bedeiah,
> Cheluhi,
> Vaniah,
> Meremoth,
> Eliashib,
> Mattaniah,
> Mattenai,
> Jaasu,
> Bani,
> Binnui,
> Shime-i,
> Shelemiah,
> **Nathan,**
> Adaiah,
> Machnadebai,
> Shashai,
> Sharai,
> Azarel,
> Shelemiah,
> Shemariah,
> Shallum,
> Amariah,
> Joseph;

43   From the clan of Nebo:
> Je-iel,
> Mattithiah,
> Zabad,
> **Zebina,**

> Jaddai,
> Joel,
> Benaiah.

44 Each of these men had heathen wives, and many had children by these wives.

Nehemiah

CHAPTER 1

The Autobiography of Nehemiah, the Son of Hecaliah:

In December of the twentieth year of the reign of King Ar-ta-xerxes of Persia,[1] when I was at the palace at Shushan,

2 One of my fellow Jews named Hanani came to visit me with some men who had arrived from Judah. I took the opportunity to inquire about how things were going in Jerusalem. "How are they getting along?" I asked. " — the Jews who returned to Jerusalem from their exile here?"

3 "Well," they replied, "things are not good; the wall of Jerusalem is still torn down, and the gates are burned."

4 When I heard this, I sat down and cried. In fact, I refused to eat for several days, for I spent the time in prayer to the God of heaven.

5 "O Lord God," I cried out; "O great and awesome God who keeps His promises and is so loving and kind to those who love and obey Him! Hear my prayer!

6, 7 Listen carefully to what I say! Look down and see me praying night and day for Your people Israel. I confess that we have sinned against You; yes, I and my people have committed the horrible

---

¹Implied.

sin of not obeying the commandments You gave us through Your servant Moses.

8 Oh, please remember what You told Moses! You said, *'If you sin, I will scatter you among the nations;*

9 *But if you return to Me and obey My laws, even though you are exiled to the farthest corners of the universe, I will bring you back to Jerusalem. For Jerusalem is the place in which I have chosen to live.'*

10 We are Your servants, the people You rescued by Your great power.

11 O Lord, please hear my prayer! Heed the prayers of those of us who delight to honor You. Please help me now as I go in and ask the king for a great favor — put it into his heart to be kind to me." (I was the king's cupbearer.)

CHAPTER 2

One day in April four months later, as I was serving the king his wine he asked me, "Why so sad? You aren't sick, are you? You look like a man with deep troubles." (For until then I had always been cheerful when I was with him.) I was badly frightened,

3 But I replied, "Sir,[1] why shouldn't I be sad? For the city where my ancestors are buried is in ruins, and the gates have been burned down."

4 "Well, what should be done?" the king asked.

With a quick prayer to the God of heaven I replied, "If it please Your Majesty and if you look upon me with your royal favor, send me to Judah to rebuild the city of my fathers!"

[1]Literally, "Let the king live forever."

5, 6 The king replied, with the queen sitting beside him, "How long will you be gone? When will you return?"

So it was agreed! And I set a time for my departure!

7 Then I added this to my request: "If it please the king, give me letters to the governors west of the Euphrates River instructing them to let me travel through their countries on my way to Judah;

8 Also a letter to Asaph, the manager of the king's forest, instructing him to give me timber for the beams and for the gates of the fortress near the Temple, and for the city walls, and for a house for myself." And the king granted these requests, for God was being gracious to me.

9 When I arrived in the provinces west of the Euphrates River, I delivered the king's letters to the governors there. (The king, I should add, had sent along army officers and troops to protect me!)

10 But when Sanballat (the Horonite) and Tobiah (an Ammonite who was a government official) heard of my arrival, they were very angry that anyone was interested in helping Israel.

11, 12 Three days after my arrival at Jerusalem I stole out during the night, taking only a few men with me; for I hadn't told a soul about the plans for Jerusalem which God had put into my heart. I was mounted on my donkey and the others were on foot,

13 And we went out through the Valley Gate toward the Jackal's Well and over to the Dung Gate to see the broken walls and burned gates.

14, 15 Then we went to the Fountain Gate and to the King's Pool, but my donkey couldn't get through the rubble. So we circled the city, and I followed the brook, inspecting the wall, and entered again at the Valley Gate.

16   The city officials did not know I had been out there, or why, for as yet I had said nothing to anyone about my plans — not to the political or religious leaders, or even to those who would be doing the work.

17   But now I told them, "You know full well the tragedy of our city; it lies in ruins and its gates are burned. Let us rebuild the wall of Jerusalem and rid ourselves of this disgrace!"

18   Then I told them about the desire God had put into my heart, and of my conversation with the king, and the plan to which he had agreed.

They replied at once, "Good! Let's rebuild the wall!" And so the work began.

19   But when Sanballat and Tobiah and Geshem the Arab heard of our plan, they scoffed and said, "What are you doing, rebelling against the king like this?"

20   But I replied, "The God of heaven will help us, and we, His servants, will rebuild this wall; but you may have no part in this affair."

CHAPTER 3

Then Eliashib the High Priest and the other priests rebuilt the wall as far as the Tower of the Hundred and the Tower of Hananel; then they rebuilt the Sheep Gate, hung its doors, and dedicated it.

2   Men from the city of Jericho worked next to them, and beyond them was the work crew led by Zaccur (son of Imri).

3   The Fish Gate was built by the sons of Has-senaah; they did the whole thing — cut the beams, hung the doors, and made the bolts and bars.

4   Meremoth (son of Uriah, son of Hakkoz) repaired the next section of wall, and beyond him were Meshullam (son of Berechiah, son of Meshezabel) and Zadok (son of Baana).

5   Next were the men from Tekoa, but their leaders were lazy and didn't help.

6   The Old Gate was repaired by Joiada (son of Paseah) and Meshullam (son of Besodeiah). They laid the beams, set up the doors, and installed the bolts and bars.

7   Next to them were Melatiah from Gibeon; Jadon from Meronoth; and men from Gibeon and Mizpah, who were citizens of the province.

8   Uzziel (son of Harhaiah) was a goldsmith by trade, but he too worked on the wall. Beyond him was Hananiah, a manufacturer of perfumes. Repairs were not needed from there to the Broad Wall.

9   Rephaiah (son of Hur), the mayor of half of Jerusalem, was next down the wall from them.

10   Jedaiah (son of Harumaph) repaired the wall beside his own house, and next to him was Hattush (son of Hashabneiah).

11   Then came Malchijah (son of Harim) and Hasshub (son of Pahath-moab), who repaired the Furnace Tower in addition to a section of the wall.

12   Shallum (son of Hallohesh) and his daughters repaired the next section. He was the mayor of the other half of Jerusalem.

13   The people from Zanoah, led by Hanun, built the Valley Gate, hung the doors, and installed the bolts

and bars; then they repaired the 1,500 feet of wall to the Dung Gate.

14 The Dung Gate was repaired by Malchijah (son of Rechab), the mayor of the Beth-haccherem area; and after building it, he hung the doors and installed the bolts and bars.

15 Shallum (son of Colhozeh), the mayor of the Mizpah district, repaired the Fountain Gate. He rebuilt it, roofed it, hung its doors, and installed its locks and bars. Then he repaired the wall from the Pool of Siloam to the king's garden and the stairs that descend from the City of David section of Jerusalem.

16 Next to him was Nehemiah (son of Azbuk), the mayor of half the Beth-zur district; he built as far as the royal cemetery, the water reservoir, and the old Officers' Club building.[1]

17 Next was a group of Levites working under the supervision of Rehum (son of Bani). Then came Hashabiah, the mayor of half the Keilah district, who supervised the building of the wall in his own district.

18 Next down the line were his clan brothers led by Bavvai (son of Henadad), the mayor of the other half of the Keilah district.

19 Next to them the workers were led by Ezer (son of Jeshua), the mayor of another part of Mizpah; they also worked on the section of wall across from the Armory, where the wall turns.

20 Next to him was Baruch (son of Zabbai), who built from the turn in the wall to the home of Eliashib the High Priest.

21 Meremoth (son of Uriah, son of Hakkoz) built a section of the wall extending from a point opposite

---

[1]Literally, "the house of the mighty men."

the door of Eliashib's house to the side of the house.

22 Then came the priests from the plains outside the city.[2]

23 Benjamin, Hasshub, and Azariah (son of Ma-as-eiah, son of Ananiah) repaired the sections next to their own houses.

24 Next was Binnui (son of Henadad), who built the portion of the wall from Azariah's house to the corner.

25 Palal (son of Uzai) carried on the work from the corner to the foundations of the upper tower of the king's castle beside the prison yard. Next was Pedaiah (son of Parosh).

26 The Temple attendants living in Ophel repaired the wall as far as the East Water Gate and the Projecting Tower.

27 Then came the Tekoites, who repaired the section opposite the Castle Tower and over to the wall of Ophel.

28 The priests repaired the wall beyond the Horse Gate, each one doing the section immediately opposite his own house.

29 Zadok (son of Immer) also rebuilt the wall next to his own house, and beyond him was Shemaiah (son of Shecaniah), the gatekeeper of the East Gate.

30 Next was Hananiah (son of Shelemiah); Hanun (the sixth son of Zalaph); and Meshullam (son of Berechiah), who built next to his own house.

31 Malchijah, one of the goldsmiths, repaired as far as the Temple attendants' and merchants' Guild Hall, opposite the Muster Gate; then to the upper room at the corner.

---

[2]Implied.

32 The other goldsmiths and merchants completed the wall from that corner to the Sheep Gate.

CHAPTER 4

Sanballat was very angry when he learned that we were rebuilding the wall. He flew into a rage, and insulted and mocked us and laughed at us, and so did his friends and the Samaritan army officers. "What does this bunch of poor, feeble Jews think they are doing?" he scoffed. "Do they think they can build the wall in a day if they offer enough sacrifices? And look at those charred stones they are pulling out of the rubbish and using again!"

3 Tobiah, who was standing beside him, remarked, "If even a fox walked along the top of their wall, it would collapse!"

4 Then I prayed, "Hear us, O Lord God, for we are being mocked. May their scoffing fall back upon their own heads, and may they themselves become captives in a foreign land!

5 Do not ignore their sin. Do not blot it out, for they have despised You in despising us who are building Your wall."

6 At last the wall was completed to half its original height around the entire city — for the workers worked hard.

7 But when Sanballat and Tobiah and the Arabians, Ammonites, and Ashdodites heard that the work was going right ahead and that the breaks in the wall were being repaired, they became furious.

8 They plotted to lead an army against Jerusalem to bring about riots and confusion.

9   But we prayed to our God and guarded the city day and night to protect ourselves.

10   Then some of the leaders began complaining that the workmen were becoming tired; and there was so much rubble to be removed that we could never get it done by ourselves.

11   Meanwhile, our enemies were planning to swoop down upon us and kill us, thus ending our work.

12   And whenever the workers who lived in the nearby cities went home for a visit, our enemies tried to talk them out of returning to Jerusalem.

13   So I placed armed guards from each family in the cleared spaces behind the walls.

14   Then as I looked over the situation, I called together the leaders and the people and said to them, "Don't be afraid! Remember the Lord who is great and glorious; fight for your friends, your families, and your homes!"

15   Our enemies learned that we knew of their plot, and that God had exposed and frustrated their plan. Now we all returned to our work on the wall;

16   But from then on, only half worked while the other half stood guard behind them.

17   And the masons and laborers worked with weapons within easy reach beside them,

18   Or with swords belted to their sides. The trumpeter stayed with me to sound the alarm.

19   "The work is so spread out," I explained to them, "and we are separated so widely from each other, that when you hear the trumpet blow you must rush to where I am; and God will fight for us."

20, 21   We worked early and late, from sunrise to sunset; and half the men were always on guard.

22   I told everyone living outside the walls to move into Jerusalem so that their servants could go on guard duty as well as work during the day.

23   During this period none of us — I, nor my brothers, nor the servants, nor the guards who were with me — ever took off our clothes. And we carried our weapons with us at all times.

CHAPTER 5

A bout this time there was a great outcry of protest from parents against some of the rich Jews who were profiteering on them.

2, 3, 4   What was happening was that families who ran out of money for food had to sell their children or mortgage their fields, vineyards, and homes to these rich men; and some couldn't even do that, for they already had borrowed to the limit to pay their taxes.

5   "We are their brothers, and our children are just like theirs," the people protested; "yet we must sell our children into slavery to get enough money to live. We have already sold some of our daughters, and we are helpless to redeem them, for our fields, too, are mortgaged to these men."

6   I was very angry when I heard this;

7   So after thinking about it I spoke out against these rich government officials. "What is this you are doing?" I demanded. "How dare you demand a mortgage as a condition for helping another Israelite?"

Then I called a public trial to deal with them.

8   At the trial I shouted at them, "The rest of us are doing all we can to *help* our Jewish brothers who

have returned from exile as slaves in distant lands, but you are forcing them right back into slavery again. How often must we redeem them?"

And they had nothing to say in their own defense.

9 Then I pressed further. "What you are doing is very evil," I exclaimed. "Should you not walk in the fear of our God? Don't we have enough enemies among the nations around us who are trying to destroy us?

10 The rest of us are lending money and grain to our fellow-Jews without any interest. I beg you, gentlemen, stop this business of usury.

11 Restore their fields, vineyards, oliveyards, and homes to them this very day and drop your claims against them."

12 So they agreed to do it and said that they would assist their brothers without requiring them to mortgage their lands and sell them their children. Then I summoned the priests and made these men formally vow to carry out their promises.

13 And I invoked the curse of God upon any of them who refused.[1] "May God destroy your homes and livelihood if you fail to keep this promise," I declared.

And all the people shouted, "Amen," and praised the Lord. And the rich men did as they had promised.

14 I would like to mention that for the entire twelve years that I was governor of Judah — from the twentieth until the thirty-second year of the reign of King Ar-ta-xerxes — my aides and I accepted no

---

[1] Literally, "then I shook out the lap of my gown . . ."

salaries or other assistance from the people of Israel.

15 This was quite a contrast to the former governors who had demanded food and wine and $100 a day in cash, and had put the population at the mercy of their aides, who tyrannized them; but I obeyed God and did not act that way.

16 I stayed at work on the wall and refused to speculate in land; I also required my officials to spend time on the wall.

17 All this despite the fact that I regularly fed 150 Jewish officials at my table, besides visitors from other countries!

18 The provisions required for each day were one ox, six fat sheep, and a large number of domestic fowls; and we needed a huge supply of all kinds of wines every ten days. Yet I refused to make a special levy against the people, for they were already having a difficult time.

19 O my God, please keep in mind all that I've done for these people and bless me for it.

CHAPTER 6

When Sanballat, Tobiah, Geshem the Arab, and the rest of our enemies found out that we had almost completed the rebuilding of the wall — though we had not yet hung all the doors of the gates —

2 They sent me a message asking me to meet them in one of the villages in the Plain of Ono. But I realized they were plotting to kill me,

3 So I replied by sending back this message to them: "I am doing a great work! Why should I stop to come and visit with you?"

4   Four times they sent the same message, and each time I gave the same reply.

5, 6   The fifth time, Sanballat's servant came with an open letter in his hand and this is what it said: "Geshem tells me that everywhere he goes he hears that the Jews are planning to rebel, and that is why you are building the wall. He claims you plan to be their king — that is what is being said.

7   He also reports that you have appointed prophets to campaign for you at Jerusalem by saying, 'Look! Nehemiah is just the man we need!'

You can be very sure that I am going to pass these interesting comments on to King Ar-ta-xerxes! I suggest that you come and talk it over with me — for that is the only way you can save yourself!"

8   My reply was, "You know you are lying. There isn't one bit of truth to the whole story.

9   You're just trying to scare us into stopping our work." (O Lord God, please strengthen me!)

10   A few days later I went to visit Shemaiah (son of Delaiah, who was the son of Mehetabel), for he said he was receiving a message from God. "Let us hide in the Temple and bolt the door," he exclaimed, "for they are coming tonight to kill you."

11   But I replied, "Should I, the governor, run away from danger? And if I go into the Temple, not being a priest, I would forfeit my life. No, I won't do it!"

12, 13   Then I realized that God had not spoken to him, but Tobiah and Sanballat had hired him to scare me and make me sin by fleeing to the Temple; and then they would be able to accuse me.

14   "O my God," I prayed, "don't forget all the

evil of Tobiah, Sanballat, No-adiah the prophetess, and all the other prophets who have tried to discourage me."

15 The wall was finally finished in early September[1] — just fifty-two days after we had begun!

16 When our enemies and the surrounding nations heard about it, they were frightened and humiliated, and they realized that the work had been done with the help of our God.

17 During those fifty-two days many letters went back and forth between Tobiah and the wealthy politicians of Judah.

18 For many in Judah had sworn allegiance to him because his father-in-law was Shecaniah (son of Arah) and because his son Jehohanan was married to the daughter of Meshullam (son of Berechiah).

19 They all told me what a wonderful man Tobiah was, and then they told him everything I had said; and Tobiah sent many threatening letters to frighten me.

CHAPTER 7

After the wall was finished and we had hung the doors in the gates and had appointed the gatekeepers, singers, and Levites,

2 I gave the responsibility of governing Jerusalem to my brother Hanani and to Hananiah, the commander of the fortress — a very faithful man who revered God more than most people do.

3 I issued instructions to them not to open the Jerusalem gates until well after sunrise, and to close and lock them while the guards were still on duty. I

---

[1]Or, "twenty-fifth day of the month Elul."

also directed that the guards be residents of Jerusalem, and that they must be on duty at regular times, and that each homeowner who lived near the wall must guard the section of wall next to his own home.

4 For the city was large, but the population was small; and only a few houses were scattered throughout the city.

5 Then the Lord told me to call together all the leaders of the city, along with the ordinary citizens, for registration. For I had found the record of the genealogies of those who had returned to Judah before, and this is what was written in it:

6 "The following is a list of the names of the Jews who returned to Judah after being exiled by King Nebuchadnezzar of Babylon.

7 Their leaders were:

> Zerubbabel, Jeshua, Nehemiah;
> Azariah, Ra-amiah, Nahamani;
> Mordecai, Bilshan, Mispereth;
> Bigvai,
> Nehum,
> Baanah.

The others who returned at that time were:

8-38
> From the subclan of Parosh, 2,172;
> From the subclan of Shephatiah, 372;
> From the subclan of Arah, 652;
> From the families of Jeshua and Joab of the subclan of Pahath-moab, 2,818;
> From the subclan of Elam, 1,254;
> From the subclan of Zattu, 845;
> From the subclan of Zaccai, 760;
> From the subclan of Binnui, 648;
> From the subclan of Bebai, 628;

From the subclan of Azgad, 2,322;

From the subclan of Adonikam, 667;

From the subclan of Bigvai, 2,067;

From the subclan of Adin, 655;

From the family of Hezekiah of the sub-clan of Ater, 98;

From the subclan of Hashum, 328;

From the subclan of Bezai, 324;

From the subclan of Hariph, 112;

From the subclan of Gibeon, 95;

From the subclans of Bethlehem and Netophah, 188;

From the subclan of Anathoth, 128;

From the subclan of Beth-azmaveth, 42;

From the subclans of Kiriath-jearim, Chephirah, and Be-eroth, 743;

From the subclans of Ramah and Geba, 621;

From the subclan of Michmas, 122;

From the subclans of Bethel and Ai, 123;

From the subclan of Nebo, 52;

From the subclan of Elam, 1,254;

From the subclan of Harim, 320;

From the subclan of Jericho, 345;

From the subclans of Lod, Hadid, and Ono, 721;

From the subclan of Sanaah, 3,930.

39-42 Here are the statistics concerning the returning priests:

From the family of Jeshua of the subclan of Jedaiah, 973;

From the subclan of Immer, 1,052;

> From the subclan of Pashhur, 1,247;
>
> From the subclan of Harim, 1,017.

43, 44, 45 Here are the statistics concerning the Levites:

> From the family of Kadmi-el of the sub-
> clan of Hodevah of the clan of Jesh-
> ua, 74;
>
> The choir members from the clan of
> Asaph, 148;
>
> From the clans of Shallum, (all of whom
> were gatekeepers), 138.

46-56 Of the Temple assistants, the following sub-clans were represented:

> Ziha, Hasupha, Tabbaoth;
>
> Keros, Sia, Padon;
>
> Lebana, Hagaba, Shalmai;
>
> Hanan, Giddel, Gahar;
>
> Re-aiah, Rezin, Nekoda;
>
> Gazzam, Uzza, Paseah;
>
> Besai, Asnah, Me-unim, Nephushesim;
>
> Bakbuk, Hakupha, Harhur;
>
> Bazlith, Mehida, Harsha;
>
> Barkos, Sisera, Temah;
>
> Neziah, Hatipha.

57, 58, 59 Following is a list of the descendants of Solomon's officials who returned to Judah:

> Sotai, Sophereth, Perida,
>
> Jaala, Darkon, Giddel,
>
> Shephatiah, Hattil, Pochereth-hazzebaim,
> Amon.

60 In all, the Temple assistants and the descendants of Solomon's officers numbered 392."

61 Another group returned to Jerusalem at that

time from the Persian cities of Tel-melah, Tel-harsha, Cherub, Addon, and Immer. But they had lost their genealogies and could not prove their Jewish ancestry;

62 These were the subclans of Delaiah, Tobiah, and Nekoda — a total of 642.

63 There were also several subclans of priests named after Habaiah, Hakkoz, and Barzillai (he married one of the daughters of Barzillai the Gileadite and took her family name),

64, 65 Whose genealogies had been lost. So they were not allowed to continue as priests or even to receive the priests' share of food from the sacrifices until the Urim and Thummim had been consulted to find out from God whether or not they actually were descendants of priests.

66 There was a total of 42,360 citizens who returned to Judah at that time;

67 Also, 7,337 slaves and 245 choir members, both men and women.

68, 69 They took with them 736 horses, 245 mules, 435 camels, and 6,720 donkeys.

70 Some of their leaders gave gifts for the work. The governor gave $5,000 in gold, 50 golden bowls, and 530 sets of clothing for the priests.

71 The other leaders gave a total of $100,000 in gold and $77,000 in silver;

72 And the common people gave $100,000 in gold, $70,000 in silver, and 67 sets of clothing for the priests.

* * * * *

73 The priests, the Levites, the gatekeepers, the choir members, the Temple attendants, and the rest of the people now returned home to their own towns and

villages throughout Judah. But during the month of September, they came back to Jerusalem.

CHAPTER 8

Now, in mid-September, all the people assembled at the plaza in front of the Water Gate and requested Ezra, their religious leader, to read to them the law of God which He had given to Moses.

So Ezra the priest brought out to them the scroll of Moses' laws. He stood on a wooden stand made especially for the occasion so that everyone could see him as he read. He faced the square in front of the Water Gate, and read from early morning until noon. Everyone stood up as he opened the scroll. And all who were old enough to understand paid close attention. To his right stood Mattithiah, Shema, Anaiah, Uriah, Hilkiah, and Ma-aseiah. To his left were Pedaiah, Misha-el, Malchijah, Hashum, Hash-baddenah, Zechariah, and Meshullam.

6 Then Ezra blessed the Lord, the great God, and all the people said, "Amen" and lifted their hands toward heaven; then they bowed and worshiped the Lord with their faces toward the ground.

7, 8 As Ezra read from the scroll, Jeshua, Bani, Sherebiah, Jamin, Akkub, Shabbethai, Hodiah, Ma-aseiah, Kelita, Azariah, Jozabad, Hanan, Pelaiah, and the Levites went among the people[1] and explained the meaning of the passage that was being read.

9 All the people began sobbing when they heard the commands of the law. Then Ezra the priest, and I as governor, and the Levites who were assisting me,

---

[1]Literally, "while the people remained in their places."

said to them, "Don't cry on such a day as this! For today is a sacred day before the Lord your God —

10 It is a time to celebrate with a hearty meal, and to send presents to those in need, for the joy of the Lord is your strength. You must not be dejected and sad!"

11 And the Levites, too, quieted the people, telling them, "That's right! Don't weep! For this is a day of holy joy, not of sadness."

12 So the people went away to eat a festive meal and to send presents; it was a time of great and joyful celebration because they could hear and understand God's words.

13 The next day the clan leaders and the priests and Levites met with Ezra to go over the law in greater detail.

14 As they studied it, they noted that Jehovah had told Moses that the people of Israel should live in tents during the Festival of Tabernacles to be held that month.

15 He had said also that a proclamation should be made throughout the cities of the land, especially in Jerusalem, telling the people to go to the hills to get branches from olive, myrtle, palm, and fig trees and to make huts in which to live for the duration of the feast.

16 So the people went out and cut branches and used them to build huts on the roofs of their houses, or in their courtyards, or in the court of the Temple, or on the plaza beside the Water Gate, or at the Ephraim Gate Plaza.

17 They lived in these huts for the seven days of the feast, and everyone was filled with joy! (This pro-

cedure had not been carried out since the days of Joshua.)

18 Ezra read from the scroll on each of the seven days of the feast; and on the eighth day there was a solemn closing service as required by the laws of Moses.

CHAPTER 9

On October 10[1] the people returned for another observance; this time they fasted and clothed themselves with sackcloth and sprinkled dirt in their hair. And the Israelis separated themselves from all foreigners.

3 The laws of God were read aloud to them for two or three hours, and for several more hours they took turns confessing their own sins and those of their ancestors. And everyone worshiped the Lord their God.

4 Some of the Levites were on the platform praising the Lord God with songs of joy. These men were Jeshua, Kadmi-el, Bani, Shebaniah, Bunni, Sherebiah, Bani, and Chenani.

5 Then the Levite leaders called out to the people, "Stand up and praise the Lord your God, for He lives from everlasting to everlasting. Praise His glorious name! It is far greater than we can think or say." The leaders in this part of the service were Jeshua, Kadmi-el, Bani, Hashabneiah, Sherebiah, Hodiah, Shebaniah, and Pethahiah.

6 Then Ezra prayed, "You alone are God. You have made the skies and the heavens, the earth and the seas, and everything in them. You preserve it all;

---

[1]Literally, "the twenty-fourth day" of the Hebrew month.

and all the angels of heaven worship You.

7 You are the Lord God who chose Abram and brought him from Ur of the Chaldeans and renamed him Abraham.

8 When he was faithful to You, You made a contract with him to forever give him and his descendants the land of the Canaanites, Hittites, Amorites, Perizzites, Jebusites, and Girgashites; and now You have done what You promised, for You are always true to Your word.

9 You saw the troubles and sorrows of our ancestors in Egypt, and You heard their cries from beside the Red Sea.

10 You displayed great miracles against Pharaoh and his people, for You knew how brutally the Egyptians were treating them; You have a glorious reputation because of those never-to-be-forgotten deeds.

11 You divided the sea for Your people so they could go through on dry land! And then You destroyed their enemies in the depths of the sea; they sank like stones beneath the mighty waters.

12 You led our ancestors by a pillar of cloud during the day and a pillar of fire at night so that they could find their way.

13 You came down upon Mount Sinai and spoke with them from heaven and gave them good laws and true commandments,

14 Including the laws about the holy Sabbath; and You commanded them, through Moses Your servant, to obey them all.

15 You gave them bread from heaven when they were hungry and water from the rock when they were thirsty. You commanded them to go in and conquer

the land You had sworn to give them;

16 But our ancestors were a proud and stubborn lot, and they refused to listen to Your commandments.

17 They refused to obey and didn't pay any attention to the miracles You did for them; instead, they rebelled and appointed a leader to take them back into slavery in Egypt! But You are a God of forgiveness, always ready to pardon, gracious and merciful, slow to become angry, and full of love and mercy; You didn't abandon them,

18 Even though they made a calf-idol and proclaimed, 'This is our God! He brought us out of Egypt!' They sinned in so many ways,

19 But in Your great mercy You didn't abandon them to die in the wilderness! The pillar of cloud led them forward day by day, and the pillar of fire showed them the way through the night.

20 You sent Your good Spirit to instruct them, and You did not stop giving them bread from heaven or water for their thirst.

21 For forty years You sustained them in the wilderness; they lacked nothing in all that time. Their clothes didn't wear out and their feet didn't swell!

22 Then You helped them conquer great kingdoms and many nations, and You placed Your people in every corner of the land; they completely took over the land of King Sihon of Heshbon and King Og of Bashan.

23 You caused a population explosion among the Israelis and brought them into the land You had promised to their ancestors.

24 You subdued whole nations before them —

even the kings and the people of the Canaanites were powerless!

25 Your people captured fortified cities and fertile land; they took over houses full of good things, with cisterns and vineyards and oliveyards and many, many fruit trees; so they ate and were full and enjoyed themselves in all Your blessings.

26 But despite all this they were disobedient and rebelled against You. They threw away Your law, killed the prophets who told them to return to You, and they did many other terrible things.

27 So You gave them to their enemies. But in their time of trouble they cried to You and You heard them from heaven, and in great mercy You sent them saviors who delivered them from their enemies.

28 But when all was going well, Your people turned to sin again, and once more You let their enemies conquer them. Yet whenever Your people returned to You and cried to You for help, once more You listened from heaven, and in Your wonderful mercy delivered them!

29 You punished them in order to turn them toward Your laws, but even though they should have obeyed them,[2] they were proud and wouldn't listen, and continued to sin.

30 You were patient with them for many years. You sent Your prophets to warn them about their sins, but still they wouldn't listen. So once again You allowed the heathen nations to conquer them.

31 But in Your great mercy You did not destroy them completely or abandon them forever. What a gracious and merciful God You are!

---

[2]Literally, "by the observance of which a man shall live."

32 And now, O great and awesome God, You who keep Your promises of love and kindness — do not let all the hardships we have gone through become as nothing to You. Great trouble has come upon us and upon our kings and princes and priests and prophets and ancestors from the days when the kings of Assyria first triumphed over us until now.

33 Every time You punished us You were being perfectly fair; we have sinned so greatly that You gave us only what we deserved.

34 Our kings, princes, priests, and ancestors didn't obey Your laws or listen to Your warnings.

35 They did not worship You despite the wonderful things You did for them and the great goodness You showered upon them. You gave them a large, fat land, but they refused to turn from their wickedness.

36 So now we are slaves here in the land of plenty which You gave to our ancestors! Slaves among all this abundance!

37 The lush yield of this land passes into the hands of the kings whom You have allowed to conquer us because of our sins. They have power over our bodies and our cattle, and we serve them at their pleasure and are in great misery.

38 Because of all this, we again promise to serve the Lord! And we and our princes and Levites and priests put our names to this covenant."

CHAPTER 10

I, Nehemiah the governor, signed the covenant. The others who signed it were:

Zedekiah, Seraiah, Azariah, Jeremiah,

3-8   Pashhur, Amariah, Malchijah,
            Hattush, Shebaniah, Malluch,
            Harim, Meremoth, Obadiah,
            Daniel, Ginnethon, Baruch,
            Meshullam, Abijah, Mija-min,
            Ma-aziah, Bilgai, Shemaiah.
            (All those listed above were priests.)

9-13   These were the Levites who signed:
            Jeshua (son of Azaniah), Binnui (son of
               Henadad), Kadmi-el,
            Shebaniah, Hodiah, Kelita, Pelaiah, Ha-
               nan,
            Mica, Rehob, Hashabiah,
            Zaccur, Sherebiah, Shebaniah,
            Hodiah, Bani, Beninu.

14-27   The political leaders who signed:
            Parosh, Pahath-moab, Elam, Zattu, Bani,
            Bunni, Azgad, Bebai,
            Adonijah, Bigvai, Adin,
            Ater, Hezekiah, Azzur,
            Hodiah, Hashum, Bezai,
            Hariph, Anathoth, Nebai,
            Magpiash, Meshullam, Hezir,
            Meshezabel, Zadok, Jaddu-a,
            Pelatiah, Hanan, Anaiah,
            Hoshea, Hananiah, Hasshub,
            Hallohesh, Pilha, Shobek,
            Rehum, Hashabnah, Ma-aseiah,
            Ahiah, Hanan, Anan,
            Malluch, Harim, Baanah.

28   These men signed on behalf of the entire nation — for the common people; the priests; the Levites; the gatekeepers; the choir members; the Temple

servants; and all the rest who, with their wives and sons and daughters who were old enough to understand, had separated themselves from the heathen people of the land in order to serve God.

29 For we all heartily agreed to this oath and vowed to accept the curse of God unless we obeyed God's laws as issued by His servant Moses.

30 We also agreed not to let our daughters marry non-Jewish men and not to let our sons marry non-Jewish girls.

31 We further agreed that if the heathen people in the land should bring any grain or other produce to be sold on the Sabbath or on any other holy day, we would refuse to buy it. And we agreed not to do any work every seventh year and to forgive and cancel the debts of our brother Jews.

32 We also agreed to charge ourselves annually with a Temple tax so that there would be enough money to care for the Temple of our God:

33 For we needed supplies of the special Bread of the Presence, as well as grain offerings and burnt offerings for the Sabbaths, the new-moon feasts, and the annual feasts. We also needed to purchase the other items necessary for the work of the Temple and for the atonement of Israel.

34 Then we tossed a coin[1] to determine when — at regular times each year — the families of the priests, Levites, and leaders should supply the wood for the burnt offerings at the Temple as required in the law.

35 We also agreed always to bring the first part of every crop to the Temple — whether it be a ground crop or from our fruit and olive trees.

---

[1]Literally, "cast lots," a form of dice.

36 We agreed to give to God our oldest sons and the firstborn of all our cattle, herds, and flocks, just as the law requires; we presented them to the priests who minister in the Temple of our God.

37 They stored the produce in the Temple of our God — the best of our grain crops, and other contributions, the first of our fruit, and the first of the new wine and olive oil. And we promised to bring to the Levites a tenth of everything our land produced, for the Levites were responsible to collect the tithes in all our rural towns.

38 A priest — a descendant of Aaron — would be with the Levites as they received these tithes; and a tenth of all that was collected as tithes was delivered to the Temple and placed in the storage areas.

39, 40 The people and the Levites were required by law to bring these offerings of grain, new wine, and olive oil to the Temple and place them in the sacred containers for use by the ministering priests, the gatekeepers, and the choir singers. So we agreed together not to neglect the Temple of our God.

CHAPTER 11

The Israeli officials were living in Jerusalem, the Holy City, at this time; but now a tenth of the people from the other cities and towns of Judah and Benjamin were selected by lot to live there too.

2 Some who moved to Jerusalem at this time were volunteers, and they were highly honored.

3 Following is a list of the names of the provincial officials who came to Jerusalem (though most of the leaders, the priests, the Levites, the Temple assis-

tants, and the descendants of Solomon's servants continued to live in their own homes in the various cities of Judah):

4, 5, 6   Leaders from the tribe of Judah:

Athaiah (son of Uzziah, son of Zechariah, son of Amariah, son of Shephatiah, son of Mahalel, a descendant of Perez);

Ma-aseiah (son of Baruch, son of Colhozeh, son of Hazaiah, son of Adaiah, son of Joiarib, son of Zechariah, son of the Shilonite).

These were the 468 stalwart descendants of Perez who lived in Jerusalem.

7, 8, 9   Leaders from the tribe of Benjamin:

Sallu (son of Meshullam, son of Joed, son of Pedaiah, son of Kolaiah, son of Ma-aseiah, son of Ithi-el, son of Jeshaiah).

The 968 descendants of Gabbai and Sallai. Their chief was Joel, son of Zichri, who was assisted by Judah, son of Hassenu-ah.

10   Leaders from among the priests:

Jedaiah (son of Joiarib);

11-14   Jachin;

Seraiah (son of Hilkiah, son of Meshullam, son of Zadok, son of Meraioth, son of Ahitub the chief priest).

In all, there were 822 priests doing the work at the Temple under the leadership of these men. And there were 242 priests under the leadership of Adaiah (son of Jeroham, son of Pelaliah, son of Amzi, son of Zechariah, son of Pashhur, son of Malchijah).

There were also 128 stalwart men under the leadership of Amashsai (son of Azarel, son of Ahzai, son of Meshillemoth, son of Immer); who was assisted by Zabdiel (son of Haggedolim).

15, 16, 17   Levite leaders:

>Shemaiah (son of Hasshub, son of Azrikam, son of Hashabiah, son of Bunni);
>
>Shabbethai and Jozabad, who were in charge of the work outside the Temple;
>
>Mattaniah (son of Mica, son of Zabdi, son of Asaph) was the one who began the thanksgiving services with prayer;
>
>Bakbukiah and Abda, (son of Shammua, son of Galal, son of Jeduthun) were his assistants.

18   In all, there were 284 Levites in Jerusalem.

19   There were also 172 gatekeepers, led by Akkub, Talmon, and others of their clan.

20   The other priests, Levites, and people lived wherever their family inheritance was located.

21   However, the Temple workers (whose leaders were Ziha and Gishpa) all lived in Ophel.

22, 23   The supervisor of the Levites in Jerusalem and of those serving at the Temple was Uzzi (son of Bani, son of Hashabiah, son of Mattaniah, son of Mica), a descendant of Asaph, whose clan became the Tabernacle singers. He was appointed by King David,[1] who also set the pay scale of the singers.

---

[1]Literally, "there was a commandment from the king concerning them."

24 Pethahiah (son of Meshezabel, a descendant of Zerah, a son of Judah) assisted in all matters of public administration.

25-30 Some of the towns where the people of Judah lived were:

> Kiriath-arba,
> Dibon,
> Jekabzeel (and their surrounding villages);
> Jeshua, Moladah, Beth-pelet,
> Hazar-shual, Beer-sheba and its surrounding villages,
> Ziklag, Meconah and its villages;
> En-rimmon, Zorah, Jarmuth,
> Zanoah, Adullam (and their surrounding villages);
> Lachish and its nearby fields,
> Azekah and its towns.

So the people spread from Beer-sheba to the valley of Hinnom.

31-35 The people of the tribe of Benjamin lived at:

> Geba, Michmash, Aija, Bethel and its surrounding villages,
> Anathoth, Nob, Ananiah,
> Hazor, Ramah, Gittaim,
> Hadid, Zeboim, Neballat,
> Lod, Ono (the Valley of the Craftsmen).

36 Some of the Levites who lived in Judah were sent to live with the tribe of Benjamin.

CHAPTER 12

Here is a list of the priests who accompanied Zerubbabel (son of She-altiel) and Jeshua:

Seraiah, Jeremiah, Ezra,
2-7   Amariah, Malluch, Hattush,
Shecaniah, Rehum, Meremoth,
Iddo, Ginnethoi, Abijah,
Mijamin, Ma-adiah, Bilgah,
Shemaiah, Joiarib, Jedaiah,
Sallu, Amok, Hilkiah, Jedaiah.

8 The Levites who went with them were:
Jeshua, Binnui, Kadmi-el,
Sherebiah, Judah, Mattaniah — who was
the one in charge of the thanksgiving
service.

9 Bakbukiah and Unno, their fellow clansmen,
helped them during the service.

10, 11   Jeshua was the father of Joiakim;
Joiakim was the father of Eliashib;
Eliashib was the father of Joiada;
Joiada was the father of Jonathan;
Jonathan was the father of Jaddu-a.

12-21   The following were the clan leaders of the
priests who served under the High Priest Joiakim:
Meraiah, leader of the Seraiah clan;
Hananiah, leader of the Jeremiah clan;
Meshullam, leader of the Ezra clan;
Jehohanan, leader of the Amariah clan;
Jonathan, leader of the Malluchi clan;
Joseph, leader of the Shebaniah clan;
Adna, leader of the Harim clan;
Helkai, leader of the Meraioth clan;
Zechariah, leader of the Iddo clan;
Meshullam, leader of the Ginnethon clan;
Zichri, leader of the Abijah clan;

> Piltai, leader of the Moadiah and Minia-
> min clans;
> Shammu-a, leader of the Bilgah clan;
> Jehonathan, leader of the Shemaiah clan;
> Mattenai, leader of the Joiarib clan;
> Uzzi, leader of the Jedaiah clan;
> Kallai, leader of the Sallai clan;
> Eber, leader of the Amok clan;
> Hashabiah, leader of the Hilkiah clan;
> Nethanel, leader of the Jedaiah clan.

22 A genealogical record of the heads of the clans of the priests and Levites was compiled during the reign of King Darius of Persia, in the days of Eliashib, Joiada, Johanan, and Jaddu-a — all of whom were Levites.

23 In *The Book of the Chronicles* the Levite names were recorded down to the days of Johanan, the son of Eliashib.

24 These were the chiefs of the Levites at that time:
> Hashabiah, Sherebiah, and Jeshua (son of
> Kadmi-el).

Their fellow-clansmen helped them during the ceremonies of praise and thanksgiving, just as commanded by David, the man of God.

25 The gatekeepers who had charge of the collection centers at the gates were:
> Mattaniah, Bakbukiah, Obadiah,
> Meshullam, Talmon, Akkub.

26 These were the men who were active in the time of Joiakim (son of Jeshua, son of Jozadak), and when I was the governor, and when Ezra was the priest and teacher of religion.

27 During the dedication of the new Jerusalem wall, all the Levites throughout the land came to Jerusalem

to assist in the ceremonies and to take part in the joyous occasion with their thanksgiving, cymbals, psaltries, and harps.

28 The choir members also came to Jerusalem from the surrounding villages and from the villages of the Netophathites;

29 They also came from Beth-gilgal and the area of Geba and Azmaveth, for the singers had built their own villages as suburbs of Jerusalem.

30 The priests and Levites first dedicated themselves, then the people, the gates, and the wall.

31, 32 I led the Judean leaders to the top of the wall and divided them into two long lines to walk in opposite directions along the top of the wall, giving thanks as they went. The group which went to the right toward the Dung Gate consisted of half of the leaders of Judah,

33 Including Hoshaiah, Azariah, Ezra, Meshullam,

34 Judah, Benjamin, Shemaiah, and Jeremiah.

35 The priests who played the trumpets were Zechariah (son of Jonathan, son of Shemaiah, son of Mattaniah, son of Micaiah, son of Zaccur, son of Asaph),

36 Shemaiah, Azarel, Milalai,
Gilalai, Maai, Nethanel,
Judah, and Hanani.

(They used the original musical instruments of King David.) Ezra the priest led this procession.

37 When they arrived at the Fountain Gate they went straight ahead and climbed the stairs which go up beside the castle to the old City of David; then they went to the Water Gate on the east.

38 The other group, of which I was a member, went around the other way to meet them. We walked

from the Tower of Furnaces to the Broad Wall,

39   Then from the Ephraim Gate to the Old Gate, passed the Fish Gate and the Tower of Hananel, and went on to the gate of the Tower of the Hundred; then we continued on to the Sheep Gate and stopped at the Prison Gate.

40, 41   Both choirs then proceeded to the Temple. Those with me were joined by the trumpet-playing priests —

> Eliakim, Ma-aseiah, Miniamin,
> Micaiah, Eli-o-enai, Zechariah, and Hana-
> niah.

42   And by the singers —

> Ma-aseiah, Shemaiah, Eleazar,
> Uzzi, Jehohanan, Malchijah,
> Elam and Ezer.

They sang loudly and clearly under the direction of Jezrahiah the choirmaster.

43   Many sacrifices were offered on that joyous day, for God had given us cause for great joy. The women and children rejoiced too, and the joy of the people of Jerusalem was heard far away!

44   On that day men were appointed to be in charge of the treasuries, the wave offerings, the tithes, and first-of-the-harvest offerings, and to collect these from the farms as decreed by the laws of Moses. These offerings were assigned to the priests and Levites, for the people of Judah appreciated the priests and Levites and their ministry.

45   They also appreciated the work of the singers and gatekeepers, who assisted them in worshiping God and performing the purification ceremonies as required by the laws of David and his son Solomon.

46 (It was in the days of David and Asaph that the custom began of having choir directors to lead the choirs in hymns of praise and thanks to God.)

47 So now, in the days of Zerubbabel and Nehemiah, the people brought a daily supply of food for the members of the choir, the gatekeepers, and the Levites. The Levites, in turn, gave a portion of what they received to the priests.[1]

CHAPTER 13

On that same day, as the laws of Moses were being read, the people found a statement which said that the Ammonites and Moabites should never be permitted to worship at the Temple.[1]

2 For they had not been friendly to the people of Israel. Instead, they had hired Balaam to curse them — although God turned the curse into a blessing.

3 When this rule was read, all the foreigners were immediately expelled from the assembly.

4 Before this had happened, Eliashib the priest, who had been appointed as custodian of the Temple storerooms and who was also a good friend of Tobiah,

5 Had converted a storage room into a beautiful guest room for Tobiah. The room had previously been used for storing the grain offerings, frankincense, bowls, and tithes of grain, new wine, and olive oil. Moses had decreed that these offerings belonged to the Levites, the members of the choir, and the gatekeepers. (The wave offerings were for the priests.)

6 I was not in Jerusalem at the time, for I had returned to Babylon in the thirty-second year of the

---

[1]Literally, "to the descendants of Aaron the priest."
[1]Deuteronomy 23:3-5.

reign of King Ar-ta-xerxes (though I later received his permission to go back again to Jerusalem).

7   When I arrived back in Jerusalem and learned of this evil deed of Eliashib — that he had prepared a guest room in the Temple for Tobiah —

8   I was very upset and threw out all of his belongings from the room.

9   Then I demanded that the room be thoroughly cleaned, and I brought back the Temple bowls, the grain offerings, and frankincense.

10   I also learned that the Levites had not been given what was due them, so they and the choir singers who were supposed to conduct the worship services had returned to their farms.

11   I immediately confronted the leaders and demanded, "Why has the Temple been forsaken?" Then I called all the Levites back again and restored them to their proper duties.

12   And once more all the people of Judah began bringing their tithes of grain, new wine, and olive oil to the Temple treasury.

13   I put Shelemiah the priest, Zadok the scribe, and Pedaiah the Levite in charge of the administration of the storehouses; and I appointed Hanan (son of Zaccur, son of Mattaniah) as their assistant. These men had an excellent reputation, and their job was to make an honest distribution to their fellow-Levites.

14   O my God, remember this good deed and do not forget all that I have done for the Temple.

15   One day I was on a farm and saw some men treading winepresses on the Sabbath, hauling in sheaves, and loading their donkeys with wine, grapes, figs, and

all sorts of produce which they took that day into Jerusalem. So I opposed them publicly.

16 There were also some men from Tyre bringing in fish and all sorts of wares and selling them on the Sabbath to the people of Jerusalem.

17 Then I asked the leaders of Judah, "Why are you profaning the Sabbath?

18 Wasn't it enough that your fathers did this sort of thing and brought the present evil days upon us and upon our city? And now you are bringing more wrath upon the people of Israel by permitting the Sabbath to be desecrated in this way."

19 So from then on I commanded that the gates of the city be shut as darkness fell on Friday evenings and not be opened until the Sabbath had ended; and I sent some of my servants to guard the gates so that no merchandise could be brought in on the Sabbath day.

20 The merchants and tradesmen camped outside Jerusalem once or twice,

21 But I spoke sharply to them and said, "What are you doing out here, camping around the wall? If you do this again, I will arrest you." And that was the last time they came on the Sabbath.

22 Then I commanded the Levites to purify themselves and to guard the gates in order to preserve the sanctity of the Sabbath. Remember this good deed, O my God! Have compassion upon me in accordance with Your great goodness.

23 About the same time I realized that some of the Jews had married women from Ashdod, Ammon, and Moab,

24 And that many of their children spoke in the

language of Ashdod and couldn't speak the language of Judah at all.

25 So I argued with these parents and cursed them and punched a few of them and knocked them around and pulled out their hair; and they vowed before God that they would not let their children intermarry with non-Jews.

26 "Wasn't this exactly King Solomon's problem?" I demanded. "There was no king who could compare with him, and God loved him and made him the king over all Israel; but even so he was led into idolatry by foreign women.

27 Do you think that we will let you get away with this sinful deed?"

28 One of the sons of Jehoiada (the son of Eliashib the High Priest) was a son-in-law of Sanballat the Horonite, so I chased him out of the Temple.

29 Remember them, O my God, for they have defiled the priesthood and the promises and vows of the priests and Levites.

30 So I purged out the foreigners, and assigned tasks to the priests and Levites, making certain that each knew his work.

31 They supplied wood for the altar at the proper times and cared for the sacrifices and the first offerings of every harvest. Remember me, my God, with Your kindness.